EUROPEAN YEARBOOK OF DISABILITY LAW

European Yearbook of Disability Law

Editors:

Prof. Gerard Quinn
National University of Ireland, Galway (IRL)

Prof. Lisa Waddington
European Disability Forum Chair in European Disability Law
Maastricht University (NLs)

Editorial Board:

Prof. Theresia Degener
Evangelischen Fachhochschule Rheinland-Westfalen-Lippe (GER)

Prof. Aart Hendriks,
Chair in Health Law, University of Leiden (NLs)

Prof. Bjørn Hvinden
Head of Research & Deputy Director NOVA, (NO)

Dovile Juodkaite
Director, Global Initiative on Psychiatry – Vilnius (LI)

Anna Lawson
Senior Lecturer in Law and Member of the Centre for Disability Studies, Leeds University
(UK)

Oliver Lewis
Executive Director, Mental Disability Advocacy Center, Budapest (HU)

John Parry
Director, Commission on Mental & Physical Disability Law, American Bar Association
(US)

Shivaun Quinlivan
Law Lecturer, National University of Ireland, Galway (IRL)

Advisory Board:

Prof. Peter Blanck
Chairman, The Burton Blatt Institute, Syracuse University (US)

Prof. Christopher McCrudden
Lincoln College, Oxford University (GB)

Prof. Michael Stein
William & Mary School of Law and Executive Director, Harvard Project on
Disability Harvard Law School (US)

Yannis Vardakastanis
President of the European Disability Forum (EU)

EUROPEAN YEARBOOK OF DISABILITY LAW

Volume 1

Edited by

Gerard QUINN

Lisa WADDINGTON

intersentia

Antwerp – Oxford – Portland

Distribution for the UK:
Hart Publishing
16C Worcester Place
Oxford OX12JW
UK
Tel.: +44 1865 51 75 30
Fax: +44 1865 51 07 10

Distribution for Switzerland and Germany:
Schulthess Verlag
Zwingliplatz 2
CH-8022 Zürich
Switzerland
Tel: + 41 1 251 93 36
Fax: + 41 1 261 63 94

Distribution for the USA and Canada:
International Specialized Book Services
920 NE 58th Ave Suite 300
Portland, OR 97213
USA
Tel.: +1 800 944 6190 (toll free)
Tel.: +1 503 287 3093
Fax: +1 503 280 8832
Email: info@isbs.com

Distribution for other countries:
Intersentia Publishers
Groenstraat 31
BE-2640 Mortsel
Belgium
Tel: + 32 3 680 15 50
Fax: + 32 3 658 71 21

European Yearbook of Disability Law. Volume 1
Lisa Waddington and Gerard Quinn (eds.)

© 2009 Intersentia
Antwerp – Oxford – Portland
www.intersentia.com

ISBN 978-90-5095-820-2
D/2009/7849/27
NUR 825

TABLE OF CONTENTS

Table of Contents

EDITORIAL
THE EUROPEAN YEARBOOK OF DISABILITY LAW: A NEW PUBLICATION FOR AN EMERGING FIELD

Welcome to the first edition of the *European Yearbook of Disability Law*.
This publication marks a coming of age in a field that has been slowly growing for nearly twenty years across Europe. Disability directly affects at least 50 million European Union citizens. Indeed, the United Nations estimates that there are 650 million persons in the world who are disabled, classifying them as the 'world's largest minority.'

In Europe, the field first exploded into life with the publication of the Invisible Citizens Report to mark the 1995 European Day of Disabled Persons. The European disability non-governmental organizations which organized the event that year chose to focus on the need for the inclusion of a non-discrimination provision in the EC Treaty, which addressed, in particular, disability. Up until that point, there had been no reference made to disability or disabled people in the Treaty whatsoever, although the upcoming Inter-Governmental Conference, scheduled for 1997 under the Dutch Presidency, held out the possibility for change. In retrospect, one can say that this event, and the Invisible Citizens Report which accompanied it, laid the basis for the subsequent (successful) campaign for the inclusion of a non-discrimination article in the EC Treaty.

Moreover, this landmark report opened a window in Europe to modern thinking about human rights and disability, as reflected in the Americans with Disabilities Act (ADA) of 1990 and the United Nations Standard Rules on the Equalization of Opportunities for Persons with Disabilities (1993). It is no exaggeration to say that it triggered profound changes in EC law and policy, which enhanced the legal capacity of the EC to respond effectively to disability discrimination. Since then, the various human rights organs of the Council of Europe – including the European Court of Human Rights, the European Social Rights Committee and the Council of Europe's High Commissioner for Human Rights – have also become increasingly engaged in ensuring justice for persons with disabilities. In addition, the European Community, through the European Commission, has participated in the negotiations on, and signed, the United Nations Convention on the Rights of Persons with Disabilities. This Convention will play an increasingly important role in stimulating and maintaining the reform process.

The output of these various organs in recent years – and their potential to leverage real change for disabled persons across Europe – has been staggering. The time is right, therefore, to begin tracking and chronicling European disability law and policy in a systematic way to enable policy-makers, lawyers and civil society groups to interact constructively to ensure that the reform process remains relevant and on track. The Yearbook of European Disability Law aims to meet that need.

The Yearbook will bring together European-level developments on disability law from both the European Union and the Council of Europe in the preceding year. We have extended the scope of this first issue to go back a little further, to give context to recent developments. We also include some coverage of other European Inter-Governmental bodies such as the OECD and the OSCE, in order to gain a more rounded picture of pan-European developments. Links to homepages and additional resources are provided, enabling further research.

Each issue will also contain a number of thematic articles, by leading authors in the field, covering topics of contemporary significance. The topics covered in this first volume include the need to redesign traditional social support systems to enable a life of choice and independence, the urgent need for the reform of European legal capacity laws, the British experience of establishing a legal duty to promote equality in favour of disabled people, and the United Nations Convention on the Rights of Persons with Disabilities. Moreover, each issue will contain (extracts from) some of the main documents which have been published in the preceding year, including legislation, position papers and court judgments.

We are indebted to our Advisory Board, which is comprised of some of the leading academics in the field worldwide. We are also indebted to our Editorial Board for their sound counsel. Finally, we thank Roisin McGrogan for her assistance in editing and compiling this first edition. We trust you will find this publication useful and instructive, and look forward to hearing from readers on how the Yearbook might be further developed to ensure it plays its part in maintaining the momentum of European disability law reform.

Gerard Quinn and Lisa Waddington

PART I

ARTICLES AND SHORT COMMENTARIES

REDISTRIBUTIVE AND REGULATORY DISABILITY PROVISIONS: INCOMPATIBILITY OR SYNERGY?

Bjørn Hvinden[1]

1. INTRODUCTION

The new UN Convention on the Rights of Persons with Disabilities (CRPD) contains two important articles related to employment and standard of living.[2] According to Article 27, State Parties recognize the right of persons with disabilities to work on an equal basis with others, and shall safeguard and promote the realization of the right to work. Under Article 28, State Parties recognize the right of persons with disabilities to an adequate standard of living for themselves and their families, including the right to social protection, and shall take appropriate steps to safeguard and promote the realization of this right. While several of the principles of Article 27 are to a considerable degree already embodied in the legislation of the European Community, and most explicitly in the Framework Directive on Equal Treatment in Employment and Occupation,[3] this is to less extent the case with Article 28. In the latter case, we must look for points of convergence in other human rights instruments, for instance the European Social Charter.[4]

Nevertheless, current trends in disability policy in many countries give reasons to reconsider the interrelationships of the principles of Articles 27 and 28 of the CRPD. This paper asks what consequences these trends – partly in policy discourse, partly in enacted policy – are likely to have for the dignity, autonomy and participation of persons with disabilities, and through this, for the overall profile of countries' systems of disability protection.

The paper will see Article 27 and 28 of CRPD as expressing two different but

---

[1]   Professor, Head of Research, Norwegian Social Research (NOVA), Oslo & Leader, Nordic Centre of Excellence in Welfare Research 'Reassessing the Nordic Welfare Model' (NordForsk 2007-11). I have benefited strongly from comments to an earlier version of this paper from Gerard Quinn, Jane Jenson and Ann Orloff and other participants at the annual conference of Research Committee 19 on Poverty, Social Welfare and Social Policy of the International Sociological Association, Stockholm, Sweden, September 4-6, 2008. None of these are to be blamed for the remaining shortcomings.
[2]   United Nations Convention on the Rights of Persons with Disabilities and Optional Protocol, (adopted 13 December 2006, entry into force 3 May 2008).
[3]   Council Directive (EC) 2000/78 establishing a general framework for equal treatment in employment and occupation, [2000] O.J. L303/16.
[4]   European Social Charter (revised 1996), ETS no. 163.

complementary approaches, related to distinct but interdependent types of rights for persons with disabilities. Article 27 partly emphasizes the promotion of equal treatment and combating discrimination, and partly points to access to training and other services to enable and strengthen the labour market prospects of persons with disabilities, and thus indirectly the means for acquiring a decent living standard. Article 28 focuses on access to basic resources and social provisions of more immediate significance for the living standards of persons with disabilities. To simplify matters a bit, Article 27 is concerned with equality of opportunities, while Article 28 goes further towards a notion of equality of outcomes.[5]

Since different countries pursue these aims to different extents, or stress them to dissimilar degrees, we start by introducing some conceptual tools to characterize the profile of the overall disability protection system of a country. Next, we review some of the main criticisms against redistribute provisions or 'social supports' related to disability. We argue that the redistributive provisions have more ambiguous and complex implications for the dignity, autonomy and participation of persons with disabilities than suggested by these criticisms. We substantiate this argument by presenting results of an analysis of cross-country variations in the living standard and economic participation of persons with disabilities. Indirectly, this analysis also suggests that the goals of equality of opportunity and equality of outcomes are strongly interrelated. As argued by Anne Philips, it is hard to assess to what extent one has achieved equality of opportunity unless one falls back on indicators of equality of outcome.[6] Finally, we will more briefly discuss to what extent human rights instruments can serve as protection against unwarranted cuts in redistributive provisions and how redistributive provisions can be used more consistently and vigorously to increase the practical impact (or 'outcomes') of legislation on equal treatment, non-discrimination, accessibility and accommodation.

By the term 'disability protection system' we refer to the total package of provisions of relevance for persons with disabilities. On the one hand, these provisions include cash transfers, social services to enable independent living and labour market services to promote labour market participation, i.e. 'redistributive provisions', as they redistribute tax-financed public resources to citizens on the basis of a set of eligibility rules and processes to assess claims to these resource. On the other hand, we have provisions to protect the person with a disability against discrimination and inaccessibility and promote equal treatment. The latter kind of provisions largely falls under the concept of 'social regulation', i.e. efforts by public authorities to influence non-governmental actors, especially actors operating in a market, to act in line with social objectives.[7] Broadly speaking, the instruments of social regulation include legal rules, financial incentives and persuasion through information. Some aspects of social regulation have the potential to strengthen citizens' scope for agency and capability, not only as workers and consumers, but also as participants in civil society and the political community. As we have reasons to assume that these different provisions or instruments in-

[5] A. Philips, 'Defending equality of outcome', 12 *Journal of Political Philosophy* 1 (2004). 1.
[6] Ibid., p. 9.
[7] G. Majone, 'The European Community between social policy and social regulation', 31 *Journal of Common Market Studies* 2 (1993), 153.

teract with each other, e.g. to weaken or reinforce the impact of the other, we should study the interdependencies between these parts of disability protection system, i.e. the relationship between civil (or 'regulatory') rights and social (or 'distributional') rights. Unfortunately, researchers have rarely analyzed how these elements of overall policy packages interact or how their interrelationships may be designed to improve the synergy between them.

While regulatory provisions have been strengthened over the last ten to fifteen years in many countries, e.g. through the incorporation of human rights instruments in national legislation and the enactment of the equal treatment and non-discrimination legislation within the European Community, redistributive provisions, especially income maintenance provisions, have become much more contested. Calls to tighten up or reduce the scope and generosity of such provisions can be heard in a great number of countries, and national governments have, to different extent, put such changes into practice.

Against the backdrop of these trends, this paper will make three claims. First, the paper will argue that cuts in disability-related redistributive provisions may have adverse effects on the living standards and well-being of many persons with disabilities, especially as it is uncertain to what extent persons who will have their benefit entitlements reduced are able to find stable employment offering adequate remuneration. Although the new regulatory provisions (e.g. non-discrimination legislation) has a potential for improving the prospects of finding and keeping suitable employment for persons with disabilities, we do not yet have precise knowledge about how large their practical impact is or will be.

Second, both the CRPD (Article 2) and the Framework Directive (Article 5) point to the need to balance an employer's duty to provide reasonable accommodation for a person with a disability with a regard for the risk that this would impose a disproportionate burden for the employer. Significantly, the Framework Directive adds 'This burden shall not be disproportionate when it is sufficiently remedied by measures existing within the framework of the disability policy of the Member State concerned'. Such measures will fall under what we here have termed redistributive provisions. To the extent that national governments introduce such measures – or make existing measures more available, generous and well-known – this could lead to a fruitful synergy between regulatory and redistributive parts of the overall disability protection system.

Third, to the extent that persons with disabilities remain excluded from employment even after the introduction of more promising mixes of regulatory and redistributive provisions, public authorities must accept their responsibility in line with Article 28 of CRPD and guarantee decent living standards and independence for all through adequate redistributive provisions.

In examining the likely impact of cuts in redistributive provisions, one should pay particular attention to potentially gendered effects of such changes. Research has rarely examined the extent to which disability policy affects women and men differently. In general, disability research has only to a limited extent investigated issues of intersectionality, i.e. how a person with a disability may also belong to other disadvantaged sections of the population. Acknowledging the limitations of existing comparative data, this paper will seek to illustrate such potentially gender-differentiated impacts of reform in redistributive provisions.

2. A NOTE ON THE CONCEPTUALIZATION AND MEASUREMENT OF DISABILITY

One of the continuous issues in disability research is the fundamental one of how to define disability. Although the existence (or attribution) of some form of bodily, psychological and/or intellectual impaired functioning (i.e. a condition with a potentially adverse impact on the individual's activity and participation), is basic, most scholars today agree that the degree of functional limitation or reduced capacity, as experienced by the individual, is rarely determined by an impairment in itself. Rather, the degree of disability is a result of the interplay between the impairment and characteristics of the person's physical, social and organizational environment. Most scholars today adhere to some version of a 'relational' or 'social-contextual' understanding of disability. Some researchers, arguing for a 'social model' (or a 'civil rights model') of disability, point to environmental factors as the main factor behind disability, but risk neglecting or downplaying the social influence on impairment and its impact on the individual's functioning and well-being.[8]

Largely because the diverse elements of current disability protection were first established at different points during the last hundred years, they tend also to be dominated by different conceptualizations of disability. *Income transfers* have the oldest roots and tend still to be associated with biomedical and impairment-oriented understandings of disability. By contrast, the new *social regulatory provisions* – giving persons with disabilities enforceable rights to equal treatment and protection against discrimination and the lack of accessible and usable environments – are strongly linked to relational or social-contextual conceptions of disability. *Employment-promoting measures* and *social services* (seeking to enable the individual to enjoy an independent everyday life) tend to fall somewhere between these poles. Formally, the latter may refer to impairment-based limitation as a condition for access to services, but in practice be much more oriented towards questions of what measures, resources and adjustments are suitable for accomplishing specific changes in the situation of the individual (i.e. an instrumental means-ends reasoning rather than subsumption under rules). While access to these measures and services tend still to be rationed on the basis of a mix of budgetary considerations and professional discretionary assessments, we also see forceful calls for providing the individual with stronger and more enforceable rights in these areas.

Despite the wider acceptance of relational or social-contextual conceptions of disability, social surveys aiming to measure the proportion of a given population who has a disability, and how this disability impacts on the situation and well-being of the person, tend to be oriented toward individual impairments or

---

[8] M. Oliver, *Social Work with Disabled People*, (Macmillan, 1983); C. Barnes *et al.*, *Exploring Disability*, (Polity Press, 1999); R. F. Drake, *Understanding Disability Policy*, (Macmillan, 1999); L. Waddington and M. Diller, 'Tensions and coherence in disability policy: the uneasy relationship between social welfare and civil rights models of disability in American, European and international employment law', in M. L. Breslin and S. Yee (eds.), *Disability Rights Law and Policy*, (Transnational Publishers, 2002); C. Barnes and G. Mercer, *Disability*, (Polity Press, 2003); T. Shakespeare, *Disability Rights and Wrongs*, (Routledge, 2006).

restriction in functioning. This is partly because surveys are usually using proba-bility samples of individuals in order to estimate the distribution of characteristics in whole populations, rather than trying to interview all members of these popula-tions. This procedure means the individual's replies to a set of questions, about whether he/she has an impairment or experiences a restriction in everyday life, are used as a screening device to identify him or her as a person with a disability. Moreover, information about the individual's relationships to his/her physical, social or organizational environments has to be gained through the replies of the individual.

3. CONVERGENCE AND DIVERGENCE IN CALLS FOR REFORM

For various reasons the whole field of disability protection is currently in flux in many countries across the world. In the rich countries, we can see strong pressures for changes to disability protection, related to concerns for growing costs and the burden on public finances, especially related to income transfers.[9] In the last two decades, these pressures have been reinforced by concerns for demographic age-ing, increasing dependency rates and the issue of long-term sustainability. For similar reasons, policy makers and analysts are worried that replacement levels of income benefits create disincentives to work and thus undermine efforts to promote the entering or return to employment for people with disabilities. There is also a fear that disability-related income transfers can undermine the goal of old age pension reforms to prolong working careers by providing early exit options. Both national governments and supra-national bodies like the OECD and the EU have expressed such concerns.

However, the prominent role of income transfers in many rich countries' systems of disability protection has also met strong criticism from a completely different point of departure. A number of scholars and spokespersons for organi-zations of persons with disabilities have argued that the main function of such transfers is to exclude persons with disabilities from participation in the main-stream labour market, and hence contribute to the *de facto* societal segregation of persons with disabilities.[10] These critics argue that redistributive provisions en-trap rather than liberate and that 'they purchase the absence of the "other"'.[11] Fur-

---

[9]   B. Hvinden, 'The uncertain convergence of disability policies in Western Europe', 37 *Social Policy & Administration* 6 (2003), 609; P. A. Kemp *et al.* (eds.), *Sick So-cieties? Trends in Disability Benefit in Post-Industrial Welfare States,* (International Social Security Association, 2006); P.A. Kemp, 'The transformation of incapacity benefits', in M. Seeleib-Kaiser (ed.), *Welfare State Transformations,* (Palgrave Mac-millan, 2008).

[10] See for instance Barnes *et al., Exploring Disability*, (Polity Press, 1999) 57, 135; Waddington and Diller, in M. L. Breslin and S. Yee (eds.), *Disability Rights Law and Policy,* (Transnational Publishers, 2002), 243-244, 247-248.

[11] G. Quinn, *Disability Rights – An American Invention*, (11th Annual Valerie Gor-dan Human Rights Lecture, National University of Ireland, Galway, Faculty of Law, 2004) and G. Quinn, 'The European Social Charter and the EU anti-discrimination law in the field of disability: two gravitational fields with one common purpose', in G. de Burca and B. de Witte (eds.), *Social Rights in Europe*, (Oxford University Press, 2005), 279.

thermore, the critics argue that claiming and receiving benefits provided through redistributive arrangements imposes categorization, passivity, and dependency on the citizens in question. From the same quarters, we also find strong calls for a reorientation of disability protection towards a focus on recognition, human rights and non-discrimination.

Hence, we are faced with two agendas of reforms in disability protection; one dominated by economic efficiency considerations, and one oriented toward social justice and equity. The two agendas differ in their premises and their goals, but they converge in some of their criticisms of the main redistributive arrangements aimed at persons with disabilities, claiming that these arrangements are associated with exclusion and passivity on the part of persons with disabilities. The analyses underpinning these agendas leave relative few openings for the potential or actual positive contributions of well-developed systems of redistributive provisions for the well-being and social integration of persons with disabilities or, for that matter, for societal cohesion. Arguably, some ways of redistributing tax-financed resources have the potential of promoting the agency and capability of citizens, while some forms of social regulation can be associated with the categorization and disciplining of citizens and diminish their relative autonomy. By and large, redistribution and regulation may to a great extent be interdependent and interwoven in practice, rather than functioning as two separate spheres of public policy and legislation.[12]

4. THE REFORM AGENDA OF THE OECD

The Organization for Economic Co-operation and Development (OECD) has given trends in redistributive disability provisions, especially income transfers, great attention since its 'Jobs Study' in the early 1990s. The organization published a major report in 2003, currently followed up with a programme of detailed country analyses and recommendations for reforms.[13] Although the OECD's engagement has produced a rich and differentiated picture of the situation and trends in the participating countries, the main underlying message is that a long-term upward trend in disability expenditure and the number of beneficiaries is a growing problem in most OECD countries. A closer look at the data produced by the OECD suggests, however, that divergence in the experience of OECD countries is more striking than convergence (see Tbl. 1 and 2).

---

[12] Orloff, 'Social provision and regulation: theories of states, social policies and modernity', in J. Adam *et al.* (eds.), *Remaking Modernity: Politics, History, and Sociology*, (Duke University Press, 2005), 199.

[13] OECD, *Transforming Disability into Ability*, (Organisation for Economic Co-operation and Development, 2003); OECD, *Sickness, Disability and Work: Breaking the Barriers, vol.1: Norway, Poland and Switzerland*, (OECD, 2006); OECD, *Sickness, Disability and Work: Breaking the Barriers, vol. 2: Australia, Luxembourg, Spain and the United Kingdom*, (OECD, 2007).

Table 1 Trends in expenditure 1990-2003 and the levels of expenditure in 2003 in selected OECD countries. Expenditure related to 'incapacity'

Level of Expenditure 2003	Main direction of trends 1990-2003		
	Downwards	Fairly stable or fluctuating	Upwards
Higher than OECD average	Finland The Netherlands	Austria New Zealand Poland Portugal	Czech Republic Denmark Iceland Luxembourg Norway Sweden Switzerland
Less than or equal to OECD average (2.5 % of GDP 2003)	Belgium Canada France Greece Italy	Ireland Japan Mexico Spain	Australia Germany Korea United Kingdom United States

Source: OECD Stat Extracts (<http://stats.oecd.org/wbos/Index.aspx?datasetcode= SOCX_REF>) (accessed 10 November 2008).

Table 2 Trends in benefit recipiency 1990-2004 and the levels of recipiency in 2004 in selected OECD countries. Benefits for persons with disabilities

Level of benefit recipiency 2004 (stocks)	Main direction of trends 1990-2004		
	Downwards	Fairly stable or fluctuating	Upwards
More than 5 per cent of the working age population	Finland The Netherlands Portugal	France Ireland Sweden	Denmark Norway United Kingdom
5 per cent or less of the working age population	Germany Spain	Canada	Australia Japan New Zealand United States

Sources: S. Carcillo and D. Grubb, *From Inactivity to Work: The Role of Active Labour Market Policies*, OECD Social Employment and Migration Working Papers, No. 36, (OECD Publishing, 2006), Fig. 3, and P.A. Kemp, *Sick societies*, Fig. 2.1.

Among the countries where time series data for expenditure are available for a longer period, only twelve of twenty-seven countries had clear upward trends in the level of spending in the period 1990-2003. However, in these twelve countries the point of departure varied substantially, leaving us with only seven countries that combined high levels and upward trends in spending (Tbl. 1). Among the fewer countries where data for benefit recipiency is available, the picture is more or less similar: seven of sixteen countries had an increase in the rate of benefit recipiency, but from different starting points, in the period 1990-2004 (Tbl. 2).

The pattern of trends and levels in spending and recipiency rates for disability-related benefits cuts across well-established typologies of welfare states, e.g. the division between 'Nordic' (or Social Democratic'), 'Anglophone' (or 'Liberal') and 'Continental' (or 'Conservative') welfare models.[14] If we combine data about spending and recipiency rates for one particular year, e.g. 2003, the three Scandinavian countries, Finland and the Netherlands make up a distinct 'Nordic group' with higher spending and recipiency rates than other rich OECD-countries (Fig. 1). The 'Continental group' tends to have somewhat higher spending and recipiency rates than the 'Anglophone' group, but here the boundaries are some-what more blurred.

Figure 1 Rates of cash benefit recipiency related to disability or incapacity by the level of spending on benefits related to incapacity. Selected OECD-countries 2003

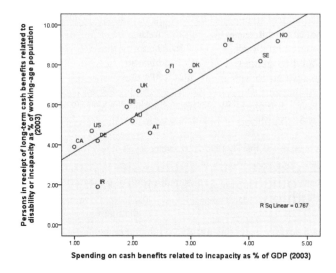

Sources of data: OECD Stat Extracts and P.A. Kemp in M. Seeleib-Kaiser (ed.), Welfare State Trans-formations.

Based on its analysis of the factors behind the trends in disability policy, the OECD has partly argued for the need for reform in many countries, to contain and possibly reduce their high level of expenditure and rate of receipt, and partly actively disseminated what it has perceived as goods models and best practice across member states. A core of the OECD recommendations is targeted at factors assumed to regulate the influx of new recipients. Some of the recommendations address the rules for eligibility for benefits, others the services aimed at support-ing entry or return to regular employment, and not least, argue for a stronger linking of the two. Governments are encouraged to introduce or enforce 'work-availability' requirements for receiving benefits, based on sanctioning in cases of non-compliance, and more restrictive conditions concerning the situations or types of impairment that give entitlement to benefit. The OECD often expresses concern for the possible disincentive effects of benefit levels or replacement rates

---

[14]   See for instance G. Esping-Andersen, *The Three Worlds of Welfare Capitalism*, (Pol-ity Press, 1990) and J. Pontusson, *Inequality and Prosperity: Social Europe vs. Lib-eral America*, (Cornell University Press, 2005).

and suggests that generous benefits might be reduced. Sometimes OECD analysts do, however, warn that such reductions may have adverse effects for persons who are 'genuinely unable to work'. Similarly, they have argued that imposing work-availability through sanctioning for persons with severe disabilities is not feasible.[15]

The OECD has been particularly concerned that the rate of outflow from disability benefits has been very low in many countries. For persons who are already in receipt of a disability-related benefit, the OECD has recommended more frequent reassessment or review of the work capacity of recipients, or a shift towards disability benefits granted only on a more short-term temporary basis.

In some contexts, the OECD has noted that the increase of beneficiary rates has been particularly strong among women with disabilities in a number of countries, and that different kinds of health problems or impairments dominate among female and male beneficiaries. Yet, what meaning these differences have and how they are related to gendered divisions of labour both in paid and unpaid work are rarely examined to any great depth.[16] Wider issues of intersectionality, e.g. whether combinations of having particular kinds of disabilities, being in a special age range, being female or male, and/or belonging to specific ethnic minorities, lead to a higher likelihood of being in receipt of disability-related benefits, seem to figure even more rarely in the analyses of the OECD.

5. THE REFORM AGENDA OF SCHOLARS WORKING WITHIN THE FRAMEWORK OF SOCIAL-CONTEXTUAL UNDERSTANDINGS OF DISABILITY

As mentioned briefly before, a number of scholars working within the new paradigm for disability research based on social-contextual understandings of disability have criticized redistributive welfare provisions as they exist in many countries for *de facto* stimulating or justifying social exclusion and segregation of persons with disabilities. These critics have often referred to how redistributive welfare provisions are associated with a narrow biomedical model of disability that locates the causes of the problem in the person in question, thus implying a biomedical deficiency explanation of disability. Consequently, the impact of environmental factors or the interaction between the person and his/her environment is disregarded; including the disabling effects of physical, organizational and social barriers and culturally based perceptions, categorizations and prejudices. The alternative to this understanding is an approach focusing on changing the societal reaction to impairments and construction of disability, leading to demands for the adoption of disability anti-discrimination and accessibility legislation to combat the systematic exclusion of persons with disabilities.

In one of the most precise analyses within this framework, Waddington and

---

15 S. Carcillo and D. Grubb, *From Inactivity to Work: The Role of Active Labour Market Policies*, OECD Social Employment and Migration Working Papers, No. 36, (OECD Publishing, 2006), 2, 4.

16 OECD, *Transforming Disability into Ability*, 27, 75-77, see also P. A. Kemp *et al.*, *Sick Societies*, 10-11, and P. A. Kemp, in M. Seeleib-Kaiser (ed.), *Welfare State Transformations*, 169, 171-172.

Diller argue that in the understanding underlying redistributive disability provisions – what they call the 'social welfare model' – we find an unsolved tension between a strategy of exclusion and a strategy of inclusion.[17] On the one hand, disability is seen as an excuse from the general social obligation to work and, on the other hand, associated with the expectation that persons with disabilities do find work, and that employers accept them as employees and facilitate their employment through appropriate forms of accommodation. This tension leads to a mixed message, both to the persons with disabilities and to potential or actual employers. Although persons with disabilities are told that it would be best if they worked as other citizens, they are in practice discouraged from doing so, for instance being offered income transfers or being pushed into sheltered work. Similarly, employers are in general terms expected to provide work opportunities for persons with disabilities, but not sanctioned if they fail to do so.

The analysis of Waddington and Diller captures ambiguities at the core of disability protection in many rich countries. We find a considerable degree of ambiguity and lack of coherence, both between policy goals and considerations, and between stated goals and the implementation of goals. The two authors are probably right that the availability of income transfers at a reasonable level may, in many instances, have served as a justification for turning down job applicants with disabilities or finding ways of terminating employment contracts for employees who acquire a disability.

At the same time, one may ask whether the ambiguous impact of redistributive provisions on the societal situation of persons with disabilities can be attributed to the design of such provisions. Arguably, the ambiguous impact of redistributive disability provisions resonates with the ambiguity of state-market relationships in the context of sharpened international competition. On one hand, private employers enjoy great freedom in deciding whom to hire and fire. On the other hand, governments seek – to different degrees – to influence the ways in which employers exercise these prerogatives, through combinations of legal rules, financial incentives and persuasion. Paradoxically, these employers' prerogatives may be even more strongly cherished and guarded in social market economies than in liberal market economies. While the state in social market economies has stronger ambitions to intervene in the market and reduce market-created inequalities through tax-based redistribution and welfare corporativism, the state seems also to be more constrained by an underlying 'contract' or settlement with the social partners than in liberal economies.[18]

Even more generally, one can argue that categorization, exclusion and segregation as societal reactions to persons who are not conforming with or fulfilling specific social norms have existed much longer than modern forms of redistributive disability provisions.[19] As argued by Deborah Stone, the social category

---

[17]   L. Waddington and M. Diller, in M. L. Breslin and S. Yee (eds.), *Disability Rights Law and Policy*, (Transnational Publishers, 2002), 243-244, 247-248.

[18]   B. Hvinden, 'Nordic disability policies in a changing Europe: is there still a Nordic model?', 38 *Social Policy & Administration* 2 (2004), 170.

[19]   See for instance Simmel, 'The Poor', in D. N. Levine (ed.), *On Individuality and Social Forms: Selected Writings of Georg Simmel*, (University of Chicago Press, 1971); M. Foucault, *Madness and Civilization*, (Vintage, 1988); D. Stone, *The Disabled State*, (Temple University Press, 1985); A. de Swaan, *In Care of the State:*

'disabled person' was constructed historically to identify working-age persons in need of exemption from the general duty to work. But this innovation can only be understood against the long-lasting issue of how public authorities were to distinguish between the 'deserving' and the 'non-deserving' poor, i.e. between those with legitimate claims on society support, leniency and consideration, and those without such legitimate claims (and who were exposed to harsh and demeaning treatment to deter and punish).[20] With the advent of universal social insurance in many welfare states, the majority of persons with disabilities were lifted out of means-tested poverty assistance and escaped the humiliation and degradation that assessment for such assistance was associated with. In other words, from a human rights perspective the type of redistributive provisions (universal or selective) available for persons with disabilities has not been a minor or trivial issue.

An important goal of disability protection systems is to diminish the number of persons who need to present claims for special consideration through preventative efforts. Such efforts should include the granting of universal rights to education and training, non-discrimination and accessibility provisions. Similarly, we should expect from public agencies that they provide all citizens with humane and respectful ways of identifying legitimate need and providing support, and it is hard to imagine a society were no working-age person will need society's support and at least temporary exemption from the general norm of being economically self-sufficient.

In spite of their fundamental criticism of the social welfare model, Waddington and Diller end up rejecting the idea of just abolishing this model and the social programmes inspired by it (i.e. redistributive disability provisions).[21] In their reasoning against abolishment, they hint at the adverse effects this would have for the well-being of many persons with disabilities. They later outline the possibility of seeing income support programmes and non-discrimination legislation as complementary and mutually supporting approaches, based on common principles of respect for human dignity. These suggestions are important and deserve to be followed up by other scholars and analysts.

Still, it is striking that Waddington and Diller have little to say about the positive gains for people with disabilities of having clear entitlements to income transfers and other redistributive disability provisions, e.g. in terms of creating conditions for personal fulfilment, autonomy and social participation. They do not acknowledge the considerable variation in the aim, quality and adequacy of existing provisions (and their administration), both within and between countries. They offer no reflections about whether the relatively high or increasing proportion of persons with disabilities, who are in receipt of redistributive welfare provisions, may weaken 'the suspicion of the poor' they claim the social welfare model rests upon, and amount to a silent development towards providing a right to decent income for all.

More generally, there is a risk that the new disability movement – and scholars who identify themselves with this movement – in the struggle for the

---

Health Care, Education and Welfare in Europe and the USA in the Modern Era, (Polity Press, 1988).

[20] D. Stone, *The Disabled State*, chs. 1-2.

[21] L. Waddington and M. Diller, in M. L. Breslin and S. Yee (eds.), *Disability Rights Law and Policy*, (Transnational Publishers, 2002), 272.

adoption of powerful anti-discrimination and accessibility legislation, based on a civil rights approach, may overstate the weaknesses and shortcomings of existing redistributive disability provisions and hence contribute to delegitimizing such provisions and justifying efforts to reduce their scope. We need a discussion of redistributive provisions that takes into account the historical development *within* such provisions (e.g. increased level and scope of benefits and services, trends towards mainstreaming of services, the shift from institutionalization and separate provisions towards deinstitutionalization and integrated provisions, the shift of emphasis from sheltered work to integration in regular work, etc), and the substantial cross-country variation in the profile of redistributive provisions for persons with disabilities.

In order to substantiate this call for a more nuanced discussion of the strengths and weaknesses of redistributive disability provisions, we will present and discuss a few findings from comparative analyses of the output and outcomes of such provisions.

6. REDISTRIBUTIVE DISABILITY PROVISIONS, POVERTY, EMPLOYMENT AND GENDER

Unfortunately, we still have fairly little comparative, representative and reliable data about the output and outcomes of redistributive disability provisions, and even less such data about the well-being, capability and agency of persons with disabilities more generally. Attempts to collect or compile such data have been made by Eurostat, ILO, OECD and the European Social Survey programme.[22] The European Community Household Panel (ECHP) study, the Labour Force Survey (LFS) Ad Hoc Module 2002 of the Eurostat and the current EU-SILC surveys, have all included disability-related questions.[23]

Attempts to produce comparative data bring us back to the fundamental issue of how to define disability for the purpose of official statistics and research. Unlike demographic characteristics like age and gender, whether a person has a disability or not is a characteristic where national statistical authorities can rely on existing registers. Knowledge about whether a person has a disability or not has to be collected through statistical surveys, based on interviews or questionnaires and large scale representative samples of the whole population. Since this approach is based on screening and self-identification, a source of error is the reluctance of some respondents to disclose to a stranger that they are a person with an impairment or disability.

---

[22]   M. Blekesaune, *Have some European countries been more successful at employing disabled people than others?*, ISER Working Paper 2007-23, Institute for Social and Economic Research, (University of Essex, 2007).

[23]   Eurostat, *Disability and social participation in Europe*, (Office for Official Publications of the European Communities, 2001); D. Dupre and A. Karjalainen, *Employment of disabled people in Europe in 2002*, Statistics in Focus, Population and Social Conditions, Population and Living Conditions, Theme 3/26, (Eurostat, 2003); T. Ward and S. Grammenos (eds.), *Men and Women with Disabilities in the EU: Statistical Analysis of the LFS Ad Hoc Module and the EU-SILC*, Final report, (APPLICA, CESEP & ALPHAMETRICS, 2007).

Another complicating factor is that, despite the goal of producing strictly comparable data from different countries and translating terms as precisely as possible between different languages, it is unavoidable that the terms used might have somewhat different associations or connotations for respondents in different countries. Possibly, the availability and scope of a country's disability provisions – both of the redistributive and regulatory kinds – influence respondents' inclination to identify themselves as having an impairment or disability. Moreover, different demographic structures of countries will affect their proportion of citizens with disabilities. Anyway, attempts to collect comparative data have been compounded by the striking and surprising difference in the proportion of respondents from different countries who reported that they had a disability. For instance in the 1996 wave of the ECHP this proportion varied from 8% (Italy) to 23% (Finland), whereas in the 2002 LFS Ad Hoc Module this proportion varied from 7% (Italy) to 32% (Finland).[24]

Bearing these shortcomings and sources of error in mind, we will use some of the existing surveys to raise the following issues:

1. To what extent do redistributive disability provisions help to reduce the risk of poverty among persons with disabilities?
2. To what extent does a high level of redistributive disability provisions increase or decrease the risk of being outside paid employment for persons with disabilities?
3. To what extent do we have reasons to expect that women with disabilities would be more adversely affected by cuts in redistributive disability provisions than men with disabilities?

6.1. LEVEL OF REDISTRIBUTIVE DISABILITY PROVISIONS AND THE POVERTY RISK FOR PERSONS WITH DISABILITIES

As a crude indicator of the level and scope of redistributive disability provisions, we use Eurostat's figures for member states' spending on disability-related benefits as per cent of the gross domestic product (GDP) of these countries.[25] In this context we can see the disability-related expenditure (as per cent of the GDP) as an indicator of a country's policy effort in this area, while the GDP tell us something about the total resources available in this country. As an indicator of poverty risk we draw on existing calculations of the proportion of respondents in the EU-SILC survey reporting considerable restrictions related to a long-standing health problem or disability with a disposable income below 60% of the median disposable income in their country. Here, income is measured on a household basis and equalized for differences in household size and composition.[26]

---

24   Eurostat, *Disability and Social Participation in Europe*; D. Dupre and A. Karjalainen, *Employment of disabled people in Europe in 2002*; T. Ward and S. Grammenos, *Men and Women with Disabilities in the EU* (2007).

25   Eurostat, *European Social Statistics, Social Protection, Expenditure and Receipts, Data 1997-2005*, (Office for Official Publications of the European Communities, 2008), Table C.1.3.2.

26   T. Ward and S. Grammenos, *Men and Women with Disabilities in the EU* (2007), 17

By combining these two indicators we find a clear negative relationship be-tween the level of spending on redistributive disability provisions and the pro-portion of persons with severe disabilities with a disposable income below the poverty line (Pearson correlation = -.68 for women and men together; see Fig. 2)

Figure 2 Relative poverty among persons with severe disabilities by spending on disability-related benefits. Selected European countries

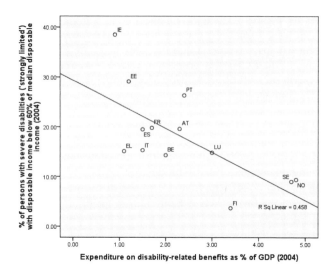

Sources of data: Eurostat, European social statistics, Social protection, Expenditure and receipts, Data 1997-2005, (Office for Official Publications of the European Communities, 2008), Table C.1.3.2 and T. Ward and S. Grammenos (eds.), Men and women with disabilities in the EU: Statistical analysis of the LFS ad hoc module and the EU-SILC, Final report, (APPLICA, CESEP & ALPHAMETRICS, 2007), Table 32.

Unfortunately, the number of countries in this subsample is rather small (n=13). We are therefore not able to control for the effect of the cross-country variation in the proportion of persons reporting to have a severe disability. Hypothetically, the correlation between spending level and the proportion of people with severe disabilities living in poverty might be the result of a spurious relationship. For instance, it could be that the questionnaire formulations used in some countries produced a higher estimate of persons with severe disabilities than the formu-lations used in other countries did, and thus created cross-country differences not reflecting real differences. What we can observe is that countries with higher levels of spending also tend to have a substantially higher proportion of people reporting to have severe disabilities (Pearson correlation = .65). Countries where a higher proportion of persons reporting severe disabilities tend to have somewhat lower proportion of persons reporting such disabilities and having disposable in-comes under the 60 % median (Pearson correlation = -.35). Hence, it is important

and Table 33.

to explore further the relationship between spending levels and poverty risk in future research. To the extent that a clear negative correlation between these two factors is replicated with a larger sample of countries, this would indicate that substantial cuts in redistributive disability provisions could lead to a considerable increase in the proportion of persons with severe disabilities who find themselves in poverty.

6.2. LEVEL OF REDISTRIBUTIVE DISABILITY PROVISIONS AND EMPLOYMENT RATES OF PERSONS WITH DISABILITIES

We have seen that critics of redistributive disability provisions have argued that such provisions in practice are associated with exclusionary processes. Such processes are supposed to be the result either of the disincentive effects of generous income benefits or the inconsistent normative and political messages behind such provisions and the tendency to categorize individuals in a rigid binary way, as either capable or incapable of working in the assessment of claims for such provisions. But are higher levels of redistributive disability provisions necessarily associated with lower levels of employment participation for persons with disabilities? Again, we use Eurostat's figures for member states' spending on disability-related benefits as per cent of the GDP as a crude indicator of the level of redistributive disability provisions in these countries. Moreover, we build on existing age-standardized estimates of the employment rates of respondents in the 2002 LFS Ad Hoc Module reporting considerable restrictions related to a long-standing health problem or disability.[27]

By combining these two indicators, we find a clear *positive* correlation between the level of spending on redistributive disability provisions and the employment rates of respondents with severe disabilities (Pearson correlation = .70 for women and men; =.78 for women, and =.64 for men, see Fig. 3).

---

[27]   Ibid., 13 and Table 18.

Figure 3 Employment rates of persons with severe disabilities by spending on disability-related benefits. Selected European countries

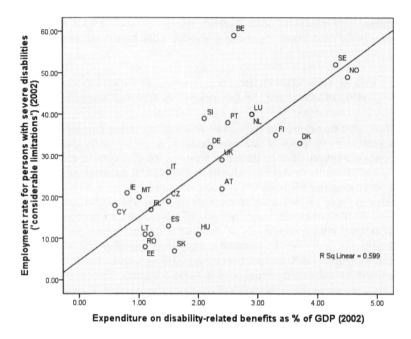

Sources of data: Eurostat, *European social statistics, Social protection, Expenditure and receipts, Data 1997-2005*, (Office for Official Publications of the European Communities, 2008), Table C.1.3.2 & T. Ward and S. Grammenos (eds.), *Men and women with disabilities in the EU: Statistical analysis of the LFS ad hoc module and the EU-SILC*, Final report, (APPLICA, CESEP & ALPHAMETRICS, 2007), Table 18.

In this case, the sample of countries is somewhat larger (n=24). Hence, we are able to control for the effect of the cross-country variation in the proportion of persons reporting to have a severe disability. When we undertake this kind of control in a regression analysis, we find that the level of spending still had a clear positive effect on employment rates of persons with severe disabilities, while the proportion of persons reporting severe disabilities has a negative and weaker effect on employment rates (standardized coefficients of .86 and -.17 respectively).

In our view, the most fruitful interpretation of the positive relationship between spending levels and employment rates is that in several countries – and particularly so in countries with a relative high level of spending – the total spending on redistributive disability provisions do not only cover the costs of income transfers and social services for persons who remain out of work for prolonged periods, but also costs related to measures of economic integration (e.g. training, services for independent living, financial support for participants in active measures or vocational rehabilitation, technical aids enabling employment, wage subsidies, etc). Moreover, even if the largest single item of the total expenditure in all countries is income maintenance for persons out of work for long periods, this item may still include income transfers to persons who are able to work on a part-time basis.

In principle, one should think that it would be straightforward to examine the relationship between employment rates and the level of spending related to 'pure' income transfers for persons out of work ('passive benefits') separately. While we find a clear and positive relationship between the spending on what has been classified as 'cash benefits' and employment rates (Pearson correlation = .55), existing classification system does not allow us to distinguish clearly between cash benefits for persons with disabilities who participate in measures to enter or return to work, and those who do not. More generally, there are reasons to doubt whether the discursive distinction between active and passive benefits lends itself to consistent operationalization.

While some of the spending on redistributive disability-related provisions relate to separate or segregated forms of employment, e.g. sheltered employment, in the large majority of European countries sheltered employment accounts for a limited part for all the jobs of persons with disabilities.[28] Even if further research is called for in the area, the results reported here do not suggest that redistributive provisions are necessarily associated with exclusionary processes that justify substantial cuts in the level and duration of such provisions.

Finally, it may not be justified to dismiss spending on redistributive provisions related to disability solely as 'social consumption'. The results presented here suggest that such provisions, to a great extent, have positive effects not only for the living standards and well-being of recipients, but also can have a positive impact on economic integration and participation on the part of persons with disabilities. In this sense, a substantial proportion of the spending on redistributive disability-related provisions – especially in high-spending countries – may also be regarded as 'social investment'.[29] Arguably, the constructive or developmental functions of redistributive provisions have not just been accidental, but reflect the original political design of these provisions in these countries. For instance, policy-makers linked active measures like education and training to the provision of fairly generous and universal benefits in order to make the latter financially sustainable and control the inflow of new recipients.[30]

[28]   T. Ward *et al.* (eds.), *Study of Compilation of Disability Statistical Data from Administrative Registers of the Member States,* Final Report, (Applica, Cesep & European Centre, 2007), 81.

[29]   G. Esping-Andersen, 'After the golden age? Welfare state dilemmas in a global economy', in G. Esping-Andersen (ed.), *Welfare States in Transition,* (Unrisd, 1996); A. Giddens, *The Third Way,* (Polity Press, 1998); J. Jenson & D. Saint-Martin, 'New routes to social cohesion? Citizenship and the social investment state', 28 *Canadian Journal of Sociology* 1 (2003), 77; Nesc, *The Developmental Welfare State,* (National Economic & Social Council, 2005).

[30]   See for instance B. Hvinden, *Divided Against Itself: A Study of Integration of Welfare Bureaucracy,* (Scandinavian University Press, 1992).

6.3. REDISTRIBUTIVE DISABILITY-RELATED PROVISIONS AND GENDER

We have already referred to the particularly strong increase in disability-related benefit recipiency rates among women in many countries during the last two-three decades. In the Scandinavian countries, women are in the majority among recipients of disability pensions.[31] Moreover, the correlation between the levels of spending on redistributive disability provisions and poverty rates are somewhat stronger for women than for men (Pearson correlation = -.67 for women and -.59 for men). We know that women, in general, tend to have lower incomes and be at a higher risk of living in poverty than men.[32] Altogether these factors suggest that reform in redistributive disability-related provisions is a gendered issue in the sense that more might be at stake for women than for men if governments were to undertake substantial cuts in such provisions.

7. THE POTENTIAL CONTRIBUTION OF HUMAN RIGHTS INSTRUMENTS IN PROMOTING AND PROTECTING THE ECONOMIC AND SOCIAL RIGHTS OF PERSONS WITH DISABILITIES

We have seen that there are strong and probably growing pressures for tightening up redistributive disability-related provisions. The demographic ageing taking place in many rich western countries are likely to reinforce such pressures, both to mobilize a greater part of the potential labour force and to improve public finances. At the same time it is not clear how prepared most employers in these countries are to see persons with disabilities as potential employees in their organization, and ensure accessibility and necessary accommodations that will enable persons with disabilities to function as employees on an equal basis with others. Many employers still appear to have prejudiced and stereotyped perceptions of persons with disabilities, to underestimate the contribution that employees with disabilities can make, and overestimate the problems that recruitment of job applicants are likely to entail.

Social regulation provisions to promote equal treatment and accessibility and combat discrimination have been introduced and strengthened in many European countries, not the least as a result of the equality strategy of the European Community. Regulatory provisions are rapidly gaining a prominent role in the disability protection system of many countries. Although such provisions have led to important progress in areas like access to physical environments, information and communication technologies and markets for goods and services, results have been more uncertain in the area of employment. Persons with disabilities still have disproportionally lower employment rates than other persons of work-

---

[31]   Nososco, *Social Protection in the Nordic Countries, 2005*, (Nordic Social Statistical Committee, 2007), Table 7.14.

[32]   In 2006 women were at higher risk of having an equivalized disposable income below 60 % of the national median disposable income in 24 of 29 European countries *before transfers* and in 22 of these countries *after transfers*, see <www.eurostat. eu>.

ing age – also in countries where non-discrimination provisions have existed for a substantial period. Social regulation's potential for improving the employment situation of persons with disabilities seems, at least partly, to depend on a combination of will and ability to enforce the legal duties and social responsibilities of employers. It is not clear how far executive authorities, legislatures and courts today are really willing – or able – to challenge the prerogatives of employers to hire and fire, especially in a context of sharpened global competition. Given a limited will and/or ability of decision-makers, the sufficiency of legal regulatory provisions, at least in themselves, is questionable. We will first concentrate on the issue of the will to enforce the duties and responsibilities of employers.

The wills of the executive branch, the legislature and the courts may obviously differ to lesser or greater extents at any given point in time. Yet, it seems reasonable to assume that all three wills are affected by the values, ideas and understandings of reality that dominate in the society in question. The dominating values, ideas and understandings are evidently to some extent – but not solely – determined by the relative powers of, and alliances between, different societal interests and sectorial forces, e.g. business, labour, the church, the military, the media, the intelligentsia, etc. Yet, values, ideas and understandings have a certain autonomy; they travel across countries and become shared in wider circles. 'Human rights' represent one important complex of interrelated values, ideas and understandings of reality that have spread out, especially through the role of international and supranational bodies. Consequently, human rights have also the potential to influence the wills of the executive, the legislature and the courts to the extent that the values, ideas and understandings behind such rights become embedded in society, as they can change established notions of what is just, fair and appropriate.

The UN High Commissioner for Human Rights has codified four core values of human rights law of particular importance in the context of disability:

> The *dignity* of each individual, who is deemed to be of inestimable value because of his/her inherent self-worth and not because s/he is economically or otherwise 'useful'; the concept of *autonomy* or self-determination, which is based on the presumption of a capacity for self-directed action and behaviour, and requires that the person be placed at the centre of all decisions affecting him/her; the inherent *equality* of all regardless of difference; and the ethic of *solidarity*, which requires society to sustain the freedom of the person with appropriate social supports.[33]

In our context the fourth core value is of particular relevance as it most directly points towards the role of redistributive welfare provisions (income transfers and services). The third core value gives the normative basis for equal treatment, including non-discrimination and accommodation in relation to employment. The stronger position these values have in society, the less legitimate it will be to leave persons with disability in poverty or to justify disregard, neglect and exclusion of persons with disabilities as potential or actual workers.

For a non-legal eye, existing human rights instruments seem to vary greatly

---

[33]   'Introduction', The Office of the United Nations High Commissioner for Human Rights, 2008, see <http://www2.ohchr.org/english/issues/disability/intro.htm> (accessed 10 November 2008).

with regard to whether they explicitly state that all human beings – or more spe-cifically human beings with disabilities – have the right to a decent living stand-ard, the right to social provisions that can ensure a decent living standard, and/or the right to work and a sufficient remuneration to obtain a decent living standard. Moreover, to the extent that the instruments give explicit statements about such rights, the instruments also differ considerably as whether they furnish individu-als with enforceable rights or not.

Interestingly, human rights instruments vary considerably in the extent to which they explicitly spell out an adequate or decent living standard as basic hu-man right, and security in the event of lack of livelihood. For instance, we find formulations to this effect in the following documents:

- The Universal Declaration of Human Rights (1948)[34]
- The United Nations Declarations on the rights of disabled persons (1975)[35]
- Convention on the Elimination of All forms of Discrimination against Women (1979)[36]
- Convention on the Rights of the Child (1989)[37]

The International Covenant on Economic, Social and Cultural Rights (1966) and the European Social Charter (revised 1996) are examples of human rights instru-ments that mainly approach the right to an adequate or decent living standard through the equal right to participate in gainful employment, i.e. as derived from the right to work.[38] The European Social Charter does, however, use terms like 'adequate social security benefits' in the context of the employed women's right to protection of maternity and 'adequate resources' in the context of the right to social and medical assistance.[39] More generally, the European Social Charter ad-dresses the right to social security 'at a satisfactory level', and at least equal to that as is necessary for the ratification of the European Code of Social Security.

In sum, it seems that most existing general human rights instruments put the main emphasis on civil and political rights, and when they deal with social rights, the equal right to work, education and services play the main role. To the extent that a right to a decent or adequate living standard is spelled out, this tends to be formulated as a general norm or ideal. For instance, the human rights instruments do not specify how the notion of a decent or adequate living standard relates to the average or median living standard of a nation's population. In the absence of this kind of operationalization, it will probably be difficult both for individuals

---

[34] Universal Declaration of Human Rights (adopted and proclaimed by General As-sembly resolution 217 A (III) of 10 December 1948), Art. 25.
[35] Declaration on the Rights of Disabled Persons (proclaimed by General Assembly resolution 3447 (XXX) of 9 December 1975), Art. 7.
[36] Convention on the Elimination of All Forms of Discrimination against Women (ad-opted by General Assembly 18 December 1979), Art. 14.3. (h).
[37] Convention on the Rights of the Child (adopted by General Assembly 20 November 1989), Arts. 26 and 27.
[38] International Covenant on Economic, Social and Cultural Rights (adopted by Gen-eral Assembly resolution 2200A (XXI) of 16 December 1966), Art. 7 (a) (ii), and European Social Charter (revised 1996), Art. 4.
[39] European Social Charter (revised, 1996), Arts. 8 and 13.

or organizations to use such formulations as argumentative ammunition against cuts in existing redistributive provisions or in favour of improved redistributive provisions. Without any yardstick or benchmark for judging whether an existing or proposed provision gives beneficiaries a decent or adequate living standard, the scope for discretionary decisions on the part of courts or monitoring bodies remains very wide.

Consequently, it is imaginable that the lack of agreement on what yardstick or benchmark to use to judge whether a given living standard is adequate, could turn out to be an Achilles-heel in efforts to use Article 28 of the CRPD. In this context, the last part of Article 23(1) is of great potential significance: 'State Parties recognize the right of persons with disabilities to an adequate standard of living for themselves and their families, including adequate food, clothing and housing, and to the continuous improvement of living conditions, and *shall take appropriate steps to safeguard and promote the realization of this right without discrimination on the basis of disability*' (our emphasis). This commitment on the part of State Parties offers the opportunity to argue that national authorities will have a duty not to dismantle or weaken existing redistributive provisions, but rather to improve them to ensure that the living standards of persons with disabilities develop in line the general living standards of the country in question.

8. TOWARD A GREATER SYNERGY BETWEEN REDISTRIBUTIVE AND REGULATORY PROVISIONS – CIVIL AND SOCIAL RIGHTS

Gerald Quinn has given a stimulating analysis of how the monitoring body for the European Social Charter has made efforts to align the social rights of persons with disabilities with their civil rights through its jurisprudence.[40] He suggests that there is a wider scope for such efforts, also in the context of the CRPD and the Committee on the Rights of Persons with Disabilities. If one looks carefully at the cases that Quinn analyzes, it seems that what the monitoring body for the European Social Charter has done is to use the Charter's principles of equality and non-discrimination to demand partly a redirection of the resources spent on redistributive provisions, to make mainstreaming and inclusion a reality, and partly oblige national authorities to improve the quality of provisions where persons with disabilities are among the beneficiaries, i.e. unavoidably increase the amount of resources spent on such provisions. From our perspective, these aspects of the cases are a forceful argument for a further strengthening of redistributive provisions for persons with disabilities, and not for a dismantlement of such provisions.

In the first part of this paper, we referred to Article 5 of the EC Framework Directive on Equal Treatment in Employment and Occupation and the obligation of employers to provide reasonable accommodation. According to this article, the costs of providing reasonable accommodation is not to be seen as a disproportionate burden when this burden is sufficiently remedied by measures existing within the framework of disability policy of the Member State. We are to expect more of employers in terms of accommodation efforts when the costs of these efforts can be shared between the employer and the public purse. Hence, a quite important

---

[40]   G. Quinn, in G. de Burca and B. de Witte (eds.), *Social Rights in Europe.*

issue is whether the employer operates in a national context where the system of redistributive disability-related provisions makes this kind of sharing possible. In a number of countries (e.g. Norway), such financial support for accommodation in the workplace is available, opening up a crucial form of synergy between redistributive and regulatory provisions. The full potential of this synergy has not been realized so far, partly because existing legislation does not include provision to reimburse some aspects of workplace accommodation, partly because provisions recognize a too narrow type of accommodation, and partly because there are shortcomings in the implementation of the provisions. Norwegian experiences suggest that the effective impact of such provision can be increased under these conditions:

- All relevant parties must be aware and fully informed both about employers' duty to provide accommodation and the legal scope for a public-private sharing of the costs. These parties include employers, the individual employee or job applicant with a disability, his/her trade union representative, front-line staff in the bodies responsible for enforcement, supervision and/or implementation, and advisors in non-governmental organizations (NGOs) of and for persons with disabilities.
- There must be a firm commitment from the relevant public authorities and agencies to use the scope for proactive action that the legislation allows them. The organizations of and for persons with disabilities, trade unions and other NGOs must put pressure on public authorities to demonstrate will and ability to use this scope.
- Individuals who see themselves as discriminated against, including by being denied an accommodation in the workplace or having the possibilities for an accommodation to be assessed properly, must be given encouragement and support to file complaints, and if necessary, to take their case to court. Public authorities or NGOs must provide funds to cover costs related to litigation in such cases, at least in test cases.
- There must be a systematic monitoring, assessment and public reporting of the enforcement of regulatory provisions related to Article 5 in the Framework Directive and the implementation of redistributive provisions that ensure the sharing of accommodation costs. Public authorities must consider whether existing support arrangements are sufficiently geared towards the kind of accommodation that are required in the emerging post-industrial working life with high-skilled, information and communication intensive jobs and 'greedy' work organizations (e.g. reorganization, reassignment of tasks, more flexible working time, increased scope for working partly from home, etc).[41]

9. CONCLUDING REMARKS

This paper has discussed the relationship between the more traditional redistributive parts and the newer regulatory parts of disability protection systems. We have argued that the current criticism against redistributive disability provisions

---

[41] B. Hvinden, 'How to get employers to take on greater responsibility for the inclusion of disabled people in working life', in B. Marin *et al.* (eds.), *Transforming Disability Welfare Policies*, (Ashgate, 2004), 333.

are somewhat one-sided, tending to exaggerate the segregating and exclusionary functions of such provisions, to disregard the complexity and development over time within such provisions, and downplay the significance of income transfers and services for the dignity, autonomy and participation for a great number of persons with disabilities. This argument has been substantiated through an analysis of existing cross-national data about poverty risk and employment participation of persons with disabilities. Even if these data are far from perfect, they indicate that the level and scope of redistributive provisions do make a substantial difference for the well-being of persons with disabilities and that the association with segregation and exclusion is not the only story that can be told about such provisions. Dismantlement or far-reaching cuts in redistributive provisions are not warranted. At the same time, it is clear that existing redistributive provisions are not sufficient in themselves.

The advance of social regulatory disability provisions based on principles of equality and non-discrimination is essential for making the rights to dignity, autonomy and participation a practical reality for persons with disabilities. Yet, it is unlikely that social regulatory provisions can replace redistributive provisions. The full practical impact of the new social regulatory provisions remains still to be seen, especially in the area of employment. In this context, we should look systematically for complementarities and synergies between regulatory and redistributive provisions. We have indicated how redistributive provisions in the form of financial support can play an important role in preventing concern for costs, which undermine the employers' duty to provide accommodations for employees or job applicants with disabilities. The provision of wage subsidies in cases where employers fear that a job applicant with a disability will be less productive than his or her colleagues, even after appropriate accommodation has been provided, may be another example of such synergy.

Finally, and in line with the spirit of Article 28 of the CRPD, we would like to emphasize that to the extent that persons with disabilities remain excluded from employment – despite the introduction of more promising mixes of legal and financial instruments to promote inclusion – public authorities must accept the responsibility to guarantee decent living standards and independence for all through adequate redistributive provisions.

'PROMOTING EQUALITY?'

Early Lessons from the Statutory Disability Duty in Great Britain

Caroline Gooding[1]

1. INTRODUCTION

Achieving greater equality requires changes at many levels, including changes in attitudes and relationships, in institutions and legal frameworks, in economic institutions, and in political decision-making structures. In relation to gender, a strategy of 'mainstreaming' has long been considered a key means of achieving such changes,[2] and this approach is increasingly being adopted for other equality issues.[3]

A paper commissioned by the European Commission identified a compulsory element, such as statutory duty to promote equality, as the critical factor for successful implementation of a mainstreaming approach.[4]

> Research suggests that while other factors are also important (such as access to practical mainstreaming instruments and equality specialists, the presence of a political environment conducive to equality mainstreaming etc.), non-discrimination mainstreaming only tends to occur systematically when supported by [such a statutory base].

---

[1]   Caroline Gooding is a former Director of Legislative Change at the Disability Rights Commission, and is currently a freelance consultant.

[2]   Gender mainstreaming was established as a major global strategy for the promotion of gender equality in the Beijing Platform for Action from the Fourth United Nations World Conference on Women in Beijing in 1995. See United Nations Office of the Special Adviser on Gender Issues and Advancement of Women, *Gender Mainstreaming An overview,* (United Nations, 2002).

[3]   C. O'Cinneide, 'Positive Duties and Gender Equality', 8 *International Journal of Discrimination and the Law,* 8 (2005), 91.

[4]   Centre for strategy and evaluation services, *Non-discrimination mainstreaming – instruments, case studies and way forwards,* (European Commission, Directorate-General for Employment, Social Affairs and Equal Opportunities, 2007).

The positive duties on the public sector to promote equality, introduced in Great Britain in relation to race,[5] disability[6] and gender,[7] along with the pre-existing Northern Ireland duty on which they are modelled,[8] are the prime examples of a statutory mainstreaming requirement.[9]

These duties have ambitious goals: to mainstream equality into the way in which the public sector carries out its business, root out institutional discrimination and change the culture of public sector organizations with the ultimate aims of improving equality outcomes, producing greater engagement of disadvantaged groups in policy making and improved accountability of public authorities. They thus represent a paradigmatic shift in the law, away from a negative and reactive focus on individual acts of discrimination, to an understanding that achieving greater equality requires purposive State action to tackle systemic discrimination and structural disadvantage arising from a number of inter-connecting sources.

Debates regarding the impact of the duties are thus of interest in Europe, and beyond. On the one hand, they have been heralded as a 'new generation' of equality law.[10] A seminal review of British equality legislation reported considerable consensus that such duties represent an essential supplement to the deficiencies of existing anti-discrimination law, with pro-active and integrative methods, based on a foundation of greater participation in decision making by disadvantaged groups.[11]

On the other hand, despite this generally positive welcome, a range of potential concerns have also been raised, most fundamentally that the duties lack a clear

---

5   S. 71 (1) Race Relations Act 1976, as substituted by Race Relations (Amendment) Act 2000.
6   S. 49A of the Disability Discrimination Act 1995, as inserted by Disability Discrimination Act 2005.
7   S. 76A Sex Discrimination Act 1975, as amended by Equality Act 2006.
8   Section 75 Northern Ireland Act 1998 applies not only to disability, gender and race but also sexuality, age, religion (marital status, political affiliation and with/without dependants). See Chaney and Rees, 'The Northern Ireland Section 75 Equality Duty: An International Perspective', 1-51 in E. McLaughlin, and N. Faris (eds), *The Section 75 Equality Duty – An Operational Review'*, volume 2 (Northern Ireland Office, 2004).
9   A similar duty exists in Finland, but only in relation to gender and race equality. Under the 2004 Equality Act, Finnish public bodies have responsibility to systematically promote equality in all their activities as well as to take remedial steps to tackle obstacles to the realization of equality. A practical means of promoting equality of opportunity provided for by the Act is the requirement on public authorities to draw up an Equality Plan. While there has been a statutory duty on public bodies to draw up a Gender Equality Plan since 1995, the 2004 Act introduced an additional requirement to produce a separate plan on race and ethnicity.
10   S. Fredman, 'Equality: A New Generation', 30 *Industrial Law Journal* 2 (2001), 145-168.
11   B. Hepple *et al*, *Equality: A New Framework, Report of the Independent Review of Anti Discrimination Legislation*, (University of Cambridge Centre for Public Law, 2000). See also C. O'Cinneide, *Taking Equal Opportunities Seriously, The Extension of Positive Duties to Promote Equality,* (Equality and Diversity Forum, 2003).

concept of equality and will merely produce tokenistic, procedural compliance.[12] Perhaps the most surprising source of criticism was the same Government that introduced the duties. In 2007 a Green Paper was published setting out proposals for combining the public sector equality duties in a new model, and considering whether to extend the duty to age, sexual orientation and/or religion or belief.[13] Despite their recent advent (the gender duty had only come into force two months earlier), and with scant evidence of their operation, the *Framework for Fairness* Green Paper, whilst acknowledging 'encouraging evidence that, to an extent it has had a positive influence on public authorities' practices', concluded that 'the success of the duty in achieving real change in our society has been more limited than had been hoped for'.[14]

This article considers the validity of these critiques through an examination of the distinctive experience of the disability equality duties (DED), their implementation and initial impact.

It argues that the novelty of the duties and their ambitious goals, combined with the lack of a sustained programme of legal enforcement, go a long way to explain the perceived limitations of their impact. In addition, many critiques have focused on the performance and design of the race equality duties,[15] due to its earlier introduction. However, lessons from the race duty were used to introduce improvements in both the design and the implementation of the DED,[16] and this article identifies where the form and practice of the two duties diverge, as well as where lessons can be drawn from the recent gender equality duty.

Notwithstanding this positive assessment, the article concludes that there are ways in which the duties need to be strengthened, without destroying their basic framework, and that the opportunity of the forthcoming Single Equality Bill should be used for this purpose. There is not space in this article to consider the case for the extension of similar duties to the private sector, nor the impact of the duties on the private sector through public procurement.[17]

---

[12] S. Fredman, 'Changing the norm: positive duties in equal treatment legislation', 12 *Maastricht Journal of European and Comparative Law* 4 (2005), 369-398; C. O'Cinneide, 'Positive Duties and Gender Equality', 8 *International Journal of Discrimination and the Law* (2005), 91.

[13] Department for Communities and Local Government *et al*, *Discrimination Law Review – A Framework for Fairness: Proposals for a Single Equality Bill for Great Britain* (Department for Communities and Local Government, June 2007).

[14] Ibid, 5.14.

[15] Schneider Ross, *Towards Racial Equality,* (Commission for Racial Equality, 2003); Audit Commission, *The Journey to Race Equality,* (Audit Commission, 2004).

[16] The race, disability and gender duties each have important differences within their common framework, the most significant of which will be identified in the course of the discussion below. These differences in drafting in part reflect the distinctive features of the issues which the duties seek to address but also stem from the institutional accident that the duties were introduced through three separate pieces of legislation from three different Government Departments.

[17] But see B. Hepple *et al*, *Equality: A New Framework*, 56-7; C. O'Cinneide, 'A New Generation of Equality Legislation? Positive Duties and Disability Rights', in A. Lawson and C. Gooding (eds.), *Disability Rights in Europe,* (Hart, 2005), 239.

2. THE DISABILITY EQUALITY DUTIES

The statutory framework for the DED is set out in the Disability Discrimination Act 2005 and its accompanying regulations (hereinafter referred to as 'the Disability Regulations)',[18] supplemented by a Statutory Code of Practice (hereinafter referred to as 'the Code').[19] Statutory Codes are admissible as evidence in determining the meaning of a statute and must be taken into account by Courts where relevant. Such Codes are influential in determining the meaning and impact of a statute, and are widely read. Codes can be thus used to address issues arising out of the bare statutory language, and this article makes extensive use of this important source.[20]

The Statutory Code for the disability equality duties was written by the Disability Rights Commission (DRC). The DRC was an independent, Government funded body established by statute[21] in 2000. Its duties were to work towards the elimination of discrimination and to promote the equalization of opportunities for disabled people.[22] It played a pivotal role in the implantation of the new duties until it was subsumed into the Equality and Human Rights Commission in October 2007.

2.1. GENERAL DUTY

The general disability duty requires that every public authority shall, in carrying out its functions, have due regard to the need to: promote equality of opportunity between disabled persons and other persons; eliminate discrimination that is unlawful under the Act; eliminate harassment of disabled persons that is related to their disabilities; promote positive attitudes towards disabled persons; encourage participation by disabled persons in public life; and take steps to take account of disabled persons' disabilities, even where that involves treating disabled persons more favourably than other persons.[23]

The entire edifice of the statutory duties to promote equality is built upon this requirement for authorities to 'have due regard' to equality in its various dimensions. The Code states:

> Due regard' comprises two linked elements: proportionality and relevance. In all their decisions and functions authorities should give due weight to

---

[18]   The Disability Discrimination (Public Authorities) (Statutory Duties) Regulations 2005, SI 2966.

[19]   Disability Rights Commission, *The Duty to Promote Disability Equality: Statutory Code of Practice*, (2005).

[20]   However, there are two clear constraints on the Commission when writing such Codes. Firstly, the Codes must receive Parliamentary approval. Secondly, where an issue is unclear in law any ambiguity cannot be resolved by a Code, although it can point in favour of a particular interpretation, but only by a Court.

[21]   Disability Rights Commission Act 1999.

[22]   Ibid., s. 2 (1).

[23]   Disability Discrimination Act 1995 s.49A.

the need to promote disability equality in proportion to its relevance. This requires more than simply giving consideration to disability equality.[24]

Looking at 'proportionality' the Code says:

> Proportionality requires greater consideration to be given to disability equality in relation to functions or policies that have the most effect on disabled people. Where changing a function or proposed policy would lead to significant benefits to disabled people, the need for such a change will carry added weight when balanced against other considerations.[25]

This duty applies to all public authorities except those exempted by the Act or by regulations. It came into force on 4th December 2006.

2.2. SPECIFIC DUTIES

The general duty is supported by specific duties, whose purpose is to ensure the better performance of the general duty. The specific duties require authorities to prepare and publish Disability Equality Schemes (DES), and to review and re-fresh them periodically thereafter (at least every three years). There is also an explicit requirement to implement the actions in the Scheme's action plan, and its arrangements for gathering and using information. Authorities must publish annual reports containing a summary of steps taken under the Action Plan and the results of its information gathering, including the uses to which the information has been put. This requirement improves transparency and accountability.

These duties are imposed upon those bodies listed in the relevant regulations, and these constitute the great majority of public authorities.[26] For most authorities schemes had to be in place by 4th December 2006.

The disability regulations prescribe the key elements that must be contained in these disability equality schemes. They must contain statements of: the way in which disabled people have been involved in the development of the scheme; arrangements for impact assessment and for gathering and using information; and an action plan for implementing the general duty.

The requirement to 'involve' disabled people in the development of the scheme is a key element of the duty, and is discussed further below. The Code states that 'involvement' requires a more active engagement of disabled stakeholders than 'consultation', [27] and goes on to give more detailed guidance on what such 'involvement' might entail. It stresses that disabled people should be involved in all key aspects of the development of the Scheme, such as setting priorities for action plans and including them in implementation and review.[28]

---

[24] Code 2.34.
[25] Ibid., 2.36.
[26] Smaller local authorities, small specialized advisory bodies and some professional bodies are not subject to the specific duties, but are subject to the general duties.
[27] Code 3.13.
[28] Code 3.10 'the involvement of disabled people in the implementation of the various aspects of the Scheme (such as conducting impact assessments and gathering evidence) will also be critical to the successful implementation of the duty. For example, involving disabled people in monitoring the success of initiatives throughout

The process of impact assessment is at the centre of the duties, designed to assist authorities in giving due regard to disability equality in all their decisions and functions and thus to ensure that equality considerations are 'mainstreamed'. Where a negative impact, or missed opportunity to better promote equality of opportunity, is identified, the authority must consider modifying the policy or practice.

For the process to work it needs to be embedded in all decision-making and policy development. The Code makes clear that the impact assessment process is supposed not only to be applied to new policies but also to be retrospectively applied to major programmes and policies, to ensure that they give consideration to disability equality.[29]

The requirement to build disability equality impact assessments into decision making is an ambitious technique for changing the culture of organizations. At the same time authorities must include in their DESs a plan to deliver more immediate improvements. Schemes are required to include a statement of steps which authorities will take to ensure they fulfil their general duty within the lifetime of the Scheme.[30] This action plan must be sufficient to demonstrate that the public authority is giving due regard to disability equality, and must give appropriate weight to the different elements of the duty. Authorities are required to carry out the steps in this action plan unless they can show that it is unreasonable and impractical to do so.[31]

The Code states that 'the action plan in a highly effective Disability Equality Scheme will reflect: the priorities of disabled people, as elicited through involvement and the strategic priorities of the authority, as well as evidence of where the problems and priorities lie.'[32]

Finally, Schemes must set out authorities' arrangements for collecting information on the recruitment, development and retention of disabled employees and on the extent to which their services and functions take account of the needs of disabled people. Education authorities are not required to produce information on this second aspect, but instead to gather information on their policies and practices' effect on educational opportunities and achievements of disabled students/pupils.[33]

Historically, there is a paucity of evidence about disability equality. The Disability Equality Duty will require authorities to work to remedy this problem. The evidence gathering and analysis process will assist authorities in deciding where action is most needed, reviewing its effectiveness and deciding what further work needs to be done.

A strong evidence base on disability equality should also improve awareness amongst policy makers and service providers, and is also essential for effective disability equality impact assessment.

A public authority must also include in its Disability Equality Scheme its

the duration of the Disability Equality Scheme will assist with evaluation, and will be critical when the time comes to review and revise the Scheme.' Code 3.11.

[29]   Code 3.40.
[30]   Disability Regulations 2(3)(c).
[31]   Disability Regulations 3.
[32]   Code 3.46; 3.48 – 49.
[33]   Disability Regulations 2 (3) (d).

arrangements for making use of the information obtained and, in particular, its arrangements for reviewing on a regular basis the effectiveness of the steps set out in the action plan and preparing subsequent Disability Equality Schemes.[34]

This statutory emphasis on making use of the data collected is a helpful improvement on the race equality duty where initial reports showed that public authorities were not doing this.[35] Unfortunately, the Statutory Code provides little guidance on precisely how the data should be used. In particular, its statements about the setting of targets are framed in a way which emphasizes good practice rather than strict legal requirements:

> Setting specific targets can play a useful role in ensuring that due regard is paid to disability equality in key employment or service delivery areas. Government departments either as part of their own Disability Equality Scheme or under the Secretary of State duty could usefully take the lead in setting targets for public authorities to meet.[36]

This recognizes the importance of target setting, but falls short of stating that such an approach is necessary to comply with the duties. I shall return to this significant point below.

2.3.   DUTY ON SECRETARIES OF STATE

Finally the DED requires certain Secretaries of State, the National Assembly for Wales and Scottish Ministers to publish a report every three years (starting from December 2008), providing an overview of the progress made by public authorities in their policy sector in relation to disability equality. They must also set out proposals for co-ordination of action by those public authorities in that policy sector, or remit area, to bring about further progress on disability equality.[37]

Whilst the exact wording might be improved (for example, by requiring a focus on national targets), this is a valuable requirement to provide national leadership and 'joined up' thinking. For a national framework to be effective, Secretaries of State and Scottish Ministers must be under a duty to provide leadership in their respective policy sectors and to ensure strategic, co-ordinated action across government. Some equality issues cut across sectors and require action across government departments.

2.4.   COMPARISON WITH RACE AND GENDER DUTIES

The race, disability and gender duties each have unique features within their common framework. These drafting differences partly reflect the distinctive issues which the duties seek to address in relation to gender, race and disability, but also stem from the institutional accident that the duties were introduced through three separate pieces of legislation from three different Government Departments.

The general duties in regard to race, disability and gender are all framed in

---

[34]   Disability Regulations 2 (3) (e).
[35]   Schneider Ross, *Towards Racial Equality*.
[36]   Code 3.2.
[37]   Disability Regulations (5).

terms of giving 'due regard' to a series of specified 'needs'. Whilst they all require due regard to the need to eliminate discrimination and promote equal opportunity, the objectives differ in other ways. Whilst the disability and gender duties require authorities to have due regard to the need to eliminate harassment, the race duty is silent on this issue. Only the race duty requires due regard to the need to promote good relations between persons of different racial groups.

The disability duty most explicitly spells out the different dimensions of equality: positive attitudes towards disabled people, participation in public life and taking account of disabled people's needs. However, the absence of an explicit reference to these dimensions in relation to race and gender should not be interpreted as signaling that they are not also relevant to these areas, and implicitly required to promote equality. For example, encouragement of participation in public life will also be relevant to gender and race. The three sets of specific duties all require authorities to prepare equality schemes and some of the elements of these schemes are the same: all must set out arrangements for gathering evidence and carrying out impact assessments.[38]

Nevertheless, there are some significant differences. The race duty is the most prescriptive and procedural, for example, requiring authorities to list all their functions which they have assessed as of relevance to the race equality duty. The disability and gender duties are more action oriented. The disability duty requires a Scheme to set out the steps that an authority will take to fulfil its general duty, while the gender duty requires schemes to set out the overall objectives which the authority judges are necessary to perform the general duty. Importantly, both the disability and the gender duties require the steps to be taken or objectives achieved within the lifetime of the scheme (unless this becomes unreasonable or impossible).

The other key difference is the specific requirement in the disability duty that authorities actively involve disabled people in the development of their DES. The gender duty only requires authorities to 'consult' employees, service users and others, and the race duty does not require any form of consultation of the Scheme (although in contrast to the other duties it does explicitly require consultation on the likely impact of proposed policies).

Finally, the Secretary of State duties, designed to ensure that Government provides leadership across different sectors of state activity, apply to disability and gender but not race.

3. ENFORCEMENT OF THE DUTIES

At the time that the disability equality duties came into effect, the Disability Rights Commission was the body which exercised the key enforcement role. This commission was dissolved, and replaced by the Equality and Human Rights Commission (EHRC) in October 2007. For simplicity, this explanation of the enforcement procedures will refer to both institutions as 'the Commission', except where the enforcement regime was altered with the advent of EHRC.

If a public authority does not comply with the general duty, its actions, or

---

[38]   Race Relations Act 1976 (Statutory Duties) Orders 2001 and Sex Discrimination Act 1975 (Public Authorities) (Statutory Duties) Order 2006 SI 2006/2930 set out the specific duties in relation to race and gender respectively.

failure to act, can be challenged by means of a claim to the High Court for judicial review. A claim for judicial review may be made by a person or a group of people with an interest in the matter, or by the Commission.

If a public authority does not comply with its specific duties, the Commission can serve a compliance notice stating that the authority must meet its duties and tell the Commission, within twenty-eight days, what it has done to comply.[39] If the public authority fails to provide the Commission with this information, the Commission may apply to a county court (in England and Wales), or sheriff court (in Scotland), for an order requiring the authority to furnish the information required by the notice.[40] If, three months after a compliance notice has been served, the Commission considers that the authority has still not met its specific duties, the Commission can apply to the county court or sheriff court for an order requiring compliance.[41] If the court makes an order and the authority does not abide by it, the authority may be found to be in contempt of court.[42]

The EHRC was given important additional enforcement powers. Firstly, it has the capacity to instigate judicial review proceedings.[43] In addition, however, the Commission has the specific power to conduct an assessment of compliance with the general and the specific duties, following which a compliance notice can be issued.[44] This specific power to assess was not available to the previous commissions.[45] It is a valuable additional power, for the first time allowing enforcement of the general duty through a compliance notice. However, it is likely to prove resource intensive and may suffer neglect in an overstretched and under-funded Commission.

4. IMPLEMENTATION OF THE DUTIES

The Commission for Racial Equality (CRE), charged with overseeing the implementation of the race duty, concentrated resources on working with individual authorities. To an extent this was inevitable, given that these were the first such duties to be introduced. However, over time they concluded that this approach was not productive. 'All anecdotal feedback has suggested that it has only been since the CRE started taking robust action against non-compliance, and using the press and public statements to advertise this, that public authorities have made this work a priority.'[46]

Learning from the CRE's experiences, the DRC moved immediately to a

---

[39] Equality Act 2006 S.32.
[40] Equality Act 2006.
[41] Equality Act 2006.
[42] Equality Act 2006.
[43] Equality Act 2006 s. 30(1).
[44] Equality Act s.31 (1) & 32.
[45] Enforcement of the specific duties is by means of the issuing of a compliance notice (Equality Act s.32 (1)). A compliance notice can also be issued in respect of the general duties, but this can only be done after an assessment and the notice must relate to the results of that assessment (Equality Act s.32(4)).
[46] Commission for Racial Equality Monitoring and Enforcement Plan – Final Report, (CRE Website, September 2007), accessed via: <http://83.137.212.42/sitearchive/ DRC/index.html> (accessed on 2 November 2008).

regulatory approach. It adopted a three-pronged strategy combining enforcement activity and awareness raising, regarding the duties with concerted efforts to strengthen the role of disabled people, and other key agents, in achieving full implementation of the duties.

Given the limited time for legal enforcement of the duties prior to its closure, the DRC decided to focus its activities on assessing the adequacy of key authorities' Schemes. It decided to focus these enforcement efforts on the most influential authorities – including central Government Departments, statutory inspection bodies and key national authorities such as the Housing Commission.[47] It conducted, and published on its website, in-depth assessments of over a hundred of these key disability equality schemes. It took steps to publicize strong performers, as well as the names of authorities which were subject to potential enforcement action. Anecdotal evidence suggested that this highly visible approach to enforcement, most often falling short of legal action, had a very positive impact.

In early 2007, the Department for Work and Pensions (the Government Department responsible for the DED) wrote to all authorities in England and Wales asking whether they had published a Scheme.[48] Those authorities which failed to reply in the affirmative (several hundred out of 43 000 authorities to whom the specific duties applied,) were written to by the DRC and threatened with legal action. In the end, all but nine produced Schemes, and these were issued with compliance notices. All have now produced Schemes. The DRC Scottish office carried out an equivalent survey and issued 2 compliance notices.[49]

Whilst it did not assist individual authorities in complying with the duties, the DRC provided public authorities with extensive guidance on the practical requirements of the duties, examining particular aspects of the duties, such as the monitoring requirements and the implications of the duty for public procurement, as well as the practical effect of the duties on particular sectors such as social care, housing, health and education.[50] The DRC was anxious to counter the bureaucratic tendencies of the duties by giving authorities very practical examples of what actions they might include in their action plans to implement the duty

---

[47] The DRC produced individual detailed assessments on nearly 100 public bodies Schemes in England: 15 central government departments, all 10 Strategic Health Authority's and all 9 Regional Development Agencies; inspectorates (Audit Commission, SCI, Healthcare Commission and Ofsted), bodies connected to a Formal Investigation (General Care Council, Nursing and Midwifery Council, General Teaching Council, and Training and Development Agency for Schools), broadcasters (BBC and Channel 4) and the Housing Corporation. In addition overview reports were produced on higher education and PCTs, based on examining a selection of Schemes.

[48] The *Monitoring and Enforcement Plan* CRE Report contrasted the supportive and proactive approach taken by DWP with the approach of the lead department on the race duties, the Home Office.

[49] This survey showed that there were some 32 bodies without schemes (about 1 in 8 of the total number of authorities in Scotland), and as a consequence a priority was adopted of ensuring that every public authority in Scotland with specific duties should have a scheme.

[50] These non statutory guidance documents did not require Parliamentary or Governmental approval, and carry no formal legal weight.

and placed a heavy emphasis on achieving improved equality outcomes. This was supplemented with a series of conferences and seminars around Britain, again targeted at particular sectors.

The DRC recognized the importance of mobilizing a range of other actors – particularly disabled people – to build external pressure on authorities to counteract tokenistic compliance and bureaucratic inertia. (A key dimension which seemed to have been neglected by the CRE in its work to implement the race duties.) The DRC therefore ran conferences for disabled people's groups with the goal of increasing their capacity to fulfil their role in shaping DESs, and produced a toolkit for groups wanting to challenge authorities for non-compliance with the duties.

The DRC also provided training for trade unions, as well as for public interest lawyers to encourage them to use the duty when challenging decisions of public bodies affecting disabled people. (In the first five years of the race equality duty, it was disappointing to note that no judicial reviews had been brought, challenging non-compliance with the general duty.)

Feedback on the race equality duty had indicated that the failure of Government Departments to give a strong lead weakened the impact of the duty on the wider public sector. The DRC sought to address this issue by encouraging Parliamentarians to use the duty in support of its scrutiny functions, providing training to both disability lobby groups and directly to Parliamentarians.

5. EARLY IMPACT OF THE DISABILITY EQUALITY DUTIES

The chief source of information regarding the impact of the DED is the DRC, through its published assessment of authorities' Schemes and the research it undertook to explore the perceptions of disability organizations and key staff in public authorities, regarding what had changed as a result of implementing the duty.

This research showed that where authorities had complied with the DED this had a very positive impact on public sector bodies' performance and culture.[51] Although the process of drawing up a DES has been portrayed in some quarters as overly bureaucratic, the research highlighted clear benefits from the process. Organizations, in particular, reported that the involvement of disabled people in

[51] The research reports, below, are on the DRC legacy website, accessed via: <http://83.137.212.42/sitearchive/DRC/index.html>. *Involvement and real equality*, (DRC and Office for Public Management, September 2007). *Equal to the task: guidance for scrutineers in local government on equality*, (Centre for Public Scrutiny, DRC, EOC and CRE, September 2007). *Up to the mark, DRC assessment of 15 government departments*, (DRC, June 2007). *Capturing the value of the disability equality duty, Office for Public Management*, (DRC legacy website, May 2007). *Meeting the duty: an assessment of higher education institutions' performance in relation to the disability equality duty, DRC review of a sample of HEIs*, (DRC legacy website, 2007). *PCTs and the DED: an assessment of primary care trusts' performance in relation to the DED*, (DRC legacy website, September 2007). *RADAR: case study examples of disability equality duty best practice*, (DRC legacy website, May 2007). *Delivering disability equality: progress report from public sector unions – the findings of a trade union survey*, (TUC, May 2007). *Assessment of the Scottish government disability equality scheme*, (DRC legacy website, September 2007).

developing the DES had very positive consequences. It was felt to have helped to create better public services, enabling organizations to become more customer-focused, particularly in terms of recognizing the diversity of the communities with which they engage.

A core objective of the public sector equality duties is to 'mainstream' equality considerations into the way the public sector conducts its business. The research produced encouraging signs that some authorities were beginning to take on board this message, as illustrated in the response from John Alty, Director-General, Department of Trade and Industry (DTI): 'The work that we've done on the DES will sit within the better policy-making team, which is one way we'll try to mainstream it – it's something that's very important to people in the DTI and part of their day-to-day work.' The process of drawing up a scheme was also felt to focus minds across complex organizations, with competing priorities. Susan Scholefield, Director-General, Communities and Local Government stated: 'This isn't an area where one can talk in generalities, you've actually got specific issues and I think that really does concentrate minds.'

The most significant piece of research outside the DRC is Schneider Ross's study of the implementation of the three public sector equality duties in the course of 2007.[52] This echoed the conclusions of the DRC regarding the potential of the duties, and the particular strength of the DED. This study found positive outcomes had been delivered by the duties, with equality issues being accorded higher priority and increasingly mainstreamed. Based on an analysis of the reports of public authorities regarding their implementation of the equality duties, Schneider Ross found that progress on disability was only slightly less than on race. The researchers described this as 'striking', given that the disability duty had only been recently introduced at the time of the research, whereas the race duty had been in force for more than six years. Indeed on one aspect disability scored higher than race: involvement. They concluded: 'This fits with anecdotal data. At the stakeholder discussions, practitioners were particularly enthusiastic about the impact of the public sector duty in encouraging consultation and (more significantly) about the on-going involvement of disabled people.' 72% of respondents said that involvement of disabled people contributed to successful implementation of the DED.

Overall, the DRC research found disability organizations expressing optimism, tempered by wariness. Rachel Hurst, a leading disability rights activist, epitomized this mixture: 'The Department for International Development should be congratulated for doing as much work as they have done already, but proof of the pudding will be in the eating – so we need to look at the implementation stages of the duty.' This expresses an important limitation of the DRC's assessments which are based purely on published plans for activity. Further research is necessary to ascertain where these plans have been put into effect, as legally required.

The DRC's legal assessments of DESs showed both the positive potential of the duties and also the scale of the enforcement challenge. Whilst there were some excellent examples that will make a significant difference to disabled people, less than half of the authorities were assessed as fully compliant.

One of the most common weaknesses was a failure to comply fully with the requirements for the involvement of disabled people. Some authorities had com-

---

[52]   A. Nathwani *et al*, *The Public Sector Equality Duties, Making an impact*, (Schneider Ross, 2007).

pletely ignored the involvement requirement, and even where disabled people had been involved all too often this was confined to disabled staff, completely ignoring external stakeholders, in breach of the regulatory requirement to involve disabled people who *have an interest in the way an authority carries out its functions*. Furthermore, many Schemes provided no clear indication of how this involvement had influenced the Scheme, simply describing which disabled people had been involved.

This non-compliance is of particular concern because of the key role which involving disabled people plays in producing a positive outcome. Again the DRC assessments reinforce this connexion. One of the best Government Department Schemes was prepared by the Department for Education and Skills, with the involvement of disabled people through focus groups, for both disabled adults and children. They supplemented this with a focus group of disabled learners in one inner city school, convened to look at their priorities for change and how the practice at their school helps overcome barriers; a critique, from the perspective of people with learning difficulties; and in-depth interviews with disabled educationalists and with members of organizations run by disabled people. The priorities for action which arose out of this process, such as tackling bullying of disabled children at school, are clearly reflected in the scheme.

The action plans within DES's most concretely illustrate the potential of the duties to produce improvements. The regional development agency, One Northeast's impressive DES had nine action plans covering all the main functions of the agency (including areas such as skills and transport where the role is primarily influencing partnerships) and different aspects of the disability equality duty. Each plan deals with the collection of information, accessibility of facilities, and level of participation of disabled people in the organization concerned. One Northeast will use its influence with its partners to promote the participation of disabled people as board members and in other senior roles, and will also run leadership and confidence workshops for disabled people. A special strength of One Northeast is its work on innovation and design, allowing disabled people to have input into product development, and providing training sessions for designers about the access needs of disabled people. One Northeast will map the accessibility of tourist facilities and promote good practice tourism destinations. It will also subsidize user-led training, access audits and project grants for tourist partners and suppliers. The action plans also include a range of measures to map and strengthen disabled people's organizations.

Debbie Heigh, Director of Diversity at the Department for Work and Pensions (DWP), is quoted in *Capturing the value of the disability equality duty*:

> I think the biggest impact from the action plan will be the training. This will take time; we have 110,000 staff. The training will make people more aware of disability equality and this will have the most benefit. This was the clearest message which came out of our involvement of disabled people and it is now prioritized in the action plan.[53]

However, the DRC assessment of Schemes also show that many action plans did not reflect the full range of functions or the relevant aspects of the duty. Many

[53]   Capturing the value of the disability equality duty, (DRC legacy website, 2007).

departments did not produce full action plans either, because they failed to cover all aspects of the duty (the Department of Communities and Local Government scheme, for example, failed to give consideration to harassment of disabled people in its Respect programme for tackling anti-social behaviour), and failed to cover all relevant functions. Some schemes focused almost exclusively on internal employment issues. The Department of Health scheme had no actions relating to social care, and the Home Office scheme, which ostensibly covered the prison service, had no planned actions regarding disabled prisoners.

Turning briefly to consider evidence of performance within particular sectors, only four out of fifteen government departments' schemes were assessed as compliant.[54] It was particularly disappointing that the majority of government departments had failed to involve any disabled stakeholders other than their own staff in the development of their schemes. As a result, they produced much weaker schemes. Most departments were also strikingly bad at setting out their evidence in relation to disability equality. This is a particular concern, given the strategic importance of the departments in setting targets and providing diversity information for policy in their sectors.

Whilst only four out of nine the regional development agencies (RDAs) were compliant, three were very good,[55] and this sector overall was strong on evidence-gathering and involvement. All the RDAs had set up mechanisms for the continuing involvement of disabled people, and most had commissioned qualitative research to identify barriers to equality (for example on self-employment of disabled people) and will use this to plan actions to overcome them. The South East England Development Agency had a good range of challenging targets, such as a 10% increase in the skills attainment levels of disabled people at all skills levels by 2016 and a reduction in the number of disabled people living in poverty in the south-east by 10% by 2016.

The health sector was in many ways the weakest. Only two out of the ten strategic health authorities (SHAs) had schemes that were compliant; and two had not produced a scheme at all. SHA schemes in general were particularly poor on evidence and involvement.

A major problem with implementing the DED in the health sector is that statistics on disabled people's use of healthcare are not adequately collected. The requirements within the specific duties on evidence collection should have begun to address this problem, and indeed some authorities indicated their intention to fill information gaps.

For example, progress on disability equality in the South Central NHS Primary Care Trust (PCT) will be tracked by monitoring trends in morbidity, survival rates, diagnosis, condition management and patient experience. In addition, the PCT states that disabled people will undertake independent reviews and evaluations of its services, functions, policies, decisions and employment.

In the further and higher education sector, the DRC's assessments are supplement by in-depth action research by trade unions. The DRC reported that eight

---

[54]   The Department for Communities and Local Government (DCLG); Department for International Development; Department for Education and Skills (now Department for Children, Schools and Families) and the Department for Work and Pensions.

[55]   London Development Agency, South East Development Agency and One Northeast.

out of twenty-one of the higher education institutions sampled were assessed as being compliant with the legislation, the remaining Schemes being non-compliant to greatly varying degrees. Union research provides a clearer analysis of the challenges in the Further Education (FE). Unison and the University and College Union undertook a project to help FE colleges develop good practice when implementing the disability equality duty. Project worker Sian Davies explained: 'There hadn't been any work done in the sector around involving disabled staff, and to make sure that involvement became a reality we decided that the trade unions needed to be proactive.'[56]

Training events around the country offered guidance and advice for the further education sector on the disability equality duty. In all, some 600 people participated, including College managers, vice principals and HR managers. In addition, the project worked closely with five pilot colleges to develop good practice that could be communicated to the wider FE sector.

A number of key sectoral problems were identified. Management often focused on individual 'problems' rather than identifying the major institutional barriers. This focus on the individual rather than a whole-organization approach to equality of opportunity for disabled people seems widespread. In the FE sector, disabled staff appear to be 'invisible' – just over 2% of staff disclose a disability, despite national estimates suggesting that 20% of the workforce has a disability. The low rate of disclosure in the FE sector is a symptom of the culture that many disabled staff feel exists around disability and their belief that they will be discriminated against. Staff are reluctant to disclose their impairments or to seek support or adjustments to their working conditions. However, if colleges do not know who their disabled staff are, they cannot ask them what barriers need to be removed. Trade union representatives sought to encourage employers to create an inclusive workplace culture that encourages disabled workers to declare their disability status and become actively involved in the college's disability equality scheme, acting as a reliable source of information regarding the potential equality impact of policies. The report concluded that achievements in the five pilot colleges demonstrate that it is possible to bring about a culture change.

6. CRITICISM OF THE PUBLIC SECTOR DUTIES

Whilst considerable enthusiasm and high expectations surround the public sector duties, nevertheless they have also attracted a number of criticisms and concerns. Indeed some of these concerns arise precisely because of their novelty and radicalness.

The two major criticisms are summarized in the *Framework for Fairness* Green Paper:

the general duty is too weak in the extent to which it requires action to be taken, and too unspecific about the outcomes it seeks to achieve. In addition, the specific duties (in particular the requirements for race equality

---

[56] K. Godwin, 'Disability Equality in Action', 172 *Equal Opportunities Review* (January 2008).

schemes) may be focused too much on bureaucratic process rather than on delivering tangible equality outcomes for service users and employees.

These two criticisms are in fact intrinsically linked; precisely because the specific duties are intended to assist authorities in complying with their general duty if there is no clear requirement in the general duty to produce substantive improvements, then the specific duties can necessarily only focus on procedural proprieties rather than outcomes.

6.1.   WEAK GENERAL DUTY?

The corner-stone of the statutory equality duties is the requirement for authorities to 'have due regard' to equality in its various dimensions. But how strong an injunction is this? Is it primarily procedural, or can it require a public body to adopt or adjust a policy in ways which it would otherwise would not have done? How important is equality in relation to competing considerations? To what extent can it command the expenditure of additional resources? Does it require that better equality outcomes are achieved?

The Statutory Code provides only limited answers to these questions. For example, the vexed issue of resources is touched on by the Code, but only cautiously:

> The general duty may also require public authorities to review the ways in which they prioritise, resource and implement their functions that are specifically intended to benefit disabled people, such as care and support services. Public authorities should expect to be more carefully scrutinised and accountable for their performance of disability-focused functions.[57]

The meaning of 'due regard' has been the subject of conflicting interpretations in the courts. The first case examining the meaning of the race equality duty was only heard in 2005, despite this duty coming into force in 2001. *Elias v Secretary of State*[58] involved Mrs. Elias who was born in Hong Kong and registered as a British subject. She and her family were interned by the Japanese until the liberation of Hong Kong in 1945. Despite suffering serious psychological effects, she could not benefit from the UK government's non-statutory compensation scheme for those who were interned by the Japanese, because, for civilian internees to qualify they either had to have been born in the UK or have a parent or grandparent born in the UK. She brought proceedings for judicial review claiming that the criteria adopted operated as direct discrimination on grounds of national origin or, alternatively, that they were indirectly discriminatory and could not be justified. She also alleged breach of the duty to have due regard to the need to eliminate unlawful racial discrimination.

The Court held that the scheme was indirectly discriminatory, and that the Secretary of State was also in breach of his race equality duty: given the obvious discriminatory effect of the scheme, the Secretary of State could not possibly have properly considered the potentially discriminatory nature of the scheme.

A similar decision was reached in relation to the disability equality duty in

---

57   Code 2.41.
58   *Elias v Secretary of State* [2005] IRLR 788.

R (on application of Chavda and Others) v Harrow LBC.[59] Ms Chavda and others argued that it was unlawful for Harrow Council to adopt a policy that had the effect of restricting the provision of community care services only to those with critical needs. One of the grounds successfully raised was that the decision was unlawful because it failed to take into account the disability discrimination duty. Whilst Harrow Council had conducted an 'equality impact assessment' into the proposal before making its decision, its focus was solely on 'differential impact' between different groups of service users. It found that there was a *risk* of such impact and that it should be monitored in future. It did not address at all the issues in the disability equality duty. In the assessment, there was a one line mention of the DDA, stating 'potential conflict with the DDA. A change in criteria could be seen as limiting access for some people to services'.[60]

Since the judicial review the Council has decided not to proceed with its policy and to retain the provision of services for those with substantive needs.

In *R (Baker) v Secretary of State for Communities* the Court of Appeal rejected a challenge to a planning inspector's dismissal of an appeal against the refusal of planning permission to gypsy families to station their mobile homes on Green Belt land.[61] Whilst the court emphasized the importance of the duty, it nevertheless held that the race duty did not require the achievement of particular outcomes. Lord Justice Dyson stated:

> In my judgment, it is important to emphasise that the section 71(1) duty is not a duty to achieve a result, namely to eliminate unlawful racial discrimination or to promote equality of opportunity and good relations between persons of different racial groups. It is a duty to *have due regard to the need* to achieve these goals. The distinction is vital....
>
> What is *due* regard? In my view, it is the regard that is appropriate in all the circumstances. These include on the one hand the importance of the areas of life of the members of the disadvantaged racial group that are affected

---

59 *R (on application of Chavda and Others) v Harrow LBC* [2007] EWHC 3064.

60 In the course of the hearing excerpts from the Statutory Code was brought to the Court's attention: 'Ensuring that services give due regard to disability equality may require an authority to consider, in relation to any services delivered specifically to disabled people, whether the way in which they are delivered maximizes disabled people's ability to exercise real choice, and promotes their equality more generally. When preparing individual community care plans, a local authority should have due regard to the need to promote disability equality. Disability equality is of particular relevance in this context. This would mean, for example, that the range and manner of assistance provided takes into account the need for a disabled person to have access to social and leisure activities, and, where relevant, employment.' The DRC also produced non statutory guidance: *The Social Care sector and the Disability Equality Duty.* An example discusses the appropriateness of resource allocation which leads to waiting lists for respite care. For example, where an authority is providing respite care for disabled children, the authority will need to consider to what extent any waiting list for such care means that the service adequately takes account of the needs of disabled people. If it does not, the authority will need to consider whether due regard is being paid to disability equality in its budget allocation.

61 *R (Baker) v Secretary of State for Communities* [2008] EWCA Civ 141.

by the inequality of opportunity and the extent of the inequality; and on the other hand, such countervailing factors as are relevant to the function which the decision-maker is performing.

The Baker case turned on whether, in the judgement of the court, the authority had performed this correct balancing function, despite the fact that it failed to explicitly refer to the duty. Courts are likely to get progressively less tolerant and more prepared to scrutinize decisions as the *R (Kaur and Shah) v LB Ealing* case[62] revealed.

This is a complex area, which is still being explored by the courts. There is a strong argument that it would be desirable to have more clarity in the wording of the duty itself, indicating that it can require substantive change. In relation to the promotion of equality, a formulation is needed which requires action that is proportionate to the inequality and other competing considerations. Sandra Fredman and Sarah Spencer, drawing on the terms of the International Covenant for Economic, Social and Cultural Rights and the South African Constitution, propose that the duty should be that: 'A public authority shall, in carrying out its functions, to eliminate discrimination and unlawful harassment, and take such steps as are necessary and proportionate to achieve the progressive realisation of equality.'[63] This emphasizes the need to differentiate with regard the need to eliminate discrimination and unlawful harassment, since these are absolute legal obligations that should not be balanced against other competing considerations.

6.2. PROCESS DRIVEN – FAILING TO DELIVER CHANGE

The charge that the specific duties become merely concerned with bureaucratic compliance, a technocratic tool co-opted to maintain the status quo, rather than with achieving real change, is one that has been voiced a number of commentators.[64] Research into the race equality duty highlighted this as a potential problem.[65] However, as we have seen, research on the disability equality duty is more encouraging, reflecting a number of factors, including the fact that specific disability equality duty is more action focused than the race duty, the DRC's forceful approach to enforcement and, perhaps above all, the stronger emphasis on the effective participation of excluded groups, which is a strong counterweight against bureaucratization.

One of the key processes required by the specific duties is equality impact assessment. The purposive nature of this requirement, and its link to the general duty, has been underlined by a number of cases, most explicitly *R (Kaur and Shah) v LB Ealing*.

In this case, the High Court considered a claim brought by two clients of the Southall Black Sisters group, which provides specialist support to victims

---

[62] *R (Kaur and Shah) v LB Ealing* [2008] EWHC (Admin) 2062.

[63] S. S. Fredman and S. Spencer, *Response to the Discrimination Law Review Proposal on Public Sector Equality Duties,* (Equality and Diversity Forum, July 2007).

[64] Ibid., C. O'Cinneide, 8 *International Journal of Discrimination and the Law* (2005), 91 and S. Fredman, 12 *Maastricht Journal of European and Comparative Law* 4 (2005), 369-398.

[65] Schneider Ross, *Towards Racial Equality.*

of domestic violence from certain minority communities. Their claim concerned a funding decision (which would have resulted in effectively the withdrawal of funding by requiring that services were provided in a race/gender neutral way) taken without first having undertaken a *proper* Race Equality Impact Assessment. According to the Judge, such an assessment was required to be undertaken 'as a matter of substance and with rigour'.

Nevertheless, there is a continuing danger that the impetus created by the duties will be diverted into bureaucratic processes – whether through the token-istic 'involvement' of disabled people, the collection of data as an end in itself rather than used to measure or facilitate progress or simply performing some lim-ited, unreflective activity – without effecting any real change.

A clear statutory requirement on authorities to set equality targets would help counteract this tendency. The gender duty provides a model here, but consid-eration needs to be given to how to ensure that such targets include both qualita-tive and quantitative indicators of progress and are set in consultation with af-fected groups.

Careful handling will be needed to avoid distortions being introduced and to guard against the danger that the only actions which are taken are those which relate to these equality targets. Targets are likely to focus on easily measured is-sues and on direct services and employment, at the expense of authorities' more indirect but hugely important role of influencing the community. Thus, it may be difficult to measure improvements in accessibility of local businesses, but local authority action to promote this is very important.

Actions which are less amenable to measurement, or simply do not make it on to the necessarily focused list of strategic priorities, can be invaluable. For example, schools may want to set strategic objectives on narrowing gaps in edu-cational attainment and reducing bullying. In addition, however, disabled chil-dren and their parents may be stressing the importance of ensuring that disabled children are fully included in non-educational, social activity (which may indi-rectly contribute to the reduction of bullying and better educational attainment but would probably be neglected if focus was entirely on achieving strategic objec-tives).

Even without amending the statutory requirements, it may be that judicial interpretation of the present specific duty requirements could be helpful in clari-fying the need for substantive action rather than mere form-filling. Up to the present, legal proceedings relating to the specific duties have only been initiated where an authority has failed to produce a Scheme, rather than where a Scheme, in the judgement of the Commission, fails to meet the statutory requirements. Amongst the issues that need to be clarified are: to what degree will Courts be prepared to scrutinize the adequacy of authorities' arrangements for involving disabled people, upholding the requirements set out in the statutory Code? To what extent will Courts be prepared to invalidate a Scheme which fails to address all the relevant functions of an authority or where an action plan is inadequate in that it fails to give due regard to the need to promote disability equality?

6.3. LACK OF CLARITY ABOUT EQUALITY

As many commentators have noted the meaning of 'equality' is unclear.[66] When the law moves beyond the reactive and limited approach of simply requiring identical treatment to require authorities to promote 'equality', this issue comes sharply into focus.

The three most common meanings of equality are described by Fredman as equal treatment, equal opportunities and equality of results.[67] At its narrowest, it [equality] requires the removal of barriers at the demand side. This may open the doors to excluded groups, but does not mean that they have the resources to progress through the doors. For example, requirements for educational qualifications not strictly necessary for the job may be relaxed. But disadvantaged groups might still lack the training which is, in fact, necessary for a wide range of jobs. A broader understanding of equal opportunities would require that resources be provided to make sure that members of disadvantaged groups can make use of new opportunities. In the above example, it would require that training be provided. In other contexts, child-care or transport might be needed.[68]

The DDA provides some statutory description of the different dimensions of equality, making it clear that freedom from harassment and civic participation are core components. However, the core issue of the meaning of equality in this context still requires further clarification. The DRC sought to address some of these issues in its statutory Code, which adopts a substantive equality approach focused on the need to improve outcomes for disabled people, requiring authorities to work towards an equalization of outcomes ranging from careers and educational attainment to uptake and satisfaction with public services or freedom from harassment.

The statutory Code explicitly draws on the 'social model of disability' in explaining the meaning of equality of opportunity in this context:

> At present disabled people do not have the same opportunities or choices as non-disabled people. Nor do they enjoy equal respect or full inclusion in society on an equal basis. The poverty, disadvantage and social exclusion experienced by many disabled people is not the inevitable result of their

---

[66]   M. Bell, 'Equality and the European Constitution', 35 *Industrial Law Journal* 3 (2004); C. McCrudden, 'Theorizing European Equality Law', in C. Costello and E. Barry (eds.), *Equality in Diversity: The New Equality Directives* (Irish Centre for European Law, 2003).

[67]   S. Fredman and S. Spencer, *Delivering Equality: Towards an Outcome-Focused Positive Duty, Submission to the Cabinet Office Equality Review and to the Discrimination Law Review,* <http://www.edf.org.uk/news/Delivering%20equality%20 submission%20030606-final.pdf> (accessed on 6 August 2009).

[68]   This above quotation also raises the need for a joined up approach to achieving equality, so that child care, and training and transport need to be addressed at the same time as employment opportunities. Arguably the Secretary of State duties, provide a stronger basis for achieving such a systemic approach to improving the delivery.

impairments or medical conditions, but rather stems from attitudinal and environmental barriers.[69]

Fredman and Spencer argue that a focus on equality of outcomes is both asking too much and too little of public authorities:

> while 'equality of outcomes' can be a meaningful goal in some contexts for groups (e.g. average attainment of ethnic minorities at GCSE) it can mask inequality within groups. It can also focus on quantitative measures to the exclusion of qualitative approaches and is not applicable as a measurement for individuals, who have differing priorities.[70]

Whilst I accept that there are some complexities entailed in the equalization of outcomes as a goal, this is capable of interpretation in a sophisticated and sensitive way and must form the core goal of the equality duty. The DRC addressed these issues, and the need to collect both qualitative and quantitative outcomes in its Code of Practice and in particular, in its non statutory guidance on evidence gathering.[71]

The objective is that disabled people should have full opportunities and choices to improve the quality of their lives, and be respected and included as equal members of society. If such equality were achieved, this would mean for example, at a very basic level, that disabled people who rely on additional assistance for their daily living, such as getting up and dressed, would have the same ability to determine the time at which they get up and go to bed as non-disabled people.[72]

Ensuring that services give due regard to disability equality may require an authority to consider, in relation to any services delivered specifically to disabled people, whether the way in which they are delivered maximizes disabled people's ability to exercise real choice, and promotes their equality more generally.[73]

This substantive equality approach is easier to adopt in relation to disability equality because of the asymmetrical formulation of the DDA: only disabled people are protected from discrimination, and no limit is thereby imposed on 'positive discrimination'. The other equality grounds are symmetrical, creating a potential conflict between the broader approach to equality of the statutory duties and the narrow restrictions in UK law on positive action. Public authorities will, on many occasions, in practice, be prohibited from treating men and women or people from different ethnic groups differently even where this is need in order to deliver more equal results.

Nor is this a mere theoretical danger. In 2007, a national advocacy group for women, on the basis of a survey of 101 women's voluntary groups, reported that the introduction of the gender duty made it harder for women's groups such as women's refuges to justify their existence.[74]

---

[69]   Code 1.6.

[70]   S. Fredman and S. Spencer, *Delivering Equality.*

[71]   Code 5.30; *The Disability Equality Duty, Guidance on gathering and Analysing evidence* (DRC legacy website, 2007).

[72]   Code 2.7.

[73]   Code 2.42.

[74]   Women's Resource Centre reported in Guardian:17/1/2007.

This contradiction is highlighted by a statement in *Framework for Fairness*:

> It needs to be remembered that, in deciding what action to take under public sector equality duties to benefit a particular disadvantaged group in the community, public authorities are limited by what is permitted by discrimination law. ... *Promoting equality is not about favouring one group over another; rather the opposite.*[75] [emphasis added]

This tension between two different versions of equality is not present within the DED, which explicitly requires authorities to provide more favourable treatment for disabled people if this is necessary in order to meet their needs. The statutory Code comments:

> The Act states that the duty requires public authorities to have due regard to the need to take steps to take account of disabled persons' disabilities, even where that involves treating disabled persons more favourably than other persons. This emphasises the fact that equality of opportunity cannot be achieved simply by treating disabled and non-disabled people alike.[76]

An example is then given of a disabled student who needs a dedicated car parking space because she is unable to use public transport. Non-disabled users might also want a parking space, but will not suffer the same degree of disadvantage if they do not get one: the disabled student will be prevented from attending the course, whilst the non-disabled student will merely be inconvenienced.[77]

As the Code recognizes, this principle is already inherent in the DDA 1995's requirement to provide reasonable adjustments. The university in the above example will have a duty under the Act to provide such a parking space if, in all the circumstances, it is a 'reasonable' adjustment to make.

The Code goes on to state that separate services for disabled people are required in some instances to enable disabled people to access mainstream activities on equitable terms, as an alternative alongside a 'mainstream' approach. '[H]aving due regard to disability equality will generally require some adaptation to existing or proposed activities. In some instances it may require an authority to consider whether additional, targeted services are required in order to deliver an equal outcome for disabled and non-disabled people.'[78] Even where the mainstream service is fully accessible, disabled people may value a separate space in which to engage in activities.

Mindful of the danger that inaccessible mainstream provision leaves for disabled people confined to 'special' and second-rate services, the Code goes on to emphasize: 'Where a separate service specifically aimed at disabled people is provided alongside a "mainstream" service this should be provided as a choice, not as an enforced, segregated provision provided purely because disabled people are unable to access the "mainstream" service.'[79]

---

[75] Department for Communities and Local Government *et al, Framework for Fairness*, 87.
[76] Code 2.13.
[77] Ibid.
[78] Code 2.41.
[79] Code 2.16-2.17.

The Code thus seeks to strike a balance, emphasizing that specialized services for disabled people must not be used as an alternative to creating accessible mainstream services, but at the same time not providing the rationale for authorities to withdraw specialized services where these provide a real benefit for disabled people.

There are encouraging signs of a shift towards this more substantive approach towards equality in other areas. The Government's proposals in relation to the Equality Bill include increasing the scope for positive action (despite the statement in the Green Paper quoted above). Moreover, the case of *R (Kaur and Shah) v LB Ealing* provides from within the present legislative framework a powerful articulation of this broader perspective on equality. The London Borough of Ealing argued that it would be unlawful to provide a domestic violence service specifically targeted at ethnic minority women. In rejecting this assertion, the judgment not only pointed to the positive action provision in Section 35 Race Relations Act 1976 (allowing facilities or services to meet the special needs of persons of particular racial group in regard to their education, training or welfare or any ancillary benefits), but also emphasized the broader principle:

> Section 35 is not an exception to the 1976 Act. It does not derogate from it in any way. It is a manifestation of the important principle of anti discrimination and equality measures that not only must like cases be treated alike but that unlike cases but must be treated differently. ... There is no dichotomy between the promotion of equality and cohesion and the provision of specialist services to an ethnic minority.

6.4. EFFECTIVE PARTICIPATION – OR WINDOW DRESSING?

Mainstreaming cannot work without the close involvement of organizations representing the interests of those at risk of experiencing inequality. Once again, this is a progressive aspect of public sector duties which creates a further set of challenges.

Fredman identifies the need for clarity about the function of participation, that it needs to be understood both as a means to better outcomes and improved decision making, and also as a valuable outcome in its own right through enhanced accountability and transparency.[80]

Even if these two goals are both accepted, there are further complexities. Thus, achieving accountability as result of transparency requires participating groups to have some sanction if public authorities fail to deliver on promises.

In relation to the goal of improving decision-making, a range of approaches can be adopted from merely allowing groups to comment on proposals, to obtaining information from them, to actually involving them in decision making. This final approach is likely to be most helpful in producing progress and enhancing the legitimacy of state services and public policy.

There are also important considerations in relation to ensuring that a representative range of groups and individuals are involved, and that those who are already marginalized are not excluded. There is a danger that public authorities may choose to listen to those with the least challenging views, playing groups off

---

[80]   S. Fredman, 12 *Maastricht Journal of European and Comparative Law* 4 (2005), 369-398.

against each other.

How does the DED fare in relation to these points? The first point to note is that the statutory provision helpfully addresses the point regarding the role of participation: the general duty requires public authorities to have due regard to the need to encourage participation by disabled people in public life. As the Code then makes clear: 'This is both an end in itself and will promote equality for disabled people more generally. Not only will disabled people bring valuable experience to public life, but such participation will encourage positive attitudes towards disabled people.'[81]

The specific duties also provide a strong statutory foundation since authorities are required to involve in the development of their Schemes 'disabled people who appear to that authority to have an interest in the way it carries out its functions'.

In addition, the DRC recognized that the participative dimension of the duties provides a strong counter-weight to the potential of the duty to become a bureaucratic exercise, and could prove critical in transforming the culture of public institutions by introducing new perspectives. It reflected this understanding both in the drafting of the statutory Code and in its approach to implementing the duty (as described above).

The Code emphasizes that 'involvement' requires a more active engagement of disabled stakeholders than 'consultation', and gives detailed guidance on what such 'involvement' might entail. It stresses that disabled people should be involved in all key aspects of the development of the Scheme, such as setting priorities for action plans and including them in implementation and review.[82] It quotes the National Audit Office on the need for long term supported engagement with stakeholders, including a realistic account of the often significant costs associated with ongoing communication and collaboration. [83]

The EU Report on mainstreaming emphasizes this issue: 'To ensure that mainstreaming is as participative as possible, NGOs need to be equipped with the necessary human and financial resources to develop the capacity to contribute to the policy making process.'[84]

The Code seeks to address this issue:

---

[81]   Code 2.28.
[82]   Code 3.10 'The involvement of disabled people in the implementation of the various aspects of the Scheme (such as conducting impact assessments and gathering evidence) will also be critical to the successful implementation of the duty. For example, involving disabled people in monitoring the success of initiatives throughout the duration of the Disability Equality Scheme will assist with evaluation, and will be critical when the time comes to review and revise the Scheme.'
[83]   Code 3.14.
[84]   Centre for strategy and evaluation services, *Non-discrimination mainstreaming*.

Capacity building of excluded groups is a clear prerequisite for success of this participatory dimension which requires a high degree of organization commitment and knowledge. The action plan is also likely to include specific measures to strengthen the capacity of the organization to work towards disability equality, such as training for staff in the disability equality dimension of their work, human resources policies, and the development and implementation of effective harassment policies.[85]

Nevertheless, these progressive provisions of the Code may be ignored by authorities, and disabled people may still be open to misuses through tokenistic involvement processes. A change to the enforcement mechanisms, strengthening the ability of disabled people to challenge authorities (as discussed below) would serve the duties' aim of delivering increased accountability, and give added power to those disabled people engaged with public authorities through the duties.

6.5. LIMITED ENFORCEMENT REGIME

A failure to build sufficient supervision or sanctions into the enforcement regime has been identified as further potential weakness of the equality duties.

John Halford emphasizes the limited sanctions at present facing public authorities who are found to breach these duties: 'A declaration that section 71 has been breached is by itself of little value, The Courts have not been so bold in determining remedies.'[86] In the Elias case, referred to above, only a small award of damages (£3000) was made for injury to feelings. Worse still, the discriminatory rule was not struck down but was allowed to be reformulated and reapplied in a way which still resulted in the exclusion of the claimant. (Mrs Elias was, in fact, awarded a pension under a new scheme in force prior to the Court of Appeal judgement, but after the original hearing).

Halford comments that such a sanction is neither effective, proportionate nor dissuasive, and that this may be contrary to the equal treatment requirements of the Employment Directive which require Member States to take the necessary measures to ensure that laws and administrative provisions contrary to equal treatment should be abolished.[87] It is true that public authorities generally seek to avoid litigation of this sort, and the adverse publicity attendant upon it, but these factors are frequently not sufficient to counteract the pressures of inertia and resistance to addressing the equality impact of programmes and policies.

A further weakness of the enforcement regime is that it relies so heavily on the Equality Commission as the prime driving force.[88] Whilst it is true that anyone with an interest in an issue can bring a judicial review alleging an authority's fail-

---

[85]   Code 3.1.

[86]   J. Halford, 'Statutory Equality Duties and the Public Law Courts', 12 *Judicial Review* 2 (2007), 89.

[87]   Council Directive 2000/78 of 27 November 2000 establishing a general framework for equal treatment in employment and occupation, [2000] OJ L303/16.

[88]   Indeed the advent of EHRC has led to a marked decline in visible research or enforcement activity in relation to the duties. It is to be hoped that this merely reflects disruption to the organizational infrastructure, rather than a conscious decision to de-prioritize enforcement activity in this area.

ure to discharge its public duty, such cases were very rare in relation to the race equality duty prior to 2007 (with only one decided decision). The reasons for this may be not solely related to restrictions in ability to fund such litigation, but also to a lack of knowledge of the potential of the equality duties amongst lawyers in disciplines such as housing and social care, where they might be relevant.

The DRC was conscious of these dangers when formulating its approach to implementing the DED. As we have seen, it sought to mobilize a number of external forces including public interest lawyers, disabled peoples' groups, trade unions and Parliamentarians. All in their different ways are able to bring pressure to bear on public authorities through litigation or other means. The last two years have indeed seen a wider use of the public sector duties by lawyers and interest groups, including a number of successful legal challenges clarifying their meaning and importance.

At the same time the DRC did not neglect the 'softer' motivators, It sought to mobilize authorities' fear of bad publicity and innate competitiveness by publishing assessments of authorities' Schemes, publicising details of those with no Schemes and publicly praising those with progressive Schemes.

This firm regulatory stance, coupled with the DRC's commitment to empowerment of community forces, has produced encouraging results. Nevertheless, given the scale of institutional change, required further forces need to be brought to bear.

O'Cinneide proposes that individuals and pressure groups should be able to challenge how the duties are being implemented, without being confined to the judicial review route, for example through specialist ombudsman mechanisms. [89]

Additionally, if the equality duties are to have real credibility, and to enable them to really improve the delivery of public services to all aspects of society, it is essential that public service inspectorates make equality an integral element of audit and inspection. The various statutory bodies, such as Ofsted and the Audit Commission, whose function it is to inspect and audit the performance of public bodies, are themselves subject to the equality duties. However, the inspectorates continue to have a patchy record; the Audit Commission was one of the first public authorities taken to task by the DRC for its failure to produce a DES. It would be helpful, in this regard, if the equality duties had a more explicit requirement on inspectorates to take authorities' performance on equality into account when measuring their performance.

The leadership role of government departments is also critical. The Secretary of State duty to report on progress disability equality in the policy sector for which they are responsible, provides a strong mechanism for this. The EHRC should ensure that these reports are effective, and this aspect of the DED should be retained in the unified and expanded public sector duty.

7. THE FUTURE OF THE EQUALITY DUTIES

A profound level of uncertainty has been introduced by the Government's proposals to combine and extend the equality duties to cover religion, gender reassignment, sexual orientation and age. The *Framework for Fairness* Green Paper identified some potential weaknesses in the design of the equality duties. However, its

---

[89]   C. O'Cinneide, 8 *International Journal of Discrimination and the Law* (2005), 91.

proposed cure would, if implemented, have fatally undermined the duties.

The Green Paper proposed narrowing the General Duty, so that authorities would only be required to set equality objectives (and take proportionate action to achieve these), rather than giving equality due regard in all their functions. Narrowing the focus, in this way, to only on those areas that public authorities choose as priorities for equality, would result in the sidelining, rather than mainstreaming, of equality considerations. Whilst a requirement to set objectives is desirable, this needs to be in addition, not as an alternative, to the requirement to mainstream equality into all the functions of public authorities.

The present duties legally mandate mainstreaming by requiring 'due regard' to be given to all public authority decisions and activities. A clear message is thereby sent that equality is 'core business' for the public sector. This legal principle needs to be retained.

In relation to the specific duties, under the guise of reducing bureaucracy, the Green Paper proposed that non-statutory 'principles' (of transparency, consultation, evidence and capability) should replace the precise legal requirements in the present framework with regard to Schemes, their content and implementation. This would have been a recipe for greater confusion and weaker activity.

The strength of the opposition which these proposals generated, not just from equality groups and trade unions but also from public authorities, is itself a testimony to the success of the duties. As a result, the Government has visibly retreated. A White Paper, published in June 2008, indicated the Government's intention to proceed with legislation combining the existing duties and extending them to religion or belief, gender reassignment, sexual orientation and age.[90] An accompanying document, *The Equality Bill – Government Response to the Consultation,* makes it clear that the existing structure of the general and specific duties will be retained.[91]

A unified duty extending to six strands will clearly require some further refinement, and these details still remain to be developed. For example, *Government Response to the Consultation* states that the Government wants to make clearer on the face of the legislation what is meant by 'advancing equality of opportunity' (suggesting that this entails addressing disadvantage, encouraging a culture which ensures that individuals' differences are accepted; meeting different needs; and encouraging participation and inclusion). The Equality Bill was published in April 2009. The general duty requires public authorities to have 'due regard to the need to a) eliminate discrimination, harassment, victimization and any other conduct that is prohibited by or under this Act; b) advance equality of opportunity between persons who share a relevant characteristic and those who do not share it; c) foster good relations between persons who share a relevant characteristic and those who do not share it.[92] Disability is a protected characteristic. Having due regard to equality of opportunity is said to involve in particular the need to 'a) remove or minimize disadvantages suffered by persons who share relevant protected characteristics that are connected to that characteristic; b) meet

---

[90] Government Equalities Office, *Framework for a Fairer Future*, (Department for Communities and Government, 2008).

[91] *The Equality Bill – Government Response to the Consultation* (Department for Communities and Government, 2008).

[92] Clause 143 (1).

the needs of persons who share a relevant protected characteristic that are different from the needs of persons who do not share it; c) encourage persons who share a relevant protected characteristic to participate in public life or in any other activity in which participation by such persons is disproportionately low'.[93]

The Bill explicitly states that 'compliance with the duties' 'may involve treating some persons more favourably than others, but that is not to be taken as permitting conduct that would otherwise be prohibited.'[94]

However, contrary to the Government's statement referred to above, a further Consultation on specific equality duties[95] retains proposals to replace a requirement to produce Equality Schemes with a requirement to set equality objective, representing a *de facto* weakening of the duties.

8. CONCLUSION

The equalities duties can provide a very powerful lever for change. As the DRC's closing report on the public sector duty states:

> Assessing and commenting on an organization's DES allowed a forensic examination of the organization's performance on disability equality. Feedback to the organization opens the doors to discussion about their performance on disability, in a way which it is very difficult to achieve through other means such as individual case work...To capitalize on this great opportunity is time-consuming and requires appropriate policy knowledge, otherwise all that can be assessed is whether the organization has gone through the correct processes.[96]

> However, the evidence also shows that there is still widespread failure to fully comply with the duties. There are many organizations with Schemes which fall far short of the legal requirements. What we do not know, because no research has been done at this point, is the extent to which organizations with Schemes are actually carrying out the actions set out in them, as they are legally required to do.[97]

As with every legislative requirement which seeks to introduce significant changes to behaviour, the duties need vigorous and effective enforcement activity (preferably from more than one source). Such activity needs to have high visibility to have a positive impact on other public authorities.

The equality duties are still relatively young. They have hugely ambitious aims – which will take time to achieve. Court interpretations are still settling, legislative change is imminent and the vigour of enforcement activity of the Equality

---

[93] Clause 143 (2).

[94] Clause 143 (5).

[95] Government Equality Office, *Equality Bill: Making it work Policy proposals for specific duties A consultation* (Department for Communities and Government, 2009).

[96] 'Tough Love': Enforcing the Disability Equality Duty' (DRC Commission Paper, September 2007).

[97] The DRC recommended that its successor body should investigate whether selected authorities have, as required, published Annual Reports, and whether these revealed that they were implementing their DES's.

Commission is uncertain.

Nevertheless, there is already evidence that they can produce real gains for disabled people, and for public authorities more generally. Similar evidence is emerging regarding the comparable duties in Northern Ireland.[98] This article has particularly emphasized the importance and potentially powerful impact of a legal mandate for the involvement of disabled people in guiding public authorities to deliver improvements.

Those in Europe concerned with advancing equality for disabled people and other groups should keep close watch on the development of British equality duties as a powerful new legislative tool.

---

[98]   The recent Northern Ireland Equality Commission review of the effectiveness of their integrated public sector duty found that: 'Over a relatively short period it has effected substantial change in how policy is made. The result is more informed and evidence based policy that reflects the needs of individuals, in terms of equality of opportunity and good relations. Effective consultation has been a particular success, giving rise to inclusive policy making process.' *S75 Review, Keeping it Effective*, (Equality Commission for Northern Ireland, May 2007).

LEGAL CAPACITY LAW REFORM IN EUROPE: AN URGENT CHALLENGE

Mary Keys[1]

1. INTRODUCTION

The right of autonomy and self determination, strongly supported in many juris-dictions, is central to full participation in society, and yet legal capacity can be achieved only if the law permits persons to make their own decisions or assists them in doing so.[2] In many countries, legal systems prevent people from reaching their full human potential by excluding them from control over their own lives.[3] Being regarded by others as having legal capacity for decision-making is what allows people to participate as fully as possible in society. Impaired cognitive functioning, resulting from intellectual disability, mental illness, brain damage or any form of neurological degeneration, may mean a person is partially or wholly unable to make decisions for himself at a particular time.[4] In these situations the state should provide a range of responses appropriate to the needs of the person, ranging from support and assistance in making a decision, through to substituted decision-making for some or all decisions. This area of law is concerned with decision-making and vulnerable people, and must balance the need for protection against the right to autonomy as far as possible. The European Court of Human Rights stated that consideration should be given to the need for 'special procedur-al safeguards...to protect the interests of persons who, on account of their mental disabilities, are not fully capable of acting for themselves.'[5]

Legal developments in this area are addressing the core of what it means to be human.

---

[1] Lecturer, School of Law, National University of Ireland, Galway, Academic Associate and a founding member of the Centre for Disability Law and Policy Research at the School of Law, Member of the Mental Health Commission (Ireland), of the National Disability Authority (Ireland) Mental Health Advisory Committee and of the board of the Brothers of Charity Services, Galway.

[2] *Schloendorff v. Society of New York Hospitals* [1914] 211 NY 125; *Malette v. Shulman* [1990] 67 DLR (4th) 321 at 336; *Department of Health v. JWB & SMB* (1992) 66 ALJR 300 at 317; *Re T* [1993] Fam 95 at 102.

[3] This article is concerned with countries in the Council of Europe region.

[4] The term 'mental disability' is used in this article as an umbrella term covering this range of conditions.

[5] *Winterwerp v. Netherlands* (App. No.6301/73), [1979] 2 EHRR 387, para. 60.

Respect for autonomy … involves respect for each person's individuality. It demands, therefore, that any criterion intended to determine when someone is incapable of being autonomous should, equally, be respectful of that person's individuality.[6]

Legal mechanisms exist in most countries to deal with decision-making by adults with impaired legal capacity. The traditional approach to the deprivation of legal capacity can often result in the exclusion of mentally disabled persons from any decision-making and participation in society, effectively resulting in their being 'socially dead' or regarded as suffering 'civil death', indicating the depth of powerlessness involved.[7] 'There is evidence from some countries that judges routinely deprive people with mental disorder of legal capacity in procedures which do not meet fair trial guarantees.'[8] This extreme approach fails to recognize partial capacity, treats everyone in the same way, and has a profound effect on a person's life and the choices open to them. Some legal systems have no alternatives to guardianship and preclude persons under guardianship from any legal activity including instructing a lawyer, taking legal proceedings or challenging guardianship.[9] Where a person is deprived of legal capacity, a guardian is appointed and makes all decisions for the person, even when he or she has functional capacity to make many of those decisions. Such an approach fails to recognize that there are gradations of capacity, that capacity can fluctuate at different times, and that capacity is not general but relates to a particular decision. An example is where a person may not have the legal capacity to make decisions about a large property transaction and may need intervention for this decision, but be fully capable of making many other less complex legal decisions. Clearly, this situation is at odds with the principle of proportionality in human rights law and means that there is need for a flexible approach.[10]

Less restrictive legal measures are in place in some countries in Europe, that deal only with those decisions the person is not capable of making, leaving the person to continue to make decisions for which he or she has functional capacity.[11] Such systems may facilitate assistance with decision-making and permit people to make decisions in anticipation of incapacity in the future.[12] These systems

---

[6]   I. Kennedy, *Treat me Right*, (Oxford University Press, 1988), 57.

[7]   Mental Disability Advocacy Center, *Report on Guardianship and Human Rights in Russia – Analysis of Law Policy and Practice*, (MDAC, 2007), 79; <www.mdac. info> (accessed 30 October 2008); E. Miller *et al, A Life Apart*, (Tavistock, 1972); T. Minkowitz, 'Legal Capacity: Fundamental to the Rights of Persons with Disabilities', 56 *International Rehabilitation Review* 1 (2007), 25; J. Morris, 'Citizenship and disabled people: A scoping paper prepared for the Disability Rights Commission', (2005), <www.disability-archive.leeds.ac.uk≥ (accessed 16 July 2008).

[8]   P. Bartlett *et al, Mental Disability and the European Convention on Human Rights,* (Nijhoff, 2007), 154.

[9]   *Shtukaturov v. Russia,* App. No. 44009/05, 27th March 2008, not yet reported; MDAC reports confirm that this is the situation in other countries including Serbia, the Czech Republic, Hungary, Bulgaria.

[10] P. Bartlett *et al, Mental Disability and the European Convention,* 157.

[11] These countries include Sweden, Germany, Denmark, Spain, England and Wales.

[12] Mental Capacity Act 2005, Principle 1(3), England and Wales; Mental Capacity Bill,

reflect 'a desire to protect the autonomy of the capable individual'.[13]

The paradigm shift from the medical to the social model of disability involves a presumption of legal capacity for all adults. This approach is reflected in the UN Convention on the Rights of Persons with Disabilities, in Council of Europe documents and decisions of the European Court of Human Rights.[14] Law reform in some jurisdictions is acknowledging this shift with the introduction of mechanisms to assist people with impaired capacity and to provide safeguards in the event of full incapacity.[15] Successful law reform presupposes a significant attitudinal change in the mind-set of public and civil servants, policy makers and other key players, like the judiciary, and medical and other assessors of capacity. Law reform, as the key change, has to be underpinned at a more substantive level by embracing the notion of capacity as an integral part of all human beings.

This article addresses the approach to the removal of legal capacity, its impact on the person involved and its practice in some Council of Europe Member States. It addresses the standards in human rights law, the CRPD, some documents from the Council of Europe relating to legal capacity, and particularly Recommendation No. R(99)4, and decisions of the ECtHR, and considers whether these standards are being met. The contribution of civil society is addressed in this regard. The legal mechanisms and the procedures leading to the removal of legal capacity are discussed in some detail, as is the resulting impact on persons subject to these mechanisms. Rights of appeal, review of continuing guardianship and rights to challenge actions by guardians are considered. The need for law reform in certain countries in Europe is discussed.

2. CONTEXT FOR CHANGE

Attitudinal change is a central element of progress recognizing the paradigm shift from the paternalistic system to one where persons with disabilities have rights on an equal basis with others as provided for in the CRPD, and particularly Article 12 on legal capacity. One commentator says that Article 12 '...lies at the very heart of the revolution in disability – treating people as "subjects" and not as "objects".'[16]

The notion of the self-fulfilling prophecy of a label of incapacity can re-

---

2007, Principle 1(c), Ireland.

[13] P. Bartlett, *Blackstone's Guide to the Mental Capacity Act 2005,* (2nd ed.), (Oxford University Press, 2008), 47.

[14] The UN Convention on Rights of Persons with Disabilities will be referred to as CRPD. Council of Europe documents are discussed later in the article. The European Court of Human Rights will be referred to as ECtHR. Other relevant documents include the World Health Organisation, *Resource Book on Mental Health, Human Rights and Legislation – Stop Exclusion, Dare to Care,* (WHO, 2005).

[15] Sweden, Germany, Scotland, England and Wales, Spain and proposed law reform in Ireland.

[16] G. Quinn, 'Resisting the "Temptation of Elegance": Can the Convention on the Rights of Persons with Disabilities Socialise States to Right Behaviour', in O. Arnardottir *et al* (eds),*United Nations Convention on the Rights of Persons with Disabilities: European and Scandanavian Perspectives*, (Brill, International Studies in Human Rights, 2009), 49.

Mary Keys

sult in the person losing confidence, due to a lack of opportunity for learning, achievement and capacity development.[17] Decisions are made by others, resulting in increased passivity and learned helplessness. The exercise of the right to self-determination is then undermined by a lack of entitlement to choice and control over the support many disabled persons require. Barriers to achieving self-determination need to be dismantled to give effect to the person's wishes.

The number of people with impaired capacity is increasing throughout Europe, mainly in the older population.[18] Advances in medical science are resulting in increased survival rates of persons with impaired capacity, following difficult births and following severe brain trauma. It is estimated that several hundreds of thousands of people within the Council of Europe region are subject to guardianship.[19]

The traditional approach to mentally disabled people, whether of full or limited functional capacity, is institutionalization in some European countries.[20] Many people with impaired capacity live in institutions because this is the only environment in which state support is provided.[21] Large numbers of people with mental disabilities, particularly older people and those with significant learning disabilities, are denied the choice to live independently in their community due to lack of support. They are forced into institutional or 'congregate' care systems, regardless of their legal capacity.[22] One commentator says that to 'describe people who have spent more than five years in a psychiatric hospital as "voluntary" is in many ways a misnomer. These people may well have nowhere else to go.'[23] It also means they are not visible in society. Living in a long stay institution clearly militates against self-determination. The hierarchical structure disempowers and

---

[17] B. Winick, 'The Side Effects of Incompetence Labelling and the Implications for Mental Health', 1 *Psychiatry, Public Policy & Law* 42 (1995), 437.

[18] World Health Organization, *Mental Health; New Understanding – New Hope,* (WHO, 2001), estimates that the number of people with Alzheimer's disease in the WHO European Region of 880 million people will double to 2.8 million by 2025.

[19] P. Bartlett *et al*, *Mental Disability and the European Convention,* 155, referring to the figures based on the MDAC research on legal incapacity in seven Council of Europe Member States: Bulgaria, Croatia, Czech Republic, Georgia, Hungary, Russia, and Serbia.

[20] MDAC research in Bulgaria, Croatia, Czech Republic, Georgia, Hungary, Russia, and Serbia.

[21] R. Kayness *et al* 'Out of Darkness into Light? Introducing the Convention on the Rights of Persons with Disabilities', 8 *Human Rights Law Review* 1 (2008), 1-34.

[22] J. Morris, 'Citizenship and disabled people': A scoping paper prepared for the Disability Rights Commission, (2005), <www.disability-archive.leeds.ac.uk> (accessed 16 July 2008). 24. See generally, O'Shea, *Improving the Quality of Life of Elderly Persons in Situations of Dependency*, (Council of Europe, 2002).

[23] M. Donnelly, 'Treatment for Mental Disorders and Protection of Patients' Rights', 8, paper presented at Mental Health and Human Rights Seminar, University College Cork, 25th October 2007, <www.ucc.ie/law/docs/mentalhealth2007>. For an overview and analysis of consent in Irish mental health law and the requirements of the ECHR see also M. Donnelly, 'Treatment for a Mental Disorder: The Mental Health Act 2001, Consent and the Role of Rights', *Dublin University Law Journal* (2005), 220.

diminishes any remaining autonomy in individuals living there.

One of the barriers, in some countries, to asserting functional capacity is the lack of recognition that functional incapacity cannot be presumed solely on the basis of having, for example, a mental illness or a disability.[24] The continuing acceptance at state level of institutional care, involving both large and small institutions, that include psychiatric hospitals and other residential centres for persons with intellectual disability, as well as smaller group homes, prevents people from leading independent and fulfilling lives. The care and treatment in closed residential care settings, social care homes, nursing homes and group homes for persons who have impaired capacity, is potentially inhuman and degrading. In *Herczgefalvy v. Austria,* the ECtHR said '... that the position of inferiority and powerlessness which is typical of patients confined in psychiatric hospitals calls for increased vigilance in reviewing whether the Convention has been complied with'.[25] The words 'inferiority', 'powerlessness' and 'confined' can equally apply to any person in an institutional setting, like a nursing or care home, or even in controlled residences in the community, where there are no safeguards around legal capacity and assisted decision-making.[26]

The policy of deinstitutionalization, underway in some jurisdictions, has resulted in the closure of large hospitals and residential centres housing people, many of whom were presumed to lack functional capacity.[27] This development has highlighted the need for care to be provided in a different way, in the community, and through support services. It also highlights the need for individual rights in decision-making. However, the emphasis on community care in state policies in many jurisdictions is not matched by the provision of necessary supports to enable people to remain outside the realm of centres of care. These supports must include access to independent advocacy and other forms of representation that enable the highest level of capacity potential to be achieved. Community living increases opportunities for people to have their autonomy respected, even if it is balanced against the need for safeguards when functional capacity is impaired. Even then, unless the paradigm shift is instilled in those planning and providing services, institutional behaviour can easily be transferred into the community setting.[28] Change will only come with appropriate law reform that recognizes and supports these elements.

3. HUMAN RIGHTS AND LEGAL CAPACITY

The CRPD came into effect in May 2008, and has brought the rights of disabled people into sharp focus.[29] The purpose of the CRPD, as stated in Article 1, is to

---

[24]   MDAC, *Report on Guardianship in Hungary,* (MDAC, 2007), 82.

[25]   Herczegfalvy v Austria (App. No. 10533/83), [1992] 15 EHRR 437 at 82. The Convention referred to is the ECHR.

[26]   D. Doherty *et al, Happy Living Here, An evaluation of community residential mental health services,* (Mental Health Commission & Health Research Board, 2007).

[27]   The closure of large psychiatric hospitals is continuing in Ireland and England. There are approximately 3,000 people with intellectual disability living in institutions in Ireland in 2008.

[28]   D. Doherty *et al, Happy Living Here,* 13.

[29]   See <www.un.org/disabilities> (accessed on 17 November 2008) for the signatories

promote, protect and ensure the full and equal enjoyment of all human rights and fundamental freedoms by all persons with disabilities, and to promote respect for their inherent dignity. The core human rights principles of dignity, autonomy, equality, and independence are set out to guide the interpretation of the CRPD in Article 3, regarded as 'the moral compass of the CRPD', and the principles are the 'legacy values of human rights theory and law'.[30] The CRPD is, effectively, a map of what is required if we are to achieve the objectives set out in Article 1. Article 1 provides that, '[p]ersons with disabilities include persons with long-term physical, mental, intellectual, or sensory impairments, which in interaction with various barriers, may hinder their full and effective participation in society on an equal basis with others'. Recognizing that people with disabilities remained invisible, despite many earlier human rights instruments, it was deemed necessary to clarify current international human rights law specifically in relation to persons with disabilities.[31] The Preamble to the CRPD provides that, '[d]isability is an evolving concept and results from the interaction between persons with impairments and the attitudinal and environmental barriers that hinders their full and effective participation in society on an equal basis with others'.[32] These barriers are highlighted in relation to the achievement of legal capacity.

Legal capacity is underpinned in Article 12 of the CRPD, entitled 'Equal recognition before the Law'. It provides:

1. States Parties reaffirm that persons with disabilities have the right to recognition everywhere as persons before the law.
2. States Parties shall recognize that persons with disabilities enjoy legal capacity on an equal basis with others in all aspects of life.
3. States Parties shall take appropriate measures to provide access by persons with disabilities to the support they may require in exercising their legal capacity.
4. States Parties shall ensure that all measures that relate to the exercise of legal capacity provide for appropriate and effective safeguards to prevent abuse in accordance with international human rights law. Such safeguards shall ensure that measures relating to the exercise of legal capacity respect the rights, will and preferences of the person, are free of conflict of interest and undue influence, are proportional and tailored to the person's circumstances, apply for the shortest time possible and are subject to regular review by a competent, independent and impartial authority or judicial body. The safeguards shall be proportional to the degree to which such measures affect the person's rights and interests.
5. Subject to the provisions of this article, State Parties shall take all appropriate

---

and ratifications.

[30] G. Quinn, 'Empowering Persons with Disabilities, the UN Convention on the Human Rights of Persons with Disabilities', Keynote Address, given at German EU Presidency Ministerial Conference, Empowering People with Disabilities, Berlin, 11th June 2007, on file with author of paper: gerard.quinn@nuigalway.ie.

[31] G. Quinn and T. Degener, *Human Rights and Disability: the Current use and Future Potential of United Nations Instruments in the context of Disability*, (Office of the UN High Commission for Human Rights, 2002).

[32] UN Convention on the Rights of Persons with Disabilities, Preamble (e).

and effective measures to ensure the equal right of persons with disabilities to own or inherit property, to control their own financial affairs and to have equal access to bank loans, mortgages and other forms of financial credit, and shall ensure that persons with disabilities are not arbitrarily deprived of their property.

There is near universal agreement among civil society organizations and academic commentators that legal capacity is a fundamental element in the CRPD, one in which, 'the old regime has finally been lifted'.[33]

The standard laid down in Article 12 contrasts with systems that use a medical model where all rights and powers affecting lives are removed based on a general assessment of capacity. Guardianship that is overly broad, and other substitute decision-making mechanisms, form part of the traditional armoury for dealing with incapacity and have negative connotations of over-intrusiveness and paternalism.[34] There have been calls for supported rather than substituted decision-making from many quarters.[35] One commentator, referring to substitute decision-making as 'the stranglehold of the past' states that the substitution of judgements by others is not prohibited by Article 12 but '... that an inclusive and universal concept of legal capacity is essential if the prejudice against persons with disability is to be "disassembled".'[36] There must be an assessment of continuing legal capacity even where there is a substitute decision-maker for all decisions and actions. A system of advocacy is essential to enable this new capacity formulation to be effective.[37]

The achievement of many other rights in the CRPD is dependent on legal capacity. The Preamble at (j) recognizes the need for more intensive supports to achieve the aim of the protection and promotion of human rights for some people. The right to independent living found in Article 19, like Article 12, is cross-cutting and all embracing, and is one of the most challenging areas from a policy standpoint, as it moves the focus away from traditional centres of care.

The important human rights principle of the least restrictive alternative necessitates the option of living in the community rather than an institution. While the connection with deprivation of legal capacity is not clear, large numbers of people who are deprived of legal capacity remain in institutional care. However,

---

[33]   T. Minkowitz, 56 *International Rehabilitation Review* 1 (2007), 25. MDAC and Rehabilitation International share this view, to name two.

[34]   England and Wales have moved from a traditional system to one which is only involved where a person is unable to make a particular decision. Ireland continues to retain the system of wardship involving removal of capacity for most legal activity, based on a general assessment, but proposed legislation, Mental Capacity and Guardianship Bill, which will follow a somewhat similar system to the Mental Capacity Act, 2005, England and Wales.

[35]   T. Minkowitz, 56 *International Rehabilitation Review* 1 (2007), 25; P. Bartlett *et al*, *Mental Disability and the European Convention,* 158; Mental Disability Advocacy Center in their state reports; World Health Organization, *Resource Book on Mental Health,* (WHO, 2005).

[36]   A. Dhanda, 34 *Syracuse Journal of International Law and Commerce* 2 (2007), 457.

[37]   Ibid., 461.

some countries have engaged in policies of law reform and active deinstitutionalization with moves towards community living.[38] The CRPD provides for the right to independent living in Article 19, recognizing:

> the equal right of all persons with disabilities to live in the community, with choices equal to others, and [States Parties] shall take effective and appropriate measures to facilitate full enjoyment by persons with disabilities of this right and their full inclusion and participation in the community, including ensuring that,
>
> (a) Persons with disabilities have the opportunity to choose their place of residence and where and with whom they live on an equal basis with others and are not obliged to live in a particular living arrangement;
>
> (b) Persons with disabilities have access to a range of in-home, residential and other community support services, including personal assistance necessary to support living and inclusion in the community and to prevent isolation or segregation from the community;
>
> (c) Community services and facilities for the general population are available on an equal basis to persons with disabilities and are responsive to their needs.

Our awareness of human rights and knowledge of the impact of institutional care mandates that institutional living should always be used as a last resort, and the deprivation of legal capacity should not automatically result in institutional living. The CRPD refers to the provision of information in an appropriate format as an essential tool enabling capacity potential to be properly addressed.[39] The absence of such an approach could result in incorrect assumptions being made about a person's legal capacity, without the person receiving the necessary assistance towards accessing information. Assistance with the interpretation and application of information will be necessary to make the right real for the person. Closely related to the right to access information is the right to informed consent to medical treatment on an equal basis with others.[40] These, and other articles, present a tight framework that presumes capacity, and supports self-determination, with or without assistance. One commentator believes that 'an evaluation of legal capacity, more than any other right, will show how the Convention challenges stereotypes surrounding disability'.[41]

Often overlooked in the legal capacity debate are references to the autonomy of children who suffer restrictions in many domestic statutes through the use of the status of age to assume incapacity, often up to age of 18 years.[42] The CRPD provides for 'respect for the evolving capacities of children with disabilities and respect for the right of children with disabilities to preserve their identities.'[43] In

---

[38] MDAC, *Report on Guardianship in Hungary*, 2007.
[39] UN Convention on Rights of Persons with Disabilities, Article 21.
[40] Ibid., Article 25.
[41] A. Dhanda, 34 *Syracuse Journal of International Law and Commerce* 2 (2007), 430.
[42] P. Fennell, *Treatment without Consent*, (Routledge, 1995), 277.
[43] UN Convention on the Rights of Persons with Disabilities, Article 3(h).

addition, Article 7 provides for support for children with disabilities on an equal basis with other children, with their best interests as a primary consideration, and that they should be given age appropriate assistance to express their views.[44] The evolving capacities of the child is a key element of the Convention on the Rights of the Child and, along with Article 6 of the Council of Europe Convention on Human Rights and Biomedicine, require that the opinion of the minor be taken into consideration as an increasingly determinative factor in proportion to age and maturity. This latter Convention states in the Explanatory Report that the minor's opinion could even lead to the conclusion that his consent should be necessary, or at least sufficient, for some treatments.[45]

3.1. COUNCIL OF EUROPE AND LEGAL CAPACITY: RECOMMENDATION NO. R(99) 4

The Council of Europe began to address the protection of incapable adults in 1995 in order to guarantee their integrity, rights and independence where possible. The leading document on legal capacity is *Recommendation No. R (99) 4 concerning the legal protection of incapable adults*. The Recommendation strongly promotes self-determination and autonomy, the essential elements to respecting the human rights and dignity of each person.[46] It 'concerns the protection of adults who, by reason of an impairment or insufficiency of their personal faculties, are incapable of making, in an autonomous way, decisions concerning any or all of their personal or economic affairs, or understanding, expressing or acting upon such decision, and who consequently cannot protect their interests'.[47] Rather than a narrow notion of decision-making the Explanatory Memorandum to Recommendation (99) 4 states that autonomy,

> ...is used in a wide sense – based on the idea of the authenticity of decisions in the light of a person's character, values and life history. An autonomous decision must be free from external coercion and internal compulsion due, for example to such factors as schizophrenic delusions or severe depressive episodes. It should also be based on sufficient understanding of the importance and consequences of the decision.[48]

---

[44] In Ireland, children with mental health difficulties who need in-patient care are, for the most part, admitted to adult in-patient mental health facilities that are inappropriate. Figures available confirm 193 children were admitted to adult mental health services in 2007, based on notifications to the Mental Health Commission 2007 available on <www.mhcirl.ie> (accessed on 17 November 2008).

[45] Council of Europe, *Explanatory Report for Convention on Human Rights and Biomedicine* (1996), DIR/JUR (97) 5, para. 44.

[46] Council of Europe, 'Recommendation (99) 4 of the Committee of Ministers to Member States on Principles Concerning the Legal Protection of Incapable Adults', 23 February 1999.

[47] Council of Europe, Recommendation No.R (99) 4, Part 1, para. 1.

[48] Council of Europe, Explanatory Memorandum to Recommendation No. (99) 4, para. 20.

Recommendation No. R(99) 4 provides for public measures of protection or other legal arrangements enabling adults to benefit from representation or assistance regarding their personal affairs. It includes detailed principles and safeguards applying to adults who lack legal capacity. Addressed to all member states, it gives detailed guidance on how to reform national legislation.

A number of principles are worth noting, the most important being that no measure of protection should be established unless it is necessary, taking individual circumstances into account. The automatic removal of legal capacity should not happen, but the Recommendation acknowledges the restriction of legal capacity as an appropriate element of protection.[49] Principle 3 provides for maximum preservation of capacity:

1. The legislative framework should, as far as possible, recognize that different degrees of incapacity may exist and that incapacity may vary from time to time. Accordingly, a measure of protection should not result automatically in a complete removal of legal capacity. However, a restriction of legal capacity should be possible where it is shown to be necessary for the protection of the person concerned.

2. In particular, a measure of protection should not automatically deprive the person concerned of the right to vote, or to make a will, or to consent or refuse consent to any intervention in the health field, or to other decisions of a personal character at any time when his or her capacity permits him or her to do so.

3. Consideration should be given to legal arrangements whereby, even when representation in a particular area is necessary, the adult may be permitted, with the representative's consent, to undertake specific acts or acts in a specific area.

4. Whenever possible the adult should be enabled to enter into legally effective transactions of an everyday nature.

The Recommendation requires that less formal procedures should be addressed first, permitting flexibility and proportionality, and any interventions should be proportional to the degree of capacity and tailored to that individual's needs. Interventions should not be automatic, in order to ensure the maximum preservation of capacity.[50] Another important principle is the consideration of the past and present wishes of the person, which are to be given due respect in providing any measure of protection. Even though these principles are regarded as soft law, it is worth noting that they have been cited authoritatively by the ECtHR in a number of cases involving legal capacity.[51] Recognizing that the principles had no force in

---

[49]   Ibid., Principle 5.
[50]   Recommendation No. R (99) 4, Principles 5, 6 and 3 respectively.
[51]   Black's Law Dictionary (8th Ed.), (Thomson West, 2004), states that soft law embraces the category of rules, recommendations, guidelines or broad principles that, while not strictly legally binding, are nonetheless legally significant. These cases are, *H.F. v. Slovakia*, App. No. 54797/00, 8th November 2005, (case in French only and not yet reported.); *Shtukaturov v. Russia*, App. No. 44009/05, 27th March 2008, not yet reported, and *X v. Croatia*. App. no. 11223/04, 17th July 2008, not yet reported.

law, the ECtHR, importantly, said they may define a common European standard in this area.[52]

A Council of Europe working party is building on Recommendation No. R(99) 4 to provide a new recommendation and elaborate principles focusing on self-determination, particularly on powers of attorney, and advance directives, recognized as less restrictive alternatives to guardianship.[53] Draft Principle 1 of the new recommendation requires states to promote self-determination for adults when they are not capable of making decisions, and that states should consider giving priority to such private measures over public measures of protection.[54] Continuing powers of attorney and advance directives are the principle means of self-determination for people who have legal capacity, but anticipate incapacity in future. The intention of law in this area is not to take over, but to assist in decision-making. The key issue in providing such a mechanism is to have an informal, simple, flexible, and inexpensive arrangement, but with protections to ensure those without capacity are safeguarded against exploitation and abuse.[55] This approach is supported also in Article 12(4) of the CRPD which refers to appropriate and effective safeguards that are proportional and tailor-made to the person's needs.

Further support is found in the *Action Plan for People with Disabilities in Europe 2006-2015* and Recommendation No. R(2006) 5 which provides that there should be no automatic loss of capacity due to disability, and there should be appropriate assistance and safeguards.[56] A key objective of the Action Plan is to ensure appropriate assistance for people with difficulty in exercising legal capacity, and that such assistance is proportionate to individual requirements.

A European based non-governmental organization, the Mental Disability Advocacy Center (MDAC), based in Hungary, carried out the first ever examination of laws relating to deprivation of legal capacity and guardianship in a number of European countries.[57] The organization has an ongoing project, since 2004, to

---

[52]   *H.F. v. Slovakia*, App. No. 54797/00, 8th November 2005, not yet reported,; *Shtukaturov v. Russia*, App. No. 44009/05, 27th March 2008, not yet reported, para. 98; *X v. Croatia*, App. no. 11223/04, 17th July 2008, not yet reported, para. 25.

[53]   Working party No. 2 on the Committee of Experts on Family Law on Incapable Adults, Draft Explanatory Report to Recommendation on principles concerning continuing powers of attorney and advance directives for incapacity, Strasbourg, 12th June 2008 CJ-FA-GT2 (2008) 7 rev. <www.coe.int/t/e/legal_affairs/legal_co-operation/family_law>.

[54]   Council of Europe, Draft Recommendation on Principles concerning continuing powers of attorney and advance directives for incapacity, 16th May 2008, CJ-FA-GT2 (2008) 7.

[55]   Council of Europe, Recommendation No. R (99) 4, Principle 2. See P. Bartlett *et al*, *Mental Disability and the European Convention*, 159.

[56]   In 2006 the Committee of Ministers of the Council of Europe adopted Recommendation No. R(2006) 5, 'Action plan to promote the rights and full participation of people with disabilities in society: improving the quality of life of people with disabilities in Europe 2006-2015'.

[57]   Mental Disability Advocacy Center (MDAC) promotes and protects the human rights of people with mental health problems or intellectual disabilities across Central and Eastern Europe and central Asia.

'identify strengths and weaknesses of existing legislative regimes'.[58] Using twenty-nine indicators, based largely on Recommendation No. R(99) 4 Principles, the Explanatory Memorandum to the Recommendations, as well as influence from America and Canada, they examined the laws applying to the removal of legal capacity and the consequences thereof. These indicators are not exclusive, but represent minimum standards, and are believed to capture the basic safeguards necessary for a person-centred and human rights orientated guardianship system, and would seem to be a very useful and important tool for both an objective and comparative examination of the systems in any country. Based on their findings, they made recommendations for urgent law reform under four headings: alternatives to guardianship, maximizing autonomy, improving procedures and preventing abuse.

Aside from the general principle in the first indicator of respect for human rights, dignity, and the fundamental freedom of persons with mental disabilities, the remaining indicators are applied in a chronological way starting with the initiation of guardianship through all the stages leading to the impact and outcome for the individual. The indicators are divided into three main areas: rights before placing the person under guardianship, rights after deprivation of capacity particularly in relation to the role of the guardian, and rights to review of guardianship, as well as a review of any less restrictive alternatives. MDAC approaches the examination in two stages: the first stage examines the legislative regimes and impact of guardianship in terms of compliance with domestic law and international human rights law standards as well as best practices, to highlight the need for reform. The second stage looks at the practices, by observing how the law works, and by reviewing implementation and how it affects persons facing guardianship.[59] This second element brings the reality of people's lives into focus and has potential for guiding the substance of law reform.

4. THE LEAST RESTRICTIVE ALTERNATIVE

Flexibility in response to any level of impaired decision-making necessitates access to a variety of measures which should apply in the least restrictive manner possible. The less restrictive measures include assisted or supported decision-making, advance directives and continuing or enduring powers of attorney, both of which are made in anticipation of future incapacity.[60] A continuing power of attorney is defined as a 'mandate given by a capable adult with the purpose that it shall remain in force, or enter into force, in the event of the granter's incapacity'.[61]

---

[58]   Reporting on Bulgaria, Croatia, Czech Republic, Georgia, Hungary, Russia, and Serbia.

[59]   The MDAC reports on Russia and Bulgaria state that access to a full range of information was not always possible due to state restrictions.

[60]   This is evident in a number of European countries, e.g., Germany, Sweden, Finland, and England and Wales.

[61]   Working party No. 2 on the Committee of Experts on Family Law on Incapable Adults, Draft Explanatory Report to Recommendation on principles concerning continuing powers of attorney and advance directives for incapacity, Strasbourg, 12th June 2008 CJ-FA-GT2 (2008) 7 rev. <www.coe.int/t/e/legal_affairs/legal_co-operation/family_law>.

It permits the appointment of a trusted person to make decisions concerning personal welfare, finance and property of the granter. Advance directives are defined as, 'statements issued by capable adults with the purpose of giving binding instructions, or expressing wishes, concerning situations that may arise in the event of their incapacity'. Some statements may be legally binding, while others may be considered and given due respect.[62] Another form of decision-making is assisted or, as it is sometimes called, supported decision-making, which is a form of interdependent decision-making and an alternative to court-ordered procedures like guardianship.[63] 'It has appeared in new adult guardianship legislation in three main ways: as a specific court-ordered alternative to substitute decision-making or guardianship; as a specifically identified and defined alternative to an application for a guardianship order; and as an indirectly identified and undefined alternative to such an application.'[64] Support for such assisted decision-making is found in some capacity laws, where a principle in the legislation in question provides that 'a person is not to be treated as unable to make a decision unless all practicable steps to *help* him to do so have been taken without success'.[65] Phrased in this way it fits the category of 'indirectly identified and undefined', leaving open, but nevertheless providing, a basis for assisted decision-making in such legislation.

5. APPROACH TO THE EVALUATION OF CAPACITY

The approach used in the evaluation of capacity is linked to the distinctions between models of disability; a medical model of disability focuses on the impairment, whereas the social or human rights model of disability is reflected in the functional approach, and involves considering the ability of the person in relation to a particular decision. Assessments of functional capacity are often carried out by medical personnel alone and, as this is a key component of the decision regarding legal capacity, it is vitally important that medical personnel have a full understanding of capacity evaluation. What is known as the status approach to capacity, focuses on factors extraneous to the person, like having a disability of any kind, and assumes, without foundation, that incapacity is an inherent part of that status. No account is taken of individual differences; one has either full capacity or is totally incapacitated.[66]

---

[62]   Austria and Denmark have provisions for binding advance directives, but some are guidelines and not legally binding, they have effect for five years and can be renewed and can be registered. Danish health law provides for living wills, and wishes regarding treatment in case of incapacity. In England the Mental Capacity Act 2005 principles on advance directives are limited only to decisions to refuse treatment. Advance directives can be part of or additional to continuing power of attorney.

[63]   R. Gordon, 'The emergence of Assisted (Supported) Decision-Making in the Canadian law of Adult Guardianship and Substitute Decision-Making', 23 *International Journal of Law and Psychiatry* 1 (2000), 61-77.

[64]   Ibid., 64.

[65]   Mental Capacity Act, 2005, s.1(3), England and Wales. Proposed Mental Capacity Bill, 2007, Ireland.

[66]   Russian Civil Code, plenary or (all encompassing) guardianship results in total legal incapacity and provides partial guardianship only for drug and alcohol addicted people.

In the case of the outcome approach, where the decision of the person conflicts with the norms of the assessor or of society, the assumption is that the person does not have capacity. However, judgements should not be made based solely on the existence of a disagreement with a proposed course of action regarded by others as being in the person's best interests. A person receiving inpatient mental health care as a voluntary patient may decide to refuse treatment for a variety of reasons. The refusal is often regarded as evidence of incapacity, while the decision to seek treatment in the first place is not. Neither the status nor the outcome approach takes account of individual differences and gradations of capacity. In many jurisdictions these approaches resulted, and continue to result, in automatic loss of legal capacity by operation of the law.[67]

Functional capacity refers to a person's ability to make a particular decision at a particular time. If, for example, someone has a mental illness or intellectual disability, this does not automatically mean that person does not have the functional capacity to make a particular decision. What is required is that the person understands the information relevant to the decision, is able to weigh up and appreciate the consequences of deciding one way or another, arrive at and communicate that choice. This approach respects the right of autonomy, is tailor-made for the individual and takes account of fluctuating capacity. Confirmation of support for this approach is to be found in decisions from the ECtHR where the Court has held that the existence of a mental disorder, even a serious one, cannot be the sole reason to justify full incapacitation and that a tailor-made approach is required.[68]

Legal capacity recognizes a person's ability to make decisions with legal consequences. Examples are entering a contract to marry, managing property or finances, or making medical care decisions. While people may have functional capacity in relation to a decision, the law may exclude them because they are under guardianship and have been judged not to have general legal capacity. The sort of general assessment of capacity in these instances questions if the person, 'is of unsound mind and unable to manage their person or property', or 'whether the person can control his or her actions as a result of a mental disease', or 'the person has a mental disorder, it is not only temporary and due to the mental disorder the person is incapable of undertaking acts in law'.[69]

If a person is placed in full guardianship because, for example, they have inherited property and are deemed legally incapable of managing their property based on a general assessment of capacity, they may also be automatically precluded by law from all other legal activity such as instructing a lawyer, getting married, making a will, regardless of their functional capacity in these contexts. This approach is regarded as a disproportionate interference with the person ac-

---

[67] Russia, Bulgaria and other countries examined by the Mental Disability Advocacy Center. The Lunacy Regulation (Ireland) Act 1871 results in the removal of capacity to enter contracts, including marriage, and prevents persons from managing property or finance.

[68] *Shtukaturov v. Russia*, App. No. 44009/05, 27th March 2008, not yet reported, para. 94.

[69] Lunacy Regulation (Ireland) Act, 1871, s.15, the Civil Code of Russian Federation, Article 29 and the Czech Republic Civil Code, Article 10.

cording to human rights law.[70] Russia and Bulgaria, for example, prevent people under guardianship from accessing court or challenging their guardianship, regardless of their capacity to do so.[71] Each decision having legal consequences necessitates a separate assessment of functional capacity.[72] This is in keeping with Recommendation No. R(99) 4, and with the CRPD, Article 12, and is evidence of the clear rejection of a one-size-fits-all approach. Decisions on legal capacity are usually made by judges, although there are examples of best practice in Australia where a multi-disciplinary approach is used by a tribunal, which is a body with judicial powers.[73] In relation to court hearings, the impact on a person of being in the formal atmosphere of the court may to be one of fear and nervousness. Observations in one report stated that, 'adult respondents were frequently stressed as the result of being in a courtroom, and/or did not understand the situation and its importance. In one particular case the adult even stated that "I am not a criminal so that I would be brought in front of a court. I shouldn't be here".'[74] The report also noted that judges were uncertain and showed discomfort in communicating with people with mental health disabilities or intellectual disabilities.[75]

6. FAIR PROCEDURES, PRIVACY AND ARBITRARY DETENTION

Although states enjoy a wide margin of appreciation when determining someone's capacity, the ECtHR has said that a fair balance between the interests of a person of unsound mind and other legitimate interests must be struck.[76] The ECtHR said that a stricter scrutiny is called for in respect of very serious limitations in the sphere of private life.[77] The deprivation of capacity, leading also to deprivation of liberty in *Shtukatorov v. Russia* was said by the ECtHR to be a 'very serious' and disproportionate interference with a person's private life, and with no tailor-made approach. Comparing the case with *Winterwerp v. Netherlands,* where both liberty and legal capacity were at stake, the ECtHR said that 'in the present case the outcome of the proceedings was at least equally important for the applicant, his personal autonomy in almost all areas of life was at issue including the eventual limitation of his liberty'.[78] This statement recognizes that removal of legal capacity necessitates careful procedural arrangements which must be fair and ensure due respect for the interests safeguarded by Article 6(1), must not result in the

---

[70]   European Convention on Human Rights, Article 8.
[71]   *Shtukatorov v. Russia,* App. No. 44009/05, 27th March 2008, not yet reported.
[72]   *X v. Croatia*, App. no. 11223/04, 17th July 2008, not yet reported.
[73]   Guardianship Tribunal in New South Wales, <www.gt.nsw.gov.au/about/>(accessed on 17 November 2008).
[74]   MDAC, *Report on Guardianship in Hungary*, para. 3.3.1.
[75]   Ibid., para. 3.4.
[76]   *Shtukatorov v. Russia,* App. No. 44009/05, 27th March 2008, not yet reported. In this case there was no evidence that the applicant had problems in the past with work, managing property, employment and the medical report was not corroborated by evidence and the court did not assess his past behaviour when it decided to restrict his legal capacity.
[77]   *Shtukatorov v. Russia*, Application No. 44009/05, 27th March 2008, not yet reported, para. 88.
[78]   Ibid., para. 71. Breaches by Russia of Articles 6(1), 8(1) and 5 were established.

arbitrary deprivation of liberty contrary to Article 5 and must ensure the right to respect for private and family life as provided for in Article 8(1) of the ECHR.

The question arises as to whether the state is under a positive obligation under Article 8 to ensure there are adequate legal protections for the rights of persons with impaired capacity.[79] If the state does not provide assistance to an individual who is unable to manage his finances and, as a result, cannot access or benefit from having money or property, this may be an unjustifiable interference with the right to private life. It means that such a right is not real for the person.[80] Further support for such obligation arises by virtue of Article 1 of the ECHR and the duty to secure to everyone the rights and freedoms in the Convention. If the ECtHR were to find that such an obligation existed, it might require states to ensure that the rights of people, believed to have impaired capacity are realized and this might require 'access to speedy, accurate and independent incapacity evaluations' as well as appointing someone to act on the person's behalf in order to maximize respect for private and family life.[81]

Fair procedures and legal rights leading to the deprivation of capacity, and legal rights after a guardianship order is made, come within the remit of Article 6(1) of the ECHR. Article 6(1) states, '[i]n the determination of his civil rights and obligations or of any criminal charge against him, everyone is entitled to a fair and public hearing within a reasonable time by an independent and impartial tribunal established by law'.

Guardianship proceedings must comply with the standards of Article 6(1) because they involve the determination of civil rights.[82] In *Winterwerp v. Netherlands* the applicant was detained in a psychiatric institution and, as a result, automatically lost the legal capacity to manage his property and affairs. Capacity to deal personally with one's affairs involves the exercise of private rights and affects 'civil rights and obligations' as provided for in Article 6(1), and removing such capacity is a determination of civil rights.[83] The ECtHR held in *Winterwerp* that the automatic loss of legal capacity to manage one's affairs under domestic law, due to compulsory admission to an institution to receive mental health care, and without any separate assessment or hearing taking place, breached the right to fair procedures as provided for in Article 6(1).[84] Whatever the justification for depriving a person of unsound mind of the capacity to administer his property, the ECtHR said it cannot warrant the total absence of that right.

This rule was reaffirmed in a case involving the restoration of legal capacity in *Matter v. Slovakia*.[85] The ECtHR had to address, '...whether or not [the applicant] is entitled, through his own acts, to acquire rights and undertake obligations set out, *inter alia* in the Civil Code. Their outcome is therefore directly decisive

---

79   P. Bartlett *et al*, *Mental Disability and the European Convention*, 153.
80   *Airey v. Ireland* (App. no. 6289/73), [1979] 2 EHRR 305, para. 24.
81   P. Bartlett *at al*, *Mental Disability and the European Convention*, 153.
82   *Winterwerp v. Netherlands*, [1979] 2 EHRR 387. See M. Wachenfeld, 'The Human Rights of the Mentally Ill in Europe', 60 *Nordic Journal of International Law* 3 (1991), 224.
83   *Winterwerp v. Netherlands*, [1979] 2 EHRR 387, para. 73.
84   Ibid., para. 75.
85   *Matter v. Slovakia*, (App. No.31534/96), [2001] 31 EHRR 32.

for the determination of the applicant's "civil rights and obligations"'.[86] Article 6(1) therefore clearly applies to the determination of legal capacity.

6.1.   NOTIFICATION

The requirement to be informed about proceedings is a requirement of fair trial as provided for under Article 6(1). It is also supported by Recommendation No.R(99) 4 which provides that, '[t]he person concerned should be informed promptly in a language, or by other means, which he or she understands of the institution of proceedings which could affect his or her legal capacity, the exercise of his or her right, of his or her interests…'.[87] The applicant in *Shtukaturov v. Russia* was not informed about the proceedings and was not heard in the decision to place him under his mother's guardianship until one year after the original decision had been taken, when he contacted a lawyer. He did not realize he was being subjected to a forensic psychiatric examination. The ECtHR held that the guardianship proceedings were unfair and breached Article 6(1) as they excluded the applicant. He was arbitrarily stripped of capacity without knowledge and had no means to challenge this action, as his detention on the application of his mother was a system of absolute exclusion.[88] While the right to notification and other rights may well be present in the procedural rules, these rights are weakened considerably due to the failure to make them real and effective.[89]

In a case involving the right of the person in guardianship to be consulted and involved in adoption proceedings, the ECtHR stated that it was not sufficient for the applicant in *X v. Croatia* to have been only summarily informed that adoption proceedings had started, while her parental rights were still intact.[90] Consent to adoption can only be dispensed with in exceptional circumstances, but the law provided that since she was in guardianship, she was automatically precluded from involvement in the proceedings or consenting to the adoption.[91] The issue in the case was whether the procedures followed respected the applicant's family life or interfered with the right to respect for family life, in a way which could not be justified as necessary in a democratic society. In this context the ECtHR said that 'it is an interference of a very serious order to split up a family'.[92] Holding a violation of Article 8(1), the ECtHR stated with regard to a situation where a child is being removed from his parents for adoption that, 'there is an even greater call than usual for protection against arbitrary interferences.'[93] Where the parents

---

[86]   Ibid., para. 51.

[87]   Council of Europe, Recommendation No. R (99) 4, Principle 4.

[88]   O. Lewis, Mental Disability Advocacy Centre, Press Release on 27th March 2008, available at: <www.mdac.info>.

[89]   MDAC, *Report on Guardianship in Russia*, 6.

[90]   *Matter v. Slovakia*, App. No.31534/96, judgment 5 July 1999, [2001] 31 EHRR 32, para. 53.

[91]   Ibid., para. 36; Family Law Act, 2003, sections 130 & 138. The ECtHR cited the United Nations Convention on the Rights of the Child prohibiting separation of parents and child unless necessary in the best interests of the child, the opportunity to participate in the proceedings and to make views known.

[92]   *X v. Croatia*, App. No. 11223/04, 17th July 2008, not yet reported, para. 47.

[93]   Ibid.

have not been involved in the decision-making process, including the right to be heard and to be fully informed, this is a failure to respect their family life. In this case, an assessment had been made resulting in the removal of legal capacity, but no separate decision had been taken about the applicant's parental rights, or regarding her relationship with her daughter, even though she continued to exercise these rights until the adoption was finalized.

6.2. ASSESSMENT OF LEGAL CAPACITY

A capacity evaluation is essential to the deprivation of legal capacity and Recommendation No. R(99) 4 calls for a thorough in-person and up-to-date assessment by 'at least one' suitably qualified person, which should be based on objective information.[94] There must be a demonstrable link between the underlying diagnosis and the alleged inability to make independent decisions, and presumptions should not be made.[95] The ECtHR said in *Shtukaturov v. Russia* that mental illness cannot be the sole reason to justify stripping someone of legal capacity.[96] By analogy with the cases concerning the deprivation of liberty, in order to justify full incapacitation the mental disorder 'must be of a kind or degree' warranting such a deprivation of legal capacity.[97] This statement matches the requirement to establish deprivation of liberty under Article 5, namely that the mental disorder 'must be of a kind or degree' warranting confinement.[98]

When a number of decisions having legal consequences are being made, the ECtHR requires that separate assessments for each decision must be carried out. This is in line with the functional approach to capacity assessment. The ECtHR in *X v. Croatia* 'had difficulty in accepting that every person divested of the capacity to act should be automatically excluded from adoption proceedings concerning his or her child…'.[99] Similarly in *Shtukaturov v. Russia*, the fact of having a mental illness in itself was not reason to deprive a person of legal capacity.[100]

6.3. FORCIBLE DETENTION FOR ASSESSMENT

The forcible examination of the applicant in *Matter v. Slovakia* was regarded as a 'serious interference with private life' under Article 8, even if it had a legal basis and was not disproportionate.[101] In *Norwicka v. Poland,* a court ordered detention

---

94   *H.F. v. Slovakia*, App. No. 54797/00, 8th November 2005, not yet reported,; *Shtukaturov v. Russia*, App. No. 44009/05, 27th March 2008, not yet reported; Council of Europe, Recommendation No. R (99) 4, Principle 12.

95   MDAC, Reports on Guardianship, Indicator 8.

96   *Shtukaturov v. Russia*, App. No. 44009/05, 27th March 2008, not yet reported, para. 94.

97   Ibid., para. 84.

98   *Winterwerp v. Netherlands*, [1979] 2 EHRR 387. See also comments by Bartlett *et al*, *Mental Disability and the European Convention,* 261-262.

99   *Matter v. Slovakia*, App. No.31534/96, judgment 5 July 1999, [2001] 31 EHRR 32.

100   *Shtukaturov v. Russia*, App. No. 44009/05, 27th March 2008, not yet reported, para. 94.

101   *Matter v. Slovakia*, App. No.31534/96, judgment 5 July 1999, [2001] 31 EHRR 32.

for assessment of capacity, amounting to almost three months, was not consistent with the purpose of the detention, which was to carry out an evaluation of capacity, and did not balance the right to liberty with the purpose of the order.[102] Detention for the purpose of a court ordered psychiatric examination is a legitimate action, but detention prior and post examination fails to balance the state's interest in the examination and the individual's right to liberty, and is a violation of Article 5.[103] Forced examinations could also violate the right to a fair trial under Article 6 and under Article 8 on the right to respect for private and family life.[104] Provision for forced examinations exist in a number of European countries including, Russia, Serbia and the Czech Republic.[105]

6.4.   ASSESSMENT OF CAPACITY AND MENTAL HEALTH DETENTION

One issue that is slightly tangential to the main issues discussed in this paper, but is relevant to the debate, concerns the compulsory treatment of detained patients who have decision-making capacity but remain excluded from the benefit of law reform on legal capacity.[106] In the case of a legally capable person detained for mental health care, the relevant legislation frequently provides for overriding a refusal to consent to treatment. Mental capacity legislation reinforces this situation by providing a specific exclusion of its provisions for people who are subject to mental health detention.[107] The ECtHR has held that the imposition of treatment for a mental disorder against the wishes of a mentally competent person who was *de facto* detained, breached Article 8.

> Even a minor interference with the physical integrity of the individual must be regarded as an interference with the right to respect for private life under Article 8, if it is carried out against the individual's will.[108]

The question of unacceptable discrimination arises in relation to mental capacity statutes that exclude those subject to compulsory mental health care. Justification is made on the basis of risk of serious harm to the patient or to others. Overriding a patient's decision should not be done simply to ensure that such decisions have a wise outcome as judged by others. 'A patient's competent refusal should only

---

[102]   *Nowicka v. Poland,* App. No. 30218/96, judgment 3 December 2002, not yet reported.

[103]   Ibid., paras. 58-61.

[104]   *Bock v. Germany* (App. No. 11118/84), [1989] 9 EHRR 562, for violation of Article 6 and *Worwa v. Poland,* App, No. 26624/95, judgment 23rd November 2003, (2006) 43 EHRR 35, for Article 8. Hungary permits detention of 30 days for evaluation, MDAC, *Report on Guardianship in Hungary.*

[105]   MDAC, Reports on Russia, Serbia and Czech Republic.

[106]   P. Bartlett, 'Capacity, Treatment and Human Rights', *Journal of Mental Health Law* (2004), 2-65. See also Church *et al;* 'Mental capacity: concepts, assessment and the law', *Irish Psychiatrist* (2008), 9-17.

[107]   Mental Health Act 1983 and Mental Capacity Act 2005 in England and Wales.

[108]   *Storck v. Germany* (App. No. 61603/00), [2006] 43 EHRR 6, para. 143.

be overridden in very strictly defined circumstances'.[109] Guidelines are needed on what might be included in such circumstances.

The first study on the practicality of assessing the capacity of people admitted for treatment to psychiatric and learning disability services found that the majority of those detained under the English Mental Health Act 1983 had capacity to make treatment decisions for themselves.[110] They also found that a proportion of those accepting treatment voluntarily were incapable of consenting to it. In relation to the former group, they would have been able to refuse treatment if it was for a physical illness. In the latter group, mental capacity legislation would have provided a solution. While capacity assessment is recognized as difficult to implement in the context of mental disorder, 'a rigorous approach to the process of capacity assessment is especially important in these situations'.[111] Another study examined prevalence rates of mental capacity to make treatment decisions in people from different diagnostic and legal groups admitted to psychiatric hospital.[112] The existence of incapacity varied according to diagnosis and, while the study found that mental incapacity to make treatment decisions was common in people admitted to psychiatric hospital, it cannot be presumed. Respect for autonomy requires governments to explain why rules for the treatment of mental disorder are different, but not discriminatory.[113]

6.5. EVIDENCE

The right to challenge evidence and have evidence presented is a key safeguard. An up-to-date evaluation of capacity by an expert must be part of the evidence.[114]

---

[109]   G. Richardson, 'Involuntary treatment: Searching for principles', in Diesfeld and Freckelton (eds.), *Involuntary Detention and Therapeutic Jurisprudence*, (Aldershot, 2003). Also Expert Committee, *Review of the Mental Health Act 1983,* (London: Department of Health, 1999), and G. Richardson, 'The European convention and mental health law in England and Wales: Moving beyond process?', *International Journal of Law & Psychiatry* 28 (2005), 127-137. Contradictory provisions recognizing capacity while also providing for overruling competent refusal of treatment are included in one statute as well as a best interests principle. Mental Health Act 2001, Ireland, sections 57, 59 and 60. See also P. Bartlett, 'The Test of Compulsion in Mental Health law: Capacity, Therapeutic Benefit and Dangerousness as possible Criteria', 11 *Medical Law Review* Autumn (2003), 326-352.

[110]   J. Belhouse *et al*, 'Capacity-based mental health legislation and its impact on clinical practice: (2) treatment in hospital', *Journal of Mental Health Law* (July/August 2003), 35-36. See also Cairns *et al*, 'Reliability of mental capacity assessments in psychiatric in-patients', 187 *British Journal of Psychiatry* 4 (2005), 371-378, where the authors found a capacity test worked and was reliable.

[111]   M. Donnelly, 'Assessing Legal Capacity: Process and the Operation of the Functional Test', 2 *Judicial Studies Institute Journal* (2007), 153.

[112]   G. Owen *et al*, 'Mental capacity to make decisions on treatment in people admitted to psychiatric hospitals: cross sectional study', available at: <www.*bmj.bmjjournals. com/cgi/content/full/337/jun*>.

[113]   G. Richardson, *International Journal of Law & Psychiatry* 28 (2005), 135.

[114]   *H.F. v. Slovakia*, App. No. 54797/00, judgment 8 November 2005, not yet reported; and *Winterwerp v. Netherlands*, [1979] 2 EHRR 387, para. 60.

The presentation of evidence by an expert should be done in person where questions can be asked. Where legal representation is not actually provided, then the person's rights cannot be ensured.[115]

Reliance on out-of-date evidence, where there had been a significant passage of time between the original assessment and the court decision, arose in *H.F. v. Slovakia.*[116] The domestic court relied on a report based on an assessment carried out some 16 months earlier and on evidence from the applicant's husband and his witnesses, without hearing the applicant. The appeal court did not seek an up-to-date assessment. There was no representation by a guardian as required under domestic law. The ECtHR affirmed that the outcome of the proceedings was extremely important to the applicant, who should have had appropriate safeguards to protect her rights and interests. Citing with authority Recommendation No. R(99) 4, and the requirement to have up-to date evidence provided by 'at least' one qualified expert, the ECtHR said that the deprivation of legal capacity was based on insufficient evidence. The ECtHR held that there was an inadequate investigation, a lack of diligence and unfairness of proceedings, resulting in the applicant being deprived of legal capacity in violation of Article 6(1). The law in some European countries such as Hungary and Bulgaria is regarded as inadequate in relation to sufficiency of evidence.[117]

The principle of prioritizing the interests and welfare of the person requires that the negative consequences of guardianship must be weighed in evidence against the necessity and benefit of guardianship. Principle 5 of Recommendation No. R(99) 4 provides that restrictions should not be imposed unless the measure is necessary, having regard to the circumstances and needs of the adult. An example is where the right to work is impacted on by guardianship and many countries prevent those in guardianship from working, and this should be tested against the requirements of necessity, subsidiarity and proportionality requirements in Principle 6.[118]

6.6. RIGHT TO BE HEARD

The right to be heard in person is an element of the right to fair trial in Article 6(1). It is further supported in Recommendation No. R(99) 4 providing for 'the right to be heard in any proceedings which could affect the person's civil rights' which might mean more than just involvement in the court proceedings, but also involvement in any discussions beforehand.[119] In *X v. Croatia*, the denial of the applicant's right to be heard in the decision-making process concerning the adoption of her daughter, due to being in guardianship, was held by the ECtHR to be crucial for the future of her relationship with her daughter. The ECtHR said, 'It was clearly a decision in which the applicant should have been closely involved if

---

[115] MDAC, *Report on Guardianship in Russia*, 53 files were examined and only one had legal representation, paid for himself and a guardianship order was not made in that case, 69.

[116] *H.F. v. Slovakia*, Application No. 54797/00, 8th November 2005, not yet reported,

[117] MDAC, *Report on Guardianship in Hungary*, 35, para. 2.6.3, Bulgaria, 39, para 2.6.3.

[118] MDAC, *Report on Guardianship in Hungary*, 36, para. 2.6.3.

[119] Council of Europe, Recommendation No. R (99) 4, Principle 13.

she was to be afforded the requisite consideration of her views and protection of her interests'.[120] The exclusion of the applicant from the hearing regarding deprivation of his legal capacity arose in *Shtukaturov v. Russia*.[121] The ECtHR stated,

> ...his participation was necessary not only to enable him to present his own case, but also to allow the judge to form his personal opinion about the applicant's mental capacity ... As he was an autonomous person it was indispensable for the judge to have at least a brief visual contact with the applicant, and preferably to question him.[122]

The fact that the applicant was neither seen nor heard by the domestic court was held by the ECtHR to have been unreasonable and in breach of Article 6(1). The case concerned serious procedural deficits in the court proceedings, resulting in the deprivation of legal capacity and ultimately deprivation of his liberty. The ECtHR said that the measures the state takes should not affect the very essence of the applicant's right to a fair trial as guaranteed by Article 6(1), where all factors are taken into account, including his exclusion from the hearing.[123]

6.7. LEGAL REPRESENTATION

Where the capacity of a person is in question, there would seem to be a particularly strong need to have legal representation, in order to challenge evidence and ensure fair proceedings and assert any appeal or review of rights. The court hearing normally involves experts as well as potentially serious outcomes for the person, as his or her mental state will be questioned in relation to capacity, and means that legal representation is essential. Otherwise, there is a danger that these Article 6(1) rights are 'theoretical and illusory' rather than practical and effective, particularly for people who may be very vulnerable.[124] Some countries have a basic right to legal representation, but there is no right to be provided with a representative or for the costs of legal representation to be met. The provision of legal representation for hearings, appeals and review of capacity should be mandatory.

6.8. CHOICE OF GUARDIAN

The choice of a guardian to represent or assist a person with impaired capacity should be governed primarily by the guardian's suitability to safeguard and promote the person's interests and welfare.[125] States are encouraged to have an adequate supply of suitably qualified guardians.[126] The past and present wishes of the person should be taken into account as far as possible, and particularly their wishes regarding the choice of guardian, representative or assistant in the

---

[120] *X. v. Croatia*, App. No. 11223/04, 17th July 2008, not yet reported, para. 53.
[121] *Shtukaturov v. Russia,* App. No. 44009/05, 27th March 2008, not yet reported.
[122] Ibid., para. 72 and 73.
[123] Ibid., para. 68.
[124] *Airey v. Ireland*, [1979] 2 EHRR 305, para. 24.
[125] Council of Europe, Recommendation No. R (99) 4, Principle 8(2).
[126] Ibid., Principle 17(1).

decision-making.[127] Some states refer to skill, experience and the duties involved as elements in choosing a guardian.[128] Any conflicts of interests concerning the guardian should be clarified and, where they exist, that person should not be a guardian.[129] Hungary precludes a person with specific conflicts of interest from guardianship. In America, the Standards of Practice from the National Guardianship Association refer to conflicts of interest and states that 'a guardian who is not a family guardian shall not directly provide housing, medical, legal or other direct services to a ward'.[130]

6.9.   LENGTH OF PROCEEDINGS

In assessing the reasonableness of the length of proceedings, a number of factors are taken into account. The particular circumstances of the case, the complexity of the issues, the conduct of the applicant and of the authorities dealing with the case will be taken into account.[131] In cases relating to capacity, the ECtHR will examine what is at stake for the applicant and has stated that 'special diligence is required in view of the possible consequences which the excessive length of proceedings may have'.[132]

The length of proceedings was an issue which arose in *Bock v. Germany*, involving divorce proceedings which continued for nine years due to the wife of the applicant insisting that the applicant husband lacked capacity to be involved in such proceedings.[133] The applicant had five reports attesting to his soundness of mind during a six-year period, along with two failed attempts by his wife to make him subject to guardianship. Finding a violation of Article 6(1), the ECtHR stated that, in principle, national courts have to proceed on the basis that an applicant has functional capacity and, should any reasonable doubt arise, they must clarify as soon as possible the extent to which the person is competent to conduct legal proceedings. The personal situation of the applicant had, for an extensive period, 'suffered by reason of the doubts cast on the state of his mental health which subsequently proved unfounded. This represented a serious encroachment on human dignity'.[134] This case raises other relevant factors such as the motivation and possible conflicts of interest of those who might allege incapacity or apply for guardianship.

The length of proceedings were impacted on by the applicant's unwillingness to submit to a capacity evaluation in *Matter v. Slovakia*, involving a seven-year delay period without justification, leading to the application to the ECtHR. Recognizing the importance of the case and 'what was at stake for the applicant', the ECtHR said that 'the domestic courts failed to act with the special diligence

---

127   Ibid., Principle 9(1)(2).
128   Guardianship Services Act, (Finland), 442/99, Chapter 2, Section 5.
129   *Shtukatorov v. Russia,* App. No. 44009/05, 27th March 2008, not yet reported, para.69.
130   MDAC, *Report on Guardianship in Hungary*, para 2.6.3, 40.
131   *Matter v. Slovakia*, App. No. 31534/96, 5 July 1999, para. 54, (2001) 31 EHRR 32.
132   Ibid.
133   *Bock v. Germany*, [1987] 9 EHRR 562.
134   Ibid., para. 48.

required by Article 6(1) of the Convention in cases of this nature'.[135] While the ECtHR recognized that the applicant had been entirely deprived of legal capacity for seven years, and even said '[t]here is no doubt that this is a serious interference with his rights under Article 8 § 1', it did not hold that there was a breach of Article 8(1).[136]

7. LEGAL RIGHTS AFTER A GUARDIANSHIP ORDER

7.1. PRESERVATION OF LEGAL CAPACITY

The principle of the maximum preservation of capacity and proportionality is to be recognized; no right should be automatically denied. The right to work and to marry are important privacy and family rights under Article 8, and their removal should be necessary and proportional to the aim of protecting the person. Article 8 of the ECHR requires proportionality relating to the aim of intervention in any person's life. Recommendation No. R(99) 4 refers to proportionality in Principle 6, and specifies that the limitation on legal capacity must be proportional to the degree of the adult's incapacity and tailored to the circumstances and needs. The Action Plan Recommendation No. R(2006) 5 refers to the right to own and inherit property, providing legal protection to manage assets on an equal basis with others.[137]

The laws in many countries automatically deprive persons who are under total guardianship of the right to vote, to work, to access court, to associate, to manage property and finance or enter into contracts including marriage.[138] Russia, for example, automatically prohibits all such rights under plenary guardianship. Article 12 of the ECHR protects the right to marry and found a family, but this right is either automatically prohibited by virtue of guardianship or in specific statutes, without there being any corresponding capacity assessment.[139] Even when some countries do not specifically remove certain rights, the lack of procedural support results in an inability to assert them.

The automatic prohibition on the right to associate following a guardianship order could engage Article 11 of ECHR, which protects the right to associate, and requires any restrictions on the right to be clearly stated in law and to be necessary. Hungarian law deprives people of the opportunity to exercise rights of association in certain areas of life as a result of guardianship, for example, as members of organizations or professional associations.[140] Membership of peer support groups may be an important source of developing empowerment skills, and particularly

---

[135] *Matter v. Slovakia*, App. No. 31534/96, 5 July 1999, para. 61, (2001) 31 EHRR 32.
[136] Ibid., para. 68.
[137] Council of Europe, Action Plan on Disability, Recommendation No. R (2006) 5, para. 3.12.3.
[138] MDAC, Reports on Bulgaria, Hungary, Russia, Serbia, Czech Republic, Georgia.
[139] In Ireland, the Lunacy Regulation (Ireland) Act 1871 results in deprivation of capacity and almost total legal incapacity, and based on the Marriage of Lunatics Act 1811 automatically prohibits marriage for wards of court without a separate capacity assessment.
[140] MDAC, *Report on Guardianship in Hungary*, para. 2.6.4, 47.

membership of advocacy associations. Article 8 protects the right to identity and personal development, and the right to establish and develop relationships with other human beings and the outside world, and is supported in the CRPD. The preservation of mental stability is, in that context, an indispensable precondition to effective enjoyment and the right to respect for private life.[141]

7.2. ROLE OF THE GUARDIAN

Countries with systems of plenary and partial guardianship grant extensive powers to guardians to make all decisions for the person. This is more likely to be true where there are limited appeal rights for the person or there is no right to challenge the actions of the guardian or to have guardianship reviewed.[142] Limitations on guardians must be clearly stated where the guardians have potentially wide powers, and the wishes of person must be taken into account where he or she is able to express them.[143] These interventions need to focus on the areas where the person needs assistance, and not permit the guardian to stray into areas of acting or decision-making for which the person has functional capacity. Limitations on substitute decision-makers in recently reformed legislation commonly exclude them from making particular significant personal decisions like consenting to marriage, adoption, or recognizing a child.[144]

Residents of institutions typically do not have the same freedom to associate, as those living independently in the community in appropriate environments. Reference to relations with other individuals underpins the link between private and family life. Where such residents are prevented from sharing family life, without justification, Article 8 may well be engaged. Positive obligations may arise to ensure that appropriate measures are taken to the greatest extent possible to ensure that disabled people have access to essential economic and social activities, and to an appropriate range of recreational and cultural activities.[145] Such a positive obligation to protect against arbitrary interference with private life includes an obligation to supervise and control private institutions.[146] The role of the guardian with regard to ensuring the least restrictive living environment is available, as an aspect of the right to exercise self-determination, should be considered.

The approach to retention of control in all areas for which the person has functional capacity, and the limitation on intervention to areas where the person is unable to make a decision, is ensured in some capacity laws, where substitute decision-making should be an intervention of last resort.[147] This means that the law is not interested in areas where the person has functional capacity and is the direct opposite approach to one that removes legal capacity for a particular decision, resulting in the automatic restriction in relation to many or all other legal rights in

---

[141] *Bensaid v. United Kingdom* (App. No.44599/98), [2001] 33 EHRR 205, para. 46.

[142] MDAC, *Report on Guardianship in Russia,* 2007.

[143] Council of Europe, Recommendation No R (99) 4, Principle 18.

[144] Council of Europe, Recommendation R (99) 4, Principle 19, Explanatory Memorandum to the Recommendation, para. 67; Mental Capacity Act 2005, England and Wales, and the proposed Mental Capacity Bill 2007, Ireland.

[145] *Botta v. Italy* (App. No. 21439/93), [1998] 26 EHRR 241.

[146] *Storck v. Germany,* [2006] 43 EHRR 6, para.103-6.

[147] Such laws are found in Sweden, Denmark, Germany, England and Wales, Ireland.

the absence of any less restrictive mechanisms. Alternatively, some countries that make partial guardianship orders actually outline the areas of legal independence for the person where they have functional capacity to make those decisions.[148]

In some instances, there is little or no communication between the guardian and the person, and the guardian may have responsibility for several people.[149] It is difficult to ensure the person remains central to decision-making if there is no contact with the guardian, and no sharing of information concerning decisions in order to permit an opinion to be given.[150] Otherwise how can a guardian, who is acting for the person, know and understand the circumstances of the person, their state of health, his or her wishes in relation to a decision which may have a major impact on his or her life, and ensure they are living in the least restrictive environment?

Robust and effective mechanisms need to be in place to prevent abuse and to ensure that any property or assets are used for the benefit of the person. Oversight of guardians is required to ensure accountability, liability and safeguards of the person subject to guardianship.[151] This could include a complaints mechanism to trigger review of the actions of a guardian. The World Health Organization supports procedures for review of a guardian's decisions as a key principle of mental health law and this should embrace availability, timeliness, accessibility and the opportunity to be heard in person.[152]

7.3. RIGHT OF APPEAL AND REVIEW OF DEPRIVATION OF LEGAL CAPACITY

A right of appeal is an important procedural right, and this is facilitated in some countries, but is limited to some ten or fifteen days within which to appeal in others.[153] These periods are short, and for vulnerable people the period would hardly be considered adequate, as required under Recommendation No. R(99)4, Principle 14(3). In addition to this restrictive period, there may well be a lack of effective legal representation, and together these elements could result in an appeal being unavailable as a right. The right of appeal should also be open to others who may activate an appeal on behalf of the person, where the person does not have capacity to understand or activate it, particularly in the absence of a legal representative.

Recommendation No. R(99) 4, Principle 14 provides that 'measures of protection should, wherever possible and appropriate, be of limited duration. Consideration should be given to the institution of periodical review'. These measures of protection should be reviewed following a change of circumstances, but particularly a change in the person's condition, or if the grounds for the protection

---

[148] For example, French Civil Code, Book 1, Title X, Chapter 11, Article 501.

[149] MDAC, *Report on Guardianship in Hungary,* 73, refers to one institution with 700 occupants, half of whom are under supervision of two guardians. Another guardian had dealt with 174 cases in nine years and only one person had guardianship terminated.

[150] Council of Europe, Recommendation No. R (99) 4, Principle 9.

[151] Ibid., Principle 16.

[152] World Health Organization, *Resource Book on Mental Health.*

[153] Russia and the Czech Republic have restrictive appeal limits.

no longer exist, it should be terminated.[154] Russian guardianship is not subject to review and people can be sent to social care institutions for the rest of their lives.[155] Guardianship in Hungary is reviewed infrequently; five years from the initial decision, and the review does not apply if the judge considers the situation to be permanent.[156] In *Shtukatorov v. Russia*, there was no right of appeal for the applicant, and only the guardian could activate an appeal under the Russian Civil Code.[157] The ECtHR stated, '[t]he applicant was trapped in his incapacitation as it applied indefinitely and had to be challenged through his guardian who had requested the guardianship and his participation was "reduced to Zero".'[158] The impact in his case was very serious. The applicant in *Shtukaturov* contacted his lawyer, but was subsequently detained in a psychiatric hospital and prevented from all contact with the outside world. Following an application to the ECtHR, the Government was ordered to permit the lawyer to have access to him and, as this was ignored, he remained in detention for seven months.[159] Although classed as a voluntary patient, requests to leave were refused. Attempts through the courts to appeal his guardianship status and his lack of access to a lawyer failed, as he had no legal standing. The ECtHR believed Shtukaturov was effectively prevented from having any independent legal remedy of a judicial character to enable him to challenge his detention.

8. LAW REFORM

Many countries have introduced, or are introducing, legislation on the assessment of capacity, less restrictive measures and the appointment of assistant or substitute decision-makers to make personal welfare decisions on behalf of people with impaired decision-making capacity. Some countries have less restrictive measures such as enduring powers of attorney and advance directives, as well as support systems based on the family and community, and the substitute decision-maker is limited to what is essential, and will not be appointed against the person's free will. In Germany, the possibility of support from family, friends and neighbours is paramount, and the person is not automatically deprived of legal capacity to act unless the guardianship court explicitly orders a reservation of consent in a particular area.[160] Likewise, in Sweden, the trend towards reform of the law has

---

[154] World Health Organization, *Resource Book on Mental Health*, 41 states that legislation should contain provision for automatic review, at specified periodic intervals, of the finding of a lack of competence.

[155] MDAC, *Report on Guardianship in Russia*, 6.

[156] MDAC, *Report on Guardianship in Hungary*, 62, Indicator 28.

[157] *Shtukatorov v. Russia*, App. No. 44009/05, 27th March 2008, not yet reported, para.99.

[158] Ibid., para. 91.

[159] *Shtukatorov v. Russia*, App. No. 44009/05, 27th March 2008, not yet reported, paras. 22-4. The applicant's complaints to the Court were under different headings: incapacitation, placement in psychiatric hospital, inability to obtain a review of his status, inability to meet his lawyer, interference with correspondence, and involuntary medical treatment.

[160] German Civil Code (BGB) Section 1901(2), entered into force 1992, and Sections 1896-1908 k.

been embraced by developing policies that reinforce rather than disregard the person's capacity for self-determination.[161] Guardianship has been replaced with two systems that focus on support: the mentor and trustee systems.[162] The mentor is the less restrictive system and has procedures in place to ensure support for the person. The mentor must have the consent of the person to act and, while the mentor can be appointed by the court, the court ensures that a tailor-made approach applies to the individual's needs. Remedies are available to challenge the mentor if he or she usurps the role or carries out an action without authority. The trustee system is used as a last resort, when all less restrictive measures have been exhausted and it allows for substitute decision-making. It is applied rarely and the person retains some civil rights. In Denmark, law reform in 1995 rejected the previous law resulting in the automatic loss of legal capacity under guardianship.[163] Under the Spanish Civil Code the fact of having a disability will not automatically result in being regarded as lacking legal capacity; the focus is on the effects of the disability rather than the disability itself.[164] In common with other countries described, there are two systems in Spain, supported guardianship and a model of guardianship providing for people declared to be fully incapacitated. Supported guardianship applies after a court hearing where the person has been declared incapable in relation to some acts or decisions, but retains capacity for other areas. Legal representation will be provided in case of conflict where the person's capacity is being questioned.

The Mental Incapacity (Scotland) Act 2000, the Mental Capacity Act 2005[165] for England and Wales and the proposed Irish law, the Mental Capacity and Guardianship Bill 2007, are each underpinned by a framework of guiding principles for action taken under the Acts. These principles support the enabling of autonomy and set the tone for the interpretation of the Acts, and are essential to any actions under the Acts. These Acts also provide a legal basis for informal decision-making for carers to act for an incapacitated person on a day to day basis, provided the decision-maker operates within the guiding principles.

These principles include the presumption of capacity, the necessity for intervention taking account of the person's possible improvement of capacity, and that the intervention should be the least restrictive possible having regard to the person's freedom. The person's past and present wishes, as well as the views of relatives, carers and others named by the incapacitated person, and any other persons interested in the welfare of the person, must be taken into account. The specified human rights principles include the right to dignity, bodily integrity, privacy and autonomy.[166]

These capacity statutes contain a range of powers from assisted decision-

---

[161]   S. Herr Stanley, 'Self Determination, Autonomy and Alternatives for Guardianship', in S. Herr et al (eds.), *The Human Rights of Persons with Intellectual Disabilities*, (Oxford University Press, 2003), 432.

[162]   Föraldräbalk (Children and Parents Code) Swedish Code of Statutes SFS 1949:231, Chapter 11, Sections 4 and 7.

[163]   Vaergemålsloven (Danish Act on Guardianship), 14th June 1995.

[164]   Spanish Civil Code. 1889, Article 200.

[165]   The title of this Act changed before enactment from the Mental Incapacity Act to Mental Capacity Act to reflect a positive approach to capacity.

[166]   Proposed Mental Capacity Bill, 2007, s4, (Ireland).

making, enduring powers of attorney and advance directives, informal day to day decisions by carers to formal court powers and full guardianship. An incapacitated person cannot be deprived of his or her liberty unless it is in accordance with Article 5 of the ECHR. There is some controversy over this matter as people in guardianship may be subject to significant levels of control, so that a deprivation of liberty may be inevitable.[167]

9. CONCLUSION

The CRPD provides a new focus, with recognition of universal legal capacity and the retention of legal capacity after intervention has taken place. While the policy shift away from paternalism to enabling decision-making, and providing safeguards around the assessment of capacity based on the functional approach is well underway in some jurisdictions, it has not begun in others.[168] There must be flexibility in the new systems providing real alternatives, to respond to the needs of those whose capacity is in question, whatever the circumstances.[169] The challenge is to 'find a balance which respects the core right of all to be recognized as persons before the law and to retain autonomy to make decisions for themselves, while not abandoning the state's historic obligation to protect vulnerable adults from abuse and exploitation'.[170] The fact that large numbers of people are in guardianship and institutional care needs to be addressed. In some countries the proportion of the population in guardianship whose legal rights are removed is as low as one in 2000, but as high as one in 130 in others, so there is great disparity throughout Europe.[171] Regard must be had to the flawed procedures leading to guardianship, beginning with the assessment and reliance by judges on one unchallenged opinion from a psychiatrist, in what seems to be little more than a routine approach.[172] The consequences for the individual are immense, with limited or no opportunity to challenge the guardianship order due to restrictive time scales, lack of effective legal representation and lack of any review mechanisms. The right to legal representation must be addressed as a key element to ensuring the person's rights are upheld.

Guardianship should be a measure of last resort and in its present form in some countries is in need of reform.[173] Guardianship should restrict the rights and freedoms of an adult, along with the legal capacity to act, only to the extent neces-

---

[167]   R. Jones, 'Deprivations of Liberty: Mental Health Act or Mental Capacity Act?', *Journal of Mental Health Law* November (2007), 171.

[168]   MDAC, *Report on Guardianship in Russia*, also P. Bartlett *et al*, *Mental Disability and the European Convention*, 262.

[169]   Recommendation No. R (99) 4, Principle 3.

[170]   C. Sundram, 'The International Convention on the Rights of Persons with Disabilities', Paper delivered at the National Disability Authority Seminar on 'Capacity and the Convention', Dublin, Ireland, 15th June 2006, available at: <www.nda.ie>.

[171]   P. Bartlett *et al*, *Mental Disability and the European Convention*, 262.

[172]   MDAC, *Reports on Guardianship in Russia and Hungary*.

[173]   MDAC reports recommend the provision of less restrictive alternatives, and abolishing plenary guardianship, see Russia, Hungary, Czech Republic, Bulgaria, and Georgia.

sary to provide adequate protection.[174] Some countries need to introduce less restrictive and less intrusive measures as real alternatives for persons with impaired capacity. Even when such measures are available, the need to review decisions in individual cases is essential in recognition of the changing nature of functional capacity over time and to tailor the measure to the needs of the individual. The right of appeal within realistic time scales, as well as the right to review both the role of the guardian or representative, and the continuing need for the restriction of legal capacity, must all be considered with regard to law reform. When less restrictive measures are available, substitute decision-making is used only when these measures are exhausted.

Successful law reform will require training in both the assessment of capacity and in interacting with people whose capacity is being assessed.[175] Training frequently focuses on doctors, and particularly psychiatrists, but the need for training and understanding is much wider and includes, not only psychiatrists and other assessors, but also legislators, policy makers, judges, guardians and others in decision-making positions, so that they understand and appreciate what they are doing and the impact this may have on the life of the person being assessed for legal capacity. Training is not a one-off exercise but will need to be refreshed from time to time, as a form of continuing professional development.

The more difficult and long-term challenge is the inculcation of solid notions of personhood into the psyche of policy makers and implementation bodies. 'There is no guarantee that the new values … will be internalised and then operationalized'.[176] Legislators must be creative in order to achieve a solution that will embrace a wide sector needing assisted and substitute decision-making, while taking full account of the right to autonomy. This is a significant challenge and one that will require considerable ingenuity. Balancing rights and ensuring appropriate safeguards requires careful consideration of all elements. With the recognition of universal legal capacity comes a new energy. Success, though, comes from the positive impact change brings to the real lives of people affected by judgements of incapacity.

---

[174]   The Explanatory Memorandum to Recommendation to No. R (99) 4, para. 40.
[175]   MDAC, *Report on Guardianship in Hungary*, 70.
[176]   G. Quinn, in O.Arnardottir *et al* (eds),*United Nations Convention on the Rights of Persons with Disabilities,* 4.

A SHORT GUIDE TO THE UNITED NATIONS CONVENTION ON THE RIGHTS OF PERSONS WITH DISABILITIES

Gerard Quinn[1]

1. VALUES: DISABILITY AS A SUBJECT OF HUMAN RIGHTS

The rights-based perspective on disability is relatively new.[2] This is despite the fact the persons with disabilities were recently described by the United Nations as 'the world's largest minority'.[3] There are approximately 650 million persons with disabilities in the world – the vast majority of whom (500 million) live in developing countries. Their status – to say the least – is precarious. For example, drawing on a variety of sources, the UN estimates that 90 per cent of children with disabilities in developing countries do not attend school, the global literacy rate for adults with disabilities is as low as three per cent (and one percent for women with disabilities), persons with disabilities are more likely to be victims of violence or rape and are much less likely to obtain police intervention, legal protection or preventive care.[4]

Notwithstanding the obvious human rights issues that affect persons with disabilities, the default setting for considering disability has not generally been human rights. It has, instead, been a mixture of charity, paternalism and social policy. Indeed, the general social policy response was to maintain people rather than to forge pathways into to the mainstream. In a way, it was a perversion of the true mission of social policy.

Migrating the disability issue to the core of the human rights agenda has been slow. Perhaps this has something to do with the way the human difference of disability was perceived. In a way, the 'natural' distribution of human capacities was seen as separating persons with disabilities. It was as if the disability was seen as eroding rather than simply complicating human existence. To paraphrase the Aristotelian concept of equality, it was as if 'separate but equal' was considered

---

[1] Professor of Law and Director of the Centre for Disability Law and Policy at the National University of Ireland (Galway).

[2] See Michael A. Stein, 'Disability Human Rights', 95 *California Law Review* (2007), 75. Based with permission on an earlier paper (Disability and Human Rights: a New Field in the United Nations) published by the author in Krause, C., and Scheinen, M., (Eds), *International Protection of Human Rights : a Textbook*, (Abo Akademi University Institute for Human Rights, Turku/Abo, 2009).

[3] Some Facts about Persons with Disabilities, available at: <http://www.un.org/disabilities/convention/pdfs/factsheet.pdf> (accessed 15 October 2008).

[4] Ibid.

not merely defendable but also somehow 'natural' when it came to disability.

All of this accumulated baggage from the past is now firmly on the defensive as the move to the human rights framework of reference takes root. This movement to a new framework of reference is significant. It enables issues (such as segregated education) to be *seen* as issues, when hitherto they were unquestioned and simply accepted as 'natural'. It also enables considered judgments to be made about existing social arrangements. And it posits a whole new agenda – one of ensuring equal respect for human rights regardless of the difference of disability.

That this revolution has taken so long to happen in the disability field is curious, since one of the main attractions of human rights is its supposedly universal quality. In its essence, therefore, the human rights revolution in the context of disability has to do with making the human being behind the disability visible and extending the benefits of 'the rule of law' to all and not just to some, or indeed to most. Most importantly, it has to do with treating persons with disabilities as 'subjects' with full legal personhood as distinct from 'objects' to be managed and cared for.

The migration of the human rights framework of reference has been taking place throughout the world in the last two decades or so. It was inevitable that it would be reflected at the global level at some point in time. The recently adopted United Nations Convention on the Rights of Persons with Disabilities (CRPD, 2007) is the single most exciting development to take place in the disability field for many decades. It reflects this ongoing and worldwide process of law reform in the field of disability. More importantly, it should clarify its underlying values and help to accelerate reform trends.[5]

It might even be said that although the notion of disability rights started in the United States, it is now truly a global challenge.[6] For example, the African Union sponsors the African Decade of Persons with Disabilities (1999–2009) to drive the process of reform throughout Africa.[7] The United Nations Economic Commission for Asia and the Pacific (UNESCAP) has adopted an Asian and Pa-

---

[5] The Convention - as well as most of the drafting history can be found at: <http://www.un.org/disabilities/> (accessed 15 October 2008). There is already a growing body of literature on the Convention: see, e.g., Don MacKay, 'The United Nations Convention on the Rights of Persons with Disabilities', 34 *Syracuse Journal Of International Law and Commerce* 2 (2007), 323-331 and *From Exclusion to Equality - Handbook for Parliamentarians on the United Nations Convention on the Rights for persons with Disabilities and its optional Protocol*, (International Parliamentary Union with the United Nations Office of the High Commissioner for Human Rights, 2007). See also, 'The Convention on the Rights of Persons with Disabilities', 56 *International Rehabilitation Review* 1 (2008).

[6] Perhaps the most famous (and copied) piece of legislation on disability is the Americans with Disabilities Act (ADA) of 1990. See generally, P. Blanck *et al*, *Disability Civil Rights Law and Policy*, (Thompson/West, 2005). The statute has been much diminished through narrow rulings from the US Supreme Court: see generally, L. Hamilton Krieger (ed.), *Backlash against the ADA - reinterpreting disability rights*, (U Michigan Press, 2003).

[7] The secretariat of the African Decade is available at: <www.secretariat.disabilityafrica.org> (accessed 16 October 2008).

cific Decade of Disabled Persons (2003–2012) with similar aims.[8] The Organization of American States (OAS) declared a Decade of the Americas for the Rights
and Dignity of Persons with Disabilities (2006–2016), with the theme 'Equality,
Dignity, and Participation',[9] and the OAS even adopted a convention as early as
1999 against disability discrimination.[10] At European regional level both the European Union (EU) has a Disability Action Plan (2003–2010)[11] and the Council
of Europe has its own Disability Action Plan (2006–2015).[12] The comparative law
literature on disability discrimination is voluminous. Our focus, however, is on
the United Nations system for the purposes of this chapter.

It is widely expected that the disability convention will become one of the
most widely ratified human rights treaties in the UN system, partly because it carries no ideological baggage from the Cold War. It has already received sufficient
ratifications to enable it to come and came into force on 3 May 2008. Fittingly, it
is the first human rights treaty of the 21st century which cleverly combines civil
and political rights as well as economic, social and cultural rights under an overarching theory of non-discrimination. It is accompanied by an Optional Protocol
which, if ratified, will enable the relevant treaty monitoring body to receive individual and group petitions.[13]

The application of human rights in the context of disability is not merely

---

[8]   UNESCAP has a very active disability programme within its Population and Social
        Integration Section. Website available at: <www.unescap.org/esid/psis/disability>
        (accessed 16 October 2008).

[9]   Information on the OAS disability activities is available at: <www.oas.org/DIL/per-
        sons_with_disabilities.htm> (accessed 16 October 2008).

[10]   The Inter-American Convention on the Elimination of All Forms of Discrimination
        against Persons with Disabilities, 1999, available at: <http://www.oas.org/DIL/inter-
        american_convention_persons_with_disabilities.htm>. At the time of writing (May
        2008), the Convention has 25 ratifications and is currently in force. The first meet-
        ing of its monitoring committee took place in 2007. Neither Canada nor the United
        States have ratified this convention.

[11]   The Disability Action Plan is set out in COM/2003/650. The history of EU disability
        law and policy is set out in G. Quinn, 'The Human Rights of People with Disabilities
        under EU Law', in P. Alston *et al, The EU and Human Rights*, (Oxford University
        Press, 1999), 281. For a detailed review of the evolving European anti-discrimina-
        tion law (including on the ground of disability) see D. Schiek *et al, Cases, Materials
        and Text on National, Supranational and International Non-Discrimination Law*,
        (Hart, 2007).

[12]   The Action Plan is contained in Recommendation Rec (2006) 5 of 5 April 2006
        of the Committee of Ministers of the Council of Europe to member states 'on the
        Council of Europe Action Plan to promote the rights and full participation of people
        with disabilities in society: improving the quality of life of people with disabilities
        in Europe 2006-2015'. For a good overview of the Council of Europe's activities
        in the broad disability field see T. Afflerbach *et al*, 'Council of Europe Actions to
        Promote Human Rights and Full Participation of People with Disabilities: Improving
        the Quality of Life of People with Disabilities in Europe', 34 *Syracuse Journal of
        International Law and Commerce* 2 (2007), 463.

[13]   The text of the Optional Protocol is available at: <http://www.un.org/disabilities/
        documents/convention/convoptprot-e.pdf\> (accessed 16 October 2008).

new – it is profoundly instructive for several reasons. First of all, it forces us to think through the concept of human difference on the ground of disability and to reflect on when or whether the difference requires separate, special treatment. For example, even after one takes due account of how the difference of disability is commonly exaggerated, are there nevertheless some sound arguments for some special, separate or even (in extreme cases) segregated treatment? Does the philosophy of 'separate but equal' have some residual value in the context of disability? As will be seen, the text of the CRPD is scattered with reference to ensuring rights for persons with disabilities 'on an equal basis with others'. Of course, this merely restates the question and does not resolve it. As will be seen, this dilemma was clearly reflected in the drafting of several key provisions in the convention, including the right to education.

Secondly, the difference of disability forces us to expand our concept of non-discrimination to require the would-be discriminator to take positive account of the disability and to reasonably accommodate' it. That is to say, a rule of law that requires a third party (for example, an employer) to ignore a difference (based, for example, on race) will be of little use where neutral treatment will not overcome obstacles that are no fault of the individual. For example, a rule that requires restaurant owners to allow everybody to enter without restriction will not be much good to a wheelchair user who is confronted with steps. This notion of 'reasonable accommodation' is a signature feature of the non-discrimination tool in most comparative disability discrimination law.[14] As will be seen, it is also a key feature of the CRPD.

Thirdly, the case of disability tends to provide tangible proof of the much vaunted – but little understood – thesis concerning the interdependence and indivisibility of both sets of human rights (civil and political as well as economic, social and cultural). In an almost unique way, disability brings out the truth in the nexus between both sets of rights. This is so because breaking down barriers in the way of persons with disabilities through, for example, non-discrimination law, is not enough. Some positive acts of social solidarity are also often required to underpin freedom. This is in fact true for all persons, and only more obviously true in the case of persons with disabilities. So the disability field vividly demonstrates how economic, social and cultural rights underpins, and do not undermine, freedom.

One caveat needs to be made at the very outset. There is a limit to what the non-discrimination tool can achieve in the disability context. Even when expanded to embrace the added obligation of 'reasonable accommodation' and even when explicit permission (and nothing more) is made for 'positive action measures', it still cannot do the full job of economic, social and cultural rights. Consequently, it is not a substitute for the substance of these rights – merely a way of ensuring parity of treatment with respect to those rights.

Fourthly, the application of economic, social and cultural rights in the context of disability brings out something often forgotten about the nature of these rights. These rights are not merely about human welfare viewed in a static sense. Primed positively, they help to forge pathways into inclusive societies and economies. They help set the terms of access, entry and participation in the mainstream.

---

[14] See, e.g., Christine Jolls, 'Accommodation Mandates', 53 *Stanford Law Review* (2000-2001), 223.

In other words, they help secure a system of 'public freedom'. In the context of this chapter, they enable people with disabilities to live a genuinely independent life and to participate in their community. As will be seen, this is how in fact the relevant economic, social and cultural rights were sculpted in the CRPD and tailored to tackle the various barriers faced by persons with disabilities in achieving a life of independence as well as inclusion. This represents economic, social and cultural rights at their best.

2. HISTORY: THE EVOLUTION OF THE RIGHTS-BASED FRAMEWORK OF REFERENCE ON DISABILITY IN THE UNITED NATIONS

Sad to relate, but the United Nations human rights machinery paid little attention to the issue of disability until very recently. This did not mean that the UN system as a whole paid no attention. To their credit, the Specialized Agencies were in fact very active on the disability issue. Bodies such as the ILO, UNICEF, UNESCO and the WHO have had long involvement in the field and indeed participated actively in the drafting of the CRPD.

The disability issue figured in the general UN system through the UN Commission for Social Development, as distinct from the Commission on Human Rights That in itself, demonstrated that the issue was framed more as a social policy issue than a human rights issue. Two resolutions of the General Assembly in the 1970s are particularly revealing in that they provided an early indication of a shift from a 'caring' agenda to a 'rights' agenda in the context of disability.[15] In 1971 the General Assembly passed a resolution entitled *Declaration on the Rights of Mentally Retarded Persons*.[16] Significantly, this resolution starts by pointing out that that persons with disabilities enjoy a parity of human rights protection with all other persons. The interesting thing about this is that it needed saying in the first place. Moreover, the General Assembly passed another milestone Resolution in 1975 entitled *Declaration on the Rights of Disabled Persons*.[17] Among other things, the Declaration specified a number of economic, social and cultural rights of importance to the development of the capacities of persons with disabilities as well as their social integration. It declared a right to have one's special needs taken into account at all stages of economic and social planning, as well as a right to protection against exploitation and treatment of an abusive nature. An innovation was its insistence that organizations of persons with disabilities 'may be consulted in all matters regarding the rights of disabled persons'. Thus the slogan '*nothing about us without us*' became an early feature in UN policy. This was to pay handsome dividends later in the drafting of the CRPD.

The year 1981 was declared by the UN as the International Year of Disabled Persons. To follow through, the General Assembly created a World Programme of Action for Persons with Disabilities (WPA) in 1982,[18] and in order to facili-

---

[15]   See generally, T. Degener and Y. Koster-Dreese (ed.), *Human Rights and Disabled Persons*, (Nijhoff, 1995).

[16]   UN General Assembly Resolution 2865 (XXVI), 20 December, 1971.

[17]   UN General Assembly Resolution 3447 (XXX), 9 December, 1975.

[18]   UN General Assembly Resolution 37/52, 3 December, 1982.

tate implementation, the UN created the UN Decade of Disabled Persons (1983–1992). The WPA is actually still in force (that is, it co-exists with the CRPD) and is regularly reported on by the UN Secretariat. Among the traditional elements of UN disability policy (such as rehabilitation and prevention), the WPA was clearly inspired by the 'equalization of opportunities' model. It defined 'equalization of opportunities' as:

> the process through which the general system of society, such as the physical and cultural environment, housing and transportation, social and health services, educational and work opportunities, cultural and social life, including sports and recreational facilities, are made accessible to all.[19]

The WPA envisioned national action plans. The implementation of the World Decade was reviewed several times.[20] Not much progress could be reported. Rather, such progress as was reported could not be positively correlated to the WPA. In recognition of the need to move the matter forward in the late 1980s, both Italy and Sweden proposed drafting a new thematic human rights convention on the rights of persons with disabilities. However, due mainly to treaty fatigue, the General Assembly declined to consider a new convention. It opted instead to issue a special resolution entitled the *UN Standard Rules for the Equalisation of Opportunities for Persons with Disabilities* (1993) which was reputedly heavily influenced by Swedish thinking on disability at the time.[21] Though comprehensive and even elegantly drafted, the Standard Rules lacked legal status.[22]

However, there was one major procedural innovation in the Standard Rules: a Special Rapporteur was appointed. This five-year mandate has been successively extended.[23] Interestingly, this mandate also co-exists with the newly adopted CRPD. From a formal point of view, the Special Rapporteur reported to the UN Commission for Social Development rather than to the (then called) UN Commission on Human Rights. Towards the end of the 1990s, the first UN Special Rapporteur (Bengt Lindquist of Sweden – who served for two successive five-year terms) developed a good relationship with the Commission on Human Rights and made frequent appearances before it. The Special Rapporteur has published a global survey on the implementation of the Standard Rules[24] and continues to contribute very actively to the deliberations of the Commission for Social Development.

A straw in the wind for change was contained in the Vienna Declaration and Programme of Action adopted by the World Conference on Human Rights

---

[19] Ibid., para. 12.
[20] The reviews as well as related documentation connected with the World Programme of Action are to be found at: <http://www.un.org/disabilities/default.asp?id=22> (accessed 11 November, 2008).
[21] UN General Assembly Resolution 48/96, 20 December, 1993.
[22] Para 14 of the Rules was to the effect that if they gained sufficient currency they might obtain the status of customary international law. This never happened.
[23] The website of the special rapporteur is at: <http://www.un.org/esa/socdev/enable/rapporteur.htm> (accessed 16 October 2008).
[24] Dimitris Michailakis, *Government Action on Disability Policy: a Global Survey*, (Office of the United Nations Special Rapporteur on Disability, 1997).

in 1993 which stated that 'persons with disabilities should be guaranteed equal opportunity'.[25]

Yet, all of this was happening in a parallel universe to the home of the UN human rights agenda; the UN Commission on Human Rights. Several things came together to make the late 1990s a pivotal moment in migrating disability to the core human rights agenda. First of all, the enactment in the USA of the Americans with Disabilities Act (ADA) in 1990 inspired many around the world to adopt similar legislation and – more importantly – to frame disability from a human rights point of view. It lent substantial authority to the migration to the human rights perspective. It emboldened civil society groups around the world to reframe their inarticulate sense of injustice into the language or rights. It probably had as much impact outside the US as it did inside.[26] Secondly, the new UN High Commissioner for Human Rights – Mary Robinson – had taken a personal interest in disability when she had served as President of Ireland and seemed determined to nudge the UN human rights machinery to embrace disability.

Meanwhile, as if engaged in a war of manoeuvre, various UN workshops on disability had all arrived at a consensus that the existing UN human rights system was – for whatever reason – proving unavailing on the issue of disability and that a convention was necessary. A United Nations Consultative Expert Group on International Norms and Standards on Disability met in 1998 in Berkeley. It recommended that the Commission on Human Rights should establish a working group to address specific violations of rights in the disability context and that disability should be considered under the various thematic procedures, including Resolutions 1235 and 1503. More importantly, it explicitly called for the UN to examine the desirability of a new international instrument. An Interregional Seminar and Symposium, held in Hong Kong in 1999, called for the appointment of a Special Rapporteur on disability answerable to the Commission on Human Rights and for the initiation of a treaty drafting process. Successive conferences came to the same conclusion. Indeed, several states themselves came to the conclusion that a convention was needed alongside continuing efforts to mainstream disability into the existing UN human rights machinery.[27]

A window opened up in the Commission on Human Rights in the late 1990s. Since the early 1990s the Commission had passed a wholly unnoticed and innocuous bi-annual resolution on disability. Its passage did not occasion any serious debate. However, slowly but surely, it acquired importance. For example, the 1994 disability resolution called on the UN human rights treaty monitoring bodies to monitor compliance by states of their obligations with respect to persons with disabilities.[28] The Commission repeated this call in another resolution in 1996.[29]

---

[25]   Vienna Declaration and Programme of Action, A/CONF.157/23, 12 July 1993, para. 64.

[26]   See M. Breslin and S. Yee, *Disability Rights Law and Policy: International and National Perspectives*, (Transnational, 2002).

[27]   See Report of an Informal Consultative Meeting on International Norms and Standards for Persons with Disabilities, UN Division for Social Policy and Development, 2001.

[28]   Commission on Human Rights Resolution 1994/27, 'human rights and disability', 4 March 1994 (Geneva).

[29]   Commission on Human Rights Resolution 1996/27, 'human rights of persons with

The 1998 resolution asserted that any violation of the right to equality for persons with disabilities is an infringement of their human rights.[30] It also called on States Parties to the various conventions to report regularly on the situation pertaining to their disabled populations.

Ireland proposed using this bi-annual resolution to place the question of a convention back on the table. In the draft resolution it presented to the Commission on Human Rights for 2000, some new language was inserted into the resolution to that effect.[31] However, this language had to be withdrawn to enable the resolution to pass on the basis of consensus. The ostensible reason against considering a convention was that more time was needed to get the existing conventions working on the disability issue. Rather than yield to this argumentation, the Irish Government decided to fund a Study through the Office of the UN High Commissioner for Human Rights on disability. The object of the Study was to show how or whether the existing human rights system could be improved in the context of disability and to evaluate the arguments for a new convention.

The 2002 Study for the Office of the United Nations High Commissioner for Human Rights contains valuable analysis of the current use and future potential of the then existing United Nations human rights instruments in the context of disability.[32] The analysis revealed that only one General Comment had been adopted on human rights and disability by the treaty monitoring bodies. Despite the normative potential, the relevant jurisprudence of the treaty monitoring bodies on disability was found to be sparse, which probably reflected a lack of awareness among disability organizations about how such claims could be ventilated at the UN level. And the treaty monitoring bodies tended not to probe States Parties on their record or plans in the area of disability. This was reflected in the lack of mention of disability on the concluding observations of most of the treaty monitoring bodies.

The one General Comment that did exist – General Comment 5 of Committee on Economic, Social and Cultural Rights (1994) on disability – is rightly famous and pioneering. It was adopted in response to a specific request put forward in a major report on disability and human rights by Leandro Despouy in 1993.[33] Despouy noted the legal disadvantage persons with disabilities were at compared to other vulnerable groups who had the benefit of thematic conventions.

General Comment 5 acknowledges the need to go beyond (traditional) anti-discrimination law to include positive action measures. Dealing with 'Means of Implementation' in the specific context of disability, General Comment 5 interest-

disabilities', 19 April, 1996 (Geneva).

[30] Commission on Human Rights Resolution 1998/31, 'human rights of persons with disabilities', 17 April, 1998 (Geneva).

[31] The new addition, if successful, would have read: 'Considers that the next logical step forward in advancing the effective enjoyment of the rights of persons with disabilities requires that the Commission for Social development should examine the desirability of an international convention on the rights of persons with disabilities'. Text on file with author.

[32] G. Quinn and T. Degener (eds), *Human Rights and Disability - the Current and Future Use of United National Human Rights Instruments in the context of disability*, (Office of the United Nations Commissioner for Human Rights, 2002).

[33] L. Despouy, *Human Rights and Disabled Persons*, (United Nations, 1993).

ingly seems to contemplate legislation that provides for enforceable remedies, not merely with respect to non-discrimination, but also with respect to such positive action measures.[34]

The aforementioned 2002 Study made several practical recommendations to improve the visibility of disability with respect to States Parties (for example, include more disability information in their periodic reports), to the treaty monitoring bodies (adopt General Comments of relevance to disability, set aside a day of discussion, to step up dialogue with States Parties on disability, etc.), to the Office of the High Commissioner on Human Rights (spread more knowledge about human rights and disability, support teaching and research, etc.) and to the Commission on Human Rights (now the Human Rights Council) (mainstream disability and start with a thematic focus, consider appointing a thematic or Special Rapporteur answerable directly to itself).

Much progress has, in fact, been made in implementing the recommendations of the 2002 Study.[35] In 2006, for example, the Committee on the Rights of the Child issued a very fine General Comment on the rights of children with disabilities.[36] In 2007 the UN Special Rapporteur on the right to education has also issued a special report on the right to education of persons with disabilities.[37] Reportedly, the Committee Against Torture is preparing a General Comment on disability and torture, inhumane and degrading treatment. This is especially welcome in the context of institutional settings where persons with disabilities are at their most vulnerable.

The Human Rights Council, in a resolution on 'human rights and persons with disabilities' adopted on 27 March 2008, decided to hold an annual interactive debate in its regular sessions, and that the first such debate would be held at its 10th session focusing on 'key legal measures for ratification and effective implementation of the' disability convention.[38] The significance of this is that it places the disability issue squarely – and regularly – at the heart of deliberations in the UN on human rights.

The 2002 UN Study went on to provide a series of arguments in favour of drafting a new thematic treaty on the rights of persons with disabilities. It argued

---

[34]　It is significant to observe that the Committee on Economic, Social and Cultural Rights, in its 2002 Concluding Observations on Ireland, specifically criticized a Bill (Disability Bill, 2002) that removed 'the rights of people with disabilities to seek judicial redress if any of the Bill's provisions are not carried out'. This Bill purported to provide a legal basis for a variety of positive action measures for persons with disabilities – but in a way that was not accountable to them.

[35]　See Report of the United Nations High Commissioner for Human Rights on progress in the implementation of the recommendations contained in the study on the human rights of persons with disabilities, Geneva, 2003, text available at: <http://www.un-hchr.ch/huridocda/huridoca.nsf/(Symbol)/E.CN.4.2003.88.En?Opendocument> (accessed 16 October 2008).

[36]　CRC General Comment No 9 (206), The Rights of Children with Disabilities, CRC/C/GC/9, 29 September 2006.

[37]　Report of the Special Rapporteur on the Right to Education (Vernor Munoz), The Right to Education of persons with disabilities, A/HRC/4/29, 19 February 2007.

[38]　See Draft Report of the Council, A/HRC/7/L11, 28 March 2008, Resolution 7/9 'Human Rights of Persons with Disabilities', 29-34, para. 15.

for a convention on the basis that it would enhance the visibility of the rights of persons with disabilities. It also argued that a convention would have the practical advantage of enabling disability groups in civil society to engage more meaningfully with the UN human rights system (with one focused convention) and that this dialectic could drive ever deeper insights into human rights and disability, that would cross-fertilize into the work of the existing treaty bodies. In other words, the convention was not seen as something that would supplant the other conventions, but instead as something that would ignite interest in the other treaty bodies on the question of disability. In this way the convention would assist – and not undermine – mainstreaming. The Study also envisaged allowing the UN Special Rapporteur's role (under the UN Standard Rules) to continue and inform the deliberations of any future treaty monitoring body.

Events were by now moving fast. By December 2001 (that is, about three months before the publication of the Study in February 2002), Mexico succeeded in getting the UN General Assembly to set up an Ad Hoc Committee to 'consider proposals for' a new thematic treaty on disability.[39] Mexico had a draft text at the ready which dealt with disability in part as a human rights issue and in part as a social development issue.

This Ad Hoc Committee met eight times (usually for two-week sessions) and once as an expert Working Group (January 2004) to draft the convention between August 2002 and December 2006. It was truly *ad hoc* in the sense that whatever state wanted to turn up could turn up. The first few sessions were inconclusive in part because the negotiations took place in New York, rather than Geneva where most of the human rights expertise both of states and of the UN is located. Indeed, most delegations at the first session had no explicit instructions.

The whole process teetered on the brink during the First Session in part because the US delegation appeared opposed to the process. The US changed its position toward the end of the initial two-week session to the effect that it would not oppose others taking the process forward. This was interpreted as a major victory. As a result, the US did not take an active part during the early negotiations (when the foundations were being laid). This was a pity, since its experience could have unravelled some key issues at an early stage in the process. This meant that the EC took a leading role along with China.

An unusual procedural innovation occurred during the first and succeeding sessions of the Ad Hoc Committee. It agreed to allow all genuinely interested civil society groups to be present and to speak (although not to vote) throughout the proceedings. Importantly, they did not need to have consultative status with the UN. This greatly expanded the range of disability groups that could attend. And this new element had a huge impact in the drafting positions of states. Indeed, a highly effective International Disability Caucus was formed to bring coherence to the positions of civil society groups which worked quite effectively.[40] Additionally, National Human Rights Institutions were also given a right of audience in the Ad Hoc Committee and in the Working Group. National Institutions intervened

---

[39] UN General Assembly Resolution 56/168, 'Comprehensive and integral convention to promote and protectect the right and dignity of persons with disabilitires', A/56/583/ Add 2, 19 December 2001 (New York).

[40] For full text of the inputs of the IDC to the drafting process see: <http://www.un.org/esa/socdev/enable/rights/idc05.htm> (accessed 16 October 2008).

frequently and prepared an elaborate and very creative position on monitoring.[41] As will be seen, their role is set to become quite crucial in transposing the majestic generalities of the convention into domestic practice.

The convention was adopted on 13 December 2006 and formally opened for signature and ratification on 30 March 2007. Twenty ratifications were needed for it to enter into force. At the time of writing (May 2008) there are twenty-seven ratifications. The Convention came into force on 3 May 2008. An election must be held within six months to the new treaty monitoring body (Committee on the Rights of Persons with Disabilities). The Committee can then begin its work toward the end of 2008. The convention is accompanied by an Optional Protocol enabling the Committee to entertain individual or group complaints.

3. LAW: THE UNITED NATIONS CONVENTION ON THE RIGHTS OF PERSONS WITH DISABILITIES

3.1. GENERAL PROVISIONS

It is important to understand that the drafters had three broad options before them. First, they could have drafted a full substantive rights treaty on the model of the Convention on the Rights of the Child. This option was favoured by most civil society groups. It would, of course, have taken quite some time to achieve. Secondly, they could have drafted a simple convention on non-discrimination and disability. Such an instrument could be short (containing no more than two or three operative provisions) and might perhaps have pegged itself to the existing conventions. Indeed, some delegations at the First Session of the Ad Hoc Committee seemed to suggest that a protocol to the existing conventions would have been enough. Or, thirdly, they could have drafted a hybrid convention containing all the relevant substantive rights drawn from both sets (civil and political as well as economic, social and cultural) and then animated by the non-discrimination/ equal opportunities philosophy. Ultimately, the latter option was chosen.

While there was no appetite for a full-blown substantive convention along the lines of the Convention on the Rights of the Child, there was also no enthusiasm for a bald convention on discrimination that did not make the effort to link the equality idea to the rights themselves. The overarching equality ideal is plain from Article 1 which proclaims that the purpose of the convention is to 'promote, protect and ensure the full and equal enjoyment of all human rights and fundamental freedoms by persons with disabilities and to promote respect for their inherent dignity'. This formulation sits well with a full and substantive conception of equality. When rendered as egalitarianism, it builds bridges between both sets of rights.

However, at other times, the convention seems to let the non-discrimination tool do most of the heavy lifting. That is, the convention seems to aim at 'equality of opportunities' as well as – or maybe in place of – 'equality of results'. This 'equal opportunities' pitch makes the convention much more marketable to states where most allocational decisions are left to market forces.

---

[41]   For an account of the engagement of National Institutions in the process see: <http://www.nhri.net/default.asp?PID=103&DID=0> (accessed 16 October 2008).

There was some contention over the definition of discrimination to be contained in the convention. The EC favoured an approach that would track the distinction between 'direct' and 'indirect' discrimination contained in its law and especially in the Framework Directive on Employment[42]. Some, especially civil society groups, were fearful that the notion of 'indirect discrimination' (which permits some limited defences) would open a Pandora's box. Eventually – and for the sake of consistency – it was decided to revert to the common understanding of discrimination in UN human rights treaties. The definition now reads (Article 2):

> 'Discrimination on the basis of disability' means any distinction, exclusion or restriction on the basis of disability which has the purpose or effect of impairing or nullifying the recognition, enjoyment or exercise, on an equal basis with others, of all human rights and fundamental freedoms in the political, economic, social, cultural, civil or any other field. It includes all forms of discrimination, including denial of reasonable accommodation

Note the specific mention of 'reasonable accommodation' at the end – which is, of course, not found in other UN human rights treaties. This also proved contentious. Recall that the non-discrimination norm is styled an 'obligation of result' under international human rights law. Recall also that most comparative disability discrimination law takes one further step in requiring 'reasonable accommodation' to the situation of persons with a disability. To a certain – limited – extent this enables the non-discrimination tool to take on some modicum of positive action. It is of course distinguishable from positive action measures as such. In contrast to positive action measures, 'reasonable accommodation' responds directly to an individual, is tailored to that individual and any failure to achieve it may trigger a suit for discrimination. But it nevertheless sweeps in some action going beyond merely abstaining from discrimination.

It was this tentative bridge to some positive measures that impelled the EU Presidency during the Working Group (January 2004) to argue for a separation of the notion of 'reasonable accommodation' from the concept of discrimination. In other words, the view was apparently taken that if the notion of 'reasonable accommodation' were tied to the notion of non-discrimination, then it could become a Trojan horse for the enforceability of more and more slices of social and economic rights. Therefore, it was pressed by the EU Presidency that while failure to achieve 'reasonable accommodation' was regrettable, it did not necessarily trigger a finding of discrimination. This, of course, was unsustainable since most comparative law forges a direct link between 'reasonable accommodation' and non-discrimination. Yet it demonstrated a deep misgiving about the judicial or administrative enforceability of the more programmatic elements of the convention. Thankfully the move did not succeed. Discrimination is now defined as specifically including a 'denial of reasonable accommodation', and the obligation not to discriminate spans every right contained in the convention.

At the outset, there was agreement that the new convention would not contain 'new' human rights or even 'disability rights'. Instead, it would tailor the existing suite of general human rights to the specific situation of persons with disabilities. So in arguing for a particular provision, civil society groups had to

---

[42]   Council directive 2000/78/EC of 27 November 2000 establishing a general framework for equal treatment in employment and occupation, [2000] O.J. L303/16.

somehow fit their claims within the existing corpus of rights – which was a very tight squeeze at times.

The animating values or principles of the convention are set up in Article 3. They include respect for inherent dignity, autonomy (including the freedom to make one's own choices) and independence, non-discrimination, full and effective participation in society, respect for difference, equality of opportunities, accessibility, equality between men and women, respect for the evolving capacities of children with disabilities, etc. These values are important, since the text of the convention contains many ambiguities which will hopefully be resolved in a manner consistent with these animating principles.

Article 4 sets out the general obligations of States Parties in addition to the more specific obligations contained in its various substantive provisions. These general obligations include an undertaking to adopt fresh legislation and other appropriate administrative measures where needed to implement the convention, to modify or repeal laws, customs or practices that constitute discrimination, to mainstream disability into all relevant policies and programmes, to refrain from any act or practice that is inconsistent with the convention, to take all appropriate measures to eliminate discrimination on the basis of disability by any person, organization or private enterprise, etc.

Article 4 on general obligations also requires effective consultation with persons with disabilities and their representative organizations in the development and implementation of legislation and policies to implement the convention (Article 4.3). In a way, this gives clear legal expression to the slogan 'nothing about us without us'.

Importantly, paragraph 2 of Article 4 sets out the general obligations of States Parties with respect to economic, social and cultural rights contained in the convention. It states, echoing Article 2(1) of the International Covenant on Economic, Social and Cultural Rights:

> With regard to social, economic and cultural rights, each State Party undertakes to take measures to the maximum of its available resources and, where needed, within the framework of international cooperation, with a view to achieving progressively the full realization of these rights, without prejudice to those obligations contained in the present Convention that are immediately applicable according to international law.

The intention was to demarcate between 'obligations of result' or immediate effect (like non-discrimination) and 'obligations of conduct' which were to be achieved progressively. However, the language adopted in Article 4(2) may well cause some interpretive problems in the future, since many of the rights contained in the convention contain both 'obligations of immediate result' as well as 'obligations of conduct', and it is sometimes difficult to disentangle the two.

The question of the definition of disability was also contentious and again – at least partly – for the reason of deflecting hard economic and social obligations. Consistent with its own domestic law, Canada and others argued that there should be no definition.[43] After all, there is no definition of a woman, or a racial minority

---

[43]   See, *Quebec (Commission de droits de la personne et des droits de la jeunesse) v Montreal et al* [2000] 1 SCR (known as the *Mercier* case). For comparative analysis on the question of the definition of disability see G. Quinn, 'Disability Discrimina-

Gerard Quinn

or a child in the relevant UN thematic human rights treaties. However, several developing countries argued strongly in favour of including a definition in order to limit their exposure to resource-intensive obligations. The definition finally adopted is nevertheless quite open-ended. It states:

> Persons with disabilities include those who have long-term physical, mental, intellectual or sensory impairments which in interaction with various barriers may hinder their full and effective participation in society on an equal basis with others.

This is in keeping with the Preamble which recognizes that disability is:

> an evolving concept and that disability results from the interaction between persons with impairments and attitudinal and environmental barriers that hinders their full and effective participation in society on an equal basis with others.

The definition may or may not become a key interpretive issue. Since the bulk of the convention is directed against the discriminatory behaviour of *third parties*, the definition may not be all that crucial. For example, Article 5 – which secures the right to equality and non-discrimination – enjoins the States Parties to prohibit all discrimination 'on the basis of disability'. This latter term is surely wider than a definition that focuses on the peculiar impairments of any given individual. For example, 'discrimination on the basis of disability' could potentially reach those who do not have impairments but who are disadvantaged because of their association with someone who has a disability (for example, mother of a child with a disability trying to re-enter the labour market).[44] It will be interesting, to say the least, to see how the Committee grapples with the conjunction/disjunction between the definition of disability (focusing on the individual with a disability) and the definition of discrimination (taking the focus *away* from the individual and placing it on the actions of third parties).

There are two transversal articles in the convention covering women with disabilities (Article 6) and children with disabilities (Article 7). Article 6 asserts the obvious which is that women and girls with disabilities are subject to multiple discrimination and that added attention is required to secure their full enjoyment

---

tion Law in the European Union', in H. Meenan (ed.), *Equality Law in an Enlarged European Union: Understanding the Article 13 Directives*, (Cambridge University Press, 2007), 132-277 at 249-251.

[44] See Case C-303/06, *Coleman v Attridge Law and Steve Law*, Opinion of the Advocate General, delivered on 31 January 2008. The net issue was whether a mother of a child with a disability who claimed she was constructively dismissed from her employment could claim the protective benefit of the EC Framework Directive even though she herself did not have a disability. The Advocate General accepted that 'discrimination by association' was covered by the EC Framework Directive in part because the Directive forbids discrimination on the ground of' disability which is not the same as actually having a disability. The Court's judgment was given on 17 July 2008. The Court agreed with that part of the Advocate General's Opinion that held that 'discrimination by association' fell within the ambit of the Directive with regard to direct discrimination and harassment.

102

Intersentia

of human rights. States Parties are specifically enjoined to 'take all appropriate measures to ensure the full development, advancement and empowerment of women'. Rights that protect women and girls against violence, exploitation and abuse, and that restore decision-making capacity and autonomy to them are particularly important (see below). Likewise, Article 7 on children with disabilities emphasizes the need for special attention. Interestingly, it was opposed by some delegations on the basis that it might undermine equivalent provisions in the Convention on the Rights of the Child. It was included because of the need to nurture, protect and empower children with disabilities and to ensure that their 'best interests' lie at the heart of all decisions affecting them. Article 7(3) goes on to give voice to children with disabilities. It is to the effect that in all matters that pertain to them, children with disabilities have the right to express their views freely and that their views should be given due weight in accordance with age and maturity 'on an equal basis with other children'. These two articles should prove important when coming to terms with the ambiguities of the text of the convention as it applies to women and children.

The one glaring – indeed remarkable – omission is the lack of any article dealing with the transversal issue of age and disability. This is an unusual omission since age correlates quite significantly with disability There is also a divide – of sorts – between those who bring a disability into old age and those who acquire a disability in old age. It is hoped that the new Committee will develop insights into this overlap and develop its jurisprudence accordingly.

A possibility is expressly allowed for reservations under Article 46, provided they are 'not incompatible with the objects and purpose of the convention'. This reflects Article 19 of the Vienna Convention on the Law of Treaties.

It is much more likely that States Parties will make interpretive declarations when ratifying the convention rather than outright reservations.

Of course, there is always the possibility that an interpretive declaration might be found by the new Committee to amount to a disguised reservation. If so, and if the Mexican interpretive declaration cuts to the heart of Article 12(2), then it would appear to be incompatible with the object and purpose of the convention. The larger point is that it is likely that the Committee will be very occupied with these vexing matters as more states ratify and enter reservations or interpretive declarations.

Article 8 enjoins the States Parties to raise awareness about the rights of persons with disabilities as well as the convention. It is perhaps one of the most significant of the general obligations, since most (not all) of the problems in the disability field is unthinking prejudice. Usefully, Article 8 requires a publicity campaign to 'nurture receptiveness to the rights of persons with disabilities' and to promote recognition of the 'skills, merits and abilities of persons with disabilities'. It also requires states to encourage all organs of the media to 'portray persons with disabilities in a manner consistent with the purpose of the' convention. This too is important, since a culture shift in attitudes and value could make the difference between rhetorical change and real improvement.

A novel provision was added to the convention dealing with 'situations of risk and humanitarian emergencies' (Article 11). This was originally resisted since there was a perception that it was – or could be – directed against a small group of states. Nevertheless, it was included on the basis that persons with disabilities had heightened vulnerabilities during situations of risk which are categorized as 'situations of armed conflict, humanitarian emergencies and the occurrence of natural disasters'. The main obligation on states in these circumstances is to take all necessary measures to ensure the protection and safety of persons with disabilities.

3.2. THE RIGHTS

The rights themselves comprise the bulk of the convention (Articles 9–30). Perhaps the easiest way of rendering them accessible is to loosely categorize them into clusters as follows: (i) rights that protect the person; (ii) rights that restore autonomy, choice and independence; (iii) rights of access and participation; (iv) liberty rights; (v) economic, social and cultural rights.

3.2.1. Rights that Protect the Person

These rights include the right to life (Article 10), freedom from torture, inhuman or degrading treatment (Article 15), freedom from violence and exploitation (Article 16) and a right to integrity of the person (Article 17).

The drafting of the right to life could have proved contentious since some wished to raise the issue of selective abortion on the basis of disability. In the result the Chair (ambassador Don MacKay of New Zealand) was successful in making it plain that the addition of Article 10 did not alter, add or subtract from existing international human rights law. That is, tailoring the right to disability did not involve any substantive re-working of the right. Rather, States Parties now undertake to take all necessary measures to ensure its effective enjoyment by persons with disabilities 'on an equal basis with others'.

Article 15(1) (freedom from torture, etc.) added one significant element in the context of disability. It adds to the normal formulation the following: '[I]n particular, no one shall be subjected without his or her free consent to medical or scientific experimentation'. As applied in the specific context of disability, this refers to the practice of clinical trials and particularly in cases where there is no direct therapeutic benefit. Of course, it begs the question as to what should occur when the individual is unable to give consent. As will be seen, this is governed by Article 12 of the convention which lies at its very heart.

Article 16 (freedom from exploitation, violence and abuse) is novel. In a way, it represents a logical entailment of general human rights norms as applied in the context of disability where many people are vulnerable and especially in institutional settings. It enjoins States Parties to take all appropriate measures to protect persons with disabilities both within and outside the home from all forms of exploitation, violence and abuse and is especially attuned to the gender aspects of such abuse. The explicit inclusion of 'home' means that States Parties will have to craft appropriate tools to investigate abuse within the family setting. It goes on to enjoin States Parties to prevent all forms of exploitation and abuse by providing assistance and supports, including information on how to recognize and report instances. It effectively requires lifting the veil surrounding institutions by demanding effective monitoring. In addition, it requires States Parties to put in place effective recovery and rehabilitation programmes in cases where violence and abuse have taken place. Importantly, it requires robust action in the form of investigation and prosecution where instances are suspected of occurring. Article

16 should prove extremely important in places where persons with disabilities are at their most vulnerable. It sends a very strong signal that there are to be no more 'no-go-areas' for the public authorities.

Article 17 rounds out this first cluster of rights by demanding that the 'physical and mental integrity' of the persons with a disability should be respected 'on an equal basis with others'. In a way, it re-states the essence of this cluster, which is really about using human rights norms to throw appropriately tailored protective shields around the person.

3.2.2. Rights that Restore Autonomy, Choice and Independence

If the first cluster can be thought of as protecting people against the abuse of power, then the second cluster can be thought of in terms of restoring power to people to make their own decisions for themselves. This is taken for granted by most people, but it is by no means assured in the disability context.

At the heart of this cluster is Article 12 (equal recognition before the law). Though technical, this lies right at the heart of the convention.[45] Recall that one of the problems with disability was the lack of visibility of the person with a disability. They tended to be treated in the past as 'objects' (to be managed) rather than as 'subjects' with their own interests and desires and their own rights to pursue them. This 'old' view of disability was best exemplified in highly restrictive laws on legal capacity. Having full legal capacity is the key to making decisions for oneself. Having it withdrawn enables others to make those decisions and effectively direct one's personal destiny.

There are three general approaches to legal capacity. One is the so-called 'status approach' which basically means that once an individual is deemed disabled (for example, as having an impairment that can impact decision-making), then legal capacity is automatically stripped away. It did not matter that the impairment might be of a kind or degree that did not warrant stripping away legal capacity. The decision to strip was not nuanced to the circumstances of the person. Another approach is called the 'outcome approach' which works backwards from particular (improvident) decisions to deduce an incapacity sufficient to trigger a loss of legal capacity. Of course, this left considerable latitude for paternalistic impulses. The third approach is the 'functional approach' which requires a very close evaluation of the actual capacities of the individual. By switching around the default, this approach gets at stereotypical assumptions about disability and places a heavy emphasis on assisting people to make their own decisions for themselves, rather than supplanting them as the deciders.

Article 12 engineers a profound shift to the 'functional approach' under international law. In essence, it centres the person and restores decision-making autonomy to them. Article 12(2) is to the effect that States Parties recognize that persons with disabilities 'enjoy legal capacity on an equal basis with others in all aspects of life'. Of course, this formulation is ambiguous. One could read to assert that persons with disabilities shall be treated equally with all others with respect to legal capacity. Or, one might read to assert that, in as much as persons

---

[45]   A. Dhanda, 'Legal Capacity in the Disability Rights Convention: Stranglehold of the past or lodestar for the future?', 34 *Syracuse Journal of International Law and Commerce* 2 (2007), 429.

with disabilities are similarly situated with others, they shall be treated equally with respect to legal capacity – but not otherwise. This ambiguity is, of course, not peculiar to Article 12, but afflicts all provisions where the relevant rights are stated to be assured 'on an equal basis with others'.

The switch to the 'functional model' can be seen in Article 12(3) which enjoins the States Parties to take appropriate measures to provide access to supports in order to exercise legal capacity. It is plain that the thrust of Article 12(3) is on 'assisted decision-making' as distinct from substituted decision-making. Paragraph 4 deals with the various safeguards that ought to apply in any interventions in the field (proportionate intervention, free from conflict of interest, individually tailored, etc.). It does not explicitly state that there will be circumstances where a complete lack of legal capacity occurs. Indeed, some civil society groups challenge the very legitimacy of the concept of legal incapacity.

Article 12 is likely to prove contentious. Mexico, for example, has made an interpretive declaration upon ratification. The declaration attaches to Article 12(2), which provides that States Parties shall recognize that persons with disabilities enjoy legal capacity on an equal basis with others (see next section below). A straightforward reservation to Article 12(2) that gives the current state of domestic law priority over it would probably be deemed inconsistent with the object and purpose of the convention, since Article 12(2) encapsulates the very essence of the convention. It goes to the heart of the convention, which is to treat persons as subjects and not as objects. The interpretive declaration of Mexico is to the effect that if there is a clash between Mexican law, on the one hand, and Article 12(2), on the other hand, then the superior norm shall prevail. This of course begs the obvious question – which is superior? If, for the sake or argument, Mexican law is superior then the need for the interpretive declaration is not obvious, since Article 4(4) of the convention is already to the effect that the norms of the convention are without prejudice to higher national standards. In that case, the interpretive declaration would appear to be superfluous. And it does look like an unusual interpretive declaration, in that it does not purport to attach any particular meaning or interpretation to Article 12.

Article 26 provides for a right of 'habilitation and rehabilitation'. Although there is such a right in the European Social Charter (Revised),[46] it does not find a strong echo elsewhere in international law. Given that the convention was not intended to create 'new' rights then how did Article 26 make it in? The answer is simple. It was argued for on the basis that it was necessary to give efficacy to other more general human rights, such as liberty. This dependence on general human rights is plain from Article 27(1), which asserts that the right is a means to the higher end of 'attain[ing] and maintain[ing] maximum independence, full physical, mental, social and vocational ability and full inclusion and participation in all aspects of life'.

Autonomy interests also animate how other – more general – human rights are tailored to disability. For example, while persons with disabilities do enjoy a formal right of freedom of expression, which is key to enabling them express their own preferences, they are often unable to use it to maximum advantage

---

[46]   See G. Quinn, 'The European Social Charter and EU Anti-Discrimination Law in the Field of Disability: Two Gravitational Fields with One Common Purpose', in G. Burca et al, Social Rights in Europe, (Oxford University Press, 2005).

either because they require supports to express themselves or because the relevant information upon which to make decisions is itself inaccessible. Article 21 (freedom of expression) seeks to remedy those obstacles by requiring States Parties to 'take all appropriate measures to ensure' that persons with disabilities can exercise their right to expression (Article 21), by providing information intended for the general public is provided to persons with disabilities in accessible formats (Article 21(a)), by facilitating the use of sign language, Braille and alternative communications (Article 21(b)), by urging private entities to provide information in accessible formats (Article 21(c)), by encouraging the mass media – including the providers of information over the Internet – to make their services accessible (Article 21(d)) and to recognize and promote the use of sign language.

Likewise the right of privacy is tailored (Article 22) to meet the particular autonomy needs of persons with disabilities. Of course, one of the legacies of being treated as an 'object' rather than a 'subject' was that private and very intimate information circulated almost without any limits, especially within the health sector. Article 22 seeks to reverse this and restore to the person decision-making capacity over which information to reveal and how. It reiterates the right of persons with disabilities – in common with all others – to the right of privacy. And it specifically adds that persons with disabilities shall have a right to privacy with respect to all health and rehabilitation 'on an equal basis with others'.

Restoring human autonomy is also evident in Article 23 on 'respect for home and the family'. This right restores to persons with disabilities the right to marry (which was heavily regulated in the past) on the basis of full and free consent (23(1)(a)). In a roundabout way this restates the issue of capacity dealt with under Article 12. It assures to persons with disabilities the right to decide on the number and spacing of children. Pointedly, it adds that persons with disabilities shall retain their fertility 'on an equal basis with others'. This gets at the practice of compulsory sterilization so prevalent even in the 20th century. Of course, again, much will depend on how the term 'on an equal bass with others' is interpreted.

Children have a right not to be separated form their parents against their will, except where necessary in their best interests (Article 23(4)). This is important given the tendency in some countries for children with disabilities to be automatically taken into care in institutions after birth. There is also relevant language in Article 23 dealing with the practice of concealment, abandonment and neglect. Furthermore, there is an interesting reference to adoption rights for prospective parents with disabilities – something that is taken for granted for most.

3.2.3. Rights of Access and Participation

Protecting persons with disabilities against the abuse of power, and restoring autonomy and decision-making capacity to them is plainly not enough. Real barriers to the mainstream of life remain, if only because the mainstream was not built to positively accommodate the difference of disability. The classic example is steps into a building that excludes those who use wheelchairs. This cluster of rights tackles those barriers in general as well as in the specific context of access to political life, access to justice and access to the cultural life of the nation. This aspect of the convention is innovative. In essence these rights serve to identify and remove obstacles that make participation – something taken for granted by most – a reality for persons with disabilities.

Article 9 deals with a general right of access. Again, it is pegged to the higher goal of enabling people with disabilities to live independently. It enjoins States Parties to take appropriate measures – again 'on an equal basis with others' – to ensure access to the built environment, transportation, information and communications technologies and other services open to the public. States Parties are obliged to develop and monitor standards, to regulate access to private entities, to provide accessibility training, to provide Braille signage in public buildings, to promote live assistance (readers, sign language interpreters), to promote access to new forms of technologies and to promote the design, development, production and distribution of accessible information technologies at an early stage. Perhaps the most far-seeing provision has to do with ensuring that the Information Society – as it evolves – takes fully into account the access needs of persons with disabilities from the very outset. It is much cheaper to do so as a design feature rather than later as an add-on.

Article 29 deals with access to the political world for persons with disabilities. This is very important since persons with disabilities typically lack political impact (despite their large numbers). This is due in part to the extremely high opportunity costs of engaging in political life (most of their time can be taken up with mere survival), but it is also due to the lack of accessibility of the political world to persons with disabilities. The most obvious example is inaccessible voting and polling stations, as well as the lack of political information (such as party manifestos) in accessible formats. Article 29 is designed to get at these and other barriers. It requires that voting procedures, facilities and materials are appropriate, accessible and easy to use (29(a)(i)). It protects the right to vote by secret ballot with appropriate assistance and to stand for election (29(a)(ii)).

Of course, a key to exercising effective political influence is the right to form civil society groups. Article 29 also requires States Parties to promote an environment in which persons with disabilities can effectively and fully participate in political parties and other groups as well as specifically in organizations of persons with disabilities themselves.

Article 30 deals with access to, and participation in, cultural life, recreation and sports. It contains a number of unusual features. In addition to specifying access rights to cultural life (for example, access to theatres) it goes on to require States Parties to take appropriate measures to enable persons with disabilities to develop and use their creative artistic and intellectual potential (Article 30(2)). It further requires States Parties (in accordance with international law) to ensure that laws protecting intellectual property rights 'do not constitute an unreasonable or discriminatory barrier' to access to cultural materials. This relates primarily to copyright issues with respect to electronic versions of documents for blind users. Furthermore, Article 30 asserts that persons with disabilities shall be entitled, 'on an equal bass with others', to 'recognition and support' of their specific cultural and linguistic identity, including sign languages and deaf culture. This was a major issue for the deaf community and marks a very significant advance – especially with respect to the legal recognition of sign language throughout the world. The remainder of Article 30 deals with sport and leisure. An interesting variant on 'mainstreaming' occurs in Article 30 (5)(d) which requires that children with disabilities have equal access to participation in play, recreation and sports including in the school system. This sweeps in integrated play and recreation in kindergardens also – where attitudes are formed in other children towards their peers with disabilities.

These access rights are rounded out by Article 13 in the context of the justice system. This is important since it enables persons with disabilities to vindicate their rights through the justice system, to defend themselves effectively against prosecutions (including at the pre-trial stage) and to otherwise participate, for example, as a witness or as a member of a jury. It calls on States Parties to provide procedural and 'age appropriate accommodations' in order to facilitate effective participation in the justice system. It also calls for appropriate training for those working in the justice system.

3.2.4. Liberty Rights

More general liberty-style rights are provided in Articles 14 (liberty), 20 (personal mobility) and 18 (nationality). These rights connect up with broader human rights and essentially take the extra step of addressing the relevant obstacles in the disability context with appropriately tailored obligations.

Article 14 reiterates the general right to liberty which shall not be forfeited unlawfully or arbitrarily. It adds that 'disability shall in no case justify a deprivation of liberty'. At one level this adds nothing to international law since disability, *per se*, has never been a justification for loss of liberty. Rather, it is always the conjunction of disability with 'danger to self' or to 'others' that justifies deprivation of liberty. At another level, however, it does signal a tightening of the criteria upon which loss of liberty can occur. Article 14(2) insists that if persons with disabilities are deprived of their liberty through any process (which presumably embraces both the criminal process and the civil commitment process), that they are entitled to all the due process guarantees available to others under international human rights law and shall be treated in conformity with the objectives and principles of the convention.

Article 20 provides a right of personal mobility as a way of exercising the general right to liberty, whereas Article 18 deals with liberty of movement and nationality. This is an important article when one considers that persons with disabilities often have great difficulty in moving from one country to another. The relevant barriers in this context do not concern issues like the 'exportability of social benefits' or inaccessible transport. Rather, the barriers aimed at were those that explicitly (or effectively) excluded persons with disabilities from entering countries or acquiring nationality. In addition to tackling these legacy issues, Article 18 also guarantees a right to children with disabilities to be registered at birth and have the right to a name, a nationality, as well as a right to know and be cared for by their parents. This is important given the stigma that may attend having child with a disability in many countries.

3.2.5. Economic, Social and Cultural Rights

Economic, social and cultural rights take on a sharp edge in the context of disability. One result of being viewed as an 'object' rather than a person was that society generally tended not to invest in developing the latest capacities of persons with disabilities, or did so in overly segregated environments. This cluster of rights is important not merely because it provides a floor of social supports to maintain people. It is important because it equips people with disabilities to take their own place in society. They include the right to education (Article 24), the right to work (Article 27), the right to an adequate standard of living (Article 28) and the right to health (Article 25). Of course, they reflect a blending of the principle of non-discrimination (immediately achievable) with obligations that are more progressive in character.

The right to education is fascinating because it merges two seemingly contradictory philosophies. On the one hand, the thrust of much modern thinking on education and disability is that 'separate but equal' is an inherent violation of the equality principle. Mainstreaming ensures that latent talents are optimized and that stereotypes are eroded. However, on the other hand, recall that the notion of equality may, on occasion *require* differential treatment. So the net question was whether there were sufficient 'objective' justifications based on different learning capacities that would warrant some separate provision of education, at least for some impairment-specific groups?

Article 24 attempts to square this circle. It assures the right to education to persons with disabilities (that is, it has a broader ambit than for children alone – an important factor when one considers the educational deficiencies of a generation gone by and now in adulthood). Such education is said to be aimed at 'development by persons with disabilities of their personality, talents and creativity' – which is, in its own way, an insistence that every human being has some such potential. Moreover, the education to be provided must be 'inclusive' at all levels. It demands that persons with disabilities should not be excluded from the general education system 'on the basis of disability'. It seeks to ensure that adequate resources are applied (including an obligation of 'reasonable accommodation') to ensure an effective right to education.

Most interestingly, Article 24(3)(c) makes specific allowance for some separate provision for children who are blind, deaf or deafblind. The relevant obligation is to ensure that their education is 'delivered in the most appropriate languages and modes and means of communication for the individual and in environments which maximize academic and social development'. This is a very interesting way of squaring separate provision with the overall goal of inclusion. It is the (tightly cabined) exception that proves the rule and the new monitoring body will have to take care to ensure that it does not undermine the thrust of mainstreaming.

Article 27 on the right to work is effectively a right to equal opportunities and non-discrimination (with an associated obligation of 'reasonable accommodation') with respect to work. It also embraces a right to just and favourable conditions of work 'on an equal basis with others' as well as trade union rights. Of course, the main problem in the context of trade unions is not so much that persons with disabilities were prohibited by law from joining unions, but more that trade unions tended in the past not to take any notice of disabled workers or prospective disabled employees.

An interesting issue is likely to challenge the new monitoring committee. What does a right to 'just and favourable conditions of work' mean in the context of sheltered employment? For example, Article 27(1)(b) speaks of a right to 'equal remuneration for work of equal value' – which begs the core question. While the convention does not expressly mention (or prohibit) such workshops, it should be read as leaning heavily in favour of employment in the open market and indeed self-employment and entrepreneurship (Article 27(1)(f)). Indeed, an interesting rider is added in Article 27(2) to the effect that States Parties are required to ensure that 'persons with disabilities are not held in slavery or servitude, and are protected, on an equal basis with others, from forced or compulsory labour'. There is certainly a lot of interpretive leeway for the new Committee to use language like this to closely interrogate the existence, and many of the egregious practices, of sheltered workshops. Much of the remainder of the article is given over to training, workplace rehabilitation and assistance to acquire and retain employment.

The right to an adequate standard of living (Article 28) includes the usual mix of a right to adequate food, clothing and housing and to a continuous improvement in living conditions without discrimination on the basis of disability. Given the high prevalence of poverty among persons with disabilities (itself the product of inadequate education and chronic under-employment), this article is particularly important. It embraces a right to clean water and affordable services (including public housing) and devices and a right to assistance for extra disability-related expenses. Effectively, Article 28 places a floor of social provision beneath persons with disabilities which co-mingles the principle of non-discrimination (immediately effective) with more programmatic elements (to be 'progressively achieved').

The substantive right to health proved controversial (Article 25). Persons with disabilities are said to have the right to the 'enjoyment of the highest attainable standard of health without discrimination'. States Parties are obliged to 'provide persons with disabilities with the same range, quality and standard of free or affordable health care' which includes 'sexual and reproductive health'. A number of delegations opposed this last reference, but it was ultimately retained. In addition Article 25(b) requires the provision of additional services specifically on account of disability (early identification, intervention as appropriate and services designed to minimize and prevent further disabilities). The text is careful not to place an emphasis on prevention as such. That would cut against the whole thrust of the convention which is not about prevention, but more about how persons with disabilities are treated by others. So it is couched in terms of preventing 'further disabilities'.

The importance of free and informed consent is also underscored in Article 25(d) which again reflects backwards to Article 12 (legal capacity). Article 25 innovates by specifically prohibiting discrimination with respect to health insurance on the basis of disability and also prohibits discrimination with respect to denial of health care or food and fluids. This presumably refers to 'do not resuscitate' orders as well as the rationing of scarce health resources on the basis of disability.

3.3. IMPLEMENTATION AND MONITORING

Normatively speaking, the obligations of states are clear – or at least much clearer than hitherto. The challenge is to translate these norms into practice.

The disability convention is innovative with respect to both implementation and monitoring. It combines a traditional treaty monitoring body (Committee on the Rights of Persons with Disabilities) with a Conference of States Parties at the international level. But, just as important, it demands the existence of an institutional architecture of change at the domestic level. It requires, for example, a 'focal point' within Government for implementation. It requires a national monitoring process independent of Government to 'promote, protect and monitor' implementation. And it requires these bodies to consult and interact effectively with civil society. And in recognition of the fact that not every country will have the resources – or indeed the domestic apparatus to drive change – it seeks to harness international cooperation and especially development aid to the achievement of its goals.

3.3.1. International Monitoring

Article 34 deals with the new treaty monitoring body. Although states had warned civil society to think innovatively about monitoring, they in fact reverted to a very traditional model. The relevant Committee (composed initially of 12 members but with a possibility of increasing its size as new states ratify) will be elected by the States Parties within six months of the coming into operation of the convention, that is by 3 November 2008. The States Parties are confined to nominating candidates from among their own nationals.

Each State Party is then obliged to submit an initial comprehensive report on measures taken and progress achieved to implement the convention. Thereafter, States Parties are obliged to submit periodic reports at least every four years and 'further when the Committee so requests' (Article 35(2)). The Committee, after evaluating the reports, is empowered to make 'such suggestions and general recommendations' as it considers appropriate. It may also transmit the reports to the Specialized Agencies and other funds within the UN system in order to address a request or indicate a need for further technical assistance or advice. The Committee is enjoined to work co-operatively with the Specialized Agencies as well as with the other treaty monitoring bodies of the UN (Article 38).

The Committee is entitled to receive individual or group complaints under the Optional Protocol (OP). These complaints can be submitted 'by or on behalf' of individuals or groups. The text does not make clear that prior authorization is needed. It could certainly be open to the Committee to dispense with authorization in circumstances of particular vulnerability (e.g., in institutional settings). Or, the Committee may initiate an examination of a situation if it 'receives reliable information indicating grave or systematic violations' (Article 6(1) of the OP). The criteria for inadmissibility are the same as obtain generally: anonymous, abuse of the right of petition, same matter already under examination, non-exhaustion of domestic remedies, manifestly ill-founded, facts precede entry into force of the convention for the State Party concerned (Article 2 of the OP). The process for considering such complaints is likewise similar to those that obtain generally. The Committee is specifically empowered to require urgent 'interim measures' to avoid possible irreparable harm (Article 4 of the OP). This could become significant, especially with respect to institutions where egregious violations can occur. The Committee may require the respondent State Party to include details of its response in its periodic report.

A Conference of States Parties will also be established (Article 40). Its functions will be 'to consider any matter with regard to the implementation of the present convention'. It remains to be seen whether civil society groups or national institutions will have a right to be present during the deliberations of the Conference or to make interventions. It is hoped that this body will become a fruitful avenue for the sharing of information as well as know-how among the States Parties.

3.3.2. Domestic Implementation and Monitoring

Article 33 on national implementation and monitoring is especially valuable. On the implementation side it requires the States Parties to establish 'one or more focal points' within Government and to give due consideration to 'the establishment or designation of a coordination mechanism' (Article 33(1)). It is obviously directed toward the need for 'joined-up' Government in the disability context. An interesting article was added dealing with statistics. Rational policy rests on an accurate picture of the status of persons with disabilities. It therefore makes sense that the convention would require the collection and analyses of such data in order to give effect to the convention. Its place in the convention was, however, questioned by one major European country in the Working Group.

Article 33(2) requires States Parties to 'designate or establish ... a framework, including one or more independent mechanisms ... to promote, protect and monitor implementation'. It enjoins States Parties to take into account the principles for establishing national human rights institutions. This is codeword for the Paris Principles. National Institutions were in fact very active in the drafting process and have begun to step up their efforts to assist one another in the demanding tasks assigned to them under Article 33(2). Article 33(3) requires that civil society groups should be fully involved in the monitoring process.

3.3.3. International Co-Operation

Plainly, many countries will require assistance in meeting their obligations. Developed countries acceded to the argument, but feared the insertion of language that might lend recognition to a legal right to development. The net effect of Article 32 (international cooperation) is that States Parties have a duty to proof their development aid programmes from the perspective of the rights contained in the convention. This does not necessarily mean they will have to spend more or even have an earmarked part of their development budget for disability. But at a minimum, it means that aid programmes should not compound the isolation of persons with disabilities (for example, by building inaccessible schools) and should ideally create pathways to inclusion. The creation of the Global Partnership on Disability and Development (GPDD) by the World Bank, and hosted by the Burton Blatt Institute at Syracuse University, offers a real step forward.

The development aid and broader international cooperation side to the convention is likely to assume major significance since in many developing countries it could be quite significant in getting a dynamic of change going – as well as raising local expectations. It should be borne in mind that a specific provision is made in the convention for approval by the European Commission representing the Institutions of the European Community and that the Commission controls the single largest development aid budget in the world (Article 44).

4. CONCLUSIONS

The disability convention should accelerate the trend underway in most corners of the world toward respecting and advancing the rights of persons with disabilities. It will reinforce reform efforts underway in many countries. It will help put in place a dynamic of reform in those countries that have yet to begin a serious reform effort.

The signs are good. As previously mentioned, the UN Human Rights Council will now consider the issue of disability every year. The Office of the UN High Commissioner for Human Rights has published a joint Handbook with the World Parliamentary Union on the convention and is steadily ratcheting up its engagement.[47] An inter-Service Taskforce combining the main Specialized Agencies of the UN has been formed to support implementation. All the signs indicate that the new Conference of States Parties will initiate a genuine sharing of experience and transfer of solutions.

The work of the incoming Committee on the Rights of Persons with Disabilities will not be easy. Key ambiguities will have to be tackled by the incoming Committee. For example, how are the progressive elements of the convention to be disentangled from obligations like non-discrimination that are immediately achievable? What will be the posture of the Committee be to the key concept that links achievement of the rights of persons with disabilities 'on an equal basis with others'? Will this be used positively or will it be used to rationalize differential treatment? How will the Committee interpret the obligation of 'reasonable accommodation'? How transferable will its insights be on 'reasonable accommodation' to an understanding of discrimination in the other UN human rights treaties? Most crucially, how will it approach and unpack Article 12 on legal capacity, which probably lies at the very root of the revolution in disability – treating people as 'subjects' and not as 'objects'. Whatever happens now, there is no going back. Disability has moved to the core of the UN human rights agenda.

---

[47] From *Exclusion to Equality - Handbook for Parliamentarians on the United Nations Convention on the Rights for persons with Disabilities and its optional Protocol*, (International Parliamentary Union with the United Nations Office of the High Commissioner for Human Rights, 2007).

A PERSONAL PERSPECTIVE ON THE DRAFTING HISTORY OF THE UNITED NATIONS CONVENTION ON THE RIGHTS OF PERSONS WITH DISABILITIES

Stefan Trömel[1]

1. INTRODUCTION

I had the privilege to represent the European Disability Forum (first as Director, later as advisor) throughout the negotiation process of the Convention on the Rights of Persons with Disabilities (from now on, the Convention), attending all meetings of the Ad Hoc Committee, which was established to draft the Convention, as well as a number of additional meetings.

Based on that participation, this paper is a brief personal testimony from the perspective of a representative of an organization of persons with disabilities.

The objective of this paper is to put on record (I repeat, a very personal record) a brief description of key elements of the negotiation process, so that this could help, together with testimonies from other participants, in the interpretation of the Convention. In order to achieve this, I have divided the paper into three parts.

The first part of this paper deals with a number of overarching issues that affected the negotiation process. The second part deals with a number of concrete articles. While all articles of the Convention are important and deserve attention, I have chosen to focus on a number of them. The main criteria for choosing these articles have been:

- The contribution they make to the paradigm shift that this Convention embodies.
- The likelihood that the final wording will be interpreted in different ways by different States, as we are already starting to see in some interpretative declarations made by States.
- The innovative character from a general human rights perspective.

In the third part of the paper, I will make some general conclusions related to the implementation of the Convention.

Because of the European dimension of the Yearbook for which this paper has been prepared, I will also pay a special attention to elements that are of particular interest from a European Community perspective.

---

[1]   International Advisor of Fundación ONCE (Spain), seconded to the Secretariat of the International Disability Alliance and its CRPD Forum.

2. BACKGROUND AND OVERARCHING ISSUES

2.1. WHY IS THERE A NEED FOR A DISABILITY-SPECIFIC CONVENTION?

The UN General Assembly resolution of 2001,[2] which started the process, established an Ad Hoc Committee to consider proposals for a comprehensive Convention on the Rights of Persons with Disabilities. Mexico, the country that promoted this initiative, had proposed that the Ad Hoc Committee should be established to draft a Convention, but the compromise solution was to establish a Committee to consider the matter.

This meant that the main objective of the first Ad Hoc Committee meeting (July-August 2002) was devoted to reflecting whether there was really the need for a new Convention. What would a thematic Convention add? Would it not put persons with disabilities in a separate ghetto? Would it undermine the efforts which had been taken to mainstream the human rights of persons with disabilities in the work of the existing human treaty bodies? These and other questions were put forward by many Member States, but also by some civil society organizations.

It is worth mentioning that the active presence of organizations of persons with disabilities at this first meeting was especially important, because they were the ones able to provide testimony of the wide ranging and diverse forms of discrimination and other human rights violations faced by persons with disabilities worldwide. These examples seemed to indicate that the way the current system was dealing with the human rights of persons with disabilities was not adequate, or at least not sufficient.

Another important element to take into account was the presentation by the High Commissioner on Human Rights, Mary Robinson, of a landmark study on persons with disabilities in the UN human rights system. The study by Gerard Quinn and Theresia Degener[3] had given clear evidence of how little the existing UN human rights machinery was considering the rights of persons with disabilities. The study included therefore, as a logical conclusion, a chapter suggesting the need for a thematic Convention on the rights of persons with disabilities.

According to this study, a thematic Convention would not undermine the mainstreaming of the rights of persons with disabilities in the current UN human rights machinery, as some were arguing, but provide a focal point of expertise on the rights of persons with disabilities which would also contribute to a better recognition and understanding of the rights of persons with disabilities within the other Treaty bodies.

Fortunately, when Member States and civil society returned to New York for the second meeting of the Ad Hoc Committee (June 2003), the issue was quickly settled. With a few exceptions, there was general agreement that there was a need for a specific Convention and the work to draft this Convention could start.

---

2   UNGA resolution Res 56/168 (19 December 2001) UN Doc A/RES/56/168.
3   UNCHR, G. Quinn and T Degener (eds), 'Human Rights and Disability: The Current Use and Future Potential of United Nations Human Rights Instruments in the Context of Disability' (2002), UN Doc. HR/PUB/02/1.

2.2.   THE ROLE OF THE INTERNATIONAL DISABILITY COMMUNITY: THE INTERNATIONAL DISABILITY CAUCUS (IDC)

I believe it is fair to say that there is a general agreement about the key role the international disability community played throughout the negotiation process.

Ambassador McKay from New Zealand, who was Chair of the Ad Hoc Committee at its last four sessions, indicated in the final session which adopted the Convention text that, according to him, 70% of the text was due to the contributions of the NGOs of persons with disabilities.

While the NGO participation in any UN process is always a controversial topic, already in the first week of the first Ad Hoc Committee meeting (July-August 2002), a resolution was adopted which would provide, in effect, for the participation of the NGOs throughout the process. While this resolution foresaw the possibility of holding closed meetings without the participation of NGOs, this happened only on a few occasions during the first and last Ad Hoc Committee meetings.

However, the key element that explains the success of the NGOs of persons with disabilities was the decision to establish a unified coordinating platform, which was to be known as the International Disability Caucus (IDC). The IDC was a network comprising international, regional and national NGOs of persons with disabilities (DPOs) as well as allied NGOs from all over the world. At the end of the process, almost a hundred organizations had become members of the IDC.

Establishing the IDC responded to a very clear conclusion: only by uniting and speaking with one voice, would NGOs of persons with disabilities be able to influence the process.

A good proof of the acknowledgement by States that organizations of persons with disabilities would need to be given an important role in the process, was the decision taken at the very end of the second Ad Hoc Committee: to establish a working group to produce a first draft Convention text which could serve as the basis for the negotiation process, composed of twenty-seven UN Member States, twelve representatives from NGOs and one representative from a national human rights institution.

While the appointment of the twenty-seven States was based on the distribution of seats among the five UN geographical regions, the allocation of the seats to the NGOs was to be decided by the UN Secretariat and NGOs were asked to submit their candidatures by a given date. This procedure could have led to a struggle between the different organizations of persons with disabilities, but, thanks to the existence of IDC, it was agreed to jointly submit a list of twelve organizations representing the different impairment groups as well as the different regions of the world.

A meeting in Madrid in December 2003 of the twelve NGO representatives in the working group, who were joined by other experts, contributed to the cohesion and coordination of the twelve representatives and the wider IDC.

The very active participation in the working group, with the same rights as Government delegates, was instrumental in confirming the role the disability community, organized as the International Disability Caucus, would play throughout the process, both as the representatives of persons with disabilities as main stakeholders in the Convention as well as in the role of experts.

'Nothing about us without us' was soon to become the slogan of the IDC, signalling to the world that the times had definitely passed when legislation and policies affecting persons with disabilities were prepared without their active involvement.

2.3. COMPREHENSIVE CONVENTION VERSUS ANTI-DISCRIMINATION CONVENTION

The mandate given to the Ad Hoc Committee was to consider proposals for a comprehensive and integral Convention to protect and promote the rights and dignity of persons with disabilities.

This was widely interpreted as meaning that this Convention was not to be a purely anti-discrimination Convention, as is the case for the Convention on the Elimination of Racial Discrimination (CERD) and the Convention on the Elimination of all Forms of Discrimination against Women (CEDAW). The Convention on the Rights of the Child (CRC) was given as a model to follow.

The initial position of the European Union[4] and some other States was that it should be a purely anti-discrimination Convention, but they soon realized that this was not supported by other Member States' delegations and also opposed by the IDC.

The IDC position was clear: the Convention had to have strong anti-discrimination provisions, but at the same time include other provisions, including positive action measures, which would achieve the effective and equal enjoyment by persons with disabilities of all human rights.

The position of the IDC and many Governments prevailed, and we have now a Convention that has very powerful anti-discrimination provisions, but includes also many other elements which would not have been in a purely anti-discrimination Convention.

2.4. NO NEW RIGHTS AND NO DIFFERENT RIGHTS THAN OTHER PERSONS

To state that the Convention was not creating new rights, was to become a recurring expression, often used to remind reticent States that the purpose of the Convention was 'just' to ensure that persons with disabilities are provided with an effective enjoyment of existing human rights.

An example of this was the discussion on whether the Convention was creating a new right to accessibility. It was argued instead that accessibility is not a right in itself, but a precondition that needs to occur to ensure the access to existing rights by persons with disabilities. The final positioning of the article on accessibility (in the first section of the Convention) is coherent with this view.

Similarly, it was discussed that the Convention was not to give rights to per-

---

[4] EU Proposal for the text of an International Convention on the Full and Equal Enjoyment of all Human Rights and Fundamental Freedoms by Persons with Disabilities (European Union, 2003), available at: <http://www.un.org/esa/socdev/enable/rights/wgcontrib-EU.htm> (accessed 5 August 2009).

sons with disabilities which other nationals from the same country do not enjoy. This became an important reminder when delicate matters were discussed, like the access to sexual and reproductive health or trade union rights. The term 'on an equal basis with others' which is to be found in many articles of the text is the phrase generally used to reflect this situation.

The IDC position on this discussion was to reiterate that persons with disabilities wanted equality and not special treatment, which of course should not exclude elements which were specific for persons with disabilities.

Now that the process is over and the Convention has been adopted, I believe one can argue that there are at least three articles that establish new rights: Article 19 on the right to living in the community, Article 20 on personal mobility and Article 26 on the right to habilitation and rehabilitation. The main justification for the inclusion of these 'additional' rights was that these rights are only relevant to persons with disabilities.

2.5.   IS IT A HUMAN RIGHTS TREATY OR A SOCIAL DEVELOPMENT TREATY?

This extremely controversial debate is obviously not related exclusively to this Convention, but is part of one of the permanent debates within the United Nations system, reflected in the division between first generation rights (civil and political) and second generation rights (economic, cultural and social).

On one hand, promoters of a 'pure' human rights treaty (mainly the developed countries) argued that the obligations of States Parties are towards their citizens and that no reference at all should be made to any obligations between States, as this could make the obligations of States conditional upon the transfer of financial resources.

The opposite view was given by some developing countries, which considered the development of their countries as a precondition for the improvement of the situation of persons with disabilities.

A large majority of Member States and the IDC held an intermediate position. While the Convention should obviously be a human rights Convention, the Convention, while insisting on the interrelated and indivisible nature of all human rights, would deal with all types of rights without establishing any hierarchy or classification by type of right. Moreover, the inclusion of an article on international cooperation would reflect the important role international cooperation could play in accelerating the process of implementation of the Convention in developing countries.

A reflection that this comprehensive objective was achieved, is best reflected in a paragraph to be found in a recent report[5] prepared by the Secretary General: 'As a human rights instrument with an explicit social development dimension, the Convention on the Rights of Persons with Disabilities is both a human rights treaty and a development tool'.

This is an important statement, as there continues to be confusion around this, arising from the claim that other UN instruments (like the World Programme

---

[5]   Report of the Secretary-General 'Implementation of the outcome of the World Summit' for Social Development and of the twenty-fourth special session of the General Assembly' (16 July 2008), UN Doc. A/63/133.

of Action concerning Disabled Persons from 1982(!)) are the relevant UN documents on disability from a social development dimension.

3. SOME KEY ISSUES

3.1. PREVENTION OF IMPAIRMENT

It is very important to highlight that the Convention does not refer to the prevention of impairment/disability (only the prevention of secondary disabilities is mentioned in Article 25 Health). This was a deliberate decision taken by the Ad Hoc Committee and is one of the elements that reflect the paradigm shift from 'disability' as an object to 'persons with disabilities' as subjects.

This discussion first came up at an expert meeting convened by the Government of Mexico in June 2002, a few months prior to the start of the process. The Government of Mexico had prepared a first draft text of a Convention which was presented to the experts. The draft included, as so many national legislations or strategies on disability do, a provision on the prevention of impairment.

At the meeting, I had the opportunity to raise the view that a Convention on the rights of persons with disabilities should not cover prevention of impairment, an opinion that was immediately seconded by others, including UN Special Rapporteur on Disability, Bengt Lindqvist.

Also, in the seminar organized in Quito (Ecuador) in June 2003[6], the issue of 'prevention' was still on the table, combined with other health and rehabilitation measures.

It seemed however obvious that when one deals with the human rights of persons with disabilities, the focus can only be on promoting the human rights of persons who have a disability. It is clearly incoherent to deal, at the same time, with prevention of disability and with the promotion of the rights of persons with disabilities.

In order to clarify the point a bit more, let me briefly refer to a similar discussion held within the drafting group of the Council of Europe action plan to promote the rights and full participation of persons with disabilities.

When the European Disability Forum (EDF) joined the drafting group in 2003 as sole representative of organizations of persons with disabilities, a first draft action plan had already been prepared. The working title of the action plan was 'Council of Europe action plan on disability' and its first section dealt with prevention of impairment.

In line with the ongoing negotiation process of the Convention, EDF proposed that the title be changed, and to move from disability as an object to 'persons with disabilities' as subjects. This was immediately supported by most Government delegates. The next proposal presented by EDF, which was supported by

---

[6]   Ad Hoc Committee on a Comprehensive and Integral International Convention on Protection and Promotion of the Rights and Dignity of Persons with Disabilities 'Compilation of proposals for a Comprehensive and Integral Convention to Promote and Protect the Rights and Dignity of Persons with Disabilities' (16-27 June 2003) UN Doc A/AC.265/CRP.13, Add.1 & Add. 2, available at: <http://www.un.org/esa/socdev/enable/rights/a_ac265_2003_crp13.htm> (accessed 5 August 2009).

some, but also met with strong resistance by others, was to eliminate the section on prevention of impairment in view of its inconsistency with the title of the action plan.

The final version of the action plan[7] does not include a section on prevention of impairment.

While not much discussion was needed to exclude the prevention of disability from the scope of the Convention, it is important for States to draw the relevant conclusions from this decision and therefore exclude the issue of prevention of impairment from any legislation and policies which are to promote the rights of persons with disabilities. Moreover, States should consider a change in terminology and refer to prevention of accidents, promotion of healthy lifestyles and other concepts, thus avoiding the use of a term which has obvious negative connotations.

3.2. DEFINITION OF DISABILITY AND DEFINITION OF PERSONS WITH DISABILITIES

It was clear from the start of the negotiation process that to try to arrive at an internationally agreed definition of disability would be an almost impossible task.

The views on having or not a definition of disability in the Convention text were split both among Governments and also initially among disability NGOs. Most European countries and European NGOs of persons with disabilities argued that it would not be possible to arrive at an acceptable definition and that a definition would soon be outdated, and that there was a risk of leaving groups outside the definition.

The main defenders of a definition argued that, in the absence of a definition in the Convention, national definitions of disability would prevail, which would mean that large groups of persons with disabilities would not be covered by the Convention in those countries with a more restricted definition. This view was finally assumed by the IDC, but leaving open the option of not having a definition, in case the proposed definition would be too restrictive.

The location of the definition of disability was supposed to be Article 2, which is the Convention article establishing different definitions. However, the discussion led to a different solution, combining a paragraph in the preamble which establishes a conceptual definition of disability based on the social model of disability and a paragraph in Article 1 related to the purpose of the Convention. The objective of the paragraph in Article 1 is no longer to come up with a definition, but more importantly to define the group to be covered by the Convention.

The paragraph in the preamble[8] provides a social model definition of disability, based on an interaction between impairment and barriers, and also includes

---

[7] Recommendation (2006) 5 of the Committee of Ministers to member states on the Council of Europe Action Plan to promote the rights and full participation of people with disabilities in society: improving the quality of life of people with disabilities in Europe 2006-2015 (5 April 2006).

[8] 'e. Recognizing that disability is an evolving concept and that disability results from the interaction between persons with impairments and attitudinal and environmental barriers that hinders their full and effective participation in society on an equal basis with others.'

the notion that disability is an evolving concept.

While the preamble text was rather easy to agree upon, agreement on the text on persons with disabilities in Article 1 was much more difficult to achieve. A key discussion point was the listing of different impairments. The IDC had argued for a very long and non-exhaustive list, including physical, sensory, psychosocial, intellectual, neurological and medical impairments and conditions.

The first circulated text included only three groups: 'mental, physical and sensory'. The IDC and others argued that the term 'mental' was no longer used and was in fact mixing up very different groups of people with disabilities. The final decision[9] was based on the addition of the term 'intellectual' alongside 'mental', which makes it clear that also people with psychosocial disabilities are to be covered by national definitions on disability. Moreover, the wording makes it clear that this is a non-exhaustive list, allowing States to use wider definitions.

IDC had opposed the inclusion of a reference to 'long term', but this was strongly opposed by some States.

Article 1 of the Convention should require the revision of the definition of disability/persons with disabilities in those countries that have more limited definitions.

3.3.   DISCRIMINATION ON THE BASIS OF DISABILITY

The definitions of discrimination used in CEDAW and CERD served as a first basis for this definition. This led to a first definition defining discrimination as 'any distinction, exclusion or restriction on the basis of disability which has the purpose or effect of impairing or nullifying the recognition, enjoyment or exercise, on an equal basis with others, of all human rights and fundamental freedoms in the political, economic, social, cultural, civil or any other field'. This was rather obvious and did not generate any significant debate.

However, the big debate was to come about whether or not to consider 'denial of reasonable accommodation' as a form of discrimination. There was an important precedent set in the General Comment number 5 to the International Covenant on Economic, Social and Cultural Rights (ICESCR) which included the denial of reasonable accommodation in its definition of 'disability-based discrimination'.[10]

Making the debate event more complicated was the fact that the concept of 'reasonable accommodation' was seen by some as identical to general accessibility measures. This led to a number of additional 'misunderstandings', as some States felt that lack of accessibility would be considered as a form of discrimination and, on the other hand, some delegates from NGOs of persons with disabilities considered that it was unacceptable to qualify the denial of reasonable

---

[9]   'Persons with disabilities include those who have long-term physical, mental, intellectual or sensory impairments which in interaction with various barriers may hinder their full and effective participation in society on an equal basis with others.'

[10]   '15. For the purposes of the Covenant, "disability-based discrimination" may be defined as including any distinction, exclusion, restriction or preference, or denial of reasonable accommodation based on disability which has the effect of nullifying or impairing the recognition, enjoyment or exercise of economic, social or cultural rights.'

accommodation (understood as general accessibility) by the words 'not imposing a disproportionate or undue burden'.

Everybody needed to be reminded (Professor Gerard Quinn was very instrumental in this) that reasonable accommodation applies to individual situations and should not be confused with general accessibility measures. The wording 'where needed in a particular case' in the definition, which is based on the definition used in the EC Employment Equality Directive of 2000,[11] reflects the individual nature of the reasonable accommodation concept.

The European Community opposed initially the inclusion of the reference to 'denial of reasonable accommodation', notwithstanding the fact that the EC Employment Equality Directive includes this concept. The fact that the denial of reasonable accommodation in this Directive is included in a separate article, and not in the same article as the other forms of discrimination, was used as a basis for some to argue that the denial of a reasonable accommodation was not considered as a form of discrimination in that Directive. Advice provided by the European Commission served to counter this argumentation.

At the end, after much discussion, the denial of reasonable accommodation was considered as a form of discrimination. This was a very important outcome in order to ensure meaningful anti-discrimination legislation as a result of the implementation of the Convention.

A somewhat peculiar corollary of this outcome is to be seen in the draft EC directive presented by the European Commission in July 2008.[12] On one hand, the denial of reasonable accommodation has been included in the same article as the other forms of discrimination, which is an improvement to the way the EC Employment Equality Directive dealt with this issue. On the other hand, the concept of disproportionate burden has been applied to general accessibility measures, a proposal which is contrary to the provisions of the Convention, as both the European Disability Forum and many EU Member States have immediately highlighted.

Another relevant discussion was whether to include, explicitly or not, the words 'direct and indirect' in the definition of discrimination. This led to the subsequent discussion on how to define these two forms of discrimination and whether or not there should be exceptions to them (the EC Employment Equality Directive has exceptions for indirect discrimination), something which the IDC strongly opposed.

Many argued, and rightly so, that the definition, when using the words 'impact or effect' covers both direct and indirect discrimination. The final decision was to not explicitly refer to 'direct and indirect', in the understanding that the reference to all forms of discrimination covers direct and indirect discrimination.

Another issue related to the definitions of disability and 'discrimination on the basis of disability' deserves to be given a bit of attention. The definition of disability as found in the preamble, which is based on the social model of dis-

---

[11]   Council Directive (EC) 2000/78 establishing a general framework for equal treatment in employment and occupation, [2000] O.J. L 303/16.

[12]   Commission (EC), 'Proposal for a Council directive on implementing the principle of equal treatment between persons irrespective of religion or belief, disability, age or sexual orientation' COM(2008) 426, 2 July 2008.

ability, includes the reference to the barriers and consequently the discrimination faced by persons with disabilities. It therefore is not really appropriate that the Convention refers to discrimination on the basis of disability, as this latter concept already incorporates the discrimination dimension.

In the absence of a definition of disability/impairment, discrimination on the basis of disability could have been the correct phrasing, in line with the definition in the EC Employment Equality Directive which refers to 'discrimination on the grounds of disability'. However, according to the final decision to include a definition of disability, this should have had as a consequence a change to 'discrimination on the basis of impairment'.

This incoherence was identified by some representatives from disability NGOs, but the efforts (not least pedagogic) such a change would have required seemed not to be a top priority in the final stages of the process.

Another relevant aspect of the 'discrimination on the basis of disability' should not be overlooked by UN Member States when implementing the Convention, and in particular when drafting national anti-discrimination legislation. Legislation which will prohibit discrimination on the basis of disability has to put the focus not on whether the person who has been discriminated has or not a (legally certified) disability, but on whether the situation faced by the person is a discriminatory situation based on disability. This would include, among others, situations faced by an associate of a person with a disability, a person who is perceived as having a disability or who has had a disability in the past.

3.4.   RIGHT TO LIFE (ARTICLE 10)

When it was first proposed to have an article on the right to life, this proposal met with some opposition. The right to life is a hugely controversial issue, as there is no agreement within the UN on when life starts, and to open such a debate immediately becomes a debate about the right (or not) to abortion and euthanasia. The presence of pro-life activists throughout the negotiation process was a permanent reminder of the delicate nature of this discussion.

Notwithstanding, the IDC provided clear examples of situations where the life of persons with disabilities had been put in danger, because of a perceived low quality and value of life. It was therefore of great relevance to include a specific article on this right in the Convention text.

While the IDC would have also liked to see the Convention outlaw the forced abortion based on the prenatal diagnosis of disability, no way could be found to cover this without entering the delicate discussion on whether life starts at conception or at birth.

It should, however, be said that the application of the non discrimination principles and the references to be found in Article 4[13] should ensure that abortion legislation, where this exists, should not discriminate on the basis of disability.

---

[13]   'States Parties undertake to (…) b) To take all appropriate measures, including legislation, to modify or abolish existing laws, regulations, customs and practices that constitute discrimination against persons with disabilities; c) To take into account the protection and promotion of the human rights of persons with disabilities in all policies and programmes.'

3.5. SITUATIONS OF RISK AND HUMANITARIAN EMERGENCIES (ARTICLE 11)

The need for this article became apparent during the debate on the article about the right to life. It was going to become one of the most contentious articles, mainly because of its link with the issue of foreign occupation.

The last Ad Hoc Committee (August 2006) was impacted on by the Lebanon war which had started on July 12, 2006. This increased the already extremely politicized nature of this article, resulting in the Arab Group and others insisting on the inclusion of a reference to foreign occupation in this article, something strongly opposed by Israel, the US and a few other States. In fact, the Arab Group presented at the outset of the eighth Ad Hoc Committee meeting a completely rephrased article, which was solely focusing on the situation of persons with disabilities under foreign occupation, leaving out any reference to any other situation of risk, such as natural disasters.

The IDC tried to keep a balanced position and insisted on the relevance of ensuring that this article covered persons with disabilities in all situations of risk. In order to address the specific coverage of persons with disabilities under armed conflict, a term which covers foreign occupation, the IDC proposed to include a reference in this article to international humanitarian law and international human rights law. This reference proved to be a relevant contribution towards finding an acceptable compromise solution for the text of this article.[14]

The final compromise was to include a reference to 'foreign occupation' in preamble paragraph (u).[15] This reference was the only paragraph of the Convention which was not approved by consensus, but required the holding of a vote.

The Government of Mauritius has made a reservation to this article upon signature.[16]

3.6. EQUAL RECOGNITION BEFORE THE LAW (ARTICLE 12)

Undoubtedly, this was one of the most controversial articles in the Convention. This is the article which best reflects the paradigm shift and which generated the

---

[14] 'Article 11 Situations of risk and humanitarian emergencies States Parties shall take, in accordance with their obligations under international law, including international humanitarian law and international human rights law, all necessary measures to ensure the protection and safety of persons with disabilities in situations of risk, including situations of armed conflict, humanitarian emergencies and the occurrence of natural disasters.'

[15] Convention on the rights of persons with disabilities, preamble paragraph (u) 'Bearing in mind that conditions of peace and security based on full respect for the purposes and principles contained in the Charter of the United Nations and observance of applicable human rights instruments are indispensable for the full protection of persons with disabilities, in particular during armed conflicts and foreign occupation.'

[16] 'The Government of Mauritius signs the present Convention subject to the reservation that it does not consider itself bound to take measures specified in article 11 unless permitted by domestic legislation expressly providing for the taking of such measures.'

most heated and complex debates.

The ambitious objective that the IDC had set itself was to ensure the recognition of the full legal capacity of all persons with disabilities on the basis of the supported decision making model, which would replace the historic substituted decision making, embodied in the legislation of most countries through the guardianship system. In order to stress the relevance of this article, and its overall impact on the lives of persons with disabilities, the IDC also insisted that being left without legal capacity would render useless most, if not all, other rights acknowledged by the Convention.

The initial wording in the working group draft was a rather good start,[17] but it was clear that for such a paradigm shift to happen, much fighting was ahead. One of the issues raised by some Member States was the distinction which is to be found in many legal systems (mainly civil law systems) between the two components of the concept of legal capacity, namely the capacity for rights, (the capacity which every person has because of being a person) and the capacity to act, a distinction that does not exist in the common law systems. Based on that distinction, some Member States argued that the reference to the recognition of legal capacity covered only the capacity for rights.

The IDC insisted that the recognition of full legal capacity had to cover both dimensions and that the wording used in CEDAW[18] could be a possible way forward to ensure that both dimensions – in those legal systems where this distinction exists – were covered. It was not an easy task, as many governments insisted on the need to maintain some form of substituted decision making for those more extreme cases, for instance to protect people in a coma. The IDC insisted that the supported decision making model was the adequate framework for all persons with disabilities, as support could range from 0 to 100%.

In addition, much concern was raised about the situations of abuse which could happen if the guardianship system was to be replaced. The IDC made clear that the guardianship system was not only abusive in itself, leading to the civil

---

[17]   'States Parties shall: recognize persons with disabilities as individuals with rights before the law equal to all other persons; a) accept that persons with disabilities have full legal capacity on an equal basis as others, including in financial matters; b) ensure that where assistance is necessary to exercise that legal capacity: – the assistance is proportional to the degree of assistance required by the person concerned and tailored to their circumstances, and does not interfere with the legal capacity, rights and freedoms of the person; c) relevant decisions are taken only in accordance with a procedure established by law and with the application of relevant legal safeguards; d) ensure that persons with disabilities who experience difficulty in asserting their rights, in understanding information, and in communicating, have access to assistance to understand information presented to them and to express their decisions, choices and preferences, as well as to enter into binding agreements or contracts, to sign documents, and act as witnesses; e) take all appropriate and effective measures to ensure the equal right of persons with disabilities to own or inherit property, to control their own financial affairs, and to have equal access to bank loans, mortgage and other forms of financial credit; e) ensure that persons with disabilities are not arbitrarily deprived of their property.'

[18]   '2. States Parties shall accord to women, in civil matters, a legal capacity identical to that of men and the same opportunities to exercise that capacity.'

death of the person, but also the entry door to many other forms of abuses often done by the legally appointed guardians.

The IDC had initially opposed any reference to safeguards in the Convention, stressing this should be left to national laws. However, to acknowledge the valid concerns raised by many Member State delegates, the IDC finally accepted safeguards based on a supported decision making model which should protect persons with disabilities from abuse by those that provide the support.

After the discussions during the seventh Ad Hoc Committee meeting, changes were made and the text which was presented to the eighth (and last) Ad Hoc Committee meeting included two alternatives, one of which maintained a reference to personal representative and a second alternative which was worded on the basis of a supported decision making model. It was this second alternative, which, with a few minor modifications, made it into the final text.[19]

However, the final 'shock' on this article was yet to come; this happened when the Chair of the Ad Hoc Committee read out the text of Article 12 at the very end of the eighth Ad Hoc Committee meeting. A footnote which had appeared in one of the previous meetings suddenly made it again into the text. The reference was incorporated as a footnote to the second paragraph of Article 12 and stated as follows: 'In Arabic, Chinese and Russian, the term "legal capacity" refers to "legal capacity for rights", rather than "legal capacity to act"'.

Although taken by surprise, as were most other delegates, the IDC managed to mobilize the EC, which speaking on behalf also of Australia and Canada, raised their concern at this last minute addition and asked for this to be revisited once the eighth Ad Hoc Committee meeting resumed for discussion and approval of the final text to be presented by the drafting group.[20] Also, the IDC made a statement explaining the implications of this footnote and supporting the proposal made by

---

[19] 'Article 12 Equal recognition before the law 1. States Parties reaffirm that persons with disabilities have the right to recognition everywhere as persons before the law. 2. States Parties shall recognize that persons with disabilities enjoy legal capacity on an equal basis with others in all aspects of life. 3. States Parties shall take appropriate measures to provide access by persons with disabilities to the support they may require in exercising their legal capacity. 4. States Parties shall ensure that all measures that relate to the exercise of legal capacity provide for appropriate and effective safeguards to prevent abuse in accordance with international human rights law. Such safeguards shall ensure that measures relating to the exercise of legal capacity respect the rights, will and preferences of the person, are free of conflict of interest and undue influence, are proportional and tailored to the person's circumstances, apply for the shortest time possible and are subject to regular review by a competent, independent and impartial authority or judicial body. The safeguards shall be proportional to the degree to which such measures affect the person's rights and interests. 5. Subject to the provisions of this article, States Parties shall take all appropriate and effective measures to ensure the equal right of persons with disabilities to own or inherit property, to control their own financial affairs and to have equal access to bank loans, mortgages and other forms of financial credit, and shall ensure that persons with disabilities are not arbitrarily deprived of their property.'

[20] The Ad Hoc Committee decided to establish an open-ended drafting group tasked with ensuring uniformity of terminology throughout the text of the draft convention and harmonizing the versions in the official languages of the United Nations.

the EC to revisit this issue.

Finally, following additional intensive advocacy work between August and December 2006, the footnote was removed at the resumed eighth Ad Hoc Committee meeting held on December 13th 2006.

It is clear to everyone that the full implementation of Article 12 will be a long lasting process, which is already reflected in some interpretative declarations (which in fact are to be considered reservations) made upon ratification by Australia[21] and Mexico[22] and upon signature by Egypt.[23]

The implementation of article 12 will not only mean the elimination of the guardianship system, but the establishment of a fully-fledged, supported decision making system providing different alternatives that respond to the different types of support required by persons with disabilities.

3.7. LIBERTY AND SECURITY OF PERSON (ARTICLE 14)

The main objective which the IDC had set itself for this article was that nobody could be deprived of their liberty based on her/his disability. This should protect persons with disabilities especially from situations of civil commitment, in which persons with disabilities are deprived of their liberty based on perceived danger to themselves or to others.

While the wording which resulted from the working group text already included most of this, there was a long paragraph dealing with the different provisions which would need to be taken into account in situations of deprivation of liberty. The IDC argued that there was no need to have these detailed provisions, as these were already foreseen in existing human rights treaties, in particular in the International Covenant on Civil and Political Rights (ICCPR).

The IDC argued that the right way to address these issues would be to ensure that these general provisions apply to persons with disabilities on an equal basis with others. The only addition which would need to be made was to take

---

[21]   'Australia recognizes that persons with disability enjoy legal capacity on an equal basis with others in all aspects of life. Australia declares its understanding that the Convention allows for fully supported or substituted decision-making arrangements, which provide for decisions to be made on behalf of a person, only where such arrangements are necessary, as a last resort and subject to safeguards;'

[22]   '...Accordingly, affirming its absolute determination to protect the rights and dignity of persons with disabilities, the United Mexican States interprets paragraph 2 of article 12 of the Convention to mean that in the case of conflict between that paragraph and national legislation, the provision that confers the greatest legal protection while safeguarding the dignity and ensuring the physical, psychological and emotional integrity of persons and protecting the integrity of their property shall apply, in strict accordance with the principle pro homine.'

[23]   'The Arab Republic of Egypt declares that its interpretation of article 12 of the International Convention on the Protection and Promotion of the Rights of Persons with Disabilities, which deals with the recognition of persons with disabilities on an equal basis with others before the law, with regard to the concept of legal capacity dealt with in paragraph 2 of the said article, is that persons with disabilities enjoy the capacity to acquire rights and assume legal responsibility ('ahliyyat al-wujub) but not the capacity to perform ('ahliyyat al-'ada'), under Egyptian law.'

into account the disability-specific needs through the provision of reasonable accommodation. This argumentation was successfully made at the seventh Ad Hoc Committee meeting and is clearly reflected in paragraph 2 of Article 14.[24]

The other discussion on this article was how to phrase the prohibition of deprivation of liberty based on disability. The initial working group text stated '… any deprivation of liberty shall be in conformity with the law, and in no case shall be based on disability'. However, during the fourth and fifth Ad Hoc Committee meetings, the EC and other States proposed wording stating that the deprivation of liberty could not be 'solely' or 'exclusively' based on disability. IDC strongly opposed this, stating that this was a clear example of discrimination based on disability. Replacing 'disability' by 'gender' was an easy way to show how unacceptable such wording in fact was. This argumentation was successfully made and the final wording states that '… and in no case shall the existence of a disability justify a deprivation of liberty'.[25]

The most recent report of the UN Special Rapporteur on Torture and other forms of cruel, inhuman and degrading treatment or punishment,[26] Manfred Nowak, confirms the implications of this and other articles when it states that 'the acceptance of involuntary treatment and involuntary confinement runs counter to the provisions of the Convention on the Rights of Persons with Disabilities'.

Nonetheless, the reservation made by Australia[27] upon ratification of the Convention, shows that the full implementation of this article, requiring the revision of most mental health laws, is another of the big challenges of this Convention.

3.8. FREEDOM FROM TORTURE OR CRUEL, INHUMAN OR DEGRADING TREATMENT OR PUNISHMENT (ARTICLE 15)

Article 15 proved to be a short but controversial article. The main part of the article was basically reiterating existing provisions of the International Covenant on Civil and Political Rights (ICCPR) and the Convention against Torture and other Forms of cruel, inhuman or degrading treatment or punishment (CAT), including

---

[24] 'States Parties shall ensure that if persons with disabilities are deprived of their liberty through any process, they are, on an equal basis with others, entitled to guarantees in accordance with international human rights law and shall be treated in compliance with the objectives and principles of the present Convention, including by provision of reasonable accommodation.'

[25] '1. States Parties shall ensure that persons with disabilities, on an equal basis with others: a) Enjoy the right to liberty and security of person; b) Are not deprived of their liberty unlawfully or arbitrarily, and that any deprivation of liberty is in conformity with the law, and that the existence of a disability shall in no case justify a deprivation of liberty'.

[26] UNCHR 'Interim report of the Special Rapporteur on torture and other cruel, inhuman or degrading treatment or punishment', (28 July 2008) UN Doc. A/63/175.

[27] 'Australia recognizes that every person with disability has a right to respect for his or her physical and mental integrity on an equal basis with others. Australia further declares its understanding that the Convention allows for compulsory assistance or treatment of persons, including measures taken for the treatment of mental disability, where such treatment is necessary, as a last resort and subject to safeguards;'

the reference to medical or scientific experimentation without free and informed consent.

The working group text produced in early 2004 had included a specific reference proposed by the IDC in paragraph 2 to protect persons with disabilities from forced interventions or forced institutionalization aimed at correcting, improving or alleviating any actual or perceived impairment.

This was, however, for many States a very controversial statement. Some States thought that this was not a matter of torture, but more appropriate for the article on violence and abuse, while others thought that forced medical interventions and forced institutionalization should be permitted in accordance with appropriate legal procedures and safeguards, as foreseen in many national and some regional and international instruments.

The paragraph on protection from forced interventions aimed at correcting, improving or correcting or alleviating any actual or perceived impairment was moved to a new article (see below on article 17).

Finally, during the last Ad Hoc Committee meeting and following a proposal from the Latin American and Caribbean Group, the first paragraph of article 15 was rephrased and brought into line with the ICCPR instead of the CAT.[28] The main reason for this was that the ICCPR applies also to private institutions, while the CAT is restricted to public settings.

The implementation of this article should mean the inclusion of disability-relevant forms of torture (electroshocks and other involuntary treatments) in the different national mechanisms which prevent these situations from occurring.

3.9. PROTECTING THE INTEGRITY OF THE PERSON (ARTICLE 17)

At first sight, this short article might give the impression of being rather irrelevant, but this is far from being the case. There was not such an article in the working group text. As mentioned above, it was during the debate on the article on torture during the fifth Ad Hoc Committee meeting when it was decided that the issue of involuntary treatments deserved to be treated in a separate article.

The new draft article[29] started with a paragraph protecting the integrity of

---

[28] '1. No one shall be subjected to torture or to cruel, inhuman or degrading treatment or punishment. In particular, no one shall be subjected without his or her free consent to medical or scientific experimentation.'

[29] Draft Article 17 'Protecting the integrity of the person 1. States Parties shall protect the integrity of the person or persons with disabilities on an equal basis with others. 2. States Parties shall protect persons with disabilities from forced interventions or forced institutionalization aimed at correcting, improving or alleviating any actual or perceived impairment. 3. In cases of medical emergency or issues of risk to public health involving involuntary interventions, persons with disabilities shall be treated on an equal basis with others. [4. States Parties shall ensure that involuntary treatment of persons with disabilities is: (a) Minimized through the active promotion of alternatives; (b) Undertaken only in exceptional circumstances, in accordance with procedures established by law and with the application of appropriate legal safeguards; (c) Undertaken in the least restrictive setting possible, and that the best interests of the person concerned are fully taken into account; (d) Appropriate for the person and provided without financial cost to the individual receiving the treatment

persons with disabilities on an equal basis with others. It had a second paragraph, the purpose of which was to protect persons with disabilities from forced treatment and institutionalization aimed at correcting, improving or alleviating any actual or perceived impairment.

More problematic were the third and fourth paragraphs of the new draft article. The third paragraph stated that persons with disabilities should be treated on an equal basis with others in medical emergencies or situations of risk to public health involving involuntary interventions. When dealing with this article, many States indicated that this would cover situations of epidemic or pandemic, but there was great concern within the IDC that this wording would become the excuse for undertaking involuntary interventions related to mental health issues.

However, the biggest problem came with the last proposed paragraph, which, when dealing with involuntary treatment of persons with disabilities, established safeguards and conditions for this. The IDC strongly opposed this, arguing that the Convention should prohibit any involuntary interventions on the basis of disability instead of legitimizing these interventions by establishing procedural safeguards.

When starting the eighth Ad Hoc Committee meeting, it became increasingly clear that there were basically two options. The first option, proposed by New Zealand, was to have a short sentence focusing on protection of integrity, a wording based on existing international human rights law, which led to the inclusion of the words 'mental and physical'.[30] The second option was to accept the article comprising the four paragraphs.

For the IDC, the second option was unacceptable and advocacy started to support the New Zealand proposal. However, it was not an easy decision for the IDC to accept the disappearance of the explicit protection 'from forced intervention and institutionalization aimed at correcting, improving or alleviating any actual or perceived impairment'. The basis for this decision was the analysis by the IDC that the short Article 17 protecting integrity, combined with the reference to informed consent in Article 25 on health,[31] as well as with Article 12 on legal capacity, provided an adequate protection against any form of forced intervention.

Another option was suggested by the European Community, using language similar to that used in Article 14. The proposed text stated 'States Parties shall protect the integrity of the person/persons with disabilities on a basis of equality with others and ensure that in no case shall the existence of disability justify an involuntary intervention or institutionalisation.' The problem with this proposal was that it implied that there could be involuntary treatment (not related to disability), something unforeseen in any human rights treaty and which would have set a dangerous precedent.

---

or to his or her family.]'

[30] 'Article 17 Protecting the integrity of the person; Every person with disabilities has a right to respect for his or her physical and mental integrity on an equal basis with others.'

[31] 'States Parties shall: (...) d) Require health professionals to provide care of the same quality to persons with disabilities as to others, including on the basis of free and informed consent by, *inter alia*, raising awareness of the human rights, dignity, autonomy and needs of persons with disabilities through training and the promulgation of ethical standards for public and private health care.'

When adopting this article during the last session of the eighth Ad Hoc Committee meeting, the first attempt to approve the proposed single line article failed, as the EC proposed the full text as an alternative. The Chair submitted the EC proposal to a vote and it was objected to by a number of States which led to the final withdrawal by the EC of its proposal and the reconsideration and adoption of the current one line article.

Undoubtedly, full implementation of Article 17 will prove to be another challenge and we have already seen a first reservation to Article 17 presented by Australia upon ratification the Convention.[32]

On a more positive note, the above quoted statement from the Special Rapporteur indicates that involuntary treatment runs counter to the provisions of the Convention and shows the way States should implement the Convention in this area.

3.10. INTERNATIONAL COOPERATION (ARTICLE 32)

This was one of the most controversial articles from the beginning to the very end of the process. It was also almost the only article where a clear North-South division could be seen.

The main arguments against a specific article were presented by the EC from the outset of the process:

- This is a Convention on human rights and not on social development;
- A human rights Convention establishes obligations between a country and its citizens, not among countries;
- No other human rights Convention includes a specific article on international cooperation.

Regarding the second argument, it was instead argued that, even if human rights treaties are different than any other international treaties (environmental, disarmament) which establish obligations among States, human rights treaties are still treaties in which States oblige themselves towards all other States Parties.

While not necessarily spelt out, the fear of developed countries about the financial implications of the Convention were clearly present. Some Governments saw this whole debate as a discussion on whether this Convention was a human rights or a social development Convention, the latter being the preferred approach by some developing countries. Many Southern countries also insisted that cooperation should not only be seen as North-South, but also South-South, as the issue was not so much about funding but about technical cooperation.

The position of the IDC was in favour of a specific article. The IDC agreed that the lack of international cooperation should not be used as an excuse for inaction by developing countries. At the same time, this article should serve the very important purpose of putting disability on the development cooperation agenda,

---

[32]   'Australia recognizes that every person with disability has a right to respect for his or her physical and mental integrity on an equal basis with others. Australia further declares its understanding that the Convention allows for compulsory assistance or treatment of persons, including measures taken for the treatment of mental disability, where such treatment is necessary, as a last resort and subject to safeguards;'

where it had been mostly absent.

Once the discussion about having or not an article had been won by those who supported a specific article, the main outstanding issue was how to define the relationship between the obligations of the State and the existence or not of international cooperation. The solution presented in final paragraph 2 was the result of a long (mainly political) discussion during the last Ad Hoc Committee meeting.[33]

In any case, the important contribution of this article is that from now on, the rights of persons with disabilities will need to be taken into account in all international cooperation programmes, including international development programmes.

3.11. NATIONAL IMPLEMENTATION AND MONITORING (ARTICLE 33)

From a general human rights treaty perspective, Article 33 is an important innovation, as no other human rights treaty had so far dealt with national implementation and monitoring.

The working group document produced in early 2004 already included a text on this issue, but some Member States argued that the Convention should not include an article on this, and that national implementation and monitoring should be left to States Parties. The main argument was that States are organized in very diverse ways and that the Convention should not be too prescriptive on this issue.

To overcome that objection, the phrase 'in accordance with their system of organization' was added to the initial paragraph of the article. In the same line, a reference to 'one or more focal points' was suggested by Canada, aiming to reflect the reality of federal and other strongly decentralized States.

Another discussion held was whether the monitoring of the implementation of the Convention should be done by a disability-specific body (which would need to be created in most countries) or a general human rights body (already existing). The final wording in paragraph 2 ('maintain, strengthen, designate or establish') allows for diverse options.[34]

Other States would have liked to see a specific reference to the Paris Principles,[35] which guide the establishment and functioning of the national human rights institutions, but others opposed this idea, as these Principles have not been accepted by all States. Ultimately, a general reference to the principles relating

---

[33] 'Article 32 International cooperation (...) 2. The provisions of this article are without prejudice to the obligations of each State Party to fulfil its obligations under the present Convention.'

[34] 'Article 33 National implementation and monitoring (...) 2. States Parties shall, in accordance with their legal and administrative systems, maintain, strengthen, designate or establish within the State Party, a framework, including one or more independent mechanisms, as appropriate, to promote, protect and monitor implementation of the present Convention. When designating or establishing such a mechanism, States Parties shall take into account the principles relating to the status and functioning of national institutions for protection and promotion of human rights.'

[35] UNGA Res 48/134 Paris Principles 'National institutions for the promotion and protection of human rights' (20 December 1993) A/RES/48/134.

to the status and functioning of national institutions for protection and promotion of human rights was included, which is an obvious reference to the Paris Principles.

3.12. THE COMMITTEE ON THE RIGHTS OF PERSONS WITH DISABILITIES (ARTICLE 34 AND FF)

The debate on the establishment or not of a Committee (a Treaty monitoring body) was influenced throughout the process by the ongoing review of the functioning of the existing United Nations human rights treaty monitoring bodies. This wider discussion led to a postponement of this important debate within the proceedings of the Ad Hoc Committee, which only at the very end dealt with this very important issue.

At the seventh meeting of the Ad Hoc Committee (January-February 2006), the Office of the High Commissioner on Human Rights (OHCHR) presented a document, which had been commissioned by the Ad Hoc Committee, on this issue.[36] The presentation of this document led to a first debate and also resulted in a first proposal prepared by the Chair.

During this Ad Hoc Committee meeting, many countries favoured some innovations to the system, which should reflect the lessons learnt from the current functioning of the system. However, quite surprisingly, at the end of the seventh Ad Hoc Committee meeting, a number of countries spoke against the establishment of a specific body, favouring as an alternative to mainstream disability in the existing Treaty bodies. This was strongly opposed by many States, including the EC, as well as the IDC, for which the establishment of a Treaty monitoring body had always been considered a fundamental issue, without which the whole Treaty would be rather useless.

Due to the pressure by all interested parties, the opposition to a specific Treaty monitoring body was gradually withdrawn, allowing therefore the start of the debate on the composition and role of the Committee.

Most of the elements related to the composition of the Committee are rather standard. The main discussion was around the participation of persons with disabilities in the Committee. The IDC had proposed that all (or at least the majority) of Committee members should be persons with disabilities themselves. Some States suggested referring to experts and persons with disabilities, which would have given the impression that persons with disabilities could not be experts. The final wording refers to 'experts with disabilities', but does not include any reference to numbers.[37]

The social development versus human rights debate also had a slight impact

---

[36]   UNCHR 'Expert paper on existing monitoring mechanisms, possible relevant improvements and possible innovations in monitoring mechanisms for a comprehensive and integral international convention on the protection and promotion of the rights and dignity of persons with disabilities' (18 January 2006) UN Doc. A/AC.265/2006/CRP.4.

[37]   '4. The members of the Committee shall be elected by States Parties, consideration being given to equitable geographical distribution, representation of the different forms of civilization and of the principal legal systems, balanced gender representation and participation of experts with disabilities.'

when the discussion was held on the location of the Committee. Some countries proposed that the Committee should be based in New York (the key location of all social development activities of the UN) and not in Geneva, where most of the UN human rights related work is done.

The final text does not specify where the Committee will meet, but in the meantime, it is clear that the Committee on the Rights of Persons with Disabilities will meet in Geneva like all other human rights treaty bodies (the CEDAW Committee had been based in New York but moved at the beginning of 2008 to Geneva).

In terms of the consideration of reports by the Committee on the Rights of Persons with Disabilities (Article 35 of the CRPD), proposals had been made for this process to be more effective, by, for instance, giving the Committee a more proactive role in the process, but finally, the provisions are very similar to other Conventions.

3.13. CONFERENCE OF STATES PARTIES (ARTICLE 40)

Article 40 on the Conference of States Parties might, at first glance, look a rather standard article. There is, however, one big potential difference between the way the Conference of States Parties under the Convention will function when compared to other meetings of States Parties under the previous international treaties. Meetings of States Parties for other human rights Conventions have one single purpose, the election of the members of the respective Treaty bodies. Yet, in the case of the Convention, its Article 40 allows the Conference of States Parties to 'consider any matter with regard to the implementation of the Convention.'[38]

The first Conference of States Parties held, on 31 October and 3 November 2008, has set an important precedent for the Conference to undertake substantive work, beyond the biennial (re)election of the members of the Committee on the Rights of Persons with Disabilities.

The IDA CRPD Forum (the structure that has replaced the International Disability Caucus) has been advocating for this approach and has presented concrete proposals on how this could be done. It has also requested the active participation of NGOs in the Conference of States Parties, in line with its level of participation throughout the negotiation process of the Convention.

3.14. THE OPTIONAL PROTOCOL TO THE CONVENTION

The initial proposal presented by the Chair included the competence by the Committee to receive individual communications and to undertake enquiry procedures in the main text of the Convention, allowing the States to opt out of these provisions.

However, a number of countries usually opposed to individual communications required these provisions to be taken out of the text and that a separate Optional Protocol be drafted. This happened at the beginning of the eight Ad Hoc

---

[38]   '1. The States Parties shall meet regularly in a Conference of States Parties in order to consider any matter with regard to the implementation of the present Convention.'

Committee meeting, which was to become the final meeting.

The IDC held the opposite view and so did several Member States (including the EC). Nevertheless, it was felt that not accepting the demands for an Optional Protocol could produce a blockage to the process.

It was finally agreed to produce an Optional Protocol to be presented to the General Assembly alongside the Convention. This Optional Protocol, to be ratified (or not) separately from the Convention, includes individual communications and enquiry procedures.

As of August 2009, forty-three of the sixty-five countries that have ratified the Convention have also ratified the Optional Protocol.

4. CONCLUSIONS

The ratification and implementation of the Convention on the Rights of Persons with Disabilities is undoubtedly a great opportunity and a challenge that States all over the world must respond to, to ensure that persons with disabilities can fully enjoy their human rights.

The fact that less than thirty months after the adoption of the Convention, already sixty-five States have ratified the Convention and an additional seventy-seven States have signed it, seems to indicate that this Convention is quickly heading towards universal ratification.

As Article 4 of the Convention clearly indicates, to implement the Convention adequately, one of the first key measures to be taken by States Parties is to undertake a systematic revision of current legislation in order to align it with the Convention.[39] This applies also to those States Parties whose legislation establishes that, upon ratification of an international treaty, this treaty becomes part of the national legislation. While in most of these countries the content of the international treaty, once ratified, would supersede any national legislation which is inconsistent with it, this does not replace the need to systematically abolish/amend any legislation, regulation or other norms which are not in line with the Convention.

It is important that representative organizations of persons with disabilities are fully involved in this process of legislative reviews and reforms, as is clearly stated in Article 4 paragraph 3.[40]

The Convention clearly prohibits any form of discrimination on the ground

---

[39] 'Article 4 General Obligations 1. States Parties undertake to ensure and promote the full realization of all human rights and fundamental freedoms for all persons with disabilities without discrimination of any kind on the basis of disability. To this end, States Parties undertake: a) To adopt all appropriate legislative, administrative and other measures for the implementation of the rights recognized in the present Convention; b) To take all appropriate measures, including legislation, to modify or abolish existing laws, regulations, customs and practices that constitute discrimination against persons with disabilities; (…).'

[40] '3. In the development and implementation of legislation and policies to implement the present Convention, and in other decision-making processes concerning issues relating to persons with disabilities, States Parties shall closely consult with and actively involve persons with disabilities, including children with disabilities, through their representative organizations.'

of disability in any area of life and guarantees equal protection and benefit of the law to all persons with disabilities. In order to ensure effective implementation of the Convention, this implies the adoption of national anti-discrimination legislation covering all areas of life, in those countries where such legislation does not yet exist, or its revision in those countries where it exists.

In the EC context, this also means the adoption of new anti-discrimination legislation by the European Community, which needs to be in full compliance with the Convention and which could complement it, among others, by setting more prescriptive accessibility standards and timelines. Moreover, the EC has more powerful competences than the UN to ensure the effective compliance by EC Member States with all the provisions of the Convention.

There can be no doubt that the full implementation of the Convention implies very important challenges for States Parties. In many areas, completely new solutions need to be found which fully respect the human rights of persons with disabilities. States Parties should not approach these challenges by making reservations to the Convention or adopting interpretative declarations which seek to modify the content of the Convention, but by accepting the fact that their existing legislation needs to be changed and by seeking assistance in doing so, when required.

Moreover, it is important that the United Nations as well as regional bodies (the European Community and Council of Europe in the European context) (re) focus their priorities in order to provide the adequate support to States to meet the objectives set out in the Convention.

IMPLEMENTING THE DIGITAL ACCESSIBILITY AGENDA OF THE UN CONVENTION ON THE RIGHTS OF PERSONS WITH DISABILITIES: CHALLENGES AND OPPORTUNITIES

Axel Leblois[1]

1. BACKGROUND TO THE UN CONVENTION ON THE RIGHTS OF PERSONS WITH DISABILITIES

The Convention on the Rights of Persons with Disabilities was adopted by the United Nations General Assembly on 13 December 2006. A major milestone for all persons living with disabilities around the world, it is the eighth Universal Convention on Human Rights and the first of this millennium. The Convention defines, for the first time, in a comprehensive international legal instrument the rights of more than 600 million people with life-altering disabilities, two thirds of which live in developing countries. 142 countries have signed it and 65 have ratified it as of August 2009, making it an enforceable legal instrument as of 5 May 2008.

The European Community, in addition to its twenty-seven members, has signed it, and is now considering adopting its Optional Protocol. Upon ratification by the European Community and its members, the Convention will have a profound influence on the evolution and mainstreaming of the rights of persons with disabilities across European countries. European Disabled Persons Organizations and Delegations to the United Nations were also very much involved with the Preparatory Committee formed by the United Nations General Assembly and charged to write the text of the Convention. It included a number of representatives of persons living with disabilities, which explains the very practical and comprehensive nature of its text. It is, therefore, no surprise that the Convention is seen by many in Europe as a universal blueprint to advance their rights and promote programmes aimed at ensuring the full participation in society and quality of life of persons living with disabilities.

---

[1] Trustee and Executive Director, G3ict, Global Initiative for Inclusive ICTs. An Advocacy Initiative of the United Nations Global Alliance for ICT and Development. G3ict, <www.g3ict.com>, A 501 (3) c not for profit corporation, 50 Hurt Plaza, suite 806, Atlanta, GA 30303.

2. ICT ACCESSIBILITY: AN IMPORTANT ASPECT OF THE RIGHTS OF PERSONS WITH DISABILITIES

In that regard, one of the most innovative components of the Convention relates to dispositions concerning ICTs – Information and Communications Technologies – both from a digital accessibility and assistive technologies standpoint. Indeed, for the first time, ICT accessibility is defined as an integral part of Accessibility Rights, on par with accessibility to the physical environment and transportation:

> 'To enable persons with disabilities to live independently and participate fully in all aspects of life, States Parties shall take appropriate measures to ensure to persons with disabilities access, on an equal basis with others, to the physical environment, to transportation, *to information and communications, including information and communications technologies and systems...*' (Article 9).

This article implies that all dispositions of the Convention which include the terms 'accessible' or 'accessibility' cover ICT applications and services, and involves a far reaching implication for industry, governments and civil society.

It is useful, to fully understand the scope and intent of Article 9 of the Convention, to step back and look at the extraordinary impact that ICTs have on society today all around the world. As of mid-2008, ICT demographics are as follows:

- 850 million personal computers
- 1 + billion Internet users (includes shared and mobile access)
- 1.3 billion telephone land lines
- 1.5 billion TV sets
- 1.8 billion text messaging users
- 2.4 billion radios
- 2.7 billion mobile phones, probably 3 billion by year-end, or one mobile phone for two human beings on the planet!

This recent explosion of new media and communications tools obviously presents significant and pervasive risks of exclusion, as it opens many new opportunities. Not surprisingly, four of the eight fundamental principles of the Convention have direct implications for the accessibility to ICTs:

1. Non-discrimination
2. Full and effective participation and inclusion in society
3. Equality of opportunity
4. Accessibility

3. SOLUTIONS ADOPTED BY THE CONVENTION

In application of those principles, the Convention addresses issues related to ICTs head-on by bringing very clear and specific answers to two fundamental challenges:

- How to ensure that barriers are not created by ICTs?
- How to better use ICT-based assistive solutions for persons with disabilities?

As a result, fourteen out of the first thirty-two non-procedural articles of the Convention mention obligations of states regarding Information and Communication Technologies. Very appropriately, given the rapid evolution of technologies and diverse ICT environments found around the world, its text defines obligations in relation to desired outcomes by application areas, rather than in specific technical terms. So, it is the responsibility of States, civil society and industry to define the required solutions in their respective jurisdictions. Meanwhile, affordability is stated as an important underlying objective across the text of the Convention, to ensure that accessible and assistive technologies are not priced out of reach for persons living with disabilities, who are often economically disadvantaged.

There are three main types of mandates which States will have to consider as they align their local legislation, regulations and programmes with the dispositions of the Convention:

1. Accessibility Mandates for: E-Government, Employment, Education, Media and Internet, Consumer Services, Freedom of Expression, Emergency Response, Personal Mobility, Independent Living, Culture and Leisure.
2. Facilitating Assistive Technologies for Education, Emergency Response, Personal Mobility and Independent Living.
3. Supporting ICT Vendors R & D via public-private partnerships for assistive technologies applied to Personal Mobility and Independent Living.

A far-reaching disposition of the Convention is that accessibility mandates cover private sector services, including ICT-based services: 'The state must insure that private entities that offer facilities and services to the public take into account the accessibility of those services' (Article 9 – also mentioned in Article 21).

Finally, it is important to note that the Convention directly addresses important issues related to the development of ICT products and services. It mandates States to:

1. 'Promote the design, development, production and distribution of accessible information and communications technologies and systems at an early stage, so that these technologies and systems become accessible at minimum cost.' (Article 9).
2. 'To undertake or promote research and development of universally designed goods, services, equipment and facilities, as defined in article 2 of the present Convention, which should require the minimum possible adaptation and the least cost to meet the specific needs of a person with disabilities, to promote their availability and use, and to promote universal design in the development of standards and guidelines.' (Article 4).
3. States are also encouraged to establish international cooperations to support new technology.

4. OBLIGATION TO ENACT LEGISLATION AND REGULATIONS FOR ICTS

The Convention presents various degrees of mandates in its text. It stipulates, however, that States Parties to the Convention shall undertake (Article 4):

To adopt all appropriate legislative, administrative and other measures for the implementation of the rights recognized in the present Convention;

To take all appropriate measures, including legislation, to modify or abolish existing laws, regulations, customs and practices that constitute discrimination against persons with disabilities;

To take into account the protection and promotion of the human rights of persons with disabilities in all policies and programs.

In regard to ICTs, however, limited references are available to policy makers to implement the many dispositions of the Convention covering ICT accessibility. In addition, two critical factors add to the complexity of the task at hand:

- The speed of change due to technological developments;
- The mandate to policy makers to ensure that accessible and assistive ICT products are available and affordable.

It is G3ict's main objective to promote regulatory, programmatic and legislative good practices, allowing ICT vendors to deliver the required product features at an affordable cost. This means leveraging global market dynamics which are driven by standards, favouring mass production, economies of scale, competition, all of which ultimately result in lower prices and better interoperability. The greatest risk may, in fact, be a high level of market fragmentation caused by the adoption of heterogeneous standards at country level, and disregarding international standards.

5. OPPORTUNITIES FOR DEVELOPING NATIONS

The availability and affordability of assistive and accessible technologies remains a difficult challenge in most developing nations. However, the advent of new accessibility standards and of open sources assistive solutions for computers, the potential of mobile phones, smart phones and PDAs to carry alternative human interfaces, the development of free web based resources, and the emergence of low cost producers of assistive devices in emerging economies, open the door to the adoption of innovative low cost solutions. This is particularly important to facilitate the employment of persons with disabilities otherwise unable to live a productive life. From an economic and social development standpoint, returns on investment on accommodations for persons with disabilities make great sense: the rates of unemployment among persons living with disabilities are typically a multiple of the national average in any country. Even in developed nations, numbers are staggering: as an example, 70% of blind adult persons in the United States are unemployed. Yet, many blind persons have full productive lives in all categories of employment, including engineering and executive positions. Well crafted programmes, as suggested by the Convention, to subsidize assistive technologies in education and the workplace can go a long way to provide equal access and opportunities to persons with disabilities, while enhancing economic development at large.

6. FACILITATING A SUCCESSFUL IMPLEMENTATION OF THE CONVENTION IN MATTERS OF ICT ACCESSIBILITY AND ASSISTIVE TECHNOLOGIES

In December 2006, shortly before the Convention was adopted by the United Nations General Assembly, the United Nations Global Alliance for ICT and Development provided the institutional framework to develop a multi-stakeholder initiative involving industry, civil society and the public sector to specifically address those issues. The European Commission has participated in this initiative since its inception. G3ict, the 'Global Initiative for Inclusive ICTs' was launched with the mission: 'To facilitate the implementation around the world of the Digital Accessibility Agenda defined by the Convention on the Rights of Persons with Disabilities'. It does so by:

- Raising awareness and good practice sharing among stakeholders involved in the implementation of the Convention;
- Promoting Harmonization and Standardization in cooperation with Standards Development Organizations, product developers and government procurement agencies;
- Benchmarking the progress of the digital accessibility of countries with the 'Digital Accessibility and Inclusion Index for Persons with Disabilities';
- Developing a live interactive 'Toolkit for Policy Makers' developed jointly with the International Telecommunications Union.

The latter project is an important initiative to advance the implementation of the Digital Accessibility Agenda of the Convention. Its objective is to provide practical resources to policy makers implementing the Convention on the Rights of Persons with Disabilities, focusing on what works, and what does not, with case studies on policy and programmes from around the world and all appropriate references to international ICT accessibility standards.

The Table of Contents of the Toolkit includes the following resources:

1. Overview of the Convention and its dispositions covering ICTs;
2. Demographics and statistical analysis of the worldwide installed base of ICT devices and telecommunications services;
3. Background on ICT Accessibility Issues;
4. Resource guide for policy making by core areas of ICTs;
5. Product development and design;
6. Public procurement policies;
7. Promoting assistive ICTs for persons with disabilities;
8. Regional and international cooperation;
9. Role of local governments;
10. Country assessment and policy development model.

Its publication date on-line is set for 2009, with live interactive features allowing all stakeholders to file commentaries and suggestions. Its format will be based upon an accessible wiki with links to useful resources. Leading academic, public and private organizations involved in accessibility issues are contributing both contents and editorial support to the Toolkit and Index, including the International Telecommunications Union, IBM, the National University of Ireland Galway, the European Commission, the National Council on Disability, the Royal National Institute for the Blind, the World Blind Union, ICDRI, the Assistive Technologies Industry Association, the Basque Regional Government, Even Grounds, WGBH, NPR, Telework, CATEA, RERC, Politecnico di Milano, the Italian Government, CIFAL Atlanta, W2i, POWERS PYLES SUTTER & VERVILLE PC, the DAISY Consortium.

G3ict would like to express its sincere gratitude to all parties involved for their active participation, continuing support, and intellectual contribution to this endeavour and welcomes the contribution and participation of all organizations or governments interested to support the implementation of the digital accessibility agenda of the Convention on the Rights of Persons with Disabilities.

7. BIBLIOGRAPHY

Convention on the Right of Persons with Disabilities. Full text available at: <http://www.un.org/disabilities/index.asp> (accessed 5 August 2009).

ICT Task Force on Disability-related Concerns, United Nations Economic and Social Commission for Asia and the Pacific (ESCAP), *Report on Access to Information and Communication for persons with disabilities with a special reference to the Biwako Millennium Framework*, August 2007, available at: <http://www.dinf.ne.jp/doc/english/twg/ict/index.html> (accessed 5 August 2009).

G3ict, the Global Initiative for Inclusive Information and Communication Technologies, *The Accessibility Imperative, implications of the Convention on the Rights of Persons with Disabilities for Information and Communication Technologies,* November 2007, available at: <www.g3ict.com> (accessed 5 August 2009).

Cynthia D. Waddell, *The Growing Digital Divide in Access for People with Disabilities: Overcoming Barriers to Participation*, commissioned in 1999 by The National Science Foundation and the U.S. Department of Commerce for the first national White House conference on the digital economy. Selected for re-publication for the World Economic Development Congress and World Bank/IMF 1999 Summit, available at: <http://www.icdri.org/CynthiaW/the_digital_divide.htm> (accessed 5 August 2009).

Cynthia D. Waddell, *Meeting Information and Communications Technologies Access and Service Needs for Persons with Disabilities.* This background paper was originally prepared for the seminar 'Sharing Experience on Best Practices and Services for People with Disabilities', held on 17 September 2007 in Geneva, Switzerland. This paper has been updated and includes the addition of the Arab

Region based on presentations at the first Arab Regional Conference on Sharing Experience on Best Practices in ICT Services for Persons with Disabilities held in Cairo, Egypt, 13-15 November 2007. It was presented at the ITU Regional Workshop on 'ICT Accessibility for Persons with Disabilities in the African Region' held in Lusaka, Zambia (July 15-16, 2008). Available via <www.g3ict.com> (accessed 5 August 2009).

Ennio V. Macagnano, *'A National Accessibility Portal for South Africa: Innovative application of ICT for Disability in the developing world'* in A. Pruski and H. Knops (eds), *Assistive Technology: From Virtuality to Reality*, (IOS Press, 2005).

Social Development Department in partnership with the Human Development Network's Social Protection, Disability & Development team, *Social Analysis and Disability: A Guidance Note: Incorporating Disability-Inclusive Development into Bank-Supported Projects,* (World Bank, 2007), available at: <http://siteresources.worldbank.org/DISABILITY/Resources/280658-1172606907476/SAnalysisDis.pdf> (accessed 5 August 2009).

From Exclusion to Equality: Realizing the rights of persons with disabilities, Handbook for Parliamentarians on the Convention on the Rights of Persons with Disabilities and its Optional Protocol, (United Nations, 2007), 96. Also available at: <http://www.un.org/disabilities/default.asp?id=212> (accessed 5 August 2009).

European Commission, Accessibility in ICT procurement, *eAccessibility Country Information, available at:* <http://www.einclusion-eu.org/SearchSpecial.asp?Definitions=YES&IDFocus0=10&IDFocus3=1&CountryID=AT,BE,DE,DK,ES,FI,FR,GR,IE,IT,LU,NL,PT,SE,UK,CZ,EE,HU,LT,LV,PL,SI,SK,MT,CY&MenuID=170> (accessed 5 August 2009).

Access IT, website of the National Disability Authority of Ireland providing guidelines for Legislation and Policy, available at: <http://accessit.nda.ie/managing-accessibility/legislation-and-public-policy> (accessed 5 August 2009).

eInclusion@EU, *Learning Examples: Accessible Procurement Toolkits Denmark, Canada and USA: Description and Synopsis*, 6, available at: <http://www.einclusion-eu.org/ShowAnalysisReport.asp?IDFocusAnalysis1=17> (accessed 5 August 2009).

Hajime Yamada, *Recent ICT Accessibility Related Activities in Japan*, 19 June 2008, at Open Seminar of Information Accessibility in the World, Tokyo, available at: <http://www.jtc1access.org/additional.htm> (accessed 5 August 2009).

Andi Snow-Weaver, *Recent Activities in the US: TEITAC Outcomes*, 19 June 2008, at Open Seminar of Information Accessibility in the World, Tokyo, Japan, available at: <http://www.jtc1access.org/additional.htm> (accessed 5 August 2009).

AN INTRODUCTION TO THE AUSTRIAN FEDERAL DISABILITY EQUALITY ACT

Anthony Williams[1]

1. A SHORT HISTORY

The Austrian Federal Disability Equality Act[2] was adopted by the Austrian parliament in 2005 and came into force on 1 January 2006. The adoption of the Act was preceded by intensive discussions with the social partners, federal ministries, various other stakeholders and representatives of organizations of people with disabilities, in which the aspirations, fears and unresolved issues were discussed. One of the main fears of trade and industry was the potential cost of compliance with the new legislation. The experience of nearly three years has shown that this fear is unfounded due to the pragmatic approach taken in the legislation.

2. SCOPE OF LEGISLATION

In the context of private law, the focus of this legislation is on consumer protection. In terms of public law, the act covers the entire *federal* administration as well as the local authorities. The legislation only applies to *federal* laws, not to provincial laws. As Austria is a Federal Republic, the legislative competences are divided between the Federal state and the provinces. However, as consumer protection, tenancy law, etc. are federal matters, many important areas are covered. In addition, many of the Austrian provinces have already adopted appropriate provincial legislation prohibiting the discrimination of disabled persons in areas that fall within their competence. The Austrian Federal Disability Equality Act does not cover discrimination in the world of work, since this has been regulated in a separate Act.[3]

---

[1] Dr. Anthony Williams is Head of the European Desk at the *Österreichische Arbeitsgemeinschaft für Rehabilitation* (Austrian National Council of Disabled Persons). This paper is based on a presentation to the Disability Intergroup meeting at the European Parliament in Brussels on 5 November 2008.

[2] *Bundesgesetz über die Gleichstellung von Menschen mit Behinderungen*, available at: <www.oeziv.org/download/060126181331.pdf> (accessed 25 August 2009).

[3] Act on the Employment of People with Disabilities, *Behinderteneinstellungsgesetz*, BGBl. Nr. 22/1970, last amended by Federal Law Gazette I Nr. 82/2005.

3. DEFINITION OF DISABILITY

The provisions in the Federal Disability Equality Act consider disability to be 'the effects of a not merely temporary impairment of a bodily, mental or psychological function or an impairment of the functions of the senses, which makes participation in the life of society more difficult'. 'Not merely temporarily' is taken to mean a period of time likely to be in excess of six months.

The target group is broadly defined: not only disabled persons themselves but certain groups of relatives are also covered by the protection afforded by the Act (e.g. parents, relatives [grandparents, siblings, spouses] and life partners who provide care to the disabled person).

4. DEFINITION OF DISCRIMINATION

The Austrian Federal Disability Equality Act differentiates between direct and indirect discrimination. The contents of these terms are analogous to Article 2, 2 (a) and (b) of the Employment Equality Directive 2000/78/EC[4] *with the exception that indirect discrimination is also prohibited with regard to 'properties of arranged/constructed areas of life'* (translation by author). These could be structural (steps, lack of sanitary installations, too small door widths, etc.), communication-technical (non-blind appropriate software design, lacking tactile, acoustic or optical orientation guides) or other barriers that prevent disabled persons accessing or being supplied with goods and services, which are available to the public.

5. DEFINITION OF ACCESSIBILITY / DISPROPORTIONATE BURDEN

The Austrian legislation does not define accessibility *per se*. It takes the approach of investigating whether indirect discrimination exists in a specific situation. Therefore, for example, the provisions of the Austrian Federal Disability Equality Act apply in the case of a disabled person attempting to access a shop, in order to conclude a legal transaction as consumer.

6. ASSESSMENT OF REASONABLENESS

In many cases, the discrimination experienced by people with disabilities is different from discrimination experienced by other groups of people, in that it is linked to structural or other barriers, the removal of which may necessitate considerable financial expenditure. When the issue of discrimination because of barriers is examined, an assessment has to be made as to whether the removal of the barriers would cause an unreasonable burden. If barriers cannot be removed, because the costs are unreasonably high, a decisive improvement in the situation still has to be attained for the person concerned, so that a situation which is as close as possible to actual equal treatment exists.

---

4   Directive 2000/78/EC establishing a general framework for equal treatment in employment and occupation, [2000] O.J. L303/16.

The issues to be considered in determining whether a barrier must be removed include:

- Cost of removing the barrier;
- Economic capability of the person/company contesting the discrimination;
- Public subsidies granted for the appropriate measure;
- The time between the coming into force of this Act and the asserted discrimination (therefore implying that the longer one had to correct the discriminating circumstances, the more likely it is that the discriminating circumstances have or could have been already been eliminated);
- The effect of the discrimination on the general interests of the community protected by the Act.

7. BURDEN OF PROOF

When drafting the Act, legislators considered that the (allegedly) discriminated person generally has a weaker economic position than the alleged discriminator (e.g. a company). For this reason the Austrian Federal Disability Equality Act foresees *a partial reversal of the burden of proof* for the benefit of the allegedly discriminated person. However, the reversal is not complete; *the allegedly discriminated person must show a probable cause,* i.e. he/she must substantiate the claim, in order for it to be heard.

8. SPECIAL SUBSIDIES FOR ACCESSIBILITY WORKS

The Federal Social Welfare Office (a disability specific department of the Federal Ministry of Social Affairs and Consumer Protection[5]) offers non-repayable funds to subsidize investments/refurbishments with the objective of achieving accessibility for offices, doctors' offices, pharmacies, shops, public transport vehicles (taxis), etc.. However, these subsidies are not available for public authorities, which are expected to bear the cost of providing accessibility themselves.

These measures to ensure accessibility can be for instance:

- Installation of a ramp;
- Installation of a lift;
- Installation of disability parking spaces;
- Installation of a guide system for blind and severely sight impaired persons;
- The disability adequate modification of workplaces, training locations, and sanitary rooms;
- Measures for the disability adequate adaptation of vehicles of transport companies.

A prerequisite for receiving a subsidy is that the proposed adaptations comply with the Austrian Standards on accessibility. Furthermore, an appropriate financial contribution of the applicant (50% of the entire costs) is required. The sub-

---

[5]   Austrian Federal Ministry for Social Affairs and Consumer Protection: <http://www. bmsk.gv.at/cms/site/liste.html?channel=CH0032> (accessed 5 August 2009).

sidy is limited to a maximum of € 50,000. The subsidy is not granted to cover the cost of adapting newly erected buildings.

The experience in Vienna is that few shops have taken advantage of these subsidies, and that they have been mainly granted to adapt doctor's offices and pharmacies. The total expenditure in 2007 was € 550,000.

9. PROGRESSIVE ACTION PLAN (*ETAPPENPLAN*)

The provisions of the legislation also apply to buildings, and specifically structural barriers, and to public transport. There are, however, transitional provisions: claims for *damages* on the grounds of discrimination due to existing structural barriers or barriers in transport can, in principle, only be asserted as of 1 January 2016. Before that, discrimination in this area can only be contested if the building, the transport infrastructure, facility or vehicle is new, or if the barriers were built unlawfully. However, claims on the grounds of discrimination due to existing structural barriers or barriers in transport can be asserted, if the cost of the removal of the barriers does not exceed a certain amount (as from 2007: € 1,000, as from 2010: € 3,000, as from 2013: € 5,000).

The operators of transport infrastructures, facilities or public transport are obligated, after hearing the Austrian National Council of Disabled Persons, to draw up a plan (*Etappenplan* – Progressive Action Plan) on the reduction of barriers for all infrastructures, facilities or public means of transport. This plan must foresee progressive realization.

Intensive discussions have taken place between the experts of the Austrian National Council of Disabled Persons and the operators of the above facilities. These discussions also resulted in the drawing up of a checklist, in order to check the accessibility of structures and means of transport. The Austrian Federal buildings are well on the path to full accessibility. In addition, some regional Austrian railways have already fully implemented the plans, whilst others are doing so progressively. This means for railways, for instance, that operators must adapt platform heights, lifts, introduce or adapt guide systems for blind and severely sight impaired persons, install ramps in order to facilitate access to the means of transport, install disability compliant sanitary installations in trains, install signal devices to the train driver/conductor, etc.

10. MANDATORY RECONCILIATION PROCEDURE BEFORE FILING A LAWSUIT

Basically, any disabled person who feels they have been the victim of discrimination has the option of bringing a court case. During the discussions before adoption of the legislation, the fear was expressed that such a possibility would result in a flood of lawsuits against transport companies, shops, service providers, etc.

The result of intensive discussions on this topic was the introduction of *compulsory* mediation as the central element of mandatory conciliation proceedings, before the Federal Social Office, *prior* to the enforcement of entitlements in court.

The procedure is as following:

The disabled person who feels they have been the victim of discrimination can file his/her complaint at the Federal Social Welfare Office. Direct recourse to the competent court is initially not possible. The Federal Social Welfare Office opens a reconciliation procedure, where the alleged discrimination is discussed with the alleged discriminator. The remit of the Federal Social Welfare Office is to find a solution between the parties, and to examine whether public funds can be used, for instance, to abolish structural discriminations. Mediators can also be called in to facilitate finding a solution. The alleged victim of discrimination is only entitled to file an action before a competent court if no solution can be found within three months. The Federal Republic of Austria bears the costs (including mediators, sign language interpreters, etc.) of this low-threshold procedure. The average duration of the reconciliation procedure is 56 to 60 days. The statistics relating to the procedure are very interesting, and show that approximately 60% of the cases can be resolved out-of-court, approximately 19% of the cases cannot be resolved, and 13% of the cases are withdrawn.

Topic	Quantity	%	Recon-ciliation with settlement	%	Recon-ciliation without settlement	%	Application withdrawn	%
Structural barriers	67	84.8	41	87.2	13	86.6	8	80.0
Communication technology barriers	2	2.5	1	2.1	-		1	10.0
Technical barriers	10	12.6	5	10.6	2	13.3	1	10.0
	79	100.0	47	100.0	15	100.0	10	100.0
%	100.0		59.49		18.99		12.66	

The experience gained during the almost three years since the Austrian Federal Disability Equality Act came into force, has shown that the competent courts are not overburdened by discrimination cases.

Part II

Annual Review of European Law and Policy

THE EUROPEAN UNION

1. BACKGROUND TO THE EUROPEAN UNION AND DISABILITY

The European Union (EU) is, in essence, an economic and political partnership between twenty-seven European states based on a series of treaties. The Treaty of Rome, establishing the European Economic Community (EEC), was signed in 1957. This was followed by the Merger Treaty in 1965, the Single European Act in 1987, the Treaty on European Union creating the EU in 1992, the Treaty of Amsterdam in 1997 and the Treaty of Nice in 2001.

The European Economic Area (EEA) is made up of all European Union Member States as well as Norway, Iceland and Liechtenstein. These latter countries enjoy free trade with the EU and they, in turn, track EU policy and adopt some equivalent legislation.

The European Community (EC) is that part of the Union with the greatest legal capacity to act at European level and is thus of major interest in the disability field. (The other two parts of the EU are concerned with foreign policy and justice and home affairs.) In a number of limited areas of policy, Member States have delegated the power to make legislation to the EC in order to implement the broad policy goals outlined in treaties. In other areas of policy, the EC and the individual Member States share competence. Unless Member States have expressly delegated some level of competence to the EC in a given policy area, they maintain full powers and responsibilities at the national level. However, this does not prevent Member States from electing to cooperate in policy areas (which do not fall within the competence of the EC). Member States have chosen to do this in the areas of employment and social inclusion. They work together in what is known as the Open Method of Coordination (OMC) to identify common objectives and establish common instruments, as well as comparative tools. The work of the OMC provides a particularly fruitful source of research and information on disability in Europe.

The work of the Community is undertaken by Member States working together through common institutions. One such institution, the European Commission, was established to identify the collective European public interest and to initiate legislation accordingly. Crucially, the Commission has the sole prerogative to propose legislation. The proposal may then be adopted by the Council of Ministers, which represents the interests of Member States. If the Commission decides not to come forward with a legislative proposal, then no legislation can be enacted. The Commission is, therefore, strategically placed to take a lead on the disability issue and has done so often in the past.

The European Commission also acts as 'Guardian of the Treaties' and polices Member States in their application of Community law. It can investigate alleged infringements and deliver a reasoned opinion should it find that a state has failed to fulfil a Treaty obligation. If the Member State does not rectify this situation, the Commission may bring the matter before the Court of Justice under Article 226 of the EC Treaty.

The work of the Commission is divided between 41 Directorates-General and overseen by a Secretariat General. The Directorate General of Employment, Social Affairs and Equal Opportunities houses three Units of particular relevance to disability policy:

- Unit for the Integration of People with Disabilities;[1]
- Unit for Equality, Action against Discrimination: Legal questions;
- Unit for Action against Discrimination, Civil Society.[2]

These three Units consider the impact of the Commission's work on people with disabilities and look at what actions would be appropriate for the Commission to take in this area. In addition, these Units provide funding for applied research in the areas of disability and non-discrimination across the European Union and they support networks of legal and academic experts, which will be discussed later in this section. These networks are important sources of knowledge about the status of persons with disabilities in Europe.

The European Parliament is directly elected by the citizens of Member States and engages in a co-decision process with the Council on the enactment of secondary legislation. Parliamentary committees may undertake 'own initiative' reports and ask Parliamentary questions of the Commission in order to influence policy on issues of concern to them. Within the Parliament, there is an informal grouping of MEPs who are committed to advancing disability rights and concerns in the Parliament's work. This 'Disability Intergroup' prepares the ground for its members and helps them to mainstream disability back into the work of the core committees in the Parliament. The recent work of this 'Disability Intergroup' will be considered later in this section.

The Council of the European Union is jointly responsible with the Parliament for adopting legislation and making policy decisions.[3] The Council consists of Ministers from each Member State with responsibility for the items on the agenda of a given meeting. The Presidency of the EU is held for a six-month period by each Member State and, during this period, the Presidency chairs and sets the agenda for Council meetings. There is now an accepted tradition whereby each Presidency holds a major Ministerial meeting on disability. This is a source of major political guidance in the field of disability. It often presages further work within the EU on disability.

European legislation can take a number of forms. 'Regulations' are directly applicable and are automatically part of national law. 'Directives' on the other hand require implementation by national legislation. 'Directives' allow a certain

---

[1] European Commission 1995-2009, <http://ec.europa.eu/social/main.jsp?catId=429&langId=en>, last accessed 16 February 2009.

[2] European Commission 1995-2009, <http://ec.europa.eu/social/main.jsp?catId=423&langId=en>, last accessed 8 April 2009.

[3] Council of the European Union 2009, <http://www.consilium.europa.eu/>, last accessed 16 February 2009.

margin of appreciation to respect the local legal culture of Member States. They also usually allow a period of time for transposition into domestic law. Should a Member State fail to implement a 'Directive' at all or correctly, there is a mechanism according to which this may become the subject of litigation in the European Court of Justice.[4] A 'Decision' is also a binding instrument, but only binds those to whom it is addressed. 'Recommendations' differ in that they are not binding, although they do have some political weight. 'Communications' usually explain the position of a European institution on a particular matter or piece of draft legislation. All of these types of instruments have been and will continue to be used in the disability context in the EC.

The competence of the European Community to take action to address disability discrimination comes from Article 13 EC (which was added by the Treaty of Amsterdam in 1997). To a limited extent it can be analogised to the 14th Amendment of the US Constitution, which enables Federal civil rights statutes to be enacted. Article 13(1) EC states:

> Without prejudice to the other provisions of this Treaty and within the limits of the powers conferred by it upon the Community, the Council, acting unanimously on a proposal from the Commission and after consulting the European Parliament, may take appropriate action to combat discrimination based on sex, racial or ethnic origin, religion or belief, disability, age or sexual orientation.

Any legislation proposed under this competence requires unanimity in the European Council before it can be adopted. Article 13 EC provided the legal competence to adopt Directive 2000/78, establishing a general framework for Equal Treatment in Employment and Occupation (hereinafter the Employment Equality Directive 2000) and Directive 2000/43 implementing the principle of equal treatment between persons irrespective of racial or ethnic origin (hereinafter the Racial Equality Directive 2000).[5]

The European Commission has now tabled a proposal for a Council Directive on implementing the principle of equal treatment between persons irrespective of religion or belief, disability, age or sexual orientation (2008), which seeks to extend the principle beyond the sphere of employment and occupation.[6] If adopted it could mark the gradual and patchwork emergence of a European equivalent of the Americans with Disabilities Act - ADA (1990).

The Treaty of Amsterdam also includes a Declaration regarding persons with a disability. This Declaration expressly provides that EC institutions shall take account of the needs of persons with disabilities in drawing up measures under Article 95 (formerly 100a) of the EC Treaty. Article 95 EC relates to the harmonization of legislation to break down barriers to give effect to the internal

---

[4]   Under certain conditions the European Court of Justice can hold (provisions) of Directive to be directly applicable, or find a State liable for failing to (properly) implement a Directive within the given time limit.

[5]   Directive 2000/78, establishing a general framework for Equal Treatment in Employment and Occupation, [2000] O.J. L303/16, Directive 2000/43 implementing the principle of equal treatment between persons irrespective of racial or ethnic origin, [2000] O.J. L180/22.

[6]   COM(08) 436 final.

market. The Declaration thus adds impetus to the mainstreaming of disability issues in all areas of EC policy.

The European Disability Forum (EDF) was established in its current form in 1996 to represent the interests of citizens of the European Union with disabilities and ensure these are taken into account in the formulation of all relevant EU policy and initiatives.[7] The EDF is a non-governmental and independent organization governed by disabled people and their families. Its voting members consist of one national council of disabled people per each EU or EEA country, European non-governmental organizations of disabled persons and/or parents of disabled persons, as well as European non-governmental organizations working for disabled persons with members in the majority of EU or EEA countries. EDF has been intimately involved in the evolution of the EC treaty competence in combating discrimination on the grounds of disability and, later, the Employment Equality Directive.[8] The Forum continues to produce influential reports, research and proposals and monitors relevant EU initiatives on an ongoing basis.

During the European Year for Equal Opportunities 2007, and to mark its tenth year of fighting for disability rights, the EDF ran a hugely significant campaign entitled '1million4disability'. It collected over one million signatures 'for a European Union in which disabled people's rights are protected through effective legislation, combating all forms of discrimination and guaranteeing the full inclusion of 50 million citizens with disabilities in the European society.'[9] This provided huge impetus to the drafting of a new proposed Directive by the European Commission in 2008 (covering goods and services).

In short, the European Commission takes the lead responsibility and initiative on disability matters across a broad range of fields in the EU. EDF adds the voice of European civil society. The European Parliament Intergroup plays a significant role in ensuring that EU law and policy moves in the right direction and the Council adds strategic direction and takes the ultimate political responsibility to enact fresh legislation in co-decision with the Parliament. All actors are important in the disability context.

---

[7] For a full history see EDF, 'European Disability Forum Ten Years of History' (2007), <http://cms.horus.be/files/99909/MediaArchive/pdf/EDF10YearsOfHistory.pdf>, last accessed 15 April 2009.

[8] Quinn, 'International Disability Law Seminar' (Beijing, 2007), <http://www.nuigalway.ie/law/documents/working/1%20CPS%202007.pdf>, last accessed 16 February 2009.

[9] European Disability Forum 2007, <www.1million4disability.eu>, last accessed 9 March 2009.

1.1. STRATEGIC DIRECTION

1.1.1. Foundations: The European Community Disability Strategy of 1996[10]

A New European Community Disability Strategy was adopted in 1996.[11] It was based explicitly on the equal opportunities model. Its inspiration was the Standard Rules on the Equalization of Opportunities for Persons with Disabilities, adopted by the United Nations in 1993.[12] This Strategy laid the policy foundations for future strategies and developments in the area of disability in the EC. The Strategy envisioned a society that is open and accessible to all. It advocated for the need to focus on the identification and removal of barriers preventing individuals with disabilities from achieving equality of opportunity and full participation in all aspects of social life. The Strategy recognized that the primary responsibility for action lies with the individual Member States and acknowledged that a truly accessible society may require significant attitudinal changes, especially in employment.

The Strategy was operationalized as follows. Firstly, the Strategy recognized the EC's role in improving co-operation among Member States and fostering the effectiveness of disability policies. It noted that this could be fulfilled through the identification and exchange of good practice and the improved collection and use of comparative information. To this end, the Commission set up an important High Level Group (HLG) of Member States' Representatives, which offers a forum for the Commission and Ministries with responsibility for disability across the EU, to reflect on future priorities and collaboration.[13] The HLG focuses on empowerment, mainstreaming the disability perspective in policy, the removal of societal barriers to participation and addressing public opinion on equal opportunities.[14] Although it acknowledges that responsibility for domestic policy lies with the Member States themselves, the HLG seeks to encourage good practice and cooperation. It is also entrusted with the task of identifying and comparing the various approaches to the implementation of disability policy in Member States. The HLG has become particularly engaged on the issue of conclusion and implementation of the United Nations Convention on the Rights of Persons with

---

[10] European Commission 1995-2009, <http://ec.europa.eu/employment_social/soc-prot/disable/com406/index_en.htm>, last accessed 16 February 2009.

[11] Communication of the Commission on Equality of Opportunity for People with Disabilities - A New European Community Disability Strategy COM (96) 406 final. This was endorsed in a Resolution of the Council and of the Representatives of the Governments of the Member States meeting within the Council of 20 December 1996 on equality of opportunity for people with disabilities, [1997] O.J. C12/1.

[12] General Assembly resolution, 'Standard Rules on the Equalization of Opportunities for Persons with Disabilities', UN doc. A/RES/48/96, <http://www.unhchr.ch/huridocda/huridoca.nsf/(Symbol)/A.RES.48.96.En?Opendocument>, last accessed 16 February 2009.

[13] European Commission 1995-2009, <http://ec.europa.eu/employment_social/soc-prot/disable/hlg_en.htm>, last accessed 17 February 2009.

[14] As per Section II of the Resolution of the Council and of the Representatives of the Governments of the Member States meeting within the Council of 20 December 1996 on equality of opportunity for people with disabilities, [1997] O.J. C 012/1.

Disabilities (see below).

Secondly, the 1996 Strategy acknowledged that it is important for the voices and experience of individuals with disabilities to be involved in the development of the Strategy. Accordingly, steps were taken to support advocacy groups and ensure greater access to information as well as opportunities for participation. The Commission engages in regular dialogue with the European Disability Forum, so that people with disabilities can express opinions and concerns and are involved in the planning, monitoring and evaluation of changes in policies. This adds an important 'reality check' to the thinking of the Commission on disability.

Thirdly, the Strategy aimed to mainstream disability into all policy forma-tion. This entails examining the impact of legislation on people with disabilities and revising any elements, which may create or reinforce barriers to equality of opportunity and/or full participation in all aspects of life. The Commission's Unit for the Integration of People with Disabilities organizes regular Interservice Group meetings of civil servants from all relevant Directorates-General. The In-terservice Group allows for discussion of draft legislative proposals before they are published and reviews them in light of the rights of persons with disabilities.

1.1.2. Current Strategy: The European Disability Action Plan 2003-2010[15]

The European Disability Action Plan carries forward the 1996 Strategy. It is grounded on mainstreaming of disability issues, achieving full application of the Employment Equality Directive 2000 (see below) and launching the debate on future anti-discrimination strategy. The EU Disability Action Plan 2003-2010 aims to provide for equality of opportunity for individuals with disabilities. This objective has been strengthened and reinforced by the signing by the European Communities and its Member States of the United Nations Convention on the Rights of Persons with Disabilities in 2007.

Every two years the Commission identifies priority areas of intervention under the Action Plan on the basis of an assessment of the situation of people with disabilities during the previous two-year phase. The 2006-2007 phase prioritized the inclusion of people with disabilities in the labour market, ensuring quality support and care services, accessibility of mainstream goods and services and increasing the EU's analytical capacity in order to promote independent living.[16]

Following a situation analysis and consultations with Member States and other stakeholders, the current phase of the Plan (2008-2009) identified the issue of accessibility as the key priority.[17] Actions to achieve this relate both to 'inclu-sive participation through accessibility' and the 'full enjoyment of fundamental rights'.

The Plan notes that 'accessible goods, services and infrastructures are es-sential to sustain non-discriminatory and inclusive forms of participation in many aspects of everyday life in an ageing society, along with the elimination of bar-riers to education and to the labour market.' The priority actions are designed to

---

[15]   COM(03) 650 final.

[16]   COM(05) 604 final.

[17]   Situation of disabled people in the European Union: the European Action Plan 2008-2009, COM(07) 738 final, <http://ec.europa.eu/employment_social/index/com_2007_738_en.pdf>, last accessed 16 February 2009.

achieve such accessibility and commit to consolidating the Commission's analytical capacity to support accessibility. The Plan also prioritizes the implementation of the new UN Convention on the Rights of Persons with Disabilities and the proposal of a new anti-discrimination directive to complement the Community's legislative framework in that regard. A new Action Plan is in preparation to cover the period of 2010 onwards.

1.2. LEGISLATIVE MEASURES

1.2.1. Non-Discrimination Legislation: Directive 2000/78 establishing a general framework for Equal Treatment in Employment and Occupation[18]

The principal EC anti-discrimination legislation in the field of disability is Directive 2000/78 establishing a general framework for Equal Treatment in Employment and Occupation (the Employment Equality Directive). This is not a disability-specific legal instrument on disability discrimination. It co-mingles disability discrimination with discrimination on other grounds such as religion or belief, sexual orientation, age and covers both public and private sector employment. The Directive introduces an obligation on employers to make 'reasonable accommodation' for employees with disabilities.

As part of the Commissions' role as 'Guardian of the Treaties', it studies national legislation of Member States to ensure this fulfils the directive's requirements. In cases of suspected infringement, a 'letter of formal notice' will be sent. If no adequate reply is received within two months, this 'letter' will be followed by a 'reasoned opinion'. Further failure to respond may result in a formal referral of the case to the European Court of Justice.[19]

In January 2008, the Commission sent reasoned opinions to ten Member States expressing concern over the implementation of the Employment Equality Directive.[20] The main problems identified were the existence of definitions of discrimination at variance to the Directive, excessive limitation on the scope of the domestic legislation and inconsistencies in protections for victims.[21] With particular reference to disability, problems were identified in the domestic implementation of measures relating to 'reasonable accommodation'. For example Estonia was criticized for a failure to enact an obligation to make 'reasonable accommodation', while the reasonable accommodation obligation in Hungary was considered too restricted. The Czech Republic failed, in the Commission's opinion, to ban direct discrimination on the grounds of disability, relying instead on a 'state of health' ground, which does not necessarily cover all workers with a disability. Germany received a letter of formal notice from the Commission,

---

[18]   Directive 2000/78, [2000] O.J. L303/16.
[19]   Europa (January 2008), *The Employment Equality Directive*, Press release Memo/08/69.
[20]   Europa (January 2008), *'Employment' Directive (2000/78/EC): list of Member States to which a reasoned opinion or letter of formal notice will be sent*, Press release Memo/08/68.
[21]   Europa (January 2008), *Commission acts to close gaps in employment equality rules*, Press release IP/08/155.

partly because the relevant national law limits the obligation to make 'reasonable accommodation' to severely disabled workers. Concern was also expressed about the fact that domestic legislation does not cover discrimination with regard to redundancy and that the limitation period for filing a complaint is, at just two months, too short.

1.2.2. Proposal for a Council Directive on implementing the principle of equal treatment between persons irrespective of religion or belief, disability, age or sexual orientation (2008)[22]

As the legal basis for this proposed Directive is Article 13 EC on non-discrimination, unanimity will be required in the European Council before it can be adopted. To date, non-discrimination legislation at EC level concerning persons with disabilities is limited to the sphere of employment (see above).

As previously mentioned, over the last few years the European Disability Forum has held consultations with its members on the need for a comprehensive directive to combat discrimination on the ground of disability in all areas of life. This culminated in their '1million4disability' campaign. In January 2008, it published a renewed proposal for such a directive with an Explanatory Memorandum explaining the necessity for adopting a disability specific directive with such wide coverage (see below). [23]

In 2008, the Commission published the findings of two studies it had commissioned to examine evidence of discrimination outside the labour market. The European Policy Evaluation Consortium completed the first such survey. It emphasized the gaps in the existing legislative framework's protection from discrimination.[24] Furthermore, it provided evidence that the introduction of a comprehensive anti-discrimination regime would not cause undue cost for service providers. The Second Survey was the Special Eurobarometer Survey. It noted that public opinion in the EU is highly supportive of measures aimed at ensuring equal opportunities in employment. It also found that European public opinion is evenly divided on the question whether national anti-discrimination efforts are adequate.[25]

In July 2008, the Commission published its Proposal for a Council Directive on implementing the principle of equal treatment between persons irrespective of religion or belief, disability, age or sexual orientation (Proposed Equal Treatment

---

[22] Proposal for a Council Directive on implementing the principle of equal treatment between persons irrespective of religion or belief, disability, age or sexual orientation, COM(08) 426 final.

[23] Proposal by the European Disability Forum for a Comprehensive Directive Fighting discrimination of Persons with Disabilities (EDF, January 2008).

[24] European Commission Directorate-General Employment, Social Affairs and Equal Opportunities, 'Study on discrimination on the grounds of religion and belief, age disability and sexual orientation outside of employment: Final Report' (June 2008).

[25] European Commission Directorate-General Employment, Social Affairs and Equal Opportunities, 'Special Eurobarometer Survey 296 on discrimination in the EU and European Policy Evaluation Consortium' (July 2008), <http://ec.europa.eu/public_opinion/archives/ebs/ebs_296_en.pdf>, last accessed 16 February 2009.

Directive). If adopted, it will establish a framework for the prohibition of discrimination on these grounds and establish a uniform minimum level of protection within the EC for people who have experienced such discrimination. This proposal seeks to extend the EC's anti-discrimination legislation beyond the sphere of employment and occupation. The proposed Directive prohibits discrimination in the fields of social protection, social advantages, education (in so far as the EC has competence) and access to and supply of public services and goods. The latter protection covers only professional or commercial activities. However, the use of disability and age in the assessment of risk for insurance or banking services is permissible if based on accurate statistical data.[26]

The obligation of 'reasonable accommodation' is addressed in the Employment Equality Directive as follows:

> In order to guarantee compliance with the principle of equal treatment in relation to persons with disabilities, reasonable accommodation shall be provided. This means that employers shall take appropriate measures, where needed in a particular case, to enable a person with a disability to have access to, participate in, or advance in employment, or to undergo training, unless such measures would impose a disproportionate burden on the employer. This burden shall not be disproportionate when it is sufficiently remedied by measures existing within the framework of the disability policy of the Member State concerned.[27]

For drafting purposes, this obligation was housed in a separate article to the non-discrimination provisions. This led some to assume that a failure to provide 'reasonable accommodation' might not amount to discrimination under the Employment Equality Directive. However, if adopted, Article 2(5) of the proposed Directive would remove any room for ambiguity. It would interpret a failure to provide 'reasonable accommodation' as discrimination. This is more in line with the UN Convention on the Rights of Persons with Disabilities, which expressly treats such a failure as a form of discrimination.[28]

Article 4(1)(a) of the proposed Directive stipulates that 'measures necessary to enable persons with disabilities to have effective non-discriminatory access to social protection, social advantages, health care, education and access to and supply of goods and services which are available to the public, including housing and transport, shall be provided by anticipation, including through appropriate modifications or adjustments.'[29] This Article goes on to refer to a 'disproportionate burden' justification – a term ordinarily associated with the principle of 'reasonable accommodation' – and it is unclear whether the article imposes an anticipatory duty with regard to 'reasonable accommodation' or if the anticipatory duty relates to different measures.

If enacted in its present form, Member States would be given two years to transpose the Directive, although obligations to ensure effective access to social protection, social advantages, health care, education and goods and services,

---

[26] Proposal for Equal Treatment Directive, Article 2.
[27] Ibid, Article 5 (Reasonable accommodation for disabled persons).
[28] Ibid, Explanatory Memorandum, 5.
[29] Ibid, Article 4(1)(a).

would not apply until four years after adoption.[30]

On 2 October 2008 the Employment and Social Affairs Ministers of the 27 Member States exchanged views regarding national positions on the proposed Directive.[31] Most Member States favoured a high level of ambition in respect of the scope to be given to the principle of equal treatment under the proposal. The UN Convention on the Rights of Persons with Disabilities was largely acknowledged as an important reference text. Many Member States expressed reservations regarding the legal clarity of the proposal and sought further information as to the financial implications it would have.

At the same time as the Commission introduced the proposed Directive, it published a Communication to the European Parliament, Council and European Economic and Social Committee and the Committee of the Regions on a renewed commitment to non-discrimination and equal opportunities.[32] The Communication seeks to give new impetus to policy dialogue and to make more effective use of all the other policy and financial instruments available. The Communication notes positive findings from its examination of the implementation of the Racial Equality Directive and highlights its support for the further development of the European Network of Equality Bodies (Equinet).[33] This Network facilitates co-operation and information exchange to support uniform and effective implementation of EC anti-discrimination law. The Communication declares a commitment to strengthening policy tools in the areas of awareness raising, non-discrimination mainstreaming, positive action and data collection. Finally, the Communication provides for Commission evaluation and monitoring of these initiatives.

The full text of the proposed Directive is contained in the Annex to the Yearbook.

1.3. THE EC AND INTERNATIONAL LEGAL DEVELOPMENTS

1.3.1. Signature & Conclusion (Affirmation) by the EC of the UN Convention on the Rights of Persons with Disabilities – current progress

The European Community signed the UN Convention on the Rights of Persons with Disabilities in March 2007. Its legal capacity to sign the UN Convention can be derived from a number of Treaty Articles. These were listed in the Commission's Proposal for a Council Decision concerning the conclusion, by the European Community, of the United Nations Convention on the Rights of Persons with Disabilities as Articles 13, 26, 47(2), 55, 71(1), 80 (2), 89, 93, 95 and 285 in conjunction with parts of Article 300 EC.[34]

Article 13 EC relates to discrimination and empowers the Council to take

---

[30]   Ibid, Article 15.
[31]   Council of the European Union (October 2008), *2393rd Council meeting, Employment, social policy, health and consumer affairs*, Press release 13405/08 (Presse 271).
[32]   COM(08) 420 final.
[33]   European Network of Equality Bodies 2008, <http://www.equineteurope.org/>, last accessed 16 February 2009.
[34]   COM(08) 530 final, 2.

appropriate action to combat discrimination based on disability. Article 26 EC allows for the fixing of common customs tariff duties. Article 47(2) EC relates to the harmonization of law in the areas of self-employment and training and access to the professions. Article 55 EC has the effect that legal persons are to be treated the in the same way as natural persons under European law in respect of services. Article 71(1) EC outlines the competence of the EC to establish common rules in relation to international transport, conditions under which non-resident carriers can operate transport services in a Member state, safety measures and 'any other appropriate provisions' in the area of transport. Article 80(2) EC allows the Council to decide on measures relating to air and sea transport. Article 89 EC deals with EC competence to regulate aid granted by Member States. Article 93 EC relates to the harmonization of indirect taxation to ensure the functioning of the internal market. Article 95 EC enables the Council to adopt harmonization measures in order to realize the functioning of the internal market. Following the Treaty of Amsterdam, such measures should consider the needs of persons with disabilities. Article 285 EC provides for the production of statistics necessary for Community activities. Article 300(2) EC provides that a Council decision is the only appropriate legal instrument for the Community to conclude an international normative text. Article 300(3) EC provides that the Council shall only conclude such agreements after consulting with the European Parliament.

On 27 February 2007, the Commission presented a proposal for a Council Decision to sign the UN Convention on the Rights of Persons with Disabilities and its Optional Protocol on behalf of the European Community.[35] By a Council Decision of 20 March 2007, the Council assumed the capacity to sign the Convention on behalf of the Community but issued a declaration stating it would consider the question of signing the Optional Protocol at a later date.[36]

On 30 March 2007, the European Community and twenty-two of its Member States signed the UN Convention on the Rights of Persons with Disabilities. At this time, fifteen Member States also signed the Optional Protocol. As of February 2008, the Convention had been signed by twenty-six Member States.[37]

In June 2007, the German Presidency of the EU hosted a ministerial conference in Berlin on 'Education, Employment, Equal Opportunities - Empowering Persons with Disabilities'.[38] This conference formed part of the calendar of the 'European Year of Equal Opportunities for All' and based its priorities (of education, employment and the promotion of equal opportunities) on Articles 9, 24 and

[35] COM(07) 77 final.
[36] Council Decision 07/7404 on the signing, on behalf of the European Community, of the United Nations' Convention on the Rights of Persons with Disabilities.
[37] Disability High Level Group, 'Report on Implementation of the UN Convention on the Rights of Persons with Disabilities' (May 2008), <http://ec.europa.eu/employment_social/index/hlg_report_en.pdf>, last accessed 16 February 2009.
[38] Conference on 'Education, Employment, Equal Opportunities- Empowering Persons with Disabilities' hosted by the German Presidency of the EU 2007, Berlin, 11-12 June 2007. Federal Foreign Office of the Federal Republic of Germany 2007, <http://www.eu2007.de/en/Meetings_Calendar/Dates/June/0611-BSGV2.html?tkSuche=ajax&globalDatum=01.01.&multiDatum=31.7.&veranstaltungsart=Fachkonferenzen%20und%20Expertentreffen&globalPolitikbereich=&visiblePath=/htdocs/en&>, last accessed 9 March 2009.

27 of the UN Convention on the Rights of Persons with Disabilities. Over 300 politicians, academics, civil servants, social partners and civil society representatives participated. Government delegations acknowledged the importance of the UN Convention and committed to developing policy to ensure its full implementation and to work together in their approach to this. Participants also agreed on the need for the swift ratification of the Convention by Member States.

The German Presidency also took the important initiative to establish an informal Ministerial meeting on disability within the conference. This was welcomed by Member States, which committed to making the meeting an annual event. The preparatory work for these conferences is to be carried out by the High Level Group on Disability.[39] High Level Group reports will, in this way, feed into the deliberations of presidency conferences. The annual informal meeting has the potential to be a key driver of cooperation and for coordination of implementation of the Convention among Member States and at EU level.

The High Level Group on Disability presented its first report on the implementation of the Convention to the second informal ministerial meeting on Disability issues in May 2008.[40] This report outlined the state of play on the signature and ratification of the UN Convention and its Optional Protocol in each of the Member States. It also considered the actions undertaken by Member States to implement and support the UN Convention. The report further considered common challenges and possible solutions identified by Member States and stakeholders in relation to the implementation of the Convention. Among the challenges noted, were the delegation of tasks to multiple actors, the coordination of a monitoring process, resources and the necessary revision of legal framework in line with a human rights based approach.[41] The report called for the development of policy, strategy and legal measures, which conform with the Convention.[42] The Second High Level Group report on the implementation of the Convention was presented in June 2009.[43]

In April 2008, the European Parliament Committee on Employment and Social Affairs took the opportunity to call for the continuation of the process of affirmation of the Convention and Protocol, noting that the proposed Equal Treatment Directive must be compliant with the Convention.[44] In their report to the Commission, the Committee reminded the Council of an earlier call for a European strategy for effective implementation of the Convention and called on the Commission 'to evaluate the need to amend secondary European legislation or to

---

[39] See EDF (June 2007), *Informal ministerial conference on disability: 'the responsibility is on our shoulders', says Vladimir Spidla*, Press release.

[40] First EU Disability High Level Group Report on the UN Convention, (May 2008) <http://ec.europa.eu/social/main.jsp?catId=431&langId=en>, last accessed 15 July 2009.

[41] Ibid, 35.

[42] Ibid, 37.

[43] Second EU Disability High Level Group Report on the UN Convention, (June 2009) <http://ec.europa.eu/social/main.jsp?catId=431&langId=en>, last accessed 15 July 2009.

[44] European Parliament (Committee on Employment and Social Affairs), 'Report on progress made in equal opportunities and non-discrimination in the EU (the transposition of Directives 2000/43/EC and 2000/78/EC)', (April 2008) A6-0000/2008, 10.

adapt the relevant policies'.[45]

On 2 September 2008, the European Commission adopted a proposal for a Council Decision concerning the conclusion, by the European Communities, of the Convention and its Optional Protocol.[46] The full text of this proposal is contained in the Annex to the Yearbook. At a Council Meeting in Luxembourg on 2 October 2008, ministers underlined the importance of the UN Convention on the Rights of Persons with Disabilities, which had been signed by all Member States and was in the process of being ratified by most of them.[47] At this meeting, some delegations expressed a desire for more ambitious measures to combat discrimination on the grounds of disability.

If and when the Community concludes the Convention, the impact will be at least threefold. Firstly, Convention obligations will have to be taken into account in any proposals for Community legislation. Secondly, the European Court of Justice may potentially look to the Convention as an interpretative guide for relevant Community legislation, which comes before it. Thirdly, the Convention should provide a spur for greater coordination among Member States in matters of disability policy.

1.4.   RECENT DEVELOPMENTS IN MISCELLANEOUS FIELDS

In March 2008, the Council adopted a Resolution on the situation of persons with disabilities in the European Union.[48] The resolution is a non-binding instrument issued in response to the Commission's European Action Plan 2008-2009.[49] It supports the recommendations of the Action Plan and calls for the earliest possible conclusion and implementation of the UN Convention on the Rights of Persons with Disabilities. It highlights the European Action Plan's call to address people with disabilities as citizens and active socio-economic actors. The resolution also notes expectations for improved access to goods, services, infrastructure, information and communication technologies employment, education and training. Finally, the importance of the participation of stakeholders is recognized, including cooperation and dialogue with people with disabilities and their organizations, as part of a human rights approach to disability.[50]

In October 2008, the Council adopted Conclusions on the situation of vulnerable adults and their cross-border legal protection.[51] This signals an engagement with one of the most vexed legal and policy questions affecting disability throughout the world – the question of the reform of legal capacity laws. Although Conclusions are not binding, they do carry some political significance. The Conclusions welcome the Hague Convention of 13 January 2000 on the International

---

[45]   Ibid.

[46]   COM(2008) 530 final (1) and (2).

[47]   Council of the European Union (October 2008), *2893ʳᵈ Council meeting, Employment, social policy, health and consumer affairs*, Press release 13405/08 (Presse 271).

[48]   [2008] O.J. C75/1.

[49]   COM(07) 738 final.

[50]   Ibid, 4.

[51]   Council of the European Union (October 2008), *2899ᵗʰ Council meeting, Justice and Home affairs*, Press release 14677/08 (Presse 299), 21.

Protection of Adults,[52] which 'applies to the protection in international situations of adults who, by reason of an impairment or insufficiency of their personal faculties, are not in a position to protect their interests.'[53] The Convention focuses on issues of jurisdiction, recognition of protection measures, the appointment and role of representatives and international co-operation. The Council Conclusions encourage Member States to conclude consultations or procedures for the signature or ratification of the Convention as soon as possible. The Conclusions suggest that additional Community measures be considered further to monitoring the application of the Hague Convention. In December 2008, the Parliament adopted a resolution on the matter requesting the Commission to a propose legislation 'on strengthening cooperation between Member States and improving the recognition and enforcement of decisions on the protection of adults, incapacity mandates and lasting powers of attorney.'[54]

A number of other recent legislative measures have been framed with disability issues in mind. In establishing a European system of integrated social protection statistics (ESSPROS),[55] the Parliament defined social protection as interventions designed to relieve burdens arising from a number of circumstances including disability.[56] ESSPROS establishes common standards and time limits for compiling comparable statistics to be used for the benefit of the Community.

In 2007, the Parliament and Council amended Council Directive 1989/552/EEC on the coordination of certain provisions laid down by law, regulation or administrative action in Member States concerning the pursuit of television broadcasting activities.[57] The objective of the new Directive is the 'creation of an area without internal frontiers for audiovisual media services whilst ensuring at the same time a high level of protection of objectives of general interest, in particular the protection of minors and human dignity as well as promoting the rights of persons with disabilities'.[58] This Directive further obliges Member States to encourage a move towards media services which are accessible to people with a visual or hearing disability and audiovisual commercial communications which are free from discrimination or the promotion of discrimination.[59]

2. ACTIVITIES OF THE EUROPEAN COMMISSION

Web resource: <http://ec.europa.eu/index_en.htm>

---

[52] Hague Convention of 13 January 2000 on the International Protection of Adults, <http://www.hcch.net/index_en.php?act=conventions.pdf&cid=71>, last accessed 16 February 2009.

[53] Ibid, Article 1(1).

[54] 2008/2123 (INI) adopting text A6-0460/2008. This resolution further calls on all Member States 'to accede to the UN Convention on the Rights of Persons with Disabilities, inasmuch as this would serve to enhance the protection of vulnerable adults within the EU.'

[55] Regulation 07/458, [2007] O.J. L113/3.

[56] Ibid, Article 2(b).

[57] Directive 2007/65, [2007] O.J. L332/27.

[58] Ibid, recital 67.

[59] Ibid, Article 3c.

The purpose of this section is to survey the activity of various Directorates General of the Commission within the relevant timeframe. This first volume of the Yearbook also covers some relevant earlier developments in order to offer a baseline of Commission activity in the disability field.

2.1.   DIRECTORATE GENERAL FOR EMPLOYMENT, SOCIAL AFFAIRS & EQUAL OPPORTUNITIES

Web resource: <http://ec.europa.eu/social/home.jsp?langId=en>

This Directorate General is mainly concerned with the creation of more and better jobs, an inclusive society and equal opportunities for all. Effectively, this DG takes the lead on disability issues within the European Commission.

Among its concerns is the low rate of participation of individuals with disabilities in the workplace. The Directorate General also deals with issues of access to quality education and lifelong learning for individuals with disabilities, believing this to promote full participation in society and to improve the quality of life of individuals concerned. Finally, the Directorate aims to provide people with disabilities with the same individual choices and control in their daily lives as all other citizens of the European Union.

As previously mentioned, This DG houses three different units which are directly engaged in disability issues:

1. Unit for the Integration of People with Disabilities Unit,
2. Unit for Equality, Action against Discrimination: Legal Questions,
3. Unit for Action against Discrimination, Civil Society.

2.1.1.   Unit for the Integration of People with Disabilities

Web resource: <http://ec.europa.eu/social/main.jsp?catId=429&langId=en>

This Unit might be considered the core unit of the European Commission on disability issues.

It chairs the Interservice Disability Group, which offers a forum where representatives from the various Directorates-General and Commission Services exchange information and develop proposals for improved cooperation in the field of disability. This group meets every two months.

The High Level Group (HLG) of Member State Representatives on Disability is hosted by this unit. The HLG is critically important in nurturing common European responses, even in some disability fields where, *strictu sensu*, there is no hard EU legal competence.

The Unit also sponsors the Academic Network of European Disability experts (ANED).[60] This Network was established at the end of 2007 to support policy development in collaboration with the Unit. The aim is to develop links between research, policy and practise and inform evidence-based policy. ANED provides a country-by-country analysis of disability law, contacts, networks and

---

[60]   ANED 2009, <http://www.disability-europe.net>, last accessed 16 February 2009.

disability groups and thus enables meaningful comparative European analysis. It is an important source of information on the status of persons with disabilities in Europe. ANED operates by drawing on the expertise of expert contacts and specialized research centres throughout the EU and from across the spectrum of academic disciplines. The Network thus coordinates academic support for European disability policy. For the year 2009, ANED will focus on independent living.

2.1.2. Unit for Equality, Action against Discrimination: Legal Questions

Web resource: <http://ec.europa.eu/social/main.jsp?catId=425&langId=en>

This Unit works on legislation, litigation and research. In the legislative arena, it focuses on the implementation of the Racial Equality Directive and the Employment Equality Directive. This Unit drafts letters to Member States in relation to supposed failures to meet their obligations under these directives. It is also engaged in work on the Proposed Equal Treatment Directive.

As part of its research dimension, this Unit sponsors the European Network of Legal Experts in Anti-Discrimination.[61] At the time of EU enlargement in 2004, this Network replaced three previous specialized networks working on disability, sexual orientation, and racial and ethnic origin and religion. The Network consists of twenty-seven country experts representing each member state with five coordinators (for each ground of race and ethnic origin, religion, disability, age and sexual orientation). The Network provides independent information and analysis on relevant developments in the Member States as well as examples of good practice in protecting against discrimination. The Network has three main productions:

- The European Anti-Discrimination Law Review (containing academic articles, ECJ and ECHR case law updates, national legal developments, etc);
- Country reports;
- Thematic Studies.

In 2008, the Network published issue 6/7 of the European Anti-Discrimination Law Review. [62] In this issue, Sandra Fredman argues that positive duties have the potential to achieve real structural change where sufficient attention is awarded to their structure and enforcement.[63] With regard to legal policy, the 2008 issue discusses the Proposed Equal Treatment Directive and the background to its introduction. The infringement procedures initiated relating to the Employment Equality Directive (as discussed above), are also mentioned. In covering European Court of Justice case law the Review considers the Opinion of Advocate General Maduro and the judgment of the Grand Chamber in the case of *Coleman*

---

[61] European Commission 1995-2009, <http://ec.europa.eu/social/main. jsp?catId=615&langId=en>, last accessed 16 April 2009.
[62] European Network of Legal Experts in the Non-Discrimination Field, 6/7 *European Anti-discrimination Law Review* (2008), <http://ec.europa.eu/social/main. jsp?catId=615&langId=en>, last accessed 1 May 2009.
[63] Fredman, 'Making a difference: the promises and perils of positive duties in the equality field', Ibid, pp. 43-53.

v. Attridge Law, Steve Law.[64] The Review also includes a summary of relevant legislative developments and case law from the Member States.

In November 2008, the Non-Discrimination Unit concerned with Legal Questions held a legal seminar in conjunction with the European Network of Legal Experts in the non-discrimination and gender equality fields to consider the implementation of EC law on equal opportunities and anti-discrimination.[65] With respect to disability, a session was held on 'reasonable accommodation'. The relevant panel considered how the obligation to provide 'reasonable accommodation' is legislated for in different Member States, and whether it would be advisable to extend the duty to provide 'reasonable accommodation' to other areas of discrimination and to grounds other than disability.

2.1.3. Unit on Action against Discrimination, Civil Society

Web resource: <http://ec.europa.eu/social/main.jsp?catId=427&langId=en>

This Unit focuses on raising awareness about fair treatment as a basic right in the European Union. The Unit supports national projects, which raise awareness about the importance of diversity and finances national training seminars in Member States, which focus on non-discrimination and diversity management. The Unit seeks to foster dialogue and strengthen networks between EU-level NGO networks. It funds Equinet, which is a network of bodies designated by Member States to promote and defend equality.[66] The Unit also engages in research and evaluation.

In March 2008, this Unit published a study entitled 'The fight against discrimination and the promotion of equality: How to measure progress done'.[67] The report recommends the creation of a European-level framework of understanding to define indicators. The purpose of a shared system of measurement would be to measure progress in each country. It would also enable a comparative evaluation of the difference in progress levels between Member States. This study envisages the role of the European Union as being one of both direction (through structuring and designing a European-wide survey on discrimination with common indicators) and data production. The study also calls on Member States to have independent authorities measure inequality and the state of progress of anti-discrimination policies.

In June 2008, a special Eurobarometer survey was published dealing with perceptions and experiences of discrimination in the EU.[68] In relation to disabil-

---

[64]   Case C-303/06, *Coleman v. Attridge Law, Steve Law* Judgment of 17July 2008, not yet reported.

[65]   European Commission 1995-2009, <http://ec.europa.eu/social/main.jsp?catId=88&l angId=en&eventsId=132&furtherEvents=yes>, last accessed 17 February 2009.

[66]   Equinet 2009, <http://www.equineteurope.org/>, last accessed 1 May 2009.

[67]   European Commission Directorate-General for Employment, Social Affairs and Equal Opportunities, 'The fight against discrimination and the promotion of equality, How to measure progress done' (March 2008).

[68]   European Commission Directorate-General Employment, Social Affairs and Equal Opportunities, 'Special Eurobarometer Survey 296 on discrimination in the EU

ity, approximately half of Europeans surveyed considered discrimination to be widespread. Of these, those with a disability themselves or who identified themselves as a friend of a person with a disability were most likely to see such discrimination as widespread. The survey also indicated that 2% of respondents were discriminated against on the grounds of disability during the previous 12 months, while 7% stated they had witnessed such discrimination.

In November, the Action against Discrimination, Civil Society Unit published a report on 'Continuing the Diversity Journey: Business Practices, Perspectives and Benefits'.[69] This report considers 'The Small to medium-sized enterprise (SME) business case for diversity', 'Diversity, innovation and productivity', 'Tools for a successful diversity journey' and 'Educating and training business leaders for tomorrow'. The report notes that an inclusion focus can help SMEs recruit and retain talented staff and also fosters product and market innovations. It states that diversity in the workplace fosters creativity and innovation by getting away from situations of like-minded people producing like-minded results. The report discusses the benefits and pitfalls of a EU-wide diversity charter and diversity awards system. It also states that business schools have a crucial role to play in sensitizing future business leaders to diversity issues. It suggests establishing a diversity network of European business schools and companies to contribute to the mainstreaming of diversity and to facilitate cross-sector partnerships and learning.

This Unit also hosts an annual thematic conference. In 2008 this conference was dedicated to communication and awareness raising.[70] The conference aimed to facilitate the exchange of experience and knowledge and inform participants of EU policy in the area. Conference presentations looked at Member State practice in working with young people, local authorities, the media and the business sector. Attention was also devoted to equality bodies and successful communication as well as the design and delivery of communication.

2.2. DIRECTORATE GENERAL FOR HEALTH AND CONSUMER PROTECTION

Web resource: <http://ec.europa.eu/dgs/health_consumer/index_en.htm>

Although competence in the area of health lies primarily with Member States, this Directorate General seeks to improve the health and safety of European Citizens. It looks at the areas in which European legislation can impact on health, for example, product safety and consumer protection. It is tasked with keeping relevant legislation up to date and monitoring implementation in Member States.

---

and European Policy Evaluation Consortium' and 'Study on discrimination on the grounds of religion and belief, age disability and sexual orientation outside of employment: Final Report' (June 2008).

[69] European Commission Directorate-General for Employment, Social Affairs and Equal Opportunities, 'Continuing the Diversity Journey: Business Practices, Perspectives and Benefits' (November 2008).

[70] Communicating Equality and Non-Discrimination in the European Union hosted by the European Commission, Belfast, 5-6 June 2008, <http://ec.europa.eu/social/main.jsp?catId=88&langId=en&eventsId=63>, last accessed 21 May 2009.

Importantly, this DG undertakes considerable work in the area of mental health.

In June 2008, the Directorate General hosted a conference entitled 'Together for Mental Health and Well-being, Communicating Equality and Non-Discrimination in the European Union' in cooperation with the Directorate General for Employment, Social Affairs and Equal Opportunities.[71] Representatives from the European Parliament, the Council, Member State Governments, sectoral organizations in health, education and employment as well as civil society representatives convened at this conference and established a 'European Pact for Mental Health and Well-being'.[72]

The Pact has five thematic priorities relating to the prevention of suicide and depression, combating stigma and social exclusion, mental health in youth and education, mental health in the workplace and mental health in older people. A background consensus document on each of these areas was produced highlighting the relevant data and policies at both European and Member State levels. The Pact commits the conference participants to exchange information and work together to avail of the opportunities and combat the challenges that present themselves in the field of mental health. The Pact is to be implemented through conferences on each priority, taking place during 2009 and 2010.

The conference and Pact follow from the 2005 Green Paper on Mental Health, which called for increased efforts by the EU to raise awareness and facilitate exchange and cooperation on common challenges in the field of mental health.[73]

2.3. DIRECTORATE GENERAL FOR ENERGY AND TRANSPORT

Web resource: <http://ec.europa.eu/dgs/energy_transport/index_en.htm>

This Directorate General manages the work of the European Commission in the interrelated fields of mobility and energy services. It recognizes that individuals with disabilities may require additional assistance in order to travel in a manner that is free from discrimination.

On 26 July 2008, new rules entered into force to ensure that disabled persons and persons with reduced mobility can access transport in a manner comparable to that enjoyed by all other passengers in European airports without discrimination or additional cost.[74] These rules resulted from a 'Regulation concerning the rights of disabled persons and persons with reduced mobility when traveling by

---

[71] Brussels, 13 June 2008, <http://ec.europa.eu/health-eu/news/live_streaming/high-levelmhconf_en.htm>, last accessed 21 May 2009.

[72] European Commission 1995-2009, <http://ec.europa.eu/health/ph_determinants/life_style/mental/docs/pact_en.pdf>, last accessed 12 March 2009.

[73] European Commission Directorate-General on Health and Consumer Protection, 'Green Paper on Improving the mental health of the population: Towards a strategy on mental health for the European Union' (October 2005).

[74] Regulation 1107/2006, concerning the rights of disabled persons and persons with reduced mobility when traveling by air, [2006] O.J. L204/1, Article 18. Articles 3 and 4, which concern prevention of refusal of carriage, derogations and special conditions came into force on 26 July 2007.

air', which was adopted in July 2006. The new rules oblige European airports to provide an appropriate set of services for persons with reduced mobility from the moment they enter the airport until they board, at both the airport of departure and of arrival.[75] The assistance is to be adapted to the individual.[76] A European carrier must provide assistance and may not charge extra for carrying wheelchairs or guide dogs,[77] even if only one port of the journey is within the EU.[78] Article 3 of the Regulation, which came into force in July 2007, prohibits refusal to carry a person on the grounds of disability or reduced mobility.

The President of the European Disability Forum considered the development as:

> a way of rehabilitation of our dignity. Hitherto we have faced different kinds of humiliating barriers and uncertainties in travel such as the requirement for medical certificate for travelling, the denial of travel because we were travelling… alone or with a guide dog, limitation of the number of disabled persons on board and so on, and so on… This regulation is a bridge for all these 50 million citizens of Europe and their families, who have been limited in their choices of movement, to the dynamic, mobile world we live in.[79]

The Regulation also obliges Member States to establish domestic enforcement bodies to ensure the Regulation is implemented.[80] The Regulation also allows for a person affected by a disability or reduced mobility who considers that his or her rights have not been respected to bring the matter to the attention of management of the relevant airport or airline. If unsatisfied with the response, the individual may make a complaint to the national enforcement body.[81]

In 2008, the Commission organized a plenary conference related to Regulation 2006/1107 for national enforcement agencies, airline associations and other interested parties.[82] One of the conclusions reached was that it was necessary for a pan-European workshop to train the trainers foreseen in the Regulation in co-operation with the European Disability Forum. This training took place in April 2008.[83]

Further to the work of this Directorate General in the area, the Commission adopted two proposals for Regulations concerning the rights of passengers when firstly, travelling by sea and inland waterway transport and secondly, in bus and

---

[75] Ibid, Article 7(6).

[76] Ibid, Article 7(7).

[77] Ibid, Article 10.

[78] Ibid, Article 1(2).

[79] European Disability Forum (25 July 2008), *New Regulation Opens Air Space for Persons with Disabilities*, Press release <http://www.edf-feph.org/Page_Generale.asp?DocID=13874&thebloc=18404>, last accessed 16 February 2009.

[80] Ibid, Article 14.

[81] Ibid, Article 15.

[82] 'Acting together to make Regulation 1107/2006 a success' (25 January 2008). Minutes available online at <http://ec.europa.eu/transport/air_portal/passenger_rights/prm/doc/2008_01_25_minutes_en.pdf>, last accessed 16 February 2009.

[83] Minutes available online at <http://ec.europa.eu/transport/passengers/air/doc/prm/2008_03_31_minutes.pdf>, last accessed 16 February 2009.

coach transport in December 2008.[84] The proposals attempt to address difficulties faced in booking a journey or boarding a vehicle or ship. Assistance is to be provided free of charge where the need has been notified to the provider, in advance, and arrival at the terminal or port is at a predetermined time prior to the scheduled departure. The proposals provide that personnel of relevant transport companies, bus terminals and ports should have appropriate knowledge of provision of assistance to disabled persons.

2.4.　DIRECTORATE GENERAL FOR DEVELOPMENT

Web resource: <http://ec.europa.eu/development/index_en.cfm>

The Directorate General for Development initiates and formulates EU policy applicable to developing countries and has endeavoured to mainstream disability issues where appropriate.

In March 2003, the Directorate General issued a 'guidance note on disability and development' explaining how EU delegations and services ought to effectively address disability issues within development co-operation.[85] The European Parliament subsequently adopted a resolution on disability and development, and called on the Commission 'to develop a detailed, technical implementation action plan to implement its Guidance Note'.[86] In an annex to the European Disability Action Plan 2008-2009, the Commission outlined priority actions at the EU level.[87] Improving the mainstreaming of disability issues in development aid was listed as a 2008-2009 priority.[88] The Disability Action Plan refers to this as contributing to the implementation to the UN Convention.

In 2006, the Community established a new financing instrument specifically for development co-operation which notes that respect for human rights is fundamental to long-term development.

Regulation 2006/1905 of the European Parliament and Council establishing a financing instrument for development cooperation includes reference to disability in respect to its sections on health, and also refers to combating discrimination and promoting social inclusion in education, employment and social cohesion.[89]

Article 32 of the UN Convention (International Cooperation) requires that States Parties take appropriate and effective measures to support international cooperation in order to realize the rights enshrined in the Convention. Article 32(1)(a) states that such measures could include, '[e]nsuring that international cooperation, including international development programmes, is inclusive of and accessible to persons with disabilities'. If and when the EC concludes the Convention,

---

[84]　COM(08) 816 final and COM(08) 817 final.
[85]　Available online at <http://ec.europa.eu/development/body/publications/docs/Disability_en.pdf>, last accessed 17 February 2009.
[86]　European Parliament resolution on disability and development, [2006] O.J. C287/336.
[87]　COM(07) 738 final, Annex 6: The EU Action Plan 2008-2009: Actions at EU Level.
[88]　Ibid, Action 4.
[89]　Regulation 1905/2006 of the European Parliament and Council establishing a financing instrument for development cooperation, [2006] O.J. L378/41.

this provision will apply to the EC development aid budget - the single largest in the world.

2.5. DIRECTORATE GENERAL FOR INTERNAL MARKET AND SERVICES

Web resource: <http://ec.europa.eu/dgs/internal_market/index_en.htm>

It is the role of this Directorate General to coordinate Commission policy on the European Single Market. Much of its work focuses on trade in services and financial trade and the removal of unjustified barriers in this area. The impact of this Directorate General's work on people with disabilities is twofold. Firstly, the growth of the internal market can itself be of assistance in opening up new opportunities for all. Secondly, market regulatory (and even deregulatory) measures can effectively sculpt market forces to ensure that they are sensitized to the rights of persons with disabilities.

A groundbreaking 2007 Commission Communication, entitled 'A single market for 21st century Europe', addresses making the Internal Market more responsive to citizens.[90] Although the Communication makes specific reference to disabled persons as consumers whose rights should be upheld, this is not the sole significance of the document in the area of disability. It speaks of avoiding a race to the bottom[91] and of taking action at a European level where 'markets do not deliver' in terms of growth, job creation and consumer welfare.[92] The Communication also demands that the social impacts of market opening and integration be considered, so that resulting benefits are shared by all.[93] This Communication offers a springboard for policy that ensures a floor of equality, non-discrimination and participation be established and that the Internal Market operates to maintain and further these principles.

This Communication views services of general interest as 'vital for the sustainable development of the EU in terms of higher levels of employment, social inclusion, economic growth and environmental quality.'[94] Services of general interest cover a broad range of activities, which are essential for the daily life of citizens and enterprises, for example energy, postal, education and health services. The commission offered the following explanation in an accompanying communication entitled 'Services of general interest, including social services of general interest: a new European commitment'.

Although their scope and organization vary significantly according to histories and cultures of state intervention, they can be defined as the services, both economic and non-economic, which the public authorities classify as being of general interest and subject to specific public service obligations. This means that it is essentially the responsibility of public authorities, at the relevant level, to decide on the nature and scope of a service of general interest.[95]

---

[90]   Com(07) 724 final.
[91]   Ibid, 7.
[92]   Ibid, 11.
[93]   Ibid, 10.
[94]   Ibid, 3.
[95]   COM(07) 725 final, para. 2.

To that effect, services of general interest are those which public authorities consider distinguishable from all other services due to their particular importance. Although regulation of these may interrupt the normal flow of commerce, this is permissible in the greater public interest.

The 2007 Communication speaks of high-quality, accessible, affordable services and an open, competitive internal market as being mutually support-ive. The Communication restates the importance of '[r]especting the diversity of services, situations, and needs and preferences of users'[96] and of promoting universal access. The Commission commits itself to conducting its work in line with these principles and to monitoring related progress under the Lisbon Treaty, if and when it comes into force. Further internal market developments will be watched by many to ensure that the internal market does indeed acquire such a 'human face.'

2.6. DIRECTORATE GENERAL FOR THE INFORMATION SOCIETY AND MEDIA

Web resource: <http://ec.europa.eu/dgs/information_society/index_en.htm>

The 'information society' refers to the modern living and working environment in so far as it is characterized by the use of information and communications tech-nologies (ICTs). The European Commission is dedicated to the further develop-ment of the Information Society and takes the view that some of the opportunities presented by the 'digital revolution' are best exploited at European level. The information society provides new opportunities for persons with disabilities – but they also risk falling further behind unless these new opportunities are intelli-gently exploited.

Related policies and activities are intended to complement and support the actions of national governments. The aims of such EC policies and actions are to improve quality of life and stimulate growth, competitiveness and jobs across Europe. Activities range from basic and applied research into cutting-edge tech-nologies, to stimulating the uptake of these technologies in different sectors of the economy throughout Europe.

In the context of disability, ensuring that the information society is accessi-ble is a high priority. In 2008, considerable attention was afforded to the determi-nation of a suitable approach with regard to e-Accessibility. E-Accessibility seeks to ensure that persons with disabilities and elderly people are able to access Infor-mation and Communication Technology (ICT) on an equal footing with others. It is a component of the e-inclusion policy, which acknowledges that technology has different rates of impact on people due to different levels of wealth, ability, education etc. E-inclusion also tries to use technology to promote and enhance inclusion of socially disadvantaged people and areas.

In November 2008, the Commission published an independent study enti-tled 'Accessibility to ICT products and services by disabled and elderly people'.[97] The study comprises two parts:

---

[96]   Com(07) 724 final, 10.
[97]   For full text see <http://ec.europa.eu/information_society/activities/einclusion/poli-cy/accessibility/com_2008/index_en.htm>, last accessed 16 February 2009.

1. 'Evidence-based analysis for a possible coordinated European approach to web accessibility' and
2. 'Towards a framework for further development of EU legislation or other coordination measures on e-accessibility'.

The first part notes that a dedicated e-Accessibility regulatory body may be useful. Such a body would identify sectoral priorities and engage in implementation and administration activities, following the introduction of EC legislation. A legislative model of initial framing of legislation, followed by the provision of detailed rules on a one-off or ongoing basis, is tentatively suggested.

The second part of the report considers the perspectives of all stakeholders in exploring possible implementation options for a coordinated approach to web accessibility. This part also acknowledges the significant disparities of priority afforded to web accessibility and of progress made among Member States. This part echoes calls for a legislative approach to achieve levels of progress and coordination.

Subsequent to the publication of that report, the Commission published a Communication in December 2008 to the European Parliament, the Council, the European Economic and Social Committee and the Committee of the Regions 'towards an accessible information society.'[98] In it, the Commission articulated the urgency in achieving a more coherent, common and effective approach to e-accessibility, (in particular web-accessibility,) to hasten the advent of an accessible information society. This is acknowledged as a means of overcoming technical barriers and difficulties which people with disabilities face when trying to participate on equal terms in the information society.

An *ad hoc* high-level group dedicated to the matter of e-Accessibility is to be established in 2009 to provide guidance for a coherent European approach and define priority action. The Communication further seeks 100% accessibility of Member States' public websites by 2010 and a rapid transition to updated web accessibility specifications in a common and coherent way. The Commission is to monitor progress and consider the need for European level guidance, including legislative action.

2.7.   EUROSTAT

Web resource: <http://ec.europa.eu/eurostat/>

Eurostat is the EC Statistical Office, which seeks to harmonize statistics throughout Europe and make them comparable. Good and comparable statistics are important in that they provide an evidence base to support rational policy development. Eurostat is based in Luxembourg. Eurostat is at the fore in providing useful statistics on disability in Europe.

The Health and Food Safety Unit of Eurostat has responsibility for disability matters. Its role may be enhanced in the disability field by Article 31 of the UN Convention, which states that 'States Parties undertake to collect appropriate information, including statistical and research data, to enable them to formulate and

---

[98]   COM(08) 804 final.

implement policies to give effect to the present Convention.'

Eurostat's principle work in the field of disability has taken the form of disability-specific questions in their 2002 Labour Force Survey (LFS)[99] and 2004 data collection of EU Statistics on Incomes and Living Conditions (EU-SILC),[100] and also in the development of modules on disability for use in future.

The findings of the first two studies were analyzed in an April 2007 report entitled, 'Men and Women with disabilities in the EU: Statistical Analysis of the LFS Ad Hoc Module and the EU-SILC'.[101] The report looks at the scale and age breakdown of disability across the EU. Issues such as access to employment, educational opportunity and attainment, state benefits and supports were also included in the analysis. The 2002 data indicated that women seem more likely than men to be limited in their activities due to a long-standing health problem or disability. Both studies found the likelihood of such a limitation increases markedly with age for both sexes. The LFS also suggested that persons born with a disability are likely to have a much lower level of education than those without restrictions. Level of education and marital status were found to impact on participation and employment rates of persons with disabilities.

In 2008, two areas of Eurostat's work were particularly relevant to the field of disability. Firstly, a survey module on Disability and Social Integration (EDSIM) is being developed to form a core element of future European Health Interview Surveys and also as a module for inclusion in non-health surveys. The EDSIM questionnaire was finalized in June 2008 after extensive consultations with country experts and pilot testing. The questionnaire seeks information about internet use, access to learning, employment and economic life, transport and mobility, community life and recreation, access to the built environment, social life and negative attitudes and behaviour. In 2009, the EDSIM module will be piloted by ten Member States.

Secondly, Eurostat prepared a proposal in 2008 for a module on the employment of disabled people for the upcoming 2011 Labour Force Survey (LFS). A task force composed of ten countries and two private experts on disability statistics presented their findings to the Eurostat Labour Market Statistics (LAMAS) Working Group in September 2008. Further to this meeting, two Member States are set to test two versions of the module. The first version, as proposed by the task force, looks at limitations in work participation relating to the amount and type of work and transport issues, before going on to consider limitations related to health conditions or diseases. The alternative version, which adheres to the medical model of disability, arose from discussions at the LAMAS Working group and identifies persons with disabilities at the outset before examining limi-

---

99   See Eurostat, 'Statistics in focus- THEME 3- 26/03' November (2003), <http://epp.
      eurostat.ec.europa.eu/cache/ITY_OFFPUB/KS-NK-03-026/EN/KS-NK-03-026-
      EN.PDF>, last accessed 1 May 2009.
100   See Eurostat, 'Income, Social Inclusion and Living Conditions' (2004) <http://epp.
      eurostat.ec.europa.eu/portal/page/portal/living_conditions_and_social_protection/
      introduction/income_social_inclusion_living_conditions>, last accessed 14 May
      2009.
101   DG Employment, Social Affairs and Equal Opportunities, 'Men and Women with
      disabilities in the EU: Statistical Analysis of the LFS Ad Hoc Module and the EU-
      SILC' (April 2007).

tations in work participation.

Both EDSIM and the proposed LFS disability module seek to incorporate the model of disability espoused by the WHO International Classification of Functioning Disability and Health (ICF), and to ensure that variables and questions in data collection reflect the interaction between social and medical dimensions to disability.[102]

3. ACTIVITIES OF THE COUNCIL OF THE EUROPEAN UNION

Web resource: <http://ue.eu.int/>

The Council is the Institution that enacts EC legislation in cooperation with the European Parliament. The relevant legislation in force and the proposed Equal Treatment Directive have been outlined above.

3.1. ACTIVITIES UNDER THE OPEN METHOD OF CO-ORDINATION (OMC)

In conjunction with the Commission and other bodies, the Council also helps to coordinate Member State activity in areas which do not fall strictly within EC Competence. In particular the Open Method of Coordination (OMC) has developed as a mechanism for Member State cooperation and coordination in policy areas where the EC lacks full legal competence. Member States use common measuring tools in order to benchmark progress towards common objectives as defined by the Council.[103]

Two OMC processes are of notable importance in the context of disability – OMC and the European Employment Strategy and OMC and Social Inclusion. Apart from their value as an aid to policy, they are a fertile source of knowledge and research on disability at European level.

3.1.1. Open Method of Coordination- European Employment Strategy

The European Employment Strategy (EES) aims to support Member States in making qualitative and quantative improvements to the job market. The EES involves the development of national action plans based on common Member State priorities. The Commission issues an annual report which analyzes national action plans, while the Council can adopt country-specific recommendations. A further component of the EES takes the form of a Joint Employment Report, which focuses on progress made in achieving the objectives of the EES during the reporting period, and implementing and prioritizing action accordingly. In this way the Report ratchets forward the dynamic of coordination and change.

Through identifying progress made and challenges that remain, the Joint Employment Report enables Member States to gauge the progress they are making. In considering each Member State's situation, the Report can provide ideas

---

[102] See WHO 2009, <http://www.who.int/classifications/icf/en/>, last accessed 16 April 2009.
[103] White Paper on European Governance, COM(01) 428.

and inspiration as to various methods and schemes for ensuring improvements in the job market. It also provides political impetus for change, as the Commission proposes country specific recommendations alongside the Report as a basis for reform. The Report is also a rich source of knowledge, information and insight on the status of people with disabilities in the context of employment.

The Joint Employment Report 2007/2008 drew attention to people with disabilities as an untapped resource of additional labour supply, noting an employment rate of just 50%.[104] The Report noted progress in enhancing work opportunities for workers with disabilities[105] while acknowledging widespread efforts to reduce non-wage labour costs with a focus on those same workers. Under the European Employment Strategy's priority of increasing labour supply and modernizing social protection systems, a number of countries' efforts to ensure an inclusive labour market were acknowledged. The Report noted that:

> Financial incentives are being created to increase the readiness of people with a disability to take up work [in Ireland, Estonia, and Slovakia], while subsidies are given to employers to hire disabled people and to adapt their workplace to their needs [in Spain, Malta, the Netherlands, Sweden, Poland, Ireland, Finland, Austria, Bulgaria, Latvia and Portugal].

Measures are also being taken to establish and develop guaranteed jobs and supported employment opportunities [in the Czech Republic, Denmark, Spain, Sweden, Slovenia, Germany, Latvia and Slovakia].[106]

The Report also discussed adapting to economic change through investment in vocational training and skills upgrades. In the field of disability, the Slovakian extension to an existing personal assistance scheme and the reinforcement of services for people with disabilities received mention.[107]

Ultimately, the Report identified 'investing in people and modernizing labour markets' as a priority action.[108] To this end, the Report stated that, 'Increasing employment rates of older workers, young people, the foreign-born, and persons with a disability is of great importance if Europe is to successfully include people outside the labour market and counter-balance the effects of an ageing population.'[109]

3.1.2. Open Method of Coordination- Social Protection and Social Inclusion

The Council and Commission also provide an annual analysis and assessment of national reports on strategies for social protection and inclusion submitted by Member States. The resulting Joint Report looks at progress made in implementing the OMC, identifies good practice and innovative approaches, as well as setting priorities for the next reporting period.

---

[104]   Council (EPSCO), 'Joint Employment Report 2007/2008' (March 2008), 7169/08, 5.
[105]   Ibid, 9.
[106]   Ibid, 11.
[107]   Ibid, 9.
[108]   Ibid, 15.
[109]   Ibid, 16.

The Joint Report on Social Protection and Social Inclusion 2008 highlighted the need to include vulnerable members of society, both socially and economically, in order to ensure the benefits of an improved economic framework.[110] The Report noted that social and economic policies should be mutually supportive. The report asserted that through improving working conditions, retraining and encouraging lifelong learning, Member States can enhance the work opportunities of people with disabilities and the less qualified.[111]

Despite a rise in employment rates for older workers, it was observed that still more people need to be brought back to the workplace. The Report viewed this as a contribution to 'a sounder base for social protection systems and adequacy and sustainability of pensions.'[112]

The Report also refers to reforms which Member States are undertaking with a view to reducing take-up of benefits resulting from an early exit from employment. Some of these reforms are affecting access to disability pensions and rehabilitation.[113] The Report also discusses health inequalities and notes that most Member States 'have adapted services to reach those who have difficulty accessing conventional services due to physical or mental disability or to linguistic or cultural differences'. However, the Report goes on to criticize the failure of most states 'to address health inequalities systematically and comprehensively by reducing social differences, preventing the ensuing health differences, or addressing the poor health that results. This would ensure in practice equal access for equal needs.'[114] In relation to education, the report calls for an equal opportunities approach resulting in 'successful educational outcomes for each child... in order to break the transmission of poverty and exclusion to the next generation.'[115]

The national reports of Member States are available publicly and so there is a strong political incentive to make progress towards the common OMC objectives in the areas of social protection, pension schemes and the fight against exclusion. The identification of best practice also provides states with effective models of implementation.

3.2. EU PRESIDENCY AND MINISTERIAL CONFERENCES ON DISABILITY

Each rotating Presidency of the Council hosts a Presidency conference on disability, as well as other Ministerial meetings. Such events help provide high-level direction on disability issues and fresh impetus for policy development.

The German Presidency Conference of June 2007 was previously discussed and set in train a process for reviewing (at Ministerial level) progress toward the implementation of the Convention the Rights of Persons with Disabilities.

---

[110] Council (EPSCO), 'Joint Report on Social Protection and Social Inclusion', 7274/08 (February 2008).
[111] Ibid, 9.
[112] Ibid, 2.
[113] Ibid, 9.
[114] Ibid, 11.
[115] Ibid, 3.

3.2.1. Slovenian Presidency Informal Meeting of Ministers for Employment and Social Affairs, Brdo pri Kranju, 31 January- 2 February 2008[116]

This meeting focussed on the importance of both flexibility and security with regard to employment - or 'flexicurity' - in a person's lifetime. This meeting (under the Slovenian Presidency) marked an effort to ensure the continued incorporation of this value into the Community fabric. Ministers in attendance paid particular attention to the young, the elderly and women in the workforce. It was agreed that 'flexicurity' is essential in confronting challenges of demographic change, globalization, rapid technological advancement and the need for heightened competitiveness. The positive impact of flexible employment arrangements on disadvantaged groups, including persons with disabilities, was noted and the need to combat discriminatory practices and ensure equal opportunities for all was emphasized.

3.2.2. Slovenian Presidency Conference on the Convention on the Rights of Persons with Disabilities – from words to reality?, Kranjska Gora, Slovenia, 22-23 May 2008[117]

The aim of the conference was to support and foster the ratification and implementation of the UN Convention by focusing on different Member States' experiences of the implementation process. The meeting also considered the new priorities of the European Disability Action Plan beyond 2010. The conference held dedicated workshops on the subjects of living in the community, employment and accessibility in the broadest sense. The discussion on the last subject considered the built environment, transport systems, information and communication as well as the media.

An informal ministerial meeting preceded this conference. The ministers supported a speedy ratification of the Convention in all Member States and by the Community. They emphasized the importance of cooperation and believed that meetings such as the one at hand promoted the enforcement of human rights. Ministers stressed the need for sustained dialogue with stakeholders and concluded that compliance of EC and Member States' non-discrimination legislation with the Convention was essential.

---

[116] Government of the Republic of Slovenia 2008, <http://www.mddsz.gov.si/en/eu2008_mddsz/dogodki/ns_zaposlovanje_sociala/>, last accessed 17 February 2009.

[117] Proceedings of the Conference available online at <http://www.mddsz.gov.si/fileadmin/mddsz.gov.si/pageuploads/dokumenti__pdf/clovekove_pravice_invalidi.pdf>, last accessed 17 February 2009.

4. CURRENT ACTIVITIES OF THE EUROPEAN PARLIAMENT

4.1. THE ROLE AND FUNCTIONING OF THE EUROPEAN PARLIAMENT

Members of the European Parliament (MEPs) are directly elected by the citizens of Member States every five years and each state has a set number of seats, which is, as a general rule, proportionate to its population. In the Parliament, the MEPs sit according to political affiliation rather than by nationality. The Parliament is also assisted by a secretariat of about five thousand officials.

Preparatory work for the plenary sittings (held in Strasbourg) is done by twenty parliamentary committees. The MEPs are divided among these Committees, whose political make-up reflects that of the Parliament as a whole. These committees meet publicly in Brussels at least once a month to work on legislative proposals and reports to be presented at the plenary sitting. The standing committees whose work is of particular relevance to the field of disability include the following:

- Committee for Employment and Social Affairs;
- Committee for Transport and Tourism;
- Committee for Environment, Public Health and Food Safety;
- Committee for Culture and Education;
- Committee for Civil Liberties, Justice and Home Affairs;
- Committee on Industry, Research and Energy;
- Committee on Foreign Affairs and its Sub-Committee on Human Rights and the Committee on Legal Affairs.

In the drafting of legislation, the Commission must present, explain and defend proposals in front of the parliamentary committees as well as take account of any changes proposed by the Parliament. The Parliament can accept, amend or reject the content of the proposed legislative texts. Under the 'co-decision' procedure, the Parliament submits its amendments to the Council. Should the Council and Parliament disagree on the legislative text at this point, they can subsequently agree upon a common position or, failing this, a 'Conciliation Committee' is convened. If agreement cannot be reached, then the legislation will not be adopted.

4.2. ACTIVITIES OF THE EUROPEAN PARLIAMENT INTERGROUP ON DISABILITY

Web resource: <http://www.disabilityintergroup.eu/>

This Intergroup consists of an informal grouping of MEPs who are committed to advancing disability rights and concerns across the spectrum of EU activities. The Intergroup assists its members who wish to ask relevant questions and propose appropriate amendments in various committees. It holds public meetings in Strasbourg every two months and produces a regular newsletter detailing its work and achievements. The Intergroup is an influential informal mechanism to ensure the mainstreaming of disability issues into Community legislation.

The Intergroup has a Bureau that meets regularly in Brussels, and approves a rolling work programme setting out work priorities on a committee-by-committee basis. In 2008, the mainstreaming of disability issues was the principal concern across the board.[118] For example, Disability Intergroup members on the Committee on Civil Liberties, Justice and Home Affairs (LIBE) were encouraged to support references to the significance of the UN Convention on the Rights of Persons with Disabilities in the *'Report on the situation of fundamental rights in the EU 2004-2007'*. Members were also asked to draw attention to the matters of deinstitutionalization and the under-representation of women with disabilities in decision-making. The Intergroup has also prioritized the proposed Equal Treatment Directive in its work on this committee.[119]

Within the Committee on Employment and Social Affairs (EMPL), the Intergroup's 2008 priorities related to social security systems,[120] the Commission's Recommendation on Active Inclusion,[121] the Commission initiative for 'A renewed commitment to social justice in Europe: deepening the open method of coordination in social protection and social inclusion'[122] as well as improving the lives of people with disabilities through the use of Information and Communications Technology. The conclusion of the UN Convention was prioritized in the Committee on Foreign Affairs (AFET), the Sub-Committee on Human Rights (DROI) and the Committee on Legal Affairs (JURI).

In the Committee on Internal Market and Consumer Protection (IMCO), the Intergroup had three priorities during 2008. Firstly the Intergroup focussed on services of general interest.[123] Secondly, it was concerned with proposals announced in the Commission's work programme 2008 for a Consumer Rights Directive. Thirdly, the Intergroup sought to mainstream disability in a review of legislation on VAT at reduced rates.

The Intergroup identified the 'telecoms package' as its priority in the work of the Committee on Industry, Research and Energy (ITRE). In this context, the Intergroup sought to ensure the provision of quality services, which are accessible, interoperable and affordable, the creation of a Community mechanism to address e-Accessibility issues, and the strengthening of the powers of the European Electronic Communications Market Authority (EECMA).

The Intergroup drew attention to the rights of persons with disabilities in the Committee on Transport and Tourism (TRAN) in the context of coach and mari-

---

[118] Disability Intergroup, 'Forthcoming Work Priorities on Disability Issues in the European Parliament', (July 2008).

[119] Ibid, 3.

[120] Also Proposal for a Regulation of the European Parliament and of the Council amending the annexes to Regulation (EC) No 883/2004 on the coordination of social security systems, COM(07) 376 final.

[121] Council Recommendation 08/867 on the active inclusion of people excluded form the labour market, [2008] O.J. L307/11.

[122] Communication from the Commission to the European Parliament, the Council, the European Economic and Social Committee and the Committee of Regions on the 'Commission Legislative and Work Programme 2008', COM(07) 640 final, p.20.

[123] Communication from the Commission to the European Parliament, the Council, the European Economic and Social Committee and the Committee of Regions on 'Services of general interest, including social services of general interest: a new European commitment', COM(07)725 final.

time travel, as well as the 2007 Commission Green Paper, 'Towards a new culture of urban mobility'.[124] This paper outlined five challenges faced by European towns and cities to ensure that urban mobility facilitates economic development, the protection of the environment and the quality of life of citizens. Accessible urban transport was identified as one of these challenges.

In the Committee on the Environment, Public Health and Food Safety (ENVI), the Intergroup's 2008 focus related to mainstreaming disability in a number of Community instruments. This included any forthcoming Community framework for safe and efficient health services, a European Action Plan in the Field of Rare Diseases and the Pharmaceuticals Package as outlined in the Commission's work programme 2008.

> Other priorities listed in the Intergroup's work programme related to the EU Budget 2008 and 2009 (Committee on Budgets, BUDG), children in external action (Committees on Culture and Education, CULT, and Development, DEVE), governance, partnership and best practice (Committee on Regional Policy, REGI) and gender equality (Committee on Women's Rights & Gender Equality, FEMM). Finally, the 2008 work programme identified as additional key issues a Special Educational Needs resource centre, accessibility and inclusion in the European Parliament electoral campaign and continued cooperation with the European Parliament Disability Support Group.

In February 2008, the Intergroup considered the accessibility of telecommunications and the opportunity afforded by the review of the current legislative framework.[125] The Intergroup concluded that consultation with stakeholders is a vital prerequisite before the proposed legislative amendment could be implemented. The proposed amendment to Article 1(1) of Directive 2002/21/EC on a common regulatory framework for electronic communications networks and services[126] reads as follows.

This Directive establishes a harmonized framework for the regulation of electronic communications services, electronic communications networks, associated facilities and associated services, and certain aspects of terminal equipment. It lays down tasks of national regulatory authorities and establishes a set of procedures to ensure the harmonised application of the regulatory framework throughout the Community.[127]

At present, terminal equipment is not covered by European accessibility standards. This amendment is significant as it would bring terminal equipment

---

[124] Green Paper 'Towards a new culture of urban mobility', COM(07) 551 final.

[125] Disability Intergroup, 'Accessible Telecommunication: An Opportunity for the Review of the Legislative Framework' (February 2008).

[126] Directive 2002/21/EC on a common regulatory framework for electronic communications networks and services [2002] O.J. L108/33.

[127] Proposal for a Directive of the European Parliament and of the Council amending Directives 2002/21/EC on a common regulatory framework for electronic communications networks and services, 2002/19/EC on access to, and interconnection of, electronic communications networks and services, and 2002/20/EC on the authorisation of electronic communications networks and services, COM(07) 697 final, Article 1(1).

within the scope of the Directive for the first time, and will thus ensure they are subject to European accessibility standards. It ought to make accessibility and interoperability issues easier to address. Heretofore, end-to-end connectivity in technology has proved a barrier to access for people with disabilities.

In April 2008, the group considered the 'Future of social security systems: ensuring full social inclusion and participation of disabled people'.[128] The discussion focused on the importance of integration into the labour market and noted the significant role that social security plays in achieving this aim. The group went on to table a number of amendments to a Report of the Committee on Employment and Social Affairs on the subject.[129] These amendments identified the main barrier to active participation in society as the inadequacy of pensions systems compensating for the extra-costs of disability, and the lack of coordination of disability pension/compensation schemes with social inclusion policies. The amendments also condemned institutionalization of persons with disabilities and promoted independent living through provision of alternative community-based services.[130]

In April 2008, the European Parliament's Committee on Employment and Social Affairs reported to the Parliament on progress made in equal opportunities and non-discrimination in the EU.[131] This Report invited Member States and the Commission to agree upon a broad definition of disability, (perhaps based on that of the UN Convention on the Rights of Persons with Disabilities), as the absence thereof to date 'has excluded some categories of disabled people from the legal protection' of the Employment Equality Directive.[132] The Report also emphasized the importance of ensuring and mainstreaming the value of non-discrimination in all areas of EC competence. It also supported the Commission's proposal for a Council Directive on implementing the principle of equal treatment between persons irrespective of religion or belief, disability, age or sexual orientation as outlined above.

On 14 May 2008 the Intergroup organized a public hearing on the future of anti-discrimination legislation and considered whether a disability specific directive was necessary.[133] This public hearing took place prior to the formal proposal of the Equal Treatment Directive by the European Commission. Opinions were

---

[128] Disability Intergroup, 'Future of social security systems and pensions: ensuring full social inclusion and participation of disabled people' (April 2008).

[129] INI/2007/2290 entitled 'Future of social security systems and pensions: their financing and the trend towards individualisation'.

[130] See Disability Intergroup, 'Forthcoming Work Priorities on Disability Issues in the European Parliament' (July 2008), 2.

[131] Parliament Committee on Employment and Social Affairs, 'Report on on progress made in equal opportunities and non-discrimination in the EU (the transposition of Directives 2000/43/EC and 2000/78/EC)' (April 2008) A6-0000/2008.

[132] Ibid, 6.

[133] Disability Intergroup, 'Future Anti-discrimination Legislation: What are the Specificities of the "Disability" ground?' (May 2008). See also Inclusion Europe, 'Report on EU Parliament Hearing on a Disability Specific Anti-Discrimination Directive' (May 2008). For further information, see Giantsidou et al, 'Report of the Public Hearing at the European Parliament: Future anti-discrimination legislation: what are the specificities of the 'disability' ground' (May 2008) contained in the Annex to the Yearbook.

divided as to the value of a disability specific directive. Some concern was expressed that it may lead to a hierarchy within the different grounds or that it would not cater for situations of discrimination on multiple grounds. On the other hand, it was acknowledged that disability is a discrete ground necessitating special considerations, such as addressing physical barriers obstructing the exercise of rights. There was broad agreement that a clear distinction should be made between 'reasonable accommodation' and 'positive action' and that any legislation introduced must be in line with the UN Convention on the Rights of Persons with Disabilities. Finally the importance of consultation with stakeholders was stressed. A report of this meeting is included in the Annex to the Yearbook.

In September 2008, the group considered what employment opportunities are available in EU institutions for prospective employees with disabilities.[134] Involvement by employees with disabilities and representative organizations was deemed imperative for successful integration in the working environment.

5. CASE LAW OF THE EUROPEAN COURT OF JUSTICE

5.1. THE POWERS OF THE EUROPEAN COURT OF JUSTICE

Web resource: <http://curia.europa.eu/>

The European Court of Justice (ECJ) is the judicial branch of the European Community. It may sit 'in Grand Chamber' with thirteen judges or in smaller Chambers of three or five judges. Its jurisdiction is specifically concerned with issues relating to the EC Treaties and secondary legislation. The domestic courts of the Member States may refer a case or question of law to the ECJ for an interpretation of EC law under Article 234 EC (the preliminary reference procedure). The Commission can also challenge Member States for failure to completely and full implement a directive, and may bring an action for infringement of Community law before the ECJ (Article 226 EC). In 1988 a Court of First Instance was created to assist in dealing with the volume of cases coming before the ECJ. Under Article 230 EC, an individual may bring a direct action against a Community institution in the Court of First Instance for a decision either addressed to the applicant, or which is of direct and individual concern to the applicant.[135]

This narrow crafting of *locus standi* limits opportunities for individuals to gain access to the Community Courts directly. It is thus more realistic for individuals to rely on national courts to make an Article 234 reference to the ECJ.

In every case coming before the ECJ, an Advocate General presents an impartial and independent opinion analyzing the legal aspects of the case and suggesting an appropriate Court response. It is not necessary for the Court to follow this Opinion. However, the Opinion of the Advocate General is helpful in its

---

[134] Disability Intergroup, 'Working for the EU Institutions: what opportunities for candidates with disabilities?' (September 2008).

[135] In Case C-25/62 *Plaumann v. Commission* [1963] ECR 95, the ECJ held that applicants are only individually concerned by a decision affecting them 'by reason of certain attributes which are peculiar to them or by reason of circumstances in which they are differentiated from all other persons'.

framing of the legal issues for the court.

In the area of disability, the Court has made significant decisions relating to employment discrimination, social policy, and welfare payments. Most notable are the decisions made under the Employment Equality Directive. This section recounts the recent case law in the field of disability.

5.2.   RECENTLY DECIDED CASES

5.2.1. *Sonia Chacón Navas v. Eurest Colectividades SA (2006)*[136]

Ms. Chacón Navas was certified as unfit to work on the grounds of sickness and had spent eight months on leave of absence, when she received notice of her dismissal from her employer. Her employer acknowledged that this was an unlawful dismissal and offered her compensation. However, Ms Chacón Navas claimed that her dismissal amounted to discrimination, which would, under Spanish law, entitle her to be reinstated and receive back pay. In its reference to the ECJ, the Spanish tribunal asked the Court to clarify if sickness falls within the personal scope of the Employment Equality Directive on the grounds of disability or, if not, if it may be regarded as an additional protected ground.

In his Opinion, Advocate General Geelhoed stated that sickness could neither be subsumed into the disability ground, nor could it amount to a separate ground on which discrimination is prohibited under the Directive. He opined that this might be otherwise where:

> during the course of the sickness long-term or permanent functional limitations emerge which must be regarded as disabilities. When relying on the prohibition of discrimination on the grounds of disability, the person concerned must then make a reasonable case that it is not the sickness itself, but the resulting long-term or permanent limitations which are the real reason for the dismissal.[137]

The Grand Chamber adopted a literal interpretation of the Directive. The Court stated that, 'by using the concept of 'disability' in Article 1 of the Directive, the legislature deliberately chose a term which differs from 'sickness'. The two concepts cannot therefore simply be treated as being the same.[138] The Court indicated that for any limitation to be considered a disability, it must be likely to last for a long time, and went on to say that 'there is nothing in Directive 2000/78 to suggest that workers are protected by the prohibition of discrimination on grounds of disability as soon as they develop any type of sickness.'[139] Although the Court acknowledged the principle of non-discrimination as an integral part of Community law, they refused to extend the principle beyond the grounds listed in Directive.

This decision presents difficulties in that it fails to provide adequate distinguishing criteria between sickness and disability, despite its insistence that the concepts are distinct. It also fails to clarify what amounts to 'a long time' in order

---

[136]   Case C-13/05 [2006] ECR I-646.
[137]   Opinion of the Advocate General of 16 March 2006, para. 85(1).
[138]   *Chacón Navas*, Judgment of the Court (Grand Chamber), para. 44.
[139]   Ibid, para. 46.

for sickness to reach the threshold of disability. It therefore seems that a person who has a temporary disability may not be protected from discrimination. Should such a person be dismissed, perhaps before long-term implications can be identified, it seems that this is compatible with Community law. However, the ECJ also stated that the concept of disability was an autonomous European legal norm, which effectively means that the Member States do not have *carte blanche* with respect to its definition.

The operative part of this judgment is contained in the Annex to the yearbook.

5.2.2. *Sharon Coleman v. Attridge Law and Steve Law (2008)*[140]

From January 2001, Ms. Coleman worked in a firm of solicitors in London as a legal secretary. In 2002, she gave birth to a disabled child whose health condition required specialized care which was provided for primarily by Ms. Coleman. On 5 March 2005, Ms. Coleman accepted voluntary redundancy from her employment, which brought her contract of employment with her employer to an end. On 30 August 2005 she lodged a claim with the South London Employment Tribunal claiming that she had been constructively dismissed from her employment and treated less favourably than her fellow employees, due to her being the primary carer for her disabled son. She claimed she had been the subject of discrimination and harassment[141] during her employment and referred to her employer's refusal to allow her return to her previous job after her maternity leave, the refusal to allow flexible working hours, as well as abusive and insulting comments being made about her and her child.

The Employment Tribunal referred the matter to the ECJ for a determination whether the prohibition against discrimination in the Employment Equality Directive extended to provide protection to a third party who had an association with a person with a disability but who was not themselves disabled (so-called associative discrimination').

In his Opinion of January 2008, Advocate General Maduro highlighted that the Directive was adopted under Article 13 EC, and must be interpreted in light of the objectives of that Article. He referred to the importance of equality, and human dignity and personal autonomy as the underlying values thereof. He stated that directly targeting someone who is disabled is one way of discriminating against him, but it is not the only way. He noted that 'the person who is the immediate victim of discrimination not only experiences a wrong himself, but also becomes the means through which the dignity of the person belonging to a suspect classification is undermined.'[142] He stated that a 'robust conception of equality entails that these subtler forms of discrimination should also be caught by anti-discrimination legislation.'[143]

The Advocate General continued to say that even in cases where the employee does not herself have a disability, the basis of the discrimination may

---

[140]   Case C-303/06, judgment of 30 August 2008, not yet reported.
[141]   As prohibited by Article 2 (3) of Directive 2000/78, establishing a general framework for Equal Treatment in Employment and Occupation.
[142]   Opinion of Advocate General, para. 13.
[143]   Ibid, para. 12.

nonetheless be disability. He stated that the hostility of an employer against people belonging to a suspect classification may not 'function as the basis for any kind of less favourable treatment in the context of employment and occupation'[144] and that the Employment Equality Directive prohibits this. Advocate General Maduro rejected the argument advanced by the United Kingdom Government that the Directive sets minimum standards, and the Member State has the discretion to decide whether to prohibit discrimination by association. The Opinion concluded that the Directive prohibited discrimination and harassment on the grounds of association with a disabled person stating that,

> if someone is the object of discrimination because of any one of the characteristics listed in [the Directive] then she can avail herself of the protection of the Directive even if she does not possess one of them herself. It is not necessary for someone who is the object of discrimination to have been mistreated on account of '*her* disability'. It is enough if she was mistreated on account of 'disability'.[145]

In delivering its judgment in July 2008, the Court stated that the purpose of the Directive was to combat all forms of discrimination by reference to the nature of the discrimination rather than to the particular category of person. The Court expressed the view that if an interpretation limiting the application of the Directive to people who are themselves disabled was given to the Directive, this would deprive the Directive of a vital element of its effectiveness and reduce the protection which it was intended to guarantee. The Grand Chamber concluded by stating that the Directive,

> must be interpreted as meaning that the prohibition of direct discrimination laid down by those provisions is not limited only to people who are themselves disabled. Where an employer treats an employee who is not himself disabled less favourably than another employee is, has been or would be treated in a comparable situation, and it is established that the less favourable treatment of that employee is based on the disability of his child, whose care is provided primarily by that employee, such treatment is contrary to the prohibition of direct discrimination laid down by Article 2(2)(a).[146]

On the subject of harassment the Court held that, '[s]ince, under Article 2(3) of Directive 2000/78, harassment is deemed to be a form of discrimination within the meaning of Article 2(1), it must be held that... that directive... must be interpreted as not being limited to the prohibition of harassment of people who are themselves disabled.'[147]

The significance of this decision is that the prohibition on discrimination in the Employment Equality Directive clearly applies equally to employees who are directly discriminated against or subjected to harassment by their employer, on the grounds of their association with disabled individuals. This is significant, as the Employment Equality Directive does not expressly provide for such

---

[144] Ibid, para. 22.
[145] Ibid, para. 23.
[146] *Coleman v. Attridge*, Judgment of the Court (Grand Chamber), para. 56.
[147] Ibid, para. 58.

protection.

The decision will apply to carers of both children with disabilities and elderly parents. However, it is worth noting that the decision has not created a new separately protected group of carers as was reported in the media.[148] Carers will only succeed in their claims if they can show that the disability of the person they care for was the reason for the treatment they received. Disability is thus still the nexus on which the prohibition on discrimination in the Directive is hinged. It is also possible, given the broad purposive approach taken by the ECJ in this case, that where a disability is incorrectly attributed to an individual, any direct discrimination arising there from may be prohibited under the Employment Equality Directive. Future cases may seek to further push the parameters of the Directive in order to establish a prohibition of indirect discrimination by association for persons associated with a person with a disability. It is certain that the extent of the protection against discrimination will be have to be tested and fleshed out further in ECJ case law.

The operative part of this judgment is contained in the Annex to the yearbook.

5.2.3. D. P. W. Hendrix v. Raad van Bestuur van het Uitvoeringsinstituut Werknemersverzekeringen (2007)[149]

This case related to the non-exportability of social entitlements. That is to say, social entitlements, such as social security benefits, provided in one Member State, do not automatically follow its citizens when they move to other EU Member States. Such entitlements are not harmonized and are not generally the subject of EU law. This does, however, conflict with the free movement of workers (and students and others) and has a pronounced negative impact on EU citizens with disabilities.

Mr. Hendrix was a citizen and resident of the Netherlands. He was employed in the wages and salaries division of a DIY store in Maastricht. He had a 'slight mental disability',[150] which reduced his capacity to work and resulted in the employer being exempt from paying up to 70% of the minimum wage. Mr. Hendrix was thus entitled to receive an incapacity benefit (*Wajong*). This is a minimum benefit paid to young persons who experience total or partial long-term incapacity for work. The *Wajong* was subject to a residency requirement.

EC Regulation No 71/1408 covers special non-contributory cash benefits that are intended either to cover against risks covered by certain branches of social security or, as a protection for disabled people. At Article 10a, the Regulation allows for residency requirements to be attached to such benefits, which, like the *Wajong*, are listed in Annex IIa.[151]

On 1st June, 1999, Mr. Hendrix moved to Belgium but retained his employ-

---

148   Barnard, 'Reporting the AG', 158 *The New Law Journal* (2008), 1095.
149   Case C-287/05 [2007] I-6909.
150   Ibid, para. 17.
151   Council Regulation (EEC) No. 1408/71 on the application of social security schemes to employed persons, to self-employed persons and to members of their families moving within the Community, [1983] O.J. L230/8.

ment in the Netherlands. The defendant decided to terminate the Wajong benefit from July 1 1999. However, the employer's exemption from an obligation to pay the minimum wage remained. On termination of his post with that employer, Mr. Hendrix proceeded to another job, also based in the Netherlands. He challenged the residency requirement attached to the *Wajong* benefit before the national court, which referred a number of questions to the ECJ. The ECJ was asked to consider whether the *Wajong* is a special non-contributory benefit for which a residency requirement is permissible. The second question was whether Mr. Hendrix could be considered a migrant worker entitled to rely on free movement of workers even though his place of work did not change. The third question for the ECJ was whether residence requirements permissible under Article 10a of EC Regulation No 71/1408 are always compatible with Community law and, if not, was the condition imposed in relation to the *Wajong* compatible.

Advocate General Kokkot asserted that a benefit under the Netherlands Law on the provision of incapacity benefit to disabled young people must be regarded as a special non-contributory benefit under Community law.[152] He felt that the transfer of residence to another Member State, while continuing to work in the state in question, did enable a worker to rely on the protections afforded to migrant workers. Advocate General Kokkot stated that although residency conditions attached to non-contributory benefits are not precluded by Community law, neither are they always compatible. Any restriction on the fundamental freedoms of the Treaty (including the freedom of movement for workers as laid down in Article 39 EC) must be justifiable by overriding reasons of general interest.

The judgment of the Grand Chamber also found Mr. Hendrix to be a migrant worker within the meaning of Article 39 of the EC Treaty. The *Wajong* was confirmed as a non-contributory benefit that may be subject to a residency requirement.[153] It was noted that any such requirement should 'not entail an infringement of the [claimant's free movement rights] which goes beyond what is required to achieve the legitimate objective pursued by the national legislation.'[154] The Court instructed the national judge to take into account the fact that the claimant was a frontier worker who maintained close economic and social links to the Netherlands as his country of origin.

The significance of this decision is that the ECJ refused to take a narrow view of the term 'migrant worker' and instead sought to ensure the principle of free movement in practice. It would seem that any measure which could hamper the enjoyment of free movement of workers in the community will be scrutinized carefully before it will be considered justified for an objective reason. Although this decision certainly chips away at the view that certain social entitlements were non-exportable, it is nonetheless confined to cross-border workers.

---

[152] Regulation 71/1408, [1997] O.J. L28/1 (consolidated version), Article 4 2(a).
[153] Article 10a of Regulation 71/1408.
[154] Operative part 2 of the judgment.

5.2.4. Halina Nerkowska v. Zakład Ubezpieczeń Społecznych Oddział w Koszalinie (2008)[155]

The respondent in this case was a Polish Social Security Institution Branch which refused to pay Ms. Nerkowska a disability pension related to damage to her health, which she had suffered as a deportee in the former USSR. Polish law provided that such payments are only paid to persons while they are resident in Polish territory. Ms. Nerkowska applied for the relevant disability pension in 2000 and, although the respondent accepted her entitlement, it suspended payment on the grounds that she was resident in Germany and not Poland. Subsequent to Polish accession to the EU, Ms. Nerkowska submitted a fresh application to receive a disability pension. She challenged the subsequent refusal in front of the national court, which asked the ECJ for a preliminary ruling under Article 234 EC . The question referred was as follows:

> Does Article 18 EC, which guarantees citizens of the European Union the right to move and reside freely within the territory of the Member States, preclude the binding force of the national rules laid down in Article 5 of the [1974 Law] in so far as they make payment of a pension benefit for incapacity for work that is linked to a stay in places of isolation subject to fulfillment of the condition that the person entitled be resident in the territory of the Polish State?[156]

The Grand Chamber determined that Article 18(1) of the EC Treaty on the free movement and residence of EU citizens is to be interpreted as precluding legislation of a Member State under which it refuses, generally and in all circumstances, to pay to its nationals a disability benefit granted to civilian victims of war or repression solely because they are not resident in the territory of that State throughout the period of payment of the benefit, but in the territory of another Member State.

This decision has the consequence of reducing barriers to free movement for all persons, including those who may claim disability benefits. This removes a financial disincentive and hurdle to free movement of persons by ensuring persons are not tied, by virtue of certain benefits, to their national territory.

5.3. CASES PENDING

5.3.1. Gottwald v. Bezirkshauptmannschaft Bregenz[157]

On 6 March 2008, an Austrian Court, Unabhängiger Verwaltungssenat des Landes Vorarlberg, lodged a reference for a preliminary ruling concerning Article 12 of the EC Treaty which prohibits discrimination on the grounds of nationality. The question referred was whether this Article precludes a residence requirement under national law for a benefit allowing the free use of federal toll roads for persons with a defined disability. This case is pending.

---

[155]   Case C-499/06, Judgment of 22 May 2008, not yet reported.
[156]   Ibid, para. 18.
[157]   Case C-103/08.

A judgment of the ECJ which rules against the residence requirement could ensure equal treatment of all European citizens with disabilities in respect of travel concessions and other such accommodations throughout the EU. This would undoubtedly make European travel and movement more feasible and less burdensome for persons with disabilities, and would amount to a step towards the realization of the principle of free movement for all.

5.3.2. Schultz-Hoff v. Deutsche Rentenversicherung Bund v (2008)[158]

The appellant was employed as a field worker in the area of tax audits with the respondent employer from 1971 to 2005. The appellant was classified under German law as severely disabled due to a serious problem with an invertebral disc. He was unable to work and on medical sick leave for extended periods of time during 2004. As a result he had not taken his annual leave entitlement for this year. Under German law, annual leave not taken cannot be carried over to a new year without permission. Even with permission, it must be taken by the end of June the following year, or it is lost and the employee is not entitled to compensation. The appellant failed to take his annual leave in advance of this deadline. This case amounted to a challenge to the national law regulating the ability of a worker to subsequently claim leave or financial compensation in such a situation. The ECJ was asked to consider whether the appellant should be allowed to carry forward his annual leave from 2004 and be paid in full for his accrued holiday entitlement when his employment ended.

The *Landesarbeitsgericht* (Higher Labour Court) referred a number of questions to the ECJ for a preliminary ruling under Article 234 EC. Firstly, the national court sought clarity as to whether Article 7(1) of Directive 2003/88 concerning certain aspects of the organization of working time requires that workers,[159] who are unable to take paid annual leave before the leave year due to illness, may carry this over to a new year. Article 7(1) states that, 'Member States shall take the measures necessary to ensure that every worker is entitled to paid annual leave of at least four weeks in accordance with the conditions for entitlement to, and granting of, such leave laid down by national legislation and/or practice.'

The second question referred to the ECJ was whether national legislation may preclude financial compensation for leave accrued, but not taken, upon termination of employment in circumstances where the worker is incapacitated for work until the end of the leave year or statutory carry-over period, or where the worker is drawing a disability or invalidity pension.

Thirdly, if the previous questions were to be answered in the affirmative, guidance was sought as to whether the worker is required to have actually worked during the leave year in order to accrue the entitlement. This question made specific reference to excusable (due to illness) and inexcusable absences.

In his Opinion, Advocate General Trsteniak stated that allowing annual leave to be lost in this manner would exclude workers from the protective scope

---

[158] Case C-350/06, Opinion of the Advocate General of 24 January 2008.

[159] Directive 2003/88/EC of the European Parliament and of the Council of 4 November 2003 concerning certain aspects of the organisation of working time, [2003] O.J. L299/9.

of the Directive and would be contrary to the objectives of the Directive.[160] Thus, in his Opinion, where workers have accrued an entitlement to annual leave but have not taken this during the leave year, they are entitled to financial compensation upon termination of employment. She expressly stated that the annual leave entitlement in the Directive applies to workers who are absent due to illness during the entire leave year.

This Opinion, if followed by the ECJ, would grant valuable entitlements to workers who are on sick leave due to incapacity. According to this view, a period of illness must be equated with a period of service for the purposes of accrual of annual leave, as the absence from work due to incapacity is due to reasons beyond the control of the worker. This could ensure significant improvements in the quality of life for persons who, heretofore, could not take annual leave, as they had been absent from work due to illness at the time the leave was accrued. It could also ensure that a person, who has absent from work due to illness, would not be left at a disadvantage in a situation of redundancy or termination of contract for other reasons. Financial compensation for annual leave accrued, but not taken, may be of particular importance to persons who have significant medical bills due to their illness.

The judgment of the European Court of Justice was delivered in January 2009.

5.3.3. Stringer v. Her Majesty's Revenue and Customs (2008)[161]

The issues considered by Advocate General Trstenjak in her Opinion were similar to those considered in *Schultz-Hoff*, above, and the cases were joined for the judgment of the Grand Chamber. In this case, the House of Lords (UK) posed a question to the ECJ in relation to Directive 2003/88 concerning certain aspects of the organization of working time. A preliminary ruling from the ECJ on whether annual leave ought be paid to a worker when on sick leave, or at a designated future time, was sought. Clarification was also sought as to the extent of the allowance-in-lieu entitlement of a worker who has been absent on sick leave, for all or part of the annual leave year, upon termination of employment.

Advocate General Trstenjak commented that

> [i]n order to protect employees and employers and to avoid undermining the fundamental right to a minimum period of paid annual leave enshrined in Community law, it must be concluded that this fundamental right is in principle not available to an employee to do with it as he wishes and therefore he is unable to waive it with legal effect.[162]

Therefore, a right to annual leave cannot be made subject to a worker's capacity to work. She went on the state that an incapacitated employee is not permitted to take annual leave during a period of sick leave.

In relation to the second question raised by the House of Lords, the Advocate General stated that where an employment relationship is terminated, an incapaci-

---

[160]   Ibid, para. 28.
[161]   Case C-520/06, Opinion of the Advocate General of 24 January 2008.
[162]   Ibid, para. 81.

tated worker is entitled to payment in lieu of leave, even where the worker was on sick leave for all or part of the leave year. She also remarked that it is incumbent on Member States to ensure that the amount of allowance paid to workers in lieu of annual leave is equivalent to his or her normal pay.

This Opinion further states that an employer cannot designate periods of sick leave as annual leave, even where an employee agrees to this. The Advocate General stated that this would be incompatible with the purpose of Directive 2003/88 concerning certain aspects of the organization of working time, which is to improve workers' health and safety.

The Court's decision in this case will provide Member States with further guidance on the obligations placed on employers by Community legislation. The view of the Advocate General, if accepted by the ECJ, would ensure that any allowance in lieu of annual leave would be equivalent to the normal pay of the employee and (as above in *Schultz-Hoff*) that annual leave would not be contingent on the employee's ability to work. As a result, persons on sick leave would not, in principle, be denied rights related to leave granted to their peers.

The judgment of the European Court of Justice is due in early 2009.

5.3.4. *Francisco Vicente Pereda v. Madrid Movilidad S.A.*[163]

In July 2008, a question relating to Directive 2003/88 concerning certain aspects of the organization of working time, was referred by the *Jazgado de lo Social No 23 Madrid*. The relevant concern was whether annual leave which was planned in advance of an accident at work that gives rise to a temporary disability, but coincides in time with that temporary disability, can then be taken on different dates - irrespective of the ending of the leave year - as a matter of entitlement.

This case is also pending, but will undoubtedly be influenced by the decisions in *Schultz-Hoff* and *Stringer* referred to above. If, as is likely, the Court decides that a situation of temporary disability may not result in a person being placed at a disadvantage in terms of annual leave, valuable rights will be conferred on persons in these circumstances. Annual leave that is additional to disability related leave would undoubtedly benefit persons recuperating from an accident, and would also ensure equality with persons who do not have such a disability.

6. EUROPEAN ECONOMIC AND SOCIAL COMMITTEE

Web resource: <http://eesc.europa.eu/>

6.1. BACKGROUND AND WORK OF THE COMMITTEE

The European Economic and Social Committee (EESC) was established under the Treaty of Rome 1957 as an advisory body representing employers, employees and civil society. The Committee has 344 members who are nominated by national governments for a renewable four-year term of office.

The primary working method of the Committee involves the adoption of Opinions addressed to the Council, Commission and European Parliament, on

---

[163] Case C-277/08.

matters of European interest. The Committee must be consulted before decisions are taken on economic and social policy, and it may issue an Opinion on other matters on its own initiative or at the request of another EU institution. The EESC also takes on the role of facilitator and promoter of civil dialogue, hosts events aimed at bringing the EU closer to its citizens, and publishes a monthly newsletter.

Committee Opinions often contain expansive reasoning and may form part of the *travaux préparatoires*, which aid the ECJ in their interpretation of EC legislation. Furthermore, reports by the European Commission on action taken pursuant to Committee Opinions show that due regard is given to at least two thirds of the Opinions.[164] The Opinions also serve to raise awareness.

This section looks at some of the Committee's Opinions of 2008 that are relevant to the disability field.

6.2.   2008 OPINIONS WITH A DISABILITY DIMENSION

July 2008 saw the Committee adopt an Opinion on 'A new European Social Action Programme', further to a referral received from the then future French Presidency.[165] In addressing the key policy area of the EU disability strategy, the Committee called for a disability specific anti-discrimination framework proposal (para 6.4), a comprehensive legislative package, as well as impact assessments of other legislation.[166] Interestingly, the Opinion called for the extension of OMC into new areas including the coordination of disability policies.[167]

In September 2008, in an Opinion on 'extending anti-discrimination measures for areas outside employment and the case for a single comprehensive anti-discrimination directive', the Committee called for:

> a single directive prohibiting discrimination on grounds of disability, religion or belief, sexual orientation or age in relation to all areas outside the field of employment within the scope of the Race Directive and requiring the establishment or enlargement of an equality body with full competence to work across all matters within the scope of the legislation.[168]

There seems to be a contradiction between the July Opinion, which called for a disability-specific anti-discrimination legislative proposal, and the September Opinion which supports a more integrated legal instrument.

This September Opinion articulated a concern regarding the hierarchy of protections afforded against discrimination on different grounds outside the employment context. The Opinion suggests this hierarchy impedes the free movement of goods and workers, social cohesion, civil participation, as well as quality of life of major groups and communities. The Committee therefore sought in its September Opinion a single comprehensive Directive in order to address the perceived hierarchy of grounds, as well as to improve transparency, consistency

---

[164]   The European Economic and Social Committee, 'The European Economic and Social Committee in ten points' (2007).

[165]   CES(08) 1209.

[166]   Ibid, 6.4.

[167]   Ibid, 7.9.2.

[168]   CES(08) 1571 'Anti-discrimination measures for areas outside employment', 8.3.

and accessibility. Reference was made to earlier drafts of the Opinion submitted to the Commission, in the hope that it may have assisted that body's decision to propose the Directive on implementing the principle of equal treatment between persons, irrespective of religion or belief, disability, age or sexual orientation. The Committee recommended any such Directive be drawn up with 'reasonable accommodation', enforcement and the role of specialized bodies in mind.

The September Opinion also called for the inclusion of a non-regression clause, such that Member States would be prevented from lowering existing national standards, which exceed the minimum requirements of the Directive. The Opinion further stated that all exceptions ought to be narrowly defined and that the issue of discrimination on multiple grounds must be adequately addressed. The Committee has since expressed disappointment at the failure of the proposed directive[169] to implement the latter recommendations.[170]

The EESC drew attention to the need to specifically support people with disabilities in a number of its other Opinions in 2008. In February, when asked by the Council for an Opinion relating to guidelines for Member State employment policies, the Committee called for greater efforts to combat discrimination, referring specifically to access to education and the labour market.[171] The Opinion called for the Commission to investigate how flexible working and supportive measures may increase the employment rate of people with disabilities.

In May 2008, the Committee adopted an Opinion on improving quality and productivity at work: 'Community Strategy 2007-2012 on health and safety at work'.[172] It identified workers with disabilities as a target group requiring specific regulation, policies and support.

In its Opinion of 11 September 2008 on 'Taking into account the needs of older people'[173] the Committee emphasized the importance of Universal Design, readable instructions and the prevention of discrimination in access to services in the consumer context. A specific Opinion on 'Ethical and social dimension of European financial institutions' adopted in October[174] referred to 'insurability [which is] free of discrimination on the grounds of age, possible disability or other social difficulties'.[175] With respect to services of general interest, the Committee once again drew attention to the principles of equality and accessibility, and the specific needs of people with disabilities, noting the purpose of these services is to address all social disadvantages resulting from disability, sickness and inability to work among others.[176]

---

[169]   COM(08) 426 final.
[170]   CES(09) 49.
[171]   CES(08) 282, 2.4.
[172]   CES(08) 994, 1.6.
[173]   CES(08) 1524.
[174]   CES(08) 1680.
[175]   Ibid, 3.3.2.4 b.
[176]   CES(08) 1665 'Policy guidelines for services of general interest and globalisation'.

7. ACTIVITIES OF THE EUROPEAN UNION FUNDAMENTAL RIGHTS AGENCY (FRA)

Web resource: <http://fra.europa.eu>

7.1. RESEARCH AND RELATED ACTIVITY

The European Union Agency for Fundamental Rights (FRA) emerged from its predecessor, the European Monitoring Centre on Racism and Xenophobia (EUMC) in 2007. It was established by a Council Regulation[177] to assist Member States and European institutions to ensure full respect for fundamental rights as set out in Article 6(2) of the Treaty on European Union, the European Convention on Human Rights and Fundamental Freedoms (ECHR), the European Social Charter of the Council of Europe and the EU Charter of Fundamental Rights (2000). Of note is the extent to which its remit extends to cover Council of Europe human rights instruments.

The FRA has a broad work programme, which covers three main areas: research and analysis, communication and awareness raising, and networking and education. In its work, the FRA looks at racism, xenophobia and related intolerance and any discrimination based on sex, race or ethnic origin, religion or belief, disability, age or sexual orientation, and against persons belonging to minorities or any combination of these. The FRA is also concerned with issues of access to efficient and independent justice and the compensation of victims. Other areas of work include the rights of the child and the rights of immigrants, especially in terms of border control, asylum and integration. In the context of the modern information society, the FRA is working to ensure respect for private life and protection of personal data. The FRA also champions the participation of the EU citizenry in the Union's democratic functioning.

To facilitate cooperation and information exchange with civil society, the Fundamental Rights Platform has been formed as a network open to all interested and qualified stakeholders.[178] The Platform is tasked with making suggestions on the FRA's Annual Work Programme, providing feedback on the FRA Annual report, communicating the outcomes of meetings and conferences and interacting with the Agency on its work priorities. The first formal consultation of the Platform took place in October 2008 in Vienna and a number of pan European Disability organizations (including EDF) were represented.

The FRA also produces a number of documents in which it raises public awareness of fundamental rights and provides data analysis. It issues thematic reports to assist the European Community and its Member States, as well as opinions on specific topics, either on its own initiative or at the request of a European institution. The FRA also publishes a bimonthly newsletter and a magazine entitled 'Equal Voices', which contains in depth analyzes and features on subjects such as successful integration. Other FRA products include educational, training

---

[177]   Council Regulation 2007/168, [2007] O.J. L53/1.
[178]   European Union Agency for Fundamental Rights 2009, <http://fra.europa.eu/fraWebsite/civil_society/fr_platform/fr_platform_en.htm>, last accessed 27 February 2009.

and promotional materials.

The FRA provides an extensive avenue to research legislation, reports, case law and monitoring organizations across Europe through its online info portal.[179] In addition the FRA continues to use the network of National Focus Points, which were contracted by its predecessor, the EUMC, to collect and disseminate information in each Member State.

A further resource of the FRA takes the form of a legal experts group, FRALEX (Fundamental Rights Agency Legal Experts), which was established in 2007 to produce reports and studies, at a national and European comparative level. In 2008, the FRA published a comparative report on 'Homophobia and Discrimination on Grounds of Sexual Orientation in the EU Member States' based on national reports undertaken by FRALEX members.[180] FRALEX also has undertaken research on child trafficking, data protection and the impact of the Racial Equality Directive. A series of national reports in the area of mental health is forthcoming.

The FRA is likely to become much more engaged on the disability issue in the future (especially as discrimination is one of its key areas of concern, and also because it takes cognisance of both ECHR case law as well as the case law of the European Social Charter) and may even have a role to play under Article 33(2) of the UN Convention on the Rights of Persons with Disabilities with respect to 'domestic' monitoring of the Convention at EU institutional level.

8. STUDIES & REPORTS

The European Commission often commissions studies and reports of major significance in the disability field. The most important reports which were published in 2008 are commented on below.

8.1. MANSELL ET AL, 'DEINSTITUTIONALISATION AND COMMUNITY LIVING – OUTCOMES AND COSTS: REPORT OF A EUROPEAN STUDY', (TIZARD CENTRE, UNIVERSITY OF KENT, 2007)[181]

This project was funded by the Commission's Directorate General for Employment, Social Affairs and Equal Opportunities, and had the goal to compile information on the number of disabled people living in residential institutions in 28 European countries. The project sought to collect and interpret existing statistical and other quantative data, and analyze arrangements necessary for an optimal transition from institutional to community services. Based on this, the report sought to report on relevant issues and make recommendations for cost-effectiveness in the process of deinstitutionalization.

---

[179] European Union Agency for Fundamental Rights 2009, <http://infoportal.fra.europa.eu/InfoPortal/infoportalFrontEndAccess.do>, last accessed 27 February 2009.

[180] Fundamental Rights Agency, 'Homophobia and Discrimination on Grounds of Sexual Orientation in the EU Member States' (June 2008).

[181] Available online at <http://www.kent.ac.uk/tizard/research/DECL_network/Project_reports.html>, last accessed 17 February 2009.

The introduction to this Report notes that the provision of a rigid programme is no longer viewed as the goal of services for people with disabilities. Instead, appropriate service ought to amount to an individualized and flexible range of aids and resources, which underpin independent living. Policy development in the reallocation of financial resources is thus required.

The Report observes that the countries studied have some way to go before they comply with Article 31 of the UN Convention on the Rights of Persons with Disabilities, which requires States to collect data 'to enable them to formulate and implement policies to give effect to the present Convention'. Comprehensive information is not yet available for all types of residential services provided, or for all the client groups involved. Even where the information exists, it is not always collected at national level. In country case studies, the importance of coordination among all agencies involved in the transition process was observed, in light of the number of agencies and different tiers of government involved.

The Report devotes considerable attention to economic and cost factors. It expresses concern at the fact that inputs and responsibilities of family and other unpaid carers often go unrecognized and unsupported, in spite of their economic value to the care system. Although the Report indicates preference for the transition from institutions to community-based services as national mandates, it cautioned policy makers against expecting lower costs. However, it concluded that '[t]here is no evidence that community-based models of care are inherently more costly than institutions, once the comparison is made on the basis of comparable needs of residents and comparable quality of care.'

Considerations relating to local employment and the indirect impact on the local economy should also be taken into account before closing a large institution. Providing deinstitutionalized accommodation in the same communities to offset any negative impact may not be sensible either, as residents may prefer to return to their place of origin. The report notes that people's needs, preferences and circumstances vary, and consequently, so do their service requirements. Thus costs are unlikely to be the same across a group of people. Also, as the needs of individuals change over time, the service systems need to be able to respond fully to these changing needs.

In its recommendations, the Report refers to the need to agree a harmonized data set at European Level. It urged the European Commission to promote joint work between Member States and Eurostat to define a minimum data set for residential services for people with disabilities. The data set ought to be workable for countries which still have services largely based in institutions as well as for countries which are in the advanced stages of replacing institutions with community-based services and independent living. The Report also recommends the publication of progress statistics in each country and calls on the Commission to work with Eurostat to this end.

8.2. SHIMA ET AL, 'THE LABOUR MARKET SITUATION OF PEOPLE WITH DISABILITIES IN EU25' (EUROPEAN CENTRE FOR SOCIAL WELFARE POLICY AND RESEARCH, 2008)[182]

The European Centre for Social Welfare Policy and Research is a UN-affiliated intergovernmental organization based in Vienna. It provides broad expertise in welfare and social policy development.[183] It produces a series of Policy Briefs to provide a synthesis of its recent research and policy advice.

In 2008 it published a 'Policy Brief on the Labour Market Situation of people with disabilities in EU25'. It details some of the results of a Study on the status of people with disabilities in the Member States of the EU' which was financed by the Directorate General for Employment, Social Affairs and Equal Opportunities of the European Commission.[184] It looks at the different methods employed to overcome the challenges causing low employment, and noted that different methods in recording information resulted in comparability difficulties between some countries.

The Policy Brief notes a high proportion of persons with disabilities who are inactive or unemployed in most countries. Increases in employment share between 2000 and 2006 were noted in most countries, with the exception of Poland and the Czech Republic.[185] A tendency for more men than women with disabilities to be in ordinary employment was also noted,[186] although males over the age of 45 constitute the highest share of unemployed people with disabilities.[187]

The Policy Brief also acknowledges the recent shift from the medical model of disability to a social and human rights based approach, evidenced by Member States' efforts to encourage social inclusion of people with disabilities, as well as inclusion in the labour market. From economic and demographic perspectives too, the Policy Brief considers it vital for Member State authorities to move away from a passive compensation system to an active integration approach. It noted that in many Member States, the method of choice is mainstream inclusion and statistics indicate increases in the numbers of disabled people in ordinary employment.[188] Alternative methods cited include the provision of special and separate employment opportunities, or a combination of both.

The Policy Brief looks at how various Member States have attempted to develop infrastructures to avoid marginalization of persons with disabilities. The Czech system of contributions for operational costs and tax advantage schemes, which are also provided in Slovenia, are discussed.[189] The Policy Brief also

---

[182]   Available online at <http://www.euro.centre.org/data/1201610451_25081.pdf>, last accessed 17 February 2009.

[183]   European Centre 2009, <http://www.euro.centre.org>, last accessed 11 March 2009.

[184]   'Study of Compilation of Disability Statistical Data from the Administrative Registers of Member States' (November 2007, Chapter III, coordinated by Applica, Brussels).

[185]   Ibid, 5.

[186]   Ibid, 8.

[187]   Ibid, 12.

[188]   Ibid, 16.

[189]   Ibid, 15.

notes the Member States which have applied public and/or private sector quota schemes. Mention is also given to what the Policy Brief terms 'sheltered employment schemes', and notes that usage of such schemes is increasing in some Member States while the opposite is the case in others.[190]

The Policy Brief recommends that active labour market policies of Member States and the EU at large should seek to attract and retain people with disabilities into the labour force, improve enterprise and worker adaptability, and invest in better education and skills training. Other measures suggested are the improvement of national and regional strategies, the modernization of social protection systems, the mobilization of local communities and the consideration of market needs when matching workers and employers.

In essence, this Policy Brief stresses the contribution people with disabilities can make to the labour force and to overall economic activity. While it acknowledges the efforts made by Member States to break down discrimination barriers, it calls for more integrative measures and programmes to ensure people with disabilities are considered as an integral part of society and the labour market.

9. ANNUAL EUROPEAN DAY OF PEOPLE WITH DISABILITIES

Since 1992, the United Nations has set December 3rd as the International Day of People with Disabilities. To mark this occasion each year, a consortium, funded by the European Commission, work with the European Disability Forum to organize a policy conference in the first week of December each year. The European Day event brings together a wide range of stakeholders on disability from across Europe.

The first European Day was held in 1993 and marked the beginning of an intensive strategic campaign for an anti-discrimination clause in the EC Treaty. Each European Day leads to a major Report. The famous 1995 report was entitled 'Disabled Persons' Status in the European Treaties: Invisible Citizens'. It argued for Community disability anti-discrimination legislation, in light of the experience of persons with disabilities in Europe. More particularly, it provided detailed arguments as to why the EC Treaty needed to be amended to confer explicit legislative power on the EC to enact EC-wide anti-discrimination laws. In a sense, it was the European equivalent to the Report of the US National Council with Disabilities in 1986 - 'Towards Independence' - which had a major impact in the drafting of the Americans with Disabilities Act (1990).

The 1995 European Day report provided the following draft clause for inclusion in the EC Treaty:

Within the scope of application of this Treaty, and without prejudice to any special provisions contained therein, any discrimination on grounds of nationality, race, sex, disability, sexual orientation or religion shall be prohibited.

This set the stage for the drafting of Article 13 EC, which introduced EC-level competence to combat discrimination on a variety of grounds.

---

[190]   Ibid, 3.

9.1. EUROPEAN DAY 2007 (5-6 DECEMBER 2007)

Web Resource: <http://ec.europa.eu/social/main.jsp?catId=88&langId=en&even
tsId=33&furtherEvents=yes>

In 2007, the EU Day focused on People with Disabilities as 'Active Players in the Internal Market'. The Conference considered both how people with disabilities can fully enjoy the four freedoms of the internal market - free movement of persons, goods, services and capital - and how they can contribute and strengthen the internal market.

The Conference acknowledged the barriers of discrimination and lack of accessibility within the internal market, and called for a legal framework to address these. It called for a comprehensive EC strategy on access to the four freedoms of the internal market, and for all new internal market legislation to by assessed in terms of its impact on people with disabilities. The Conference also sought the provision of clear information on products and services, and the establishment of a complaints mechanism to address related accessibility issues. It recommended that the principles of accessibility and non-discrimination be applied in public-private partnerships in Member States and in the administration of European Structural Funds. The importance of the UN Convention was also emphasized.

9.2. EUROPEAN DAY 2008 (1-2 DECEMBER 2008)

Web Resource: <http://ec.europa.eu/social/main.jsp?catId=88&langId=en&even
tsId=104>

In 2008, the EU Day was themed 'acting locally for a society for all' and focused on examples of mainstreaming and the local impact of EU action. The event also focused on the UN Convention on the Rights of Persons with Disabilities. This discussion concerned Convention provisions, which may be best implemented at the supranational level, as well as how the European institutions can support domestic implementation of the Convention. The Conference also looked at the future development of the European Disability Action Plan and the use of European Structural Funds to provide people with disabilities with training and accessible infrastructure. Conference presentations looked at Member State practice in the areas of accessible air travel, the provision of UN Convention training and education, dialogue and participation and accessible infrastructure.

THE COUNCIL OF EUROPE

Web Resource: <http://www.coe.int>

1. BACKGROUND TO THE COUNCIL OF EUROPE AND DISABILITY

The Council of Europe is Europe's premiere human rights institution. Therefore, one should logically look to the Council of Europe for positive guidance and jurisprudence on disability and human rights.

1.1. THE ROLE AND INSTITUTIONS OF THE COUNCIL OF EUROPE

The 'Statute of the Council of Europe' is contained in the Treaty of London, 5 May 1949.[1] The principal aim of the organization is to 'promote unity among its members for the purpose of safeguarding and realizing the ideals and principles which are their common heritage and facilitating their economic and social progress' (Article 1.a of the Statute). Chief among these ideals and principles are human rights, democracy and the rule of law.

The Council of Europe - unlike the EU - is a classic inter-governmental organization with no supra-national legal competence. Most of its powers and functions derive from a web of treaty obligations entered into voluntarily by its Member States.[2] From 1949-2003, these treaties were collected in the European Treaty Series - ETS (193 treaties in all). Since 2004, they are collected in the Council of Europe Treaty Series (CETS). From the original ten Member States, membership has expanded to forty-seven Member States, with over eight hundred million citizens between them. The Holy See, the United States, Canada, Japan and Mexico have observer status. The Council has its headquarters in Strasbourg.

The Council of Europe is directed by a Committee of Ministers that is a high-level political body responsible for decision-making. The Minister of Foreign Affairs from each Member State of the Council of Europe sits on the Committee. Effectively, however, the bulk of the business of the Committee of Ministers is carried out by the permanent representatives (ambassador) of each Member State

---

[1] ETS No. 001, Statute of the Council of Europe, <http://conventions.coe.int/treaty/en/Treaties/Html/001.htm>, last accessed 23 February 2009. The Council of Europe emerged during the post war reconciliation phase with the aim of greater unity, and facilitating the economic and social progress of members (Article 1(a)). The original ten signatories were Belgium, Denmark, France, Ireland, Italy, Luxemburg, the Netherlands, Norway, Sweden and the United Kingdom.

[2] The treaty website of the Council of Europe is available at <http://conventions.coe.int/>.

to the Council of Europe. The Presidency of the Council of Europe rotates every six months. Some Presidencies have included disability among their priority activities. The Council is administered through its Secretariat, which is directed by a Secretary General.

The Council of Europe advances its main aims by adopting legally binding treaties (Conventions and agreements), of which there are over two hundred. The most significant human rights treaties adopted by the Council of Europe include the European Convention on Human Rights (ECHR), the European Social Charter (ESC), the Revised European Social Charter (RESC), the European Convention against Torture (CPT) and the Framework Convention for the Protection of National Minorities. The Committee of Ministers supervises the execution of judgments of the European Court of Human Rights and the Decisions of the European Committee on Social Rights – both of which are active on the issue of disability (see below).

The Council of Europe also has a Commissioner for Human Rights, mandated to promote awareness and protect human rights in all Member States.[3] This Commissioner's Office is, in effect, an early warning system. To this end, the Commissioner conducts country visits and follows up with Member States and the Committee of Ministers. The current Commissioner has made a point of drawing attention to the rights of persons with disabilities within his country visits and reports to Governments. It is likely that the role of the Commissioner in the disability context will grow and it is therefore important to follow his relevant activities.

The Committee of Ministers can also adopt Recommendations that provide high-level policy guidance to the Member States. Some of these have been especially influential in the disability field. The Committee may also adopt Resolutions that, although of a lesser status, are nonetheless important from a political perspective.

Where European-level cooperation is anticipated by the Statute of the Council of Europe, then the relevant inter-governmental activities may proceed using the support of the Council's secretariat. This may result in the adoption, by the Committee of Ministers, of a new legally binding treaty or a policy Recommendation. Where, however, the Statue does not provide explicit grounding for a particular activity, then such activities may nevertheless proceed if a 'Partial Agreement' has been concluded. Basically, these 'Partial Agreements' allow the machinery of the Council of Europe to be used where some (but not all) Member States want to get involved. The 'Partial Agreement' in the Social and Public Policy field is especially relevant in the disability context. It led to the establishment of the Unit for the Integration of Persons with Disabilities within the Council of Europe's secretariat.[4] This Unit has been pioneering in its disability activities. It supports a web of inter-governmental activities focused on disability. It also produces or commissions important European-level research on disability. Its website contains a comprehensive library of policy Recommendations, conference reports and an extensive range of disability publications.

---

3   The website of the Commissioner for Human Rights is available at <http://www.coe.int/t/commissioner/Activities/mandate_en.asp>.

4   The website of the Unit for the Integration of Persons with Disabilities is available at <http://www.coe.int/T/E/Social%5FCohesion/soc%2Dsp/Integration/>.

The Parliamentary Assembly of the Council of Europe (PACE) is comprised of 636 representatives from the national parliaments of its Member States.[5] It is not a classic Parliament, in the sense that it does not debate and adopt legislation. It is essentially a consultative chamber. It has, from time to time, expressed the conscience of Europe on many disability issues, and indeed its reports and deliberations can act as a spur to the initiation of inter-governmental activities that may lead to binding treaties. From a technical perspective, the Parliamentary Assembly adopts three types of texts: Recommendations, Resolutions and Opinions - none of which are legally binding. It meets four times a year in Strasbourg to discuss areas of common concern.

1.2. THE STRATEGIC DIRECTION OF THE COUNCIL OF EUROPE ON DISABILITY

Before reviewing the recent output of the various Council of Europe organs on disability, it should be emphasized that the Council has gradually elevated its profile on the issue. Separate from - but building upon - the outputs of its various organs over the years on disability, the Committee of Ministers adopted a major Recommendation in 2006 that sets out a coherent policy framework on disability. Appended to this Recommendation is a Council of Europe Action Plan 'to promote the rights and full participation of people with disabilities in society - improving the quality of life of people with disabilities in Europe 2006-2015'.[6] This is a high-level political instrument. As befits a Recommendation, it exhorts national Governments to integrate the elements of the Action Plan into their own legislation, policies and practice as well as giving guidance to the future activities of the Council itself.

In adopting the Action Plan, the Council of Ministers called on Member States to integrate the Plan into domestic policy, and to promote it in sectors where public authorities do not have direct responsibility. Member States are also asked to promote the Action Plan to the widest audience possible. They are called upon to screen their policies and legislation in light of the Action Plan and implement specific measures under each of the action lines. The Action Plan encourages collaboration with civil society in both implementation and evaluation. It makes provision for 'effective follow up' at European level and asks that Member States provide regular updates on their progress to the Council of Europe. It envisages a forum to manage that process of reporting. This should reveal extremely useful information on disability, and will become an important resource for researchers in the future.

The 2006-2015 Action Plan contains fifteen lines of action. The first two lines of action relate to participation in political, public and cultural life. The Action Plan goes on to address the importance of access to information and communication and refers to both public and private providers. With a view to furthering

---

[5]   The website of the Parliamentary Assembly of the Council of Europe is available at <http://assembly.coe.int/default.asp>.

[6]   Council of Europe Action Plan to promote the rights and full participation of people with disabilities in society: improving the quality of life of people with disabilities in Europe 2006- 2015 <http://www.coe.int/t/e/social_cohesion/soc%2Dsp/ Rec_2006_5%20Disability%20Action%20Plan.pdf>, last accessed 28 April 2009.

social inclusion and economic independence, the Action Plan contains lines of action on equal access to education, training and employment. Accessibility of the built environment and transport are also promoted in the context of equal opportunities and independent living. The Action Plan also calls on governments to enhance community living. Other action lines relate to healthcare, rehabilitation and social and legal protection. The Action Plan also contains specific provisions on protecting persons with disabilities from abuse, on the collection and analysis of data and on awareness raising.

The Action Plan contains a section dealing with cross-cutting aspects of discrimination. It looks at the added difficulties faced by women and girls with disabilities. The Action Plan considers the rights of the child and the position of young people, as well as elderly people with disabilities. It calls for planning and coordination of services to improve the quality of life of persons with disabilities who, due to the nature of their disability, require a high level of support.

The Action Plan should be consulted regularly since it sets out benchmarks for change that the Member States have agreed. Moreover it provides a roadmap for the intergovernmental activities of the Council of Europe. It is probable that more of the treaty bodies of the Council of Europe (e.g., the European Court of Human Rights) will refer to it when reinforcing their own efforts in the field.

What follows is an account of the relevant output of the main organs of the Council of Europe in the disability field.

2. THE EUROPEAN COURT OF HUMAN RIGHTS AND RECENT CASE LAW ON DISABILITY

Web Resource: <http://www.echr.coe.int/echr/>

The Convention for the Protection of Human Rights and Fundamental Freedoms (ECHR) was signed in Rome on 4 November 1950 and is the most famous of the Council of Europe treaties.[7] It was intended to give European expression to the values contained in the Universal Declaration of Human Rights (1948) at the global level.

2.1. BACKGROUND AND JURISDICTION OF THE COURT

The European Court of Human Rights (ECtHR) was established under the Convention (as amended by Protocol No.11).[8] The ECtHR can sit as a three-member Committee, a Chamber or a Grand Chamber, depending on the case before it. Any party to a case may request that a case be referred to the Grand Chamber. The request should state 'the serious question affecting the interpretation or application of the Convention, or the Protocols thereto, or the serious issue of general importance' which, in the view of the party, warrants consideration by the Grand Chamber (Article 43 ECHR and Rule 73 of the Rules of Court).

---

[7] ETS No. 005, <http://www.echr.coe.int/NR/rdonlyres/D5CC24A7-DC13-4318-B457-5C9014916D7A/0/EnglishAnglais.pdf>, last accessed 23 February 2009.

[8] ETS No. 155, <http://conventions.coe.int/Treaty/en/Treaties/Html/155.htm>, last accessed 24 February 2009.

The jurisdiction of the Court extends to 'all cases concerning the interpretation and application' of the Convention. As befits a court whose 'outer supervision' is considered subsidiary to the legal responsibilities of the Member States, all applicants must first exhaust domestic remedies before lodging an application. The Committee of Ministers may itself seek interpretations from the ECtHR on any of the provisions of the Convention or its Protocols.

The judgments of the ECtHR are not self-executing. Rather, they are enforced politically by the Committee of Ministers whose role it is to supervise the execution of judgments. Although the Committee cannot compel compliance, its recommendations are held in high regard by the Member States and are usually respected. The political costs of non-compliance are extremely high. Indeed, both the Council of Europe and the European Union see non-compliance as unacceptable, and even as grounds for expulsion.

The 'Rules of Court' provide detailed procedural and other guidance.[9] When an application is sent to the ECtHR, it is assigned to one of five Sections. The President of the section then appoints a rapporteur to decide whether a Chamber or Committee should deal with it. The application may be declared inadmissible by the Committee or be sent on to a Chamber. A Chamber may refer cases to the Grand Chamber where there is a serious question of interpretation of the Convention, or where there exists a risk of departure from existing case law.

The ECtHR has a growing practice of accepting amicus curia briefs (Rule 44, 'Third Party Intervention' in the Rules of Court). This opens up the opportunity for civil society organizations of persons with disabilities and human rights commissions and similar bodies to intervene in cases. This growing window is of exceptional importance to European-level disability NGOs interested in advancing the engagement of the Court in the field.

The Chamber or its President where appropriate, may, at the request of a party or of any other person concerned or of its own motion, indicate to the parties any 'interim measure' which it considers should be adopted 'in the interests of the parties or of the proper conduct of the proceedings before it' (Rule 39, 'Interim Measures', Rules of Court). Notice of these measures is given to the Committee of Ministers. This is important in the context of institutional settings where certain practices might be forestalled even before a case can be heard on its merits before the ECtHR. Given that it could take quite some time for a case to reach judgment, this is extremely important.

The Chamber may request information from the parties on any matter connected with the implementation of any 'interim measure' it has requested. If an application is deemed admissible, the Chamber may then invite parties to submit further evidence and written observations. If there was no hearing conducted during the admissibility procedure, the Chamber may decide to hold a hearing on the merits of the case at this point.

While all of the provisions of the ECHR are relevant in the context of disability, a number of them are of especial relevance to people with disabilities. The right to liberty (Article 5 and especially Article 5(1)e which allows for the detention of 'persons of unsound mind') is critically important for people with disabilities. Detention in institutions has proven to be a highly contentious issue in recent

---

9   European Court of Human Rights, Rules of Court, Registry of the Court, December 2008.

years and has arisen before the European Court of Human Rights on a number of occasions. To a certain extent, this provided the Court with a classic civil liberties rights window onto disability (limiting the loss of liberty). The Court has managed to produce a sophisticated jurisprudence over the years that narrows down considerably the substantive grounds on which persons 'of unsound mind' can be deprived of their liberty and which enhances the relevant procedural safeguards. The term 'person of unsound mind' is dated and objectionable. The Court has treated it as a term of art. In effect, disability as such (no matter how it is phrased), is never deemed to be a legitimate ground for loss of liberty. Rather, it is the risk of danger of the person to others and to him/herself that is most reckonable (the so-called 'police power' of States).

In the context of detention in public institutions, the right to protection against torture, degrading and inhuman treatment is also of critical importance (Article 3). This article frequently relates to the quality of the conditions of detention. The case law of the Court on this issue is quite extensive. The Convention for the Prevention of Torture and Inhuman and Degrading Treatment or Punishment adds strength to this provision by putting in place a robust prevention system. Reports of the relevant treaty monitoring body - the Committee for the Prevention of Torture - have highlighted grave abuses in institutional settings for persons with disabilities (especially intellectual disabilities). The case law of this Committee should also be actively consulted when examining how institutions for persons with disabilities - as well as other institutions such as prisons - function.

The notion of 'positive obligations' is important generally under the ECHR, but particularly so for persons with disabilities. The relevant case law under Article 8 (respect for private and family life) is becoming extremely significant in the context of disability. Embedded in this jurisprudence is some notion of the human personality (or personhood). This concept has proven extremely important, both in terms of potential 'positive obligations', but also in terms of the important debate about legal capacity law reform across Europe (see case law below).

Advancing equality and non-discrimination (Article 14) is obviously important for people with disabilities. As is well known, however, Article 14 has some inherent weaknesses. Firstly, it does not explicitly mention disability as a protected ground, although there is the option of interpreting 'other status' as covering people with disabilities. Secondly, the scope of Article 14 is limited to the application of Convention rights and cannot form an independent (or 'autonomous') cause of action. Protocol 12 to the European Convention was intended to cure this.[10] It was adopted in 2000 by the Committee of Ministers and crafted to extend the applicability of the non-discrimination norm beyond the rights protected under the ECHR itself. Article 1(1) prohibits discrimination with respect to the enjoyment of 'any right set forth by law' on the grounds covered under the original Article 14 (e.g., sex, race, colour, etc). The occasion was not taken to expand these grounds to explicitly encompass disability. The phrase 'any right set forth by law' has the potential to apply the prohibition on discrimination to, for example, social benefits such as independent living entitlements. Although now in force (with seventeen ratifications), Protocol 12 has not been ratified by most major Member States of the Council of Europe. The only exceptions are the Netherlands and Finland.

---

[10] Protocol 12 to the Convention for the Protection of Human Rights and Fundamental Freedoms, Rome, 4 November 2000, ETS 177.

2.2. RECENT DISABILITY RELATED CASE LAW

The recent case law emanating from the European Court of Human Rights in the field of disability will now be considered.

2.2.1. DH and Others v. the Czech Republic (Judgment of Grand Chamber, November 2007)[11]

From a disability perspective the decision of the Grand Chamber in the case of *DH and Others v. the Czech Republic* will have far reaching repercussions. It considerably expands and deepens the conception of discrimination under the European Convention for the Protection of Human Rights.

Before DH the case law of the ECtHR on discrimination had been disappointing, and had failed to develop a clear approach to indirect discrimination. It had equivocated on whether statistical evidence could be used to lay a prima facie case of indirect discrimination and whether, or how, the burden of proof might shift to the would-be discriminator once a well-founded prima facie case of discrimination had been established. As a consequence, the case law on discrimination of the European Court of Justice was increasingly seen to be far ahead of that of the European Court on Human Rights.

The applicants in this case were 18 Czech nationals of Roma origin who had all been assigned to special schools for children with learning difficulties between 1996 and 1999, following psychological tests designed to assess their intellectual capacity. The consent of a child's guardians is required under Czech law for these tests. It had been reported in 1997 that 80-90% of pupils in some special schools in the Czech Republic were Roma.[12] It was argued that the segregation of Roma children at the primary educational level had long-term impacts and, in particular, diminished their prospects of being able to enter secondary education.

Fourteen of the applicants sought a review of their segregation by the Ostrava Education Department on the grounds that the assessment tests performed had been unreliable. They also sought a review on the basis that they had not been sufficiently informed as to the consequences of giving consent to the testing. The Education Department found that the placements had been made in accordance with the statutory rules that were then in place. Twelve of the applicants appealed to the Czech Constitutional Court, arguing that their placement in special schools amounted to a general practice that created segregation on the basis of unlawful racial discrimination.[13]

The Chamber of the Court had ruled (February 2006) that, despite clear statistical evidence to the contrary, it could not find that there was indirect discrimination against Roma children. This decision stood in contrast to a multitude of sources (some from within the Council of Europe itself) attesting to this dis-

---

[11] Application No. 57325/00, Grand Chamber Judgment of 13 November 2007.

[12] European Roma Rights Centre, 'A Special Remedy: Roma and Schools for the Mentally Handicapped in the Czech Republic' (June 1999), chapter 3.

[13] The two systems consisted of special schools for the Roma and mainstream primary schools for the majority of the population. The Constitutional Court dismissed that appeal on 20 October 1999.

crimination. The Chamber held that there had been no violation of Article 14 read in conjunction with Article 2 of Protocol No 1 on the right to education.

The Chamber found that the Government had established a system of special schools and had made considerable efforts in those schools to help certain categories of pupils to acquire a basic education. The Chamber observed that the rules governing the placement of children in special schools did not refer to pupils' ethnic origin and that the schools pursued the legitimate aim of adapting the education system to the needs, aptitudes and disabilities of the children concerned.

The essence of the case was that Roma children were disproportionately and wrongly placed in segregated educational settings for children with intellectual disabilities. Of course, a much deeper question is the justifiability of these segregated settings on the ground of disability in the first place. The Chamber broached this issue indirectly. On the matter of segregation of children with intellectual disabilities, the lower Chamber stated that:

> ...(47) In its admissibility decision in the present case, the Court also reiterated that the setting and planning of the curriculum falls in principle within the competence of the Contracting States. This mainly involves questions of expediency on which it is not for the Court to rule and whose solution may legitimately vary according to the country and the era (*Valsamis v. Greece*, judgment of 18 December 1996, Reports 1996-VI, § 28).

> With regard to pupils with special needs, the Court accepts that the choice between having a single type of school for everyone, highly specialised structures or unified structures with specialist sections is not an easy one and there does not appear to be an ideal solution. It involves a difficult exercise in balancing the various competing interests. The Court wishes to reiterate with regard to the States' margin of appreciation in the education sphere that the States cannot be prohibited from setting up different types of school for children with difficulties or implementing special educational programmes to respond to special needs.

In a concurring opinion, Judge Costa referred to previous case law to the effect that a 'States' educational choices were more a question of expediency than of legitimacy under the Convention.'[14] This gave the appearance that the principle of segregated education on the grounds of disability - or its extent - were not cognisable matters under the Convention.

The applicants requested a hearing in the Grand Chamber. They made submissions to the Grand Chamber to the effect that the restrictive view of discrimination taken by the Chamber was incompatible with both the Convention and previous case law. Extracts from the Grand Chamber's assessment are contained in the Annex to the Yearbook.

The Grand Chamber began its assessment by taking judicial notice of the fact that the Roma - as a result of their turbulent history and constant uprooting - had become a highly disadvantaged and vulnerable minority throughout Europe. Therefore, the Grand Chamber stated that the Roma required special protection and this protection extended to the sphere of education. The applicants argued

---

[14]   Chamber Judgment in *DH and Others v. the Czech Republic* delivered on 7 February 2006, Concurring Opinion of Judge Costa, at para. 7.

that by being placed in segregated schools, they had, without objective and reasonable justification, been treated less favourably than non-Roma children in a comparable situation. In support of that claim they had submitted statistical data based on information provided by head teachers that showed that more than half the pupils in special schools in Ostrava were from the Roma community. The Grand Chamber accepted that the evidence submitted by the applicants could be regarded as sufficiently strong to give rise to a presumption of indirect discrimination. Thereafter, the burden of proof should shift to the Government to show that the differential impact was the result of objective factors unrelated to ethnic origin.

Significantly, for our purposes, the Grand Chamber stated that it:

(198). ... accepts that the Government's decision to retain the special-school system was motivated by the desire to find a solution for children with special educational needs. However, it shares the disquiet of the other Council of Europe institutions who have expressed concerns about the more basic curriculum followed in these schools and, in particular, the segregation the system causes.

At first sight, this would appear to put the question of segregated education on the ground of disability on the defensive. However, it went on to state:

(205). As the Chamber noted in its admissibility decision in the instant case, the choice between a single school for everyone, highly specialised structures and unified structures with specialised sections is not an easy one. It entails a difficult balancing exercise between the competing interests. As to the setting and planning of the curriculum, this mainly involves questions of expediency on which it is not for the Court to rule.

Taken together and on balance, these two statements would at least appear to leave an opening for arguments challenging segregated education on the ground of disability.

With regard to the actual tests and assessments themselves, it was acknowledged by the Grand Chamber that all the children examined had sat the same tests, irrespective of their ethnic origin. The Grand Chamber noted that the Czech authorities had themselves acknowledged in 1999 that 'Romany children with average or above-average intellect' were often placed in schools on the basis of the results of psychological tests and that the tests were conceived for the majority population and did not take Roma specifics into consideration. The Grand Chamber considered that there was a danger that the tests were biased and that the results were not analyzed in light of the particularities and special characteristics of the Roma children who sat them. In that connection, the Grand Chamber observed that the European Commission against Racism and Intolerance had noted that 'the practice of channelling of Roma/Gypsy children into special schools for the mentally-retarded' was often 'quasi-automatic' and needed to be examined to ensure that any testing used was 'fair' and that the true abilities of each child were 'properly evaluated'.[15] The Grand Chamber also noted that Council of Europe's Commissioner for Human Rights had reported that Roma children were

---

[15] Grand Chamber Judgment in *DH and Others v. Czech Republic* of 13 November 2007, paras. 63-64.

frequently placed in classes for children with special needs 'without an adequate psychological or pedagogical assessment, the real criteria clearly being their ethnic origin'.[16] In these circumstances, the results of the tests could not serve as justification for the difference in treatment.

In relation to parental consent, which the Czech Government had considered to be the decisive factor justifying the difference in treatment, the Grand Chamber was not satisfied that the parents of the Roma children, who were often themselves poorly educated, were capable of weighing up all the aspects of the situation and the consequences of giving their consent. In any event, and in view of the fundamental importance of the prohibition of discrimination, no waiver (voluntary or otherwise) of the right to education could be accepted under the Convention.

While recognizing the efforts the Czech authorities had made to ensure that Roma children received schooling, the Grand Chamber was not satisfied that the difference in treatment between Roma children and non-Roma children was objectively and reasonably justified. While noting new Czech legislation providing for children with special educational needs in mainstream schools, the Grand Chamber concluded that the national legislation at the relevant time had had a disproportionately prejudicial effect on the Roma community. It held that the applicants had suffered discriminatory treatment and that there had been a violation of Article 14 of the Convention, read in conjunction with Article 2 of Protocol No. 1.

The Grand Chamber judgment is highly significant for the following reasons.

First of all, the judgment revitalizes the prohibition on discrimination under the Convention. For the first time, the ECtHR clearly accepted the notion of 'indirect discrimination'. According to the Grand Chamber judgment there is no need to prove a discriminatory intent. Furthermore, the Court now requires the burden of proof to be reversed once a well-grounded prima facie case of 'indirect discrimination' has been laid. It is then incumbent on the respondent State to show that the difference in the impact of the legislation was the result of objective factors. The key here is whether the legislation pursues a 'legitimate aim' and whether the means used are 'proportionate'. These developments in the notion of discrimination are relevant to all but may become especially relevant in future disability cases.

Secondly, while the Grand Chamber did not directly address the underlying issue of the legitimacy of segregated education on the grounds of disability, it did at least intimate that it is open to arguments. It did refer, obliquely, to the views of other Council of Europe institutions on this issue. This hints strongly at Action line 4 of the aforementioned Council of Europe Action Plan on disability, which points decidedly away from an over-reliance on segregated education and refers to a more inclusive model with mainstreaming as the primary policy default. Certainly, the European Social Committee (see below) does not view the right to integrated education as a question of 'expediency'.

Thirdly, the emphasis placed by the Grand Chamber on appropriate testing, assessments and examinations could prove extremely important in the disability

---

[16]   Commissioner for Human Rights, 'Human Rights Situation of the Roma, Sinti and Travellers in Europe', (February 2006).

context. Of course, the main issue in the disability context is not merely the use of tests to segregate (as in the DH case), but also the design of tests. It is certainly arguable that some (unmodified) tests might reveal more about a disability and less about a candidates' knowledge of a subject. It is obvious that some form of 'reasonable accommodation' is required lest such tests give a skewed view of a candidate's true abilities. It might just be possible – resting on the logic of DH – to argue for such accommodations to avoid indirect discrimination and the disparate impact that the administration of standardized tests might have on children with disabilities.

2.2.2. Shtukaturov v. Russia (Judgment of Chamber, March 2008)[17]

In this case, the applicant was a Russian national who had a mental disability. In 2004 and at the age of 22, the applicant was placed in a hospital for in-patient treatment. Shortly afterwards, his mother initiated legal proceedings to remove her son's legal capacity and have herself appointed as his guardian. The applicant was not formally notified of these proceedings. An expert psychiatric examination of the applicant was commissioned in the legal proceedings to determine whether the applicant had a mental illness and whether he was able to understand his actions or control them. In December 2004 a hearing on his legal capacity took place. This lasted approximately 10 minutes and the applicant was declared legally incapable and his mother appointed guardian. The applicant was not informed about the hearing and therefore did not attend. As he was unaware of the decision, he did not (and could not) lodge an appeal within the 10-day period allowed under national law.

The applicant first became aware of the relevant domestic legal proceedings in November 2005 when he found documentation among his mother's belongings. Two days later he was placed in hospital at the request of his mother. As his mother was his legal guardian, her consent ensured he was admitted as a voluntary patient. It followed that an authorization from a court for an involuntary placement was not required. The hospital management refused to allow the applicants' lawyer to visit him.

Following a number of failed attempts in the Russian courts to challenge the legal basis of his client's detention, the applicant's lawyer requested the ECtHR to indicate 'interim measures' to the Russian Government under Rule 39 of the Rules of the Court. The ECtHR directed the respondent Government to allow a meeting between the applicant and his legal counsel. However, the chief doctor of the hospital informed the lawyer that he did not regard the ECtHR's decision on 'interim measures' as binding. On appeal to the St. Petersburg City Court it was held that the Russian Federation – as a special subject of international relations – enjoys immunity from foreign jurisdiction and is not bound by coercive measures applied by foreign courts. The St. Petersburg City Court also concluded that the lawyer had no authority to act on behalf of the applicant, as the applicant's mother was his sole legal guardian with authority to act on behalf of the applicant in all legal transactions.

The applicant's complaints under the European Convention related to Articles 5 (right to liberty), 6 (the right to fair trial), 8 (the right to respect for private

---

17   Application no. 44009/05, Chamber Judgment of 27 March 2008.

life), 13 (right to an effective national remedy), 14 (prohibition of discrimination), 34 (the right to individual petition to the European Court of Human Rights) and 41 (the right to just satisfaction). Extracts from the ECtHR's assessment are contained in the Annex to this Yearbook.

In its judgment, the Chamber held that there was a violation of Article 6 as regards the incapacity proceedings. In the context of Article 6(1) of the Convention, the ECtHR case law affords a certain margin of appreciation to the domestic courts in cases involving mentally ill persons. For example, the domestic court can make relevant procedural arrangements in order to secure the good administration of justice and the protection of the health of the person concerned. However, these measures should not detract from the essence of the applicant's right to a fair trial. In assessing whether or not the exclusion of the applicant from the relevant domestic hearing was necessary, the Chamber took into account all relevant factors. This included an examination of the nature and complexity of the issue before the domestic courts, the gravity of the issues for the applicant and whether his appearance in person would have represented any threat to others or to himself. The Chamber accepted that the applicant was an individual with a history of psychiatric problems. However, it took due account of the fact that despite his mental illness, he had led a relatively independent life. As such, it was crucial for the judge in the incapacity proceedings to have at least a brief visual contact with the applicant, and preferably the judge should have questioned the applicant. Therefore, the Chamber concluded that the decision of the judge to decide the capacity issue on the basis of documentary evidence alone and without seeing or hearing the applicant, was unreasonable and in breach of the principle of 'equality of arms' that is an integral part of the adversarial proceedings envisioned by Article 6(1).

The Chamber considered the Russian Government's counter-argument that a representative of the hospital and the district prosecutor attended the hearing, and that this was a sufficient procedural safeguard. However, the Chamber considered this presence insufficient in ensuring that the proceedings were truly adversarial. The representative of the hospital acted on behalf of an institution that had prepared a report on the applicant, and was referred to in the judgment of the domestic Russian court as an 'interested party'. The Chamber also stated that the Government failed to explain the role of the prosecutor in the proceedings and that the record of the hearing showed that both the prosecutor and the hospital representative remained passive during the ten-minute hearing. The Chamber concluded that the proceedings before the Vasileostrovskiy District Court were not fair and violated Article 6(1) of the Convention.

The Chamber also reiterated that any interference with an individual's right to respect for his private life constitutes a breach of Article 8 of the Convention (the right to respect for private and family life) unless it is 'in accordance with the law', pursues a legitimate aim or aims, and is 'necessary in a democratic society' in the sense that it is proportionate to the aims sought. It is evident, from this element of the decision, that to interfere with an individual's legal capacity can amount to an interference with his legal personality. In the instant case, the Chamber noted:

that the interference with the applicant's private life was very serious. As a result of his incapacitation the applicant became fully dependant on his official guardian in almost all areas of life. Furthermore, 'full incapacitation' was applied for an indefinite period and could not, as the applicant's case shows, be challenged otherwise than through the guardian, who opposed any attempts to discontinue the measure.[18]

The applicant in this case claimed that full incapacitation had been an inadequate response to the problems he experienced. Under Article 8 the authorities are required to strike a fair balance between the interests of a person and any other legitimate interests concerned. A stricter scrutiny is required in respect of very serious limitations in the sphere of private life.

In concluding that there had been a violation of the right to respect for private and family life, home and correspondence as protected by Article 8, the Chamber considered three distinct factors. First was the seriousness of the interference with the applicant's private life. It resulted in his full incapacitation for an indefinite period and he became fully dependant on his official guardian in almost all areas of his life. She was the only person in a position to challenge the 'full incapacitation', but she opposed any attempts to discontinue the measure. The second factor related to the procedural flaws, under which the applicant was unable to participate in the proceedings, was not questioned by the judge in person and was unable to challenge the judgment. The Chamber was particularly concerned by the fact that the hearing on the merits in the applicant's case had lasted only ten minutes. The third factor of concern to the Chamber was the fact that the Russian District Court relied solely on the findings of a medical report, which was not sufficiently clear on a number of points.

The Chamber stated that the existence of a mental disorder, even a serious one, could not be the sole reason to justify full incapacitation. In an analogy to cases concerning deprivation of liberty, the Chamber stated that the mental disorder must be 'of a kind or degree' warranting full legal incapacitation. In this case, there was no assessment of 'the kind and degree' of the applicant's mental illness or incapacity.

The Chamber noted that the legislative framework in Russia did not leave the judge with any other choice.[19] In respect of the Russian Civil Code, the Chamber referred to Recommendation No. R(99)4 of the Committee of Ministers of the Council of Europe on principles concerning the legal protection of incapable adults.[20] In particular, the Chamber emphasized the need for safeguards including flexibility in the legal response, the maximum preservation of capacity, the principle of proportionality, the right to be heard in person and matters of duration and appeal. The Chamber acknowledged that Recommendation No. R(99)4 does not have the force of law, but that the principles therein represent a common European standard in this area.

The applicant also complained that his placement in the psychiatric hospital

---

[18]   Chamber Decision of 27 March 2008, para. 90.

[19]   The Russian Civil Code draws a sharp distinction between capacity and incapacity. It does not provide for any 'borderline' situation other than for drug or alcohol addicts.

[20]   As adopted by the Committee of Ministers on 23 February 1999, <http://www.coe. int/t/e/legal_affairs/legal_co-operation/family_law_and_children's_rights/Documents/Rec_99_4.pdf>, last accessed 23 February 2009.

had been unlawful under Article 5(1) of the Convention protecting his right to liberty. The Chamber stated that it must take account of a whole range of factors arising in a particular case such as the type, duration, effects and manner of deprivation of liberty in question.[21] The Chamber concluded the applicant was in fact deprived of his liberty.

The applicant also complained that he was unable to obtain release from the psychiatric hospital in contravention of Article 5(4) of the Convention providing for procedures to obtain release from unlawful detention. The Chamber stated that a person of unsound mind compulsorily confined in a psychiatric institution for an indefinite or lengthy period is entitled to periodic review of his detention.[22] This includes a right to take proceedings at reasonable intervals before a court to test the 'lawfulness' of the detention.[23]

The Chamber found that Russian law does not provide for automatic judicial review of confinement in a psychiatric hospital in situations such as the applicant's. It also determined that the review could not be initiated by the person concerned, if that person has been deprived of his legal capacity. On that basis, the Chamber concluded that the applicant was prevented from independently pursuing any legal remedy of judicial character to challenge his continued detention.[24]

On the question of an effective national remedy under Article 13 of the Convention, the Chamber held that the complaint was intimately linked to the complaints submitted under Article 6 and 8 of the Convention and so the complaint under Article 13 was deemed inadmissible. Using this same rationale, the Chamber further held that there was no need to examine the applicant's complaint of discrimination under Article 14 of the Convention.

The Chamber noted that it is of the greatest importance for the effective operation of the system of individual petition, instituted by Article 34, that applicants or potential applicants should be able to communicate freely with the Convention organs without being subjected to any form of pressure from the authorities to withdraw or modify their complaints.[25] The Chamber noted that in this case, there was a ban on the applicant's contact with his lawyer, which lasted from his hospitalization on 4 November 2005 until his discharge on 16 May 2006. The Chamber also noted that telephone calls and correspondence were also banned for almost all of that period. The Chamber considered that these restrictions made it impossible for the applicant to pursue his case before the ECtHR while in hospi-

---

[21] It referred to its case law on this point. See *Guzzardi v. Italy*, judgment of 6 November 1980, Series A no. 39, s.92, and *Ashingdane v. the United Kingdom*, judgment of 28 May 1985, Series A no. 93, para. 41.

[22] This is a well established point of ECtHR jurisprudence see *Luberti v. Italy*, judgment of 23 February 1984, Series A no. 75, para. 31; *Rakevich v. Russia*, no. 58973/00, paras. 43 et seq., 28 October 2003.

[23] Ibid.

[24] The Russian Government claimed that the applicant could have initiated legal proceedings through his mother. However, the Chamber concluded that this remedy was not directly accessible to that applicant as it was his mother who had requested his placement in hospital and opposed his release.

[25] On this point the Chamber referred to the following cases: *Akdivar and Others v. Turkey*, judgment of 16 September 1996, Reports 1996-IV; *Ergi v. Turkey*, judgment of 28 July 1998, Reports 1998-IV, para. 105).

tal. Thus, by restricting the applicant's contact with the outside world, the authorities interfered with his rights under Article 34 of the Convention.

In March 2006, by way of an 'interim measure', the President of the Chamber directed the respondent Government to allow the applicant to meet his lawyer on the premises of the hospital and under the supervision of the hospital staff. The measure was intended to ensure that the applicant was able to pursue his case before the ECtHR. The Chamber noted the authorities' refusal to comply with that measure. The domestic court had found that the 'interim measure' was addressed to the Russian State as a whole, but not to any of its bodies in particular and further, that Russian law did not recognize the binding force of an 'interim measure' indicated by the Court. The domestic court also considered that the applicant could not act without the consent of his mother. Therefore, the applicant's lawyer was not regarded as his lawful representative either in domestic terms, or for the purposes of the proceedings under the Convention. The Chamber held that this interpretation of the Convention was wrong. The Chamber stated that an 'interim measure' is binding to the extent that non-compliance with it may lead to a finding of a violation under Article 34 of the Convention.

The Chamber was not ready to pronounce upon the application of Article 41 of the Convention, regarding the right to just satisfaction. This question was reserved and the Chamber invited the Russian Government and the applicant to submit, within three months from the date on which the judgment became final (in accordance with Article 44(2) of the Convention), their written observations on the matter and, to notify the Chamber of any agreement that they may reach.

What is of particular significance in this decision is that the Chamber took the view that any loss of legal capacity has severe repercussions for human personhood. It therefore places legal capacity laws – especially those that are overbroad – on the defensive. It specifically referred to a major 1999 Recommendation of the Committee of Ministers on the topic. It is to be noted that this Recommendation was quite influential in the drafting of Article 12 of the United Nations Convention on the Rights of Persons with Disabilities (which also deals with the right to legal capacity). The Chamber stated that 'the existence of a mental disorder, even a serious one cannot be the sole reason to justify full incapacitation.'[26] This case has opened the door for further legal developments on the issues of legal capacity and guardianship. It is reasonable to expect further litigation on the issue of legal capacity before the ECtHR.

2.2.3. Paladi v. Moldova (Judgment of Chamber, July 2007: case referred to the Grand Chamber)[27]

In this case, a Chamber of the Court held that the medical treatment of a prisoner with a disability within a remand centre and a prison hospital was inadequate. The Chamber held that the failure to treat him as an in-patient at a hospital where he could receive the necessary neurological and hyperbaric oxygen treatment amounted to a violation of the prohibition on torture and other cruel, inhuman or degrading treatment under Article 3 of the Convention.

---

[26] Application no. 44009/05, Chamber Decision of 27 March 2008, para. 94.
[27] Application no. 39806/05, Chamber Decision of 10 July 2007.

In its recent case law, the Court has held that although there is no general right to healthcare, an obligation to provide such might arise in the peculiar circumstances of detention.[28] It has held that arguments of scarce resources or logistical service delivery difficulties, cannot justify inadequate provision of medical treatment to prisoners. Such constraints cannot justify torture, cruel, inhuman or degrading treatment. Prisoners are in an especially vulnerable position and authorities are therefore under a special duty to protect them.

In the instant case, Ion Paladi was remanded in custody in the Centre for Fighting Economic Crime and Corruption (CFECC) in Moldova from 24 September 2004, on suspicion of abuse of his position and power. He submitted that he had been recognized as having 'second degree disability'.[29] Following a recommendation from a medical examination in March 2005, he was transferred to a prison hospital with inadequate facilities for the prescribed neurological treatment, and his condition worsened. On 20 September 2005, he was transferred to a neurological centre for thirty days where he underwent the recommended hyperbaric oxygen therapy (HBO), which yielded positive results. This treatment was discontinued after five of the twelve prescribed sessions when the District Court decided to transfer the applicant back to the prison hospital. This transfer was in spite of an 'interim measure' requested by the ECtHR stating that 'the applicant should not be transferred from the RNC until the Court has had the opportunity to examine the case'.

The applicant relied on Article 3 (prohibition of inhuman and degrading treatment), Article 5 (right to liberty and security) and Article 34 (right of individual petition) of the Convention.

With respect to the arguments under Article 3, the Chamber reiterated the long-standing principle, last enunciated in the case of *Sarban v. Moldova*[30] that ill treatment must attain a minimum level of severity to fall within the scope of the Article. In Sarban, the Court stated that the assessment of this minimum level depended upon the circumstances of the case, including the duration of the treatment, its physical and mental effects and, in some cases, the sex, age and state of health of the applicant. The Chamber noted that the purpose of such treatment is a factor to be taken into account, and, in particular, whether it was intended to humiliate or degrade the victim. However, the Chamber emphasized that a violation of Article 3 could occur even in the absence of such an intention.

The Chamber concluded that although Article 3 of the Convention cannot be interpreted to give rise to a general obligation to release detainees on health grounds, it does impose an obligation to protect detainees' physical well-being. In this case, that could have been achieved through the provision of appropriate medical treatment. The Chamber considered that the lack of proper medical assistance at the remand centre and in prison, the incomplete treatment of the applicant in the prison hospital and the failure to continue the recommended neu-

---

[28]   See for example: *Holomiov v. Moldova* [2007] ECHR 30649/05; *Istratii and others v. Moldova* [2007] ECHR 8721/05.

[29]   The applicant, in a letter to the ECtHR, provided a certificate stating that on 20 June 2006 he had been recognized as having a second-degree disability. The applicant was diagnosed with a number of serious illnesses that included: diabetes, angina, heart failure, hypertension, chronic bronchitis, pancreatitis and hepatitis.

[30]   Application no. 3456/05, para. 51, 4 October 2005.

rological treatment 'unnecessarily exposed the applicant to a risk to his health'.[31] The Chamber went on to state:

> that by interrupting the applicant's HBO treatment, which had been recommended by the doctors and had already yielded positive results, the domestic court further undermined the effectiveness of his belated treatment. It also caused stress and anxiety to the applicant in excess of the level inherent in any deprivation of liberty.[32]

The Chamber concluded that the lack of proper medical assistance at the remand centre, the incomplete treatment of the applicant at the prison hospital after 20 May 2005, and the abrupt termination of his neurological treatment each amounted to a violation of Article 3 of the Convention.

With respect to the arguments under Article 5(1), the Chamber concluded that the applicant was unlawfully detained after the expiry of the last court order regarding his detention pending trial on 22 October 2004, as the detention lacked a sufficient legal basis. The applicant also complained that the failure to comply with the 'interim measure' violated his right of petition to the Court as safeguarded under Article 34 of Convention. The Chamber reiterated its previous ruling in *Mamatkulov and Askarov v. Turkey*[33] that '[a] failure by a Contracting State to comply with "interim measures" is to be regarded as preventing the Court from effectively examining the applicant's complaint and as hindering the effective exercise of his or her right and, accordingly, as a violation of Article 34'. The Chamber held that, notwithstanding the relatively short period of a delay in complying with an 'interim measure', there had been a violation of Article 34 of the Convention.

The Chamber noted that the applicant was in a serious condition that put his health at immediate and irremediable risk. It considered that this risk was the very reason for the Chamber's decision to indicate the 'interim measure'. The Chamber noted that it was good fortune that no adverse consequences to the applicant's life or health resulted from the delay in implementing that measure. However, the Chamber refused to accept that a State's responsibility for failing to comply with their obligations undertaken under the Convention should depend on unpredictable circumstances such as the (non-)occurrence of a medical emergency during the period of non-compliance with 'interim measures'. The Chamber considered that it would be contrary to the object and purpose of the Convention to require evidence not only of a risk of irremediable damage to one of the core Convention rights, but also of actual damage, before the Chamber was empowered to find a State in breach of its obligation to comply with 'interim measures'.

This case underpins the longstanding case law of the Court to the effect that positive obligations may arise in an institutional environment where health needs may arise (whether as a result of disability or not). Such decisions are especially useful in institutional settings such as prisons and detention centres.

This case was referred to the Grand Chamber that will deliver its judgment in 2009.

---

[31]   para. 81.
[32]   para. 84.
[33]   Application nos. 46827/99 and 46951/99, para. 128.

2.2.4. Saoud v. France (Judgment of Chamber, October 2007)[34]

The applicants in this case were the Tunisian mother, brothers and sisters of Mohamed Saoud. Mohamed Saoud, aged 26, was diagnosed as having schizophrenia.[35] The Saoud family called the French police on 20 November 1998 when Mohamed Saoud attacked his mother and two sisters. The applicants informed the police of Mohamed's medical condition and disability and requested that a doctor be called. This did not occur, and a violent altercation ensued upon the arrival of the police.

The police restrained Mohamed Saoud by handcuffing his hands to the front of his body. He was also pinned to the ground on his stomach by three police officers. Members of the fire services arrived at the scene and administered first aid to the police officers. Shortly afterwards, Mohamed Saoud went into cardio-respiratory arrest and died. Possible 'slow mechanical asphyxia' was revealed by an autopsy as the probable cause of death.

A week before the events leading to his death, Mohamed Saoud had requested admission to a clinic where he had previously received treatment for depression. However, there were no places available and he was informed that he could not be admitted until 23 November 1998.

In January 1999 the applicants lodged a complaint for murder of an especially vulnerable person and sought leave to initiate civil proceedings alleging, in particular, that no doctor had been provided - though requested - at the time of the events. On 12 October 2000, the investigating judge ordered that the proceedings be discontinued on the ground that there was insufficient evidence of a criminal wrong justifying the arrest of the police officers concerned. The order was upheld in a judgment dated 4 January 2001.

The applicants lodged appeals on points of law. On 24 July 2001 the delegate of the President of the Court of Cassation granted full legal aid to the applicants who had lodged an application for a fresh decision in the matter. A lawyer was appointed to assist the applicants before the Court of Cassation. On 18 September 2001 the Court of Cassation declared the appeal inadmissible. Their legal aid lawyer informed them that, as the decision of 24 July 2001 had not been served on him until 10 September 2001, he had been unable to file pleadings with the Court of Cassation before it ruled on the appeals.

The applicants took the case to the European Court of Human Rights, complaining that the death of Mohamed Saoud was unlawful. The applicants in this case relied on Articles 2 (right to life) and Article 3 (prohibition of inhuman or degrading treatment). In addition, they relied on Article 6(1) (right to a fair hearing), they complained that the criminal proceedings instituted after his death had been unfair.

In its deliberations under Article 2 of the Convention, the Chamber observed that the police officers' intervention could be justified to protect Mohamed Saoud's mother and one of his sisters. The ECtHR noted the injuries inflicted on his sisters who had been the subject of a medical report, and that some police

---

34   Application no. 9375/02, Chamber Decision of 9 October 2007. This judgment is unavailable in English and thus the writer has relied on the Court's press release when compiling this summary.

35   Ibid at para. 6.

officers had also been seriously injured during the struggle. However, the police officers on the scene were also aware of Mohamed Saoud's vulnerable state. Despite his illness, his obvious injuries and the fact that, with his hands and feet immobilized, he no longer presented a danger to others, the police officers had not relaxed their hold on Mohamed Saoud at any time. The Chamber noted that no medical examination, however superficial, was carried out at the scene of the struggle. The only course of action considered by the police and fire officers at the scene was the administration of a tranquillizer, which required waiting for the emergency medical service to arrive.

An initial French judicial enquiry appointed medical experts, who identified the restraint of Mohamed Saoud on the ground for thirty-five minutes as the direct cause of his death from slow asphyxia. The Chamber was critical of the lack of official instructions with regard to the use of this type of immobilization technique. The Chamber was also very critical of the fact that no treatment was given to Mohamed Saoud prior to his cardiac arrest, despite the presence of professionals trained in emergency assistance. For that reason, the Chamber held that the authorities had failed in their obligation to protect the life of Mohamed Saoud, and that there had been a violation of Article 2. The Chamber noted that the complaint under Article 3 related to the same facts as those examined under Article 2, and took the view that there was no need to consider it separately.

With respect to the right to a fair hearing, the Chamber noted that although the initial application for legal aid by the Saoud family was refused, the Court of Cassation overturned that decision. Nevertheless, the decision was too late for their legal representative to make effective interventions. For those reasons the Chamber held that there had been a violation of Article 6(1).

Under Article 41 (right to just satisfaction), the Chamber awarded the applicants jointly €20,000 in respect of non-pecuniary damage and €5,000 for costs and expenses.

The Court acknowledged that had Mohamed Saoud been provided with appropriate services in the week leading up to the incident at issue, his death could have been avoided. However, the judgment focused more on the failure of the French State to provide proper regulation as to the use of the face down restraint technique. The Council of Europe Committee for the Prevention of Torture and Amnesty International had previously highlighted the risks of asphyxia associated with this technique.

This judgment reflects the approach taken by the court in *Makaratzis v. Greece*,[36] to the effect that arrest operations in violent situations need to be regulated and organized in a way that minimizes to the greatest extent possible any risk to life, especially with respect to vulnerable people. The judgment is also relevant to the question on the interplay and inter-dependence of civil and political rights (in this instance the right to life) with economic, social and cultural rights (in this instance the right to health). Indeed, it vividly highlights how deficiencies with respect to economic, social and cultural rights (lack of an appropriate place in a medical facility) can themselves lead to – or at least contribute towards – violations of core civil rights. This is especially significant in the disability context since some persons with disabilities depend more than most on public resources.

---

[36]   Application no. 50385/99, Grand Chamber Decision of 20 December 2004.

2.2.5. Hüseyin Yıldırım v. Turkey (Judgment of Chamber, May 2007)[37]

In the instant case, the applicant was a person with disabilities. He had sustained spinal contusion, a parietal fracture on the right side, paresis on the left side and general hyperaesthesia in a serious road traffic accident.

In July 2001, he was arrested at his home under an arrest warrant dating back several years. His arrest related to his presumed involvement in the activities of the TKP ML/TİKKO – a faction of the extreme left wing armed organization TKP-ML (Communist Party of Turkey – Marxist-Leninist). He had already been sentenced to seven years' imprisonment in connection with the same.

He was incapable of moving or looking after himself. He was placed in pre-trial detention in Bayrampaşa Prison, where he was in the hospital unit for a few days, before being transferred to prison wing of Tekirdağ Public Hospital. He was placed on a foam mattress and questioned.

On 17 July 2001, the applicant was diagnosed with quadriparesis and atrophy of the hands, and declared medically unfit to remain incarcerated. His health deteriorated during his detention and on 13 November 2001 he was obliged to undergo a bifrontal craniotomy on account of a rupture of the cerebral membrane. He subsequently began to experience sphincterial problems and required a urethral catheter, and was subject to various dermatological, neurological and respiratory illnesses. The applicant also showed signs of chronic depression. In January 2002, a specialist board of the Istanbul Institute of Forensic Medicine asserted that the applicant's state of health was incompatible with his imprisonment. Furthermore, in November 2002 the board of health at Tekirdağ Public Hospital noted that the applicant was experiencing permanent after effects. Months later, specialists from the Istanbul Institute of Forensic Medicine found that he needed to use a wheelchair and that his illness was incurable.

During his detention, the applicant was assisted by other prisoners in his cell, who prepared his food and fabricated a commode by making a hole in a plastic stool. However, on occasion, they were reluctant to help him. From October 2002, his siblings took turns looking after him in the prison wing of Tekirdağ Public Hospital.

In September 2002, the applicant appeared before a hearing at Istanbul State Security Court. On this occasion, his police escorts allegedly dropped him, and the press published photographs depicting his efforts to get up from the ground. On 11 December 2002, the applicant was sentenced to life imprisonment, but he was released on 25 June 2004 under a Presidential pardon.

The applicant alleged that the circumstances in which he had been detained and the conditions in which he had been transferred had amounted to inhuman and degrading treatment contrary to Article 3. Article 3 of the Convention imposes both a negative obligation on a state to refrain from inflicting torture or inhuman and degrading treatment, and a positive obligation to protect against the infliction of torture or inhuman and degrading treatment at the hands of others.[38] The Chamber has also held that Article 3 requires states to provide adequate

---

[37]   Application no. 2778/02, Chamber Decision of 3 May 2007. This judgment is unavailable in English and thus the writer has relied on the Court's press release when compiling this summary.

[38]   For further information see Lawson, 'The Human Rights Act 1998 and Disabled

medical treatment for prisoners and others in its care.[39]

The Chamber noted that there were national legal provisions that allow for the release of prisoners on health grounds. The Chamber considered the reasons put forward by Turkey to be insufficient to justify the applicant's continued detention until 25 June 2004, in defiance of medical reports recommending his release. The Chamber concluded that the applicant's detention 'had infringed his dignity and had undoubtedly caused him both physical and psychological suffering, beyond that inevitably associated with a prison sentence and medical treatment.'[40] It found a violation of Article 3.

The Chamber noted that the applicant was disabled to such an extent that he could not carry out the majority of basic everyday tasks without the assistance of others. The Chamber stated that the national court should have taken particular care to ensure that the conditions of detention corresponded to the requirements of his disability. This had not been the case. Instead, the task of assisting the applicant to feed, wash, dress himself and go to the toilet fell to his fellow prisoners and family. The Chamber determined that this situation, which continued for three years, stimulated constant feelings of anguish, inferiority and humiliation that were sufficiently strong to amount to 'degrading treatment' within the meaning of Article 3.

With respect to the incident in September 2002, the Chamber expressed surprise that responsibility for a prisoner with the applicant's disabilities could have been entrusted to police, who were certainly not qualified to foresee the medical risks inherent in the transportation of such a disabled prisoner. As a result, the Chamber concluded that the events of that day had also amounted to degrading treatment contrary to Article 3 ECHR. Having held this, the Chamber considered that it was unnecessary to re-examine the case under Article 5 of the Convention (right to liberty and security).

The judgment is typical of the approach of the Court on the issue of health and well-being of prisoners, and especially vulnerable prisoners such as those with disabilities.

People: A Right to be Human?', in Harvey (ed.), *Human Rights in the Community* (Hart Publishing, 2005), 135; Nowak and Suntinger, 'The Rights of Disabled People not to be subjected to Torture, Inhuman and Degrading Treatment or Punishment' in Degener *et al* (eds), *Human Rights and Disabled Persons: Essays and Relevant Human Rights Instruments* (Martinus Nijhoff, 1995), 117. In the United Nations there is a Special Rapporteur on torture, inhuman and degrading treatment or punishment and another on disability. Both Rapporteurs look at the situation of persons with disabilities in this context.

[39] See for example *McGlinchey v. UK*, Application no. 50390/99, 29 April 2003. This case concerned the failure of prison authorities in the United Kingdom to provide adequate medical care to an asthmatic prisoner who was also experiencing severe withdrawal symptoms from heroin that resulted in her death. In *Keenan v. UK*, Application no. 27229/95 (2001) 33 EHRR 38, the ECtHR considered the adequacy of medical support provided to a prisoner with a mental illness.

[40] See European Court of Human Rights (May 2007), Chamber Judgment Hüseyin Yıldırım v. Turkey, Press release.

2.2.6. Tysiąc v. Poland (Judgment of Chamber, March 2007)[41]

The applicant in this case was a Polish national who experienced severe myopia for many years. She was diagnosed as having a disability of medium severity. Upon becoming pregnant she consulted several doctors, as she feared the pregnancy would impact further upon her eyesight. Under Polish law, abortions are permissible for therapeutic reasons only. However, it was suggested that doctors in Poland were reluctant to carry out such abortions for fear of criminal prosecution if it subsequently transpired that the abortion could not be justified.[42]

By the second month of her pregnancy, the applicant's myopia had deteriorated significantly. It was clear from medical evidence that, were she to proceed with the pregnancy, she was likely to lose her sight. She argued that in the circumstances, her case should be treated as falling within the therapeutic exception and she should therefore be allowed an abortion in Poland. Nonetheless, the head of the gynaecology and obstetrics department at the public hospital in Warsaw found no grounds for performing a therapeutic abortion and it did not take place.

Following the birth of the child, the applicant's sight deteriorated further as a result of a retinal haemorrhage. The applicant was then diagnosed as having a significant disability. She is unable to see objects more than 1.5 metres away and may become fully blind in time.

The applicant based her complaint on Articles 3 (prohibition of inhuman or degrading treatment), 8 (respect for private and family life), 13 (right to an effective remedy) and 14 (prohibition of discrimination) of the Convention.

The Chamber found that the facts did not reveal a breach of Article 3 and considered that it was more appropriate to examine the case under Article 8 of the Convention. As already mentioned, abortion is lawful in Poland if the pregnancy poses a threat to the woman's life or health. It did not, therefore, fall to the Chamber to examine whether the Convention, as such, guaranteed a right to have an abortion. Instead, the Chamber examined the complaint from the viewpoint of the State's positive obligation under Article 8 to secure the physical well-being of expectant mothers.[43]

The Chamber found that the relevant provision of Polish national law allowing therapeutic abortions did not provide any particular procedural framework to address disagreements as to the whether such abortions should proceed. This was so whether the disagreement was between the pregnant woman and her doctor or

---

[41] Application no. 5410/03, Chamber judgment of 20 March 2007.

[42] This was according to the Polish Federation for Women and Family Planning. The ECtHR noted that doctors were particularly reticent in the absence of transparent and clearly defined procedures to determine whether the legal conditions for a therapeutic abortion were complied with.

[43] The Grand Chamber observed that it was not in dispute that from 1977 Ms Tysiąc suffered from severe myopia. The Grand Chamber stressed that it was not its role to question the doctors' clinical judgment as regards the seriousness of the applicant's condition but found it sufficient to note that Ms Tysiąc feared that the pregnancy and birth might further endanger her eyesight. The Grand Chamber considered that those fears, in the light of her medical history and the advice she had been given, could not be said to have been irrational.

between doctors themselves.

The Chamber duly noted a provision in national legislation allowing a doctor, in the event of doubts, or at a patient's request, to obtain a second medical opinion. However, the Chamber emphasized that this legislation, which was addressed exclusively to members of the medical profession, did not give patients themselves a procedural right to obtain a second opinion.

In effect, the Chamber considered that the legislation did not contain any effective mechanism to determine whether the conditions for obtaining a lawful abortion had been met. It considered that this created a situation of prolonged uncertainty for the applicant and, as a result, she suffered severe distress and anguish about the possible negative consequences on her health of her pregnancy and the imminent birth.

With respect to the adequacy of available national remedies, the Chamber held that, as provisions of the Polish civil code were retroactive and could only result in a grant of compensation, they did not provide the opportunity to uphold the right to respect for private life. In these circumstances, retrospective remedies did not offer a satisfactory solution. Compensation would be insufficient to address the wrong done in the form of damage to the applicant's sight. The Chamber was also of the opinion that criminal proceedings after the fact against a doctor could not prevent the damage to the applicant's health from arising.

The resulting failure to provide appropriate protection for the physical integrity of individuals in a vulnerable position was considered by the Chamber to be a breach of Article 8. The Court found it unnecessary to examine separately whether there had been violations of Articles 13 and 14 since it had already concluded that Poland had, in the circumstances, breached Article 8.

It is important to note that this judgment does not interpret the ECHR to guarantee a substantive right to an abortion. Nor does it deal – directly or otherwise – with the notion of selective abortion on the ground of disability. Narrowly understood, it simply calls for a procedural mechanism of protection to be put in place, where the substantive right is already provided for under national law. It does not itself call for such a substantive right to be put in place.

2.2.7. DD v. Lithuania, Application Number 13469/06 (pending)

This pending case involves the placement of a Lithuanian national into a social care home for intellectually disabled persons. The applicant alleges that her confinement and forced treatment in the Kédainiai Social Care Home is unlawful and in violation of Articles 3 (prohibition on inhuman or degrading treatment), 5 (right to liberty and security), 6 (right to a fair trial), 8 (right to respect for family and private life) and 9 (freedom of thought, conscience and religion) of the Convention.

The respondent Government denies these claims. This case raises issues of fundamental importance concerning legal capacity and human rights. Effectively, it appears that legal capacity can be lost through operation of law in Lithuania.

In February 2008, the ECtHR authorized the European Group of National Human Rights Institutions[44] to intervene in the proceedings as an amicus

---

[44]   The European Group is a representative group of those national human rights institutions within the Council of Europe who are deemed to be fully compliant with

curiae and submit written submissions as per the Convention and the Rules of the Court.

3. EUROPEAN SOCIAL CHARTER AND RECENT DISABILITY CASE LAW

Web Resource: <http://www.coe.int/socialcharter>

3.1. BACKGROUND OF THE EUROPEAN SOCIAL CHARTER

The European Social Charter is a Council of Europe treaty which complements the European Convention on Human Rights. While the Convention protects civil and political rights, the Charter protects economic, social and cultural rights.

The term 'European Social Charter' is actually shorthand for a web of five treaties. The original Charter was adopted in 1961[45] and was revised and updated in 1996.[46] Ratification of the 1961 Charter was near universal. Ratification of the Revised Social Charter currently stands at twenty-seven Member States of the Council of Europe. These two core treaties sit side-by-side until there is universal ratification of the revised version. That is to say, for those States that ratified the original Charter and not the revised version, the original remains in force for them. This is naturally confusing, since the relevant treaty monitoring body (the 'European Committee of Social Rights') now monitors the implementation of both the old and the revised Charters - using different benchmarks of assessment.

The Charter is somewhat unique as a human rights instrument, in that the States Parties have the freedom to pick and choose their obligations (beyond a certain core). Of the core rights guaranteed under the Charter, with respect to which there is no opt-out possible, the work-related rights protected under Part II are regarded as particularly significant. Part I of the Charter (both original and revised) contains principles to be accepted by the States Parties as constituting the 'aim of their policy'. Part II of both instruments contains the rights to be protected. It spans nineteen substantive articles under the original Charter and thirty-one under the revised Charter. Unusually, Part III of each instrument follows an a la carte approach to obligations. Part III of the original Charter requires States Parties to accept at least five of seven articles deemed to be core. That is increased to six out of nine in the Revised Charter. Most of these 'core' articles deal with labour law matters (right to work, right to collective bargaining, etc.).

The 1961 Charter does not have a substantive provision dealing with non-discrimination. Instead, it was provided for in the preamble. This did not, however, stop the European Committee of Social Rights from developing its discrimination jurisprudence. The Revised Charter now provides for a substantive prohibition on discrimination: Article E. It reads:

---

the United Nations 'Paris Principles' governing independent national human rights institutions. The Group consists of sixteen national institutions. The homepage of the network of NHRIs is available at: <www.nhri.net/>.

[45]   European Social Charter, Turin, 18 October 1961, ETS 035.
[46]   Revised European Social Charter, Strasbourg, 3 May 1996, ETS 163.

The enjoyment of the rights set forth in this Charter shall be secured without discrimination on any ground such as race, colour, sex, language, religion, political or other opinion, national extraction or social origin, health, association with a national minority, birth or status.

Although Article E does not explicitly enumerate 'disability' as a ground of discrimination, it is clear that the European Committee of Social Rights extends Article E to embrace discrimination on the ground of disability (see below). Interestingly, Article E does include 'health' as a prohibited ground of discrimination – something that goes well beyond disability. It will be recalled that the European Court of Justice declined to extend 'disability' by analogy to include health status as a prohibited ground of discrimination under EC law.

All of the substantive rights provided for in Part II of both the 1961 and Revised instruments are relevant in the context of disability. However, Article 15 is unusual in that it specifically deals with disability. This was a very far-reaching provision in 1961. Article 15 under the original Social Charter reads:

The right of physically or mentally disabled persons to vocational training, rehabilitation and social resettlement

With a view to ensuring the effective exercise of the right of the physically or mentally disabled to vocational training, rehabilitation and resettlement, the Contracting Parties undertake:

1. to take adequate measures for the provision of training facilities, including, where necessary, specialised institutions, public or private;
2. to take adequate measures for the placing of disabled persons in employment, such as specialised placing services, facilities for sheltered employment and measures to encourage employers to admit disabled persons to employment.

As befits an instrument that was drafted against the background of the Second World War, there is a focus on rehabilitation, vocational training and employment (including sheltered employment). It was obvious that the drafters were very conscious of the need to integrate war veterans back into social and economic life.

Article 15 under the Revised Social Charter of 1995 was informed by the more modern philosophy of equal opportunities. It reads:

The right of persons with disabilities to independence, social integration and participation in the life of the community

With a view to ensuring to persons with disabilities, irrespective of age and the nature and origin of their disabilities, the effective exercise of the right to independence, social integration and participation in the life of the community, the Parties undertake, in particular:

1. to take the necessary measures to provide persons with disabilities with guidance, education and vocational training in the framework of general schemes wherever possible or, where this is not possible, through specialized bodies, public or private;
2. to promote their access to employment through all measures tending to encourage employers to hire and keep in employment persons with disabilities

in the ordinary working environment and to adjust the working conditions to the needs of the disabled or, where this is not possible by reason of the disability, by arranging for or creating sheltered employment according to the level of disability. In certain cases, such measures may require recourse to specialized placement and support services;
3. to promote their full social integration and participation in the life of the community in particular through measures, including technical aids, aiming to overcome barriers to communication and mobility and enabling access to transport, housing, cultural activities and leisure.

The change of emphasis is even detectable in the new title of the article. The new Article 15 reflects a paradigm shift in thinking in the field of disability. While the old Article placed an emphasis on welfare, the new Article focuses on inclusion and independence.

The European Committee of Social Rights recently issued a useful Factsheet on Article 15 of the Revised Charter. It summarizes its case law, or benchmarks under Article 15 against which State practice is to be measured. The Conclusions reached by the Committee (below) make the most sense in light of these benchmarks. It is worth quoting the relevant part of the Factsheet in full:

Para 1 - the right to education and training

All persons with disabilities have a right to education and training. Education encompasses general education; basic compulsory education and further education as well as vocational training in the traditional sense.

Persons with disabilities (children, young persons and adults) should be integrated into mainstream facilities; education and training should be made available within the framework of ordinary schemes and only where this is not possible through special facilities. Education in special schools or adapted education in mainstream schools should be of a sufficient quality.

Under this provision of the Revised Charter non-discrimination legislation in relation to disability in the field of education is required. Such legislation should as a minimum require compelling justification for special or segregated educational systems and confer an effective remedy on those who have been found to have been unlawfully excluded, segregated or otherwise denied an effective right to education.

Para 2 - the right to employment

This provision requires states to guarantee access to employment on the open labour market for persons with disabilities. States enjoy a margin of appreciation in the measures they adopt to enable this, however anti-discrimination legislation and protection against dismissal is required.

Sheltered employment facilities must be reserved for those persons with disabilities who cannot and only by reason of their disability be integrated into the open labour market - should be the exception - and should aim to assist workers to migrate to the open labour market. People working in sheltered employment facilities, where production is the main activity, must enjoy the usual benefits of labour law and in particular the right to fair remuneration and respect for trade union rights.

Para 3 - the right to social integration and participation in the life of the community

The third paragraph obliges states to adopt a coherent policy in the disability context: positive action measures to overcome the barriers to communication (which includes telecommunications and new information technology) and mobility in order to enable access to transport (land, rail, sea, air) housing (public, social and private), cultural activities and leisure (social activities and sporting activities). Such measures should have a clear legal basis, people themselves should have a voice in the design, implementation and review of such measures and there must be non-discrimination legislation providing effective remedies in relation to disability covering all areas mentioned in this paragraph.

In Collective Complaint No 13/2002 *Autism-Europe v. France*, the European Committee of Social Rights found a violation of Articles 15(1) and Article 17(1) (right of children and young persons to social, legal and economic protection, including the right to education), (whether alone or in conjunction with Article E (non-discrimination)) of the Revised Charter on the grounds that France had failed to achieve sufficient progress in advancing the provision of education for persons with autism.

The European Committee of Social Rights is the treaty monitoring body responsible for monitoring the States Parties' implementation of Charter provisions. In order to do so effectively, the Committee utilizes a monitoring procedure based on periodic national reports as well as a Collective Complaints procedure.

Under the national reporting procedure, States Parties submit a report regarding some of the accepted provisions of the Charter over a particular reference period and in accordance with an agreed schedule. These reports should indicate how the relevant provisions are being implemented in domestic law and practice. The Committee examines the national reports and draws its 'Conclusions', setting out whether a particular State Party is acting in conformity with the Charter. Importantly, it sometimes 'defers' its Conclusions pending the receipt of further information or particulars in the next round of reporting. It's Conclusions are published on an annual basis. The Committee's 'case law' is yielded through this reporting procedure.

Each Article of the Charter is reported upon once every four years. Article 15 was considered in 2008 and will next be considered in 2012. Curiously, States Parties to the Revised Charter do not report separately on Article E (Non-discrimination). Article E falls outside Part III and so States Parties have no option but to accept it.

Where a Conclusion (of conformity or non-conformity) is deferred this could mean (1) that there is insufficient information on which to base a Conclusion or (2) that the normative requirements of the relevant provision have been revised (usually upwards) by the Committee and more information is sought to enable a definitive Conclusion. A deferral also serves the purpose of putting the States Parties on notice that the 'case law' has changed - thus raising the bar. Therefore, a deferred Conclusion is not necessarily a negative sign - it can actually indicate an advance in the jurisprudence.

The Conclusions (whether positive, negative or deferred) are usually accompanied by extensive questions posed by the Committee to the States concerned, which should be answered in the next reporting cycle. The (evolving) thinking of the Committee, with respect to State obligations can be gleaned from the direction these questions take. In other words, the questions put forth by the Committee are a clue to the future normative requirements of the Charter in the eyes of the European Committee of Social Rights. That is why it is worth including them in the review that follows.

States Parties are obliged to take action in response to a Conclusion of non-conformity by the Committee. If no such action is taken, the Committee of Ministers may issue a Recommendation to the Party, asking it to address the area of concern. This Recommendation is drawn up after consideration of both a report prepared by a committee comprised of representatives of the governments of States Parties (Governmental Committee), as well as the Conclusions of the European Committee of Social Rights.

Article 15 is not designated a 'core' provision under the 1961 Social Charter or the Revised Charter of 1996. Nonetheless, States Parties must still report periodically on their 'non-accepted' obligations indicating how they intend moving towards full ratification. In other words, there is an expectation that States Parties will progressively remove legal and other barriers to full ratification. These reports on 'non-accepted' provisions can also be a useful source of information on disability issues from States that have yet to subscribe to Article 15. Furthermore, the Committee visits Member States to discuss non-accepted provisions, which effectively revolves around a discussion of whether a State's laws and practices are sufficient to enable opt-in to the relevant non-accepted provision. A good example which included a focus on Article 15 (which was non-accepted in toto) was the 2005 visit of the Committee to Bulgaria.[47]

An Additional Protocol to the European Social Charter providing for a system of Collective Complaints was adopted by the Committee of Ministers in 1995 and entered into force on 1 July 1998.[48] Fourteen States Parties have ratified the Protocol. There have been fifty-four Collective Complaints to date. This Collective Complaint procedure is, effectively, a quasi-judicial method of entertaining complaints of violations of the Charter. Although the outcome of a Collective Complaint is only directly relevant to the State Party concerned, the jurisprudence it generates will also inform how the Committee will assess periodic State reports. So, even if a State does not opt in to the Collective Complaints system, it will inevitably be impacted by the case law that it generates.

As befits their title, Collective Complaints cannot be brought by individuals. They may be submitted by national employer organizations and trade unions of Contracting Parties, international employer organizations and trade unions that

---

[47] Report of the Meeting with Representatives of the Bulgarian Government on Provisions of the Revised European Social Charter not accepted by Bulgaria, 4-5 October 2005, Sofia. The text of this report is available at <http://www.coe.int/t/dghl/monitoring/socialcharter/Non-acceptedProv/Bulgaria2005_en.pdf>, last accessed 8 June 2009.

[48] ETS No. 158, <http://conventions.coe.int/treaty/en/Treaties/Html/158.htm>, last accessed 19 February 2009.

are involved in the work of the Council's Governmental Committee, international non-governmental organizations with Council of Europe consultative status and national non-governmental organizations recognized by their government as having a right to do so (Article 1 of the 1995 Protocol). Non-governmental organizations may only submit complaints in relation to those matters regarding which they have been recognized as having competence. Eleven European disability organizations are already registered and entitled to lodge Collective Complaints. They include the European Disability Forum, Inclusion International, Mental Disability Advocacy Centre, International Association-Autism Europe, European Blind Union, European Union of the Deaf, Disabled People's International, etc.

Together with the 1995 Additional Protocol, the 'Rules of the European Committee of Social Rights' govern the relevant procedure concerning Collective Complaints (Rules 29-35). The European Committee of Social Rights examines the Complaint and, if the formal requirements have been fulfilled, declares it admissible. After admissibility is established, a written procedure is set in motion. There is an exchange of memorials between the parties and the Committee may, if appropriate, decide to hold a public hearing. Third party interventions are allowed, but (unlike the situation pertaining to the European Court of Human Rights) seem to be confined under the current Rules to the States Parties and organizations of employers and trade unions. A Decision is then taken on the merits of the complaint, which is forwarded to the Parties concerned and to the Committee of Ministers in a report. The report is made public within four months of being so forwarded. On the basis of the report drawn up by the European Committee of Social Rights, the Committee of Ministers adopts a Resolution. If deemed appropriate, it may issue a Recommendation to the State concerned asking it to take the necessary action to bring its laws and policies in line with the Charter.

3.2. RECENT CONCLUSIONS OF THE EUROPEAN COMMITTEE OF SOCIAL RIGHTS ON STATE PARTY REPORTS ON DISABILITY.

The 2008 Conclusions on State Party Reports with respect to Article 15 will now be considered on a country-by-country basis. Some states have selected particular paragraphs of the Article by which to be bound. In those cases, the Committee of Social Rights has only issued 'Conclusions' on the accepted provisions of Article 15. Paragraphs that have not been accepted are labelled 'non-accepted provisions' below.

In future cycles of the Yearbook, the analysis will be expanded to include other relevant Articles, such as Article 7 on the rights of children and young persons to protection and Article 17 on the right of children and young persons to social, legal and economic protection (which includes the substantive right to education). As previously mentioned, the States Parties do not report on Article E in their periodic reports.

The General Introduction to the 2008 Conclusions under the Revised European Social Charter contains the following important 'statement of interpretation' with respect to Article 15(3):

9. Statement on technical aids and support services (Article 15(3))

Under Article 15(3) states undertake to promote the full social integration and participation in the life of the community of persons with disabilities, in particular through measures, including technical aids, aiming to overcome barriers to communication and mobility and enabling access to transport, housing, cultural activities and leisure.

To give meaningful effect to this undertaking:

- Mechanisms must be established to assess the barriers to communication and mobility faced by persons with disabilities and identify the support measures that are required to assist them in overcoming these barriers.
- Technical aids must be available either for free or subject to an appropriate contribution towards their cost and taking into account the beneficiary's means. Such aids may for example take the form of prostheses, walkers, wheelchairs, guide dogs and appropriate housing support arrangements.
- Support services, such as personal assistance and auxiliary aids, must be available, either for free or subject to an appropriate contribution towards their cost and taking into account the beneficiary's means.

First, the 2008 Conclusions of the Committee under the Revised Charter (1996) are considered, followed by the relevant Conclusions under the original 1961 Charter. Links to the relevant national reports are also provided.

3.2.1. Armenia - Revised Charter (reference period: 2001-2004)[49]

National report available at:
<http://www.coe.int/t/dghl/monitoring/socialcharter/Reporting/StateReports/Armenia1_en.pdf>

Article 15(1): non accepted provision.
Article 15(2): Conclusion - non-conformity.
Article 15(3): Conclusion - deferred

This was Armenia's first report under the Social Charter system.
In reaching a Conclusion of non-conformity with respect to Article 15(2), the Committee stated that the national report failed to show that persons with disabilities enjoyed effective protection against discrimination in employment. The Committee noted that the rate of employment of persons with disabilities, though increasing, remained very low. The Committee requested up-to-date data so that it could make an accurate assessment of the situation.
The Committee also wished to know whether the WHO International Classification of Functioning, Disability and Health was incorporated into relevant national legislation. The Committee reiterated previous requests seeking clarification concerning the status and enactment of anti-discrimination legislation. It

---

[49]   European Committee of Social Rights, 'Conclusions 2008 (ARMENIA)' (November 2008), <http://www.coe.int/t/dghl/monitoring/socialcharter/conclusions/State/Armenia2008_en.pdf>, last accessed 24 February 2009.

asked if national legislation on social protection of disabled persons covered the public sector. The Committee asked how a 'reasonable accommodation' provision was implemented in practice, whether there had been resulting case law and whether the legislation improved the situation of employment of persons with disabilities in practice.

The Committee asked for specific data on the number of individuals with disabilities in the labour market and benefiting from national measures, the number of persons with disabilities progressing from sheltered employment to the ordinary labour market, as well as details of salary calculation in sheltered employment. The Committee also asked whether trade unions were active in sheltered employment facilities. The Committee acknowledged increased levels of involvement by persons with disabilities in vocational training activities and the establishment of an Employment Rehabilitation Centre to help integrate persons with disabilities into the open labour market. It sought information on the practical results emanating from this Centre.

On the matter of conformity with Article 15(3) on social integration and participation in the life of the community, the Committee deferred its decision pending the receipt of requested information. The Committee sought further information on any legislation relevant to Article 15(3). The Committee also sought information on how a new procedure for issuing prosthetics, orthopaedic apparatus and other technical aids was applied in practice. The Committee asked who was responsible for the cost of technical aids and support services, the individual or the State or both. The Committee noted the development of accessible media and asked whether measures had been put in place to ensure access to new information and telecommunication technologies.

Regarding mobility and transport, the Committee requested information on the practical implementation of measures to improve transport for people with disabilities using adapted street furniture, ramps, light and sound signals. The Committee acknowledged the appointment of special teams to help people with disabilities at airports and sought information on similar measures for transport by rail, road and sea. In the area of housing, the Committee asked about any financial assistance provided for the conversion of an existing house to suits the needs of a person with a disability.

3.2.2. Belgium - Revised Charter (reference period: 2005-2006)[50]

National report available at:
<http://www.coe.int/t/dghl/monitoring/socialcharter/Reporting/StateReports/Belgium2_en.pdf>

Article 15(1): Conclusion - non-conformity.
Article 15(2): Conclusion - non-conformity.
Article 15(3): Conclusion - non-conformity.

---

[50] European Committee of Social Rights, 'Conclusions 2008 (BELGIUM)' (November 2008), <http://www.coe.int/t/dghl/monitoring/socialcharter/conclusions/State/Belgium2008_en.pdf>, last accessed 24 February 2009.

The Committee noted that not all previously requested data had been supplied and further information was still required. The missing data related to attendance by children / adults with disabilities at mainstream and special compulsory and upper education facilities, as well as in vocational training and university education. The Committee also requested information on the definition of disability for the purposes of obtaining 'reasonable accommodation', and its impact in terms of integration of persons with disabilities in education and training. The Committee sought information on the steps taken to generally promote integration into mainstream education, whether end qualifications are identical for all children and the success rate for children with disabilities as regards further education or training and entry into the ordinary labour market. With respect to new national anti-discrimination legislation, the Committee concluded that the situation in Belgium was not in conformity with Article 15(1), as the law covering education for persons with disabilities was inadequate.

The Committee did not find conformity with Article 15(2) either, as the Belgian Report failed to establish that persons with disabilities were guaranteed effective equal access to employment. Figures as to the numbers of persons with disabilities, the number of persons with disabilities of employment age, and the number of persons with disabilities in employment (both sheltered and not) were not furnished. The Committee questioned how 'reasonable accommodation' under anti-discrimination law is implemented in practice. Information on remedies for persons aggrieved and details of relevant case law were sought. The Committee noted numerous new measures in the field of employment, and asked about their practical impact in increasing the employment rate of persons with disabilities. The Committee requested details on the progress achieved towards employment rate objectives. Information was also sought on the number of persons with disabilities transferring from the sheltered market to the open market.

The Committee also concluded that Belgium failed to conform with Article 15(3), due to the absence of general anti-discrimination legislation to protect persons with disabilities in the fields of housing, transport, telecommunications and cultural and leisure activities. It also cited a lack of information provided on mobility, transport and housing. It noted that a new Anti-Discrimination Act was adopted outside the reference period and would be analyzed in the next supervision cycle. To assist that analysis, the Committee sought all necessary information on the application of the legislation and the available remedies.

While information was provided on access policy coordination and planning and technical aids and supports in the Flemish Community, the Committee asked that it be furnished with corresponding information for the French and German speaking Communities also. The Committee asked about the financial aid provided for the purchase of technical aids and supports in all communities. The Committee acknowledged developments made in the Flemish Community regarding accessibility of communications and requested information on similar developments in the French and German Communities. It also asked for a clarification of the legal status of sign language in these latter two communities. With regard to culture and leisure, the Committee acknowledged positive developments in the Flemish Community, but required further information on developments within the French and German speaking Communities.

3.2.3. Cyprus - Revised Charter (reference period: 2003-2006)[51]

National report available at:
<http://www.coe.int/t/dghl/monitoring/socialcharter/Reporting/StateReports/Cyprus5_en.pdf>

Article 15(1): Conclusion - conformity.
Article 15(2): Conclusion - deferred.
Article 15(3): Conclusion - deferred.

The Committee found that the situation in Cyprus was in conformity with Article 15(1).

The Committee requested further and up-to-date figures regarding the situation of education and training for persons with disabilities. In the context of domestic complaints regarding a lack of 'reasonable accommodation' for dyslexic children in exams, the Committee noted criticism from the national equality body on the national Law on Education and Training of Children with Special Needs and the Pancyrian School Exams Law. It noted an amendment to the latter law to protect students with dyslexia, but it sought information as to any envisaged or adopted amendment of the former law. The Committee also sought follow-up information on a decision of the national equality body, which found the termination of a trainee who had acquired a disability during training to be discriminatory.

The Committee deferred its Conclusion with respect to Article 15(2). The Committee sought more accurate data on the current situation as regards employment and access to employment for persons with disabilities. The Committee sought clarification on the availability and adequacy of remedies for discriminatory practices. The Committee questioned apparent disparities between Cypriot law and the EC Employment Equality Directive in terms of the provision for 'reasonable accommodation' and national understandings of when the defence of 'disproportionate burden' might apply. The Committee acknowledged new schemes to promote employment of persons with disabilities. With regard to the principle that a specific category of employment should not be reserved for a particular category of disability (such as blind people), the Committee asked for examples of good practice. The Committee also sought comments on criticism levelled at sheltered employment practices in Cyprus.[52]

The Committee also deferred its decision of conformity with Article 15(3), again requesting further information, such as information on the scope of general anti-discrimination legislation which expressly refers to mobility, transport, tel-

---

[51]   European Committee of Social Rights, 'Conclusions 2008 (CYPRUS)' (November 2008), <http://www.coe.int/t/dghl/monitoring/socialcharter/conclusions/State/Cyprus2008_en.pdf>, last accessed 24 February 2009.

[52]   Demetriades, 'Report on the situation of fundamental rights in Cyprus in 2005' (December 2005), <http://cridho.cpdr.ucl.ac.be/documents/Download.Rep/Reports2005/NationalReport/CFRCyprus2005.pdf>, last accessed 24 February 2009, p. 84. This report was submitted to the EU Network of independent experts on fundamental rights and criticized the Christos Stelios Ioannou Foundation for sheltered employment.

ecommunications, culture and leisure, legal remedies available and any relevant case law. Information was also sought as to whether individuals were required to contribute to the costs of technical aids and supports. It was noted that public assistance is granted to persons residing lawfully in Cyprus whose basic income is inadequate and the Committee asked for further details.

Regarding communication, the Committee requested information on whether measures were being taken to have sign language recognized as an official language and what progress was being made in access to new information and telecommunication technologies. The Committee expressed concerns about access to transport and asked if measures were being taken to improve the situation for persons with disabilities. The Committee noted that persons with disabilities do not have free or reduced-rate access to culture and leisure facilities and therefore the Committee sought information on what was being done in this regard.

3.2.4. Estonia - Revised Charter (reference period: 2005-2006)[53]

National report available at:
<http://www.coe.int/t/dghl/monitoring/socialcharter/Reporting/StateReports/Estonia5_en.pdf>

Article 15(1): Conclusion - non-conformity.
Article 15(2): Conclusion - non-conformity.
Article 15(3): Conclusion - non-conformity.

The Committee reached a Conclusion of non-conformity with respect to Article 15(1), as the relevant anti-discrimination legislation governing education and training for persons with disabilities was inadequate. The Committee sought clarification on the actual number of persons with disabilities and the proportion of these persons living in institutions. The Committee requested information on the practical impact of disability awareness training provided to local government and education specialists. The Committee also asked whether draft anti-discrimination legislation previously notified was adopted and if it explicitly protected persons with disabilities against discrimination in education and training. The Committee found the legislation in the field of education to be wholly inadequate and reiterated previous requests for evidence of case law in this area. The Committee expressed concern about the adequacy of education provided to children in segregated institutional settings and asked how this was monitored. The Committee also sought information on how a new regulation relating to conditions and procedures for persons with special needs in vocational education affected the opportunities for persons with disabilities to acquire this education. The Committee noted developments in including children with disabilities in mainstream schools.

The Committee found non-conformity with Article 15(2) of the Revised Charter, as it failed to establish that persons with disabilities were guaranteed

---

[53]   European Committee of Social Rights, 'Conclusions 2008 (ESTONIA)' (November 2008), <http://www.coe.int/t/dghl/monitoring/socialcharter/conclusions/State/Estonia2008_en.pdf>, last accessed 25 February 2009.

effective protection against discrimination in employment. The Committee expressed concerns about the inadequate data provided regarding the total number of persons with disabilities employed both in the open market and in sheltered employment, those benefiting from employment promotion measures and those seeking employment. The Committee also sought details on the implementation of the 'reasonable accommodation' provision and any related case law.

The Committee highlighted a lack of awareness of measures to promote and facilitate the employment of persons with disabilities, in particular, employment services, tax concessions and subsidies. The Committee noted the absence of evidence as to how many people with disabilities actually benefited from these measures. The Committee sought comment on the issue of integration of persons with intellectual disabilities in employment and considered current measures to this end to be insufficient. Regarding people with disabilities in sheltered employment, the Committee requested information on their level of pay.

The situation in Estonia was also considered to be in non-conformity with Article 15(3) due to the absence of anti-discrimination legislation to protect persons with disabilities in the context of housing, transport, telecommunications and cultural and leisure activities. The Committee reiterated the importance of such legislation and the availability of effective remedies. The Committee asked for information on a legislative proposal on equal treatment, and its expected application to the areas covered by Article 15(3). The Committee also requested information on progress achieved on measures to improve access to transport by rail under the Estonian transport development plan.

3.2.5. Finland - Revised Charter (reference period: 2005-2006)[54]

National report available at:
<http://www.coe.int/t/dghl/monitoring/socialcharter/Reporting/StateReports/Finland3_en.pdf>

Article 15(1): Conclusion - conformity.
Article 15(2): Conclusion - conformity.
Article 15(3): Conclusion - non-conformity.

In Finland, the situation was considered to be in conformity with Article 15(1), pending the receipt of certain information. The Committee noted that the Finnish Non-Discrimination Act (no.630/1998) prohibits discrimination on the basis of disability in access to education, vocational training and re-training. The Committee sought accurate and detailed statistics with respect to the high number of students with disabilities still in institutions and not integrated into the mainstream education system. Other information sought related to training try-outs provided to persons with disabilities, access to higher education and the take-up and success of rehabilitation and guidance provided to prepare for work and independent life.

---

[54]   European Committee of Social Rights, 'Conclusions 2008 (FINLAND)' (November 2008), <http://www.coe.int/t/dghl/monitoring/socialcharter/conclusions/State/Finland2008_en.pdf>, last accessed 25 February 2009.

With respect to Article 15(2), the Committee also concluded that the situation in Finland was in conformity. However, it sought clarification on the implementation of the 'reasonable accommodation' obligation under the relevant non-discrimination law, as well as information on any measures in place to promote the employment of persons with disabilities and their impact in practice. The Committee also expressed concerns regarding sheltered employment and sought details on whether persons with disabilities involved in such employment enjoyed the usual benefits under labour law and whether trade unions were active.

Article 15(3) was the only part of this Article with which the situation in Finland was considered not to be in conformity. The Committee asked whether a 2006 Government report on Finnish disability policy had resulted in any progress in the development of integrated programming. The Committee also sought details on a Design for All initiative in the field of communications. With regard to technical aids and supports, the Committee asked whether costs were born by the individual, the State or both. The Committee requested information on the results of an accessibility project for public transport completed by the Ministry of Transport and Communication.

3.2.6. France - Revised Charter (reference period: 2005-2006)[55]

National report available at:
<http://www.coe.int/t/dghl/monitoring/socialcharter/Reporting/StateReports/ France7_en.pdf>

Article 15(1): Conclusion - non-conformity.
Article 15(2): Conclusion - deferred.
Article 15(3): Conclusion - deferred.

The Committee concluded that the relevant French legislation on equal rights and opportunities, participation and citizenship of persons with disabilities was in line with Article 15(1). Details were sought on the implementation of legislative arrangements and their impact on the integration of disabled persons in education. However, further to its Decision in Collective Complaint No. 13/2002, *Autism-Europe v. France* (see below), the Committee concluded that the French situation was not in conformity with Article 15(1). This was because of the absence of statistics provided to show that persons with autism were guaranteed equal access to education in an effective manner.

The national report referred to resources authorized for the creation of places for autistic persons in special establishments, educational and domiciliary care services, Maisons d'Accueil Spécialisées (MAS), and Foyer d'Accueil Medicalisé (FAM). The Committee sought accurate information on the number places actually created, and how many persons, in fact, took advantage of them.

The Committee also considered the system of 'collective schooling' in place, whereby children with the same type of special needs are educated in

---

[55]   European Committee of Social Rights, 'Conclusions 2008 (FRANCE)' (November 2008), <http://www.coe.int/t/dghl/monitoring/socialcharter/conclusions/State/ France2008_en.pdf>, last accessed 25 February 2009.

units within mainstream schools. As the national report acknowledged that the number of these units was inadequate to cater for all disabled pupils, the Committee requested further statistics and information on the progress of the 'collective schooling' initiative. The Committee also raised questions as to the nature of the qualifications that the special education syllabi led to and, whether these were recognized for the purposes of continuing education or, entering vocational education, or the open labour market. The Committee asked for details of the success rate in progressing from the 'collective schooling' system into vocational training programmes, further education and the open labour market.

The Committee sought accurate figures on places taken by young intellectually disabled persons in so-called educational and domiciliary care services, and requested information on measures being taken to reduce the total number of disabled persons receiving no education at all. The Committee further reiterated an earlier request for information relating to the provision of vocational training to persons with disabilities.

With regard to the right to employment under Article 15(2), the Committee noted that French legislation was satisfactory. However, it deferred its conclusion of conformity pending receipt of further information. It sought information on the implementation of the 'reasonable accommodation' duty and its practical impact for persons with disabilities in employment. The Committee also expressed interest in the findings of a statutory monitoring group. The Committee requested up-dates on the progress of assisted employment establishments and services initiatives, as well as uptake figures relating to new social assistance and medical service initiatives. The Committee also requested additional information on systems of sheltered employment.

In relation to Article 15(3), the Committee deferred its Conclusion. It requested further information on whether the relevant anti-discrimination legislation applied to the areas covered by Article 15(3), who bore the costs of technical aids and support services, what evidence there was of progress in practice to achieve access to public transport, and whether the state financed sporting activities for people with disabilities.

3.2.7. Georgia - Revised Charter (reference period: 2005-2006)[56]

National report available at:
<http://www.coe.int/t/dghl/monitoring/socialcharter/Reporting/StateReports/Georgia1_en.pdf>

Article 15(1): Non accepted provision
Article 15(2): Non accepted provision.
Article 15(3): Conclusion - deferred.

The Committee deferred its conclusion as to conformity with Article 15(3) - the only paragraph accepted by Georgia - pending the receipt of information

---

[56] European Committee of Social Rights, 'Conclusions 2008 (GEORGIA)' (November 2008), <http://www.coe.int/t/dghl/monitoring/socialcharter/conclusions/State/Georgia2008_en.pdf>, last accessed 25 February 2009.

requested.

The information requested related to the existence of any anti-discrimination legislation covering the areas set out in the Charter provision. Details of available remedies and relevant case law were also sought. The Committee asked whether all authorities involved in the implementation of disability rights policy applied integrated programming, and whether organizations representing persons with disabilities were involved in the design, review and implementation of measures for persons with disabilities. The Committee further requested information on the forms of economic assistance available to persons with disabilities, and asked who had responsibility for covering the costs of technical aids and support services.

The Committee asked what mechanisms existed to assess barriers to communication and mobility. In the context of mobility and transport, the Committee sought information on the implementation of new rules for the construction of public buildings with disability access and asked about the availability of free or reduced fares for disabled persons. The Committee also sought information on grants available for housing renovations or adaptations, and on any measures taken to guarantee access in sport and cultural activities.

3.2.8. Italy - Revised Charter (reference period: 2005-2006)[57]

National report available at:
<http://www.coe.int/t/dghl/monitoring/socialcharter/Reporting/StateReports/ Italy7_en.pdf>

Article 15(1): Conclusion - deferred.
Article 15(2): Conclusion - non-conformity.
Article 15(3): Conclusion - deferred.

The Committee deferred its decision on conformity with Article 15(1) pending the receipt of information. Information was sought on the impact of training given to persons involved in applying the definition of disability in light of the World Health Organization's (WHO) International Classification of Functioning, Disability and Health. The Committee confirmed the need for anti-discrimination legislation to combat discrimination. Although it considered Italian legislative measures on non-discrimination and the rights of persons with disabilities to be in conformity with Article 15(1), the Committee sought further information on implementation, and asked to be furnished with any relevant case law.

The Committee also requested information on the methods in place to achieve the objective of educating children and young people with disabilities in mainstream education from preschool level to university. The Committee reiterated concerns voiced in its 2003 Conclusions as to quality control mechanisms in place in special schools. The Committee had questions regarding the type of qualifications obtained in special schools and asked for indicators of success for

---

[57] European Committee of Social Rights, 'Conclusions 2008 (ITALY)' (November 2008), <http://www.coe.int/t/dghl/monitoring/socialcharter/conclusions/State/Italy2008_en.pdf>, last accessed 25 February 2009.

students educated in special schools who went on to further education and/or employment. In the context of vocational education, the Committee requested figures for the system of one-year recruitment-oriented work placements.

With respect to Article 15(2), the Committee made a finding of non-conformity. The Committee requested an explanation for the massive increase in the numbers of persons with disabilities in employment between 2003 and 2005, as figures given in the national report did not add up. The Committee indicated that it required a breakdown of the number of persons with disabilities in ordinary employment, the number of those in sheltered employment, the rate at which workers were moving from sheltered to ordinary employment, as well as information on trade union activity in sheltered employment. The Committee also sought further information about the practical impact of relevant anti-discrimination legislation, especially in relation to 'reasonable accommodation'. The Committee had sought information in its previous Conclusions on the sanctions in place for offending employers. In reply, the national report cited legislation that excludes access to employment and labour law from its scope of application. Thus, the Committee requested clarification on the matter.

With regard to measures in place to promote the employment of persons with disabilities, the Committee noted that the trade union, Federonlus, had received a large number of complaints of discrimination against disabled persons in the workplace. The Committee wanted to know what was being done and being planned to improve this situation. The Committee went on to request information on compliance and monitoring of an obligation of employers to create posts that they can assign to unskilled workers.

The Committee deferred its final Conclusion on Article 15(3), pending receipt of the requisite information. The Committee believed that the legislative framework provided disabled persons with adequate protection from the perspective of the provision, but sought details on implementation. Regarding technical aids and supports, the Committee sought clarification as to who bore the burden of costs. The Committee also asked for information on the application of draft legislation to encourage the full participation of deaf persons in the life of the community. Regarding mobility and transport, the Committee requested evidence of compliance with a statutory obligation to make buildings and sports facilities accessible. The Committee also sought evidence of the amount of people actually benefiting from a legislative provision authorizing central and regional governments to make non-repayable contributions for housing adaptations. Finally, the Committee requested additional information on the numerous initiatives undertaken in the field of culture and leisure.

3.2.9. Lithuania - Revised Charter (reference period: 2005-2006)[58]

National report available at:
<http://www.coe.int/t/dghl/monitoring/socialcharter/Reporting/StateReports/Lithuania5_en.pdf>

---

[58]   European Committee of Social Rights, 'Conclusions 2008 (LITHUANIA)' (November 2008), <http://www.coe.int/t/dghl/monitoring/socialcharter/conclusions/State/Lithuania2008_en.pdf>, last accessed 25 February 2009.

Article 15(1): Conclusion - conformity.
Article 15(2): Conclusion - non-conformity.
Article 15(3): Conclusion - non-conformity.

Pending the receipt of information requested, Lithuania was considered to be in conformity with Article 15(1). Accurate data was sought on the number of people with disabilities, the number of children with disabilities, and the number of those in mainstream and special education as well as in institutions. The Committee also requested information on any case law relating to discrimination in education on the basis of disability. Further information was sought on the matter of mainstreaming, related teacher training and the vocational education scheme whereby funds follow the student. The Committee also asked whether decisions of the Lithuanian Equal Opportunities Ombudsman and its Office are subject to judicial appeal.

The Committee could not justify a finding of conformity with Article 15(2) due to the absence of a legislative requirement on employers to make 'reasonable accommodation'. The Committee was concerned about inaccurate data received and requested figures on the number of disabled persons of working age, the number in ordinary and sheltered employment, and the rate of progression from sheltered to mainstream jobs. The Committee sought information on the impact of employment support legislation and specifically on whether employment opportunities are available in the open market, or solely in the sheltered one. It also requested information on conditions of employment in the sheltered market. The Committee asked whether the national strategy for social integration had led to an increase in the integration of persons with disabilities.

In concluding that Lithuania was not in conformity with Article 15(3), the Committee found that Lithuania lacked essential general anti-discrimination legislation covering the areas of housing, transport, telecommunications, cultural and leisure activities and providing effective remedies. On the question of technical aids and support services, the Committee asked who bore the cost of such necessary measures. The Committee requested information on the impact and outcomes of a government programme for the renovation of housing for people with motor impairments in the time period 2007-2011. The Committee acknowledged changes and improvements that had occurred in the area of culture, but requested specific information on measures in place to ensure the accessibility of sports and cultural activities in an ordinary environment.

3.2.10. Malta - Revised Charter (reference period: 2005-2006)[59]

National report available at:
<http://www.coe.int/t/dghl/monitoring/socialcharter/Reporting/StateReports/
Malta1_en.pdf>

---

[59]   European Committee of Social Rights, 'Conclusions 2008 (MALTA)' (November 2008), <http://www.coe.int/t/dghl/monitoring/socialcharter/conclusions/State/Malta2008_en.pdf>, last accessed 25 February 2009.

Article 15(1): Conclusion - non-conformity.
Article 15(2): Conclusion - non-conformity.
Article 15(3): Conclusion - deferred.

The Committee concluded that Malta was not in conformity with Article 15(1), as it failed to prove that mainstreaming of persons with disabilities in training was guaranteed in practice. The Committee reiterated its previous request for accurate data on the number of people with disabilities, and requested clarification on the Maltese social model of 'disability' and its relationship with the model endorsed by the WHO. The Committee requested details on the outcomes of a review of inclusive and special education undertaken in 2004. Referring to previous Conclusions on the absence of educational supports necessary to integrate students with disabilities into mainstream schools, the Committee asked what had been done to remedy this situation. Information on the number of children with intellectual disabilities in mainstream and special education was sought along with details of special education training provided to teachers. The Committee requested data on the number of persons with disabilities in mainstream vocational training or higher education.

Having examined the data available to it, the Committee concluded that Malta failed to demonstrate that people with disabilities enjoyed equal access to employment and was thus not in conformity with Article 15(2). The Committee sought further information on the practical effects of national equal opportunities legislation, a training scheme for persons with disabilities and a supported employment scheme. It asked whether the number given for placements made under the latter scheme included persons with severe disabilities only, and whether they were placed in the ordinary market or not. The Committee requested accurate data on the number of persons with disabilities in sheltered employment and asked for details on the practical effects of a supported employment programme for unemployed persons with mental health difficulties. The Committee also requested further information on the outcomes of a scheme designed to assist persons with disabilities to find open employment and the number of persons with disabilities who made use of day services.

Pending the receipt of the requested information, the Committee deferred its decision on conformity with Article 15(3). It queried whether equal opportunities legislation applied to the areas covered by the provision. It also asked whether integrated programming was utilized when implementing policy for persons with disabilities. The Committee sought clarification on measures taken to ensure access to public transport and asked about the availability of free or reduced fares for persons with disabilities. Regarding housing, the Committee asked about the availability of grants for people with disabilities for necessary adaptations. The Committee also asked about measures taken to ensure the accessibility of sport, leisure and cultural activities.

3.2.11. Moldova - Revised Charter (reference period: 2005-2006)[60]

National report available at:
<http://www.coe.int/t/dghl/monitoring/socialcharter/Reporting/StateReports/
Moldova4_en.pdf>

Article 15(1): Conclusion - non-conformity.
Article 15(2): Conclusion - non-conformity.
Article 15(3): Non accepted provision.

In line with previous Conclusions, the Committee concluded that the situation in
Moldova was not in conformity with Article 15(1), on the ground of an absence
of legislation explicitly protecting persons with disabilities from discrimination in
education and training. The Committee asked whether any steps had been taken
to move away from the medical definition of disability to a more social model,
such as that endorsed by WHO. The Committee reiterated previous requests for
information relating to vocational guidance and training and asked whether there
was any guarantee of an effective right to education in law and/or practice.

Regarding non-discrimination in employment, the Committee also maintained its previous conclusion of non-conformity and again highlighted the need
for legislation prohibiting discrimination on the grounds of disability (including
a 'reasonable accommodation' obligation). The Committee sought clarification
as to whether this existed, and, if so, how it was implemented in practice and
whether there was case law on the issue. The Committee reiterated its 2005 requests for information as to what measures were in place to encourage employers
to hire, and keep in employment, persons with disabilities. The Committee asked
for details on measures taken to raise awareness about facilities to access employment for persons with disabilities.

3.2.12. The Netherlands - Revised Charter (reference period: 2006)[61]

National report available at:
http://www.coe.int/t/dghl/monitoring/socialcharter/Reporting/StateReports/
Netherlands1_fr.pdf

Article 15(1): Conclusion - deferred.
Article 15(2): Conclusion - deferred.
Article 15(3): Conclusion - deferred.

The Committee deferred its Conclusion on Dutch conformity with Article 15(1).
The Committee highlighted the fundamental requirement for anti-discrimination

---

[60]   European Committee of Social Rights, 'Conclusions 2008 (MOLDOVA)' (Novem-
         ber 2008), <http://www.coe.int/t/dghl/monitoring/socialcharter/conclusions/State/
         Moldova2008_en.pdf>, last accessed 25 February 2009.
[61]   European Committee of Social Rights, 'Conclusions 2008 (NETHERLANDS)' (No-
         vember 2008), <http://www.coe.int/t/dghl/monitoring/socialcharter/conclusions/
         State/Netherlands2008_en.pdf>, last accessed 25 February 2009.

legislation to protect the right to education for persons with disabilities and reiterated its request for information on the existence of such legislative provisions. The Committee asked whether the criteria used in granting special educational support were based on the social model of disability endorsed by the WHO. It requested accurate data on the number of persons with disabilities in the Netherlands. The Committee sought up-to-date information regarding the progress being made to mainstream children with disabilities in the education system and training provided to teachers.

The Committee also requested clarification on the numbers of people with disabilities in secondary, vocational and higher education, as well as the impact of such education and training on labour market integration. The Committee noted that adult and vocational educational institutions in the Netherlands were entitled to funding for every learner assessed as having special needs. The Committee requested information as to the uptake of this funding. The Committee acknowledged the existence of employment legislation requiring that a person's ability be considered rather than his/her disability, and requested information on the practical impact of this, including relevant data.

Pending the receipt of the requested information in the context of employment, the Committee also deferred its conclusion on Article 15(2). It reiterated requests for up-to-date figures concerning the number of persons with disabilities of working age, those in employment and those unemployed, the number in both the open and sheltered markets and the rate of progression from the sheltered to the open market. It also sought details on how 'reasonable accommodation' requirements were implemented in practice, if they gave rise to cases before the courts and if they have resulted in an increase in the employment of persons with disabilities in the open market.

The Committee also deferred its Conclusion on Article 15(3). The Committee requested details of any relevant legislation and case law. It asked whether all authorities involved in the implementation of policy for persons with disabilities applied integrated programming. The Committee also requested information on the workings of organizations and pressure groups that protect the rights of persons with disabilities groups and that receive financial support from the government. The Committee requested further information on what aids and supports were available as of right, and who bore the cost of such aids and supports. The Committee asked if measures had been taken to promote access to new telecommunication technologies and what the legal status of sign language was. Regarding mobility and transport, the Committee asked what was being done to ensure the implementation of relevant legislation, and how access to all forms of public transport was being guaranteed. It also asked if free or reduced fares were available to persons with disabilities. With respect to housing, the Committee sought information on grants available for individual persons with disabilities for housing renovations or adaptations and, in the context of sport and cultural activities, the Committee asked how accessibility was being ensured.

3.2.13. Norway - Revised Charter (reference period: 2005-2006)[62]

National report available at:
<http://www.coe.int/t/dghl/monitoring/socialcharter/Reporting/StateReports/Norway5_fr.pdf>

Article 15(1): Conclusion - non-conformity.
Article 15(2): Conclusion - non-conformity.
Article 15(3): Conclusion - non-conformity.

The Committee believed the situation in Norway was not in conformity with Article 15(1) due to inadequate anti-discrimination legislation covering education for persons with disabilities. The Committee requested information on the status and scope of a new Anti-Discrimination and Accessibility Act. In particular, it asked if there was a requirement for a compelling justification for segregation in education and if there were effective remedies for violations. The Committee asked that it be furnished with details of any case law relating to discrimination in education on the basis of disability, and sought information on special education services. Noting the responsibility of Higher Education Institutions to draw up action plans for the integration of disabled persons, the Committee requested information on the practical impact of such plans.

In terms of the employment situation, the Committee noted considerable developments and concluded that Norway was in conformity with Article 15(2). However, further information was requested on the number of persons with disabilities of working age, including the number who are either employed or unemployed, the progression rate of persons with disabilities from the sheltered market to the open one, and also on the implementation of the 'reasonable accommodation' requirement. The Committee noted that a national Labour Inspection Authority may issue orders if an employer fails to respect their 'reasonable accommodation' obligation. The Committee requested details on the impact of these orders in practice. The Committee also requested information on the outcome of a pilot project to ensure the provision of necessary aids and supports in employment for persons with disabilities, which began in 2007.

The Committee concluded that the situation in Norway was not in conformity with Article 15(3), due to inadequate anti-discrimination legislation that did not explicitly cover the relevant fields. The Committee sought information as to who bore the cost of necessary technical aids and supports and what grants were available for housing renovations or adaptations. The Committee concluded the situation in relation to culture and leisure to be in conformity with the Charter.

---

[62] European Committee of Social Rights, 'Conclusions 2008 (NORWAY)' (November 2008), <http://www.coe.int/t/dghl/monitoring/socialcharter/conclusions/State/Norway2008_en.pdf>, last accessed 25 February 2009.

3.2.14. Portugal - Revised Charter (reference period: 2005-2006)[63]

National report available at:
<http://www.coe.int/t/dghl/monitoring/socialcharter/Reporting/StateReports/Portugal3_fr.pdf>

Article 15(1): Conclusion - conformity.
Article 15(2): Conclusion - deferred.
Article 15(3): Conclusion - deferred.

Pending the receipt of requested information, the Committee concluded that the situation in Portugal was in conformity with Article 15(1). Information requested included accurate and up-to-date figures on the number of persons with disabilities, the number of disabled children integrated into mainstream schools and in special schools, whether general teacher training incorporated special needs education, details on the practical impact of resource centres, vocational training and certification for persons with disabilities and whether places reserved for persons with physical and sensory disabilities in higher education corresponded with demand. In considering the legislative framework, which provides inter alia for equal opportunities in lifelong education and training and prohibits direct and indirect discrimination on the basis of disability with respect to education and training, the Committee requested information on implementation and remedies available. It asked if the constitutional right to education was judicially enforceable and asked for details of any case law or complaints relating to discrimination in education on the basis of disability.

The Committee noted that, despite a progressive move towards a social definition of disability, a medical model was still in use in the area of rehabilitation. The Committee sought clarification as to when the social model would be adopted fully in this area, and what progress was being made in applying this model in the areas of education and training.

The Committee deferred its decision on conformity with Article 15(2), again pending the receipt of requested information. The Committee requested to be systematically informed of the number of persons with disabilities of working age, the number of those employed in the ordinary and sheltered markets, the rate of progression from sheltered to open employment, as well as of any measures taken to ensure the integration of persons with disabilities into the ordinary labour market. It found the number of economically inactive persons with disabilities to be very high. The Committee made note of numerous measures taken during the reference period to promote and increase the levels of employment of persons with disabilities and sought details on the practical impact of these.

The Committee highlighted the necessity for comprehensive anti-discrimination legislation in the field of employment, including a requirement for the provision of 'reasonable accommodation'. The Committee requested further information on the application and implementation of laws adopted during the reference period and asked whether they had led to an increase in the employment

---

[63]   European Committee of Social Rights, 'Conclusions 2008 (PORTUGAL)' (November 2008), <http://www.coe.int/t/dghl/monitoring/socialcharter/conclusions/State/Portugal2008_en.pdf>, last accessed 25 February 2009.

rate of persons with disabilities. The Committee asked what steps employers took in practice to fulfil the obligation of 'reasonable accommodation'. The Committee noted the existence of a system of quotas, whereby a certain number of persons with disabilities must be recruited. The Committee asked what percentage of enterprises, institutions and organizations achieved the quota and what sanctions, if any, were provided for those who do not.

The Committee also deferred its conclusion on conformity with Article 15(3) pending receipt of the further information. It asked if legislation prohibited discrimination based on disability in the areas covered by the provision and if there was any resulting case law. The Committee also asked for detailed information on the benefits and other forms of financial assistance to which persons with disabilities were entitled. The Committee asked if persons with disabilities were entitled to free technical aids or if they had to contribute to the cost themselves. The Committee also asked what was being done to guarantee access to public transport by air and sea. The Committee noted various arrangements introduced to ensure new buildings complied with regulations and standards and requested further details. In relation to housing, the Committee asked what grants were available to persons with disabilities for home renovations.

3.2.15. Romania - Revised Charter (reference period: 2005-2006)[64]

National report available at:
<http://www.coe.int/t/dghl/monitoring/socialcharter/Reporting/StateReports/Romania7_fr.pdf>

Article 15(1): Conclusion - non-conformity.
Article 15(2): Conclusion - deferred.
Article 15(3): Non accepted provision.

The Committee concluded that the situation in Romania was not in conformity with Article 15(1), due to the fact that the mainstreaming of persons with disabilities is not effectively guaranteed in education and training. The Committee requested information on the practical effects of a new law providing for equal and free access to any form of education and training for persons with disabilities. In particular, questions were raised about the mainstreaming of students with disabilities and the remedies available, should a case be brought before the courts. Despite improvements under the 2005 national strategy on the social protection, integration and inclusion of persons with disabilities, the number of children with disabilities in special schools was still higher than the number in ordinary schools. The Committee had also previously found a high number of children with disabilities receiving no education at all. The national report did not comment on this and the Committee requested further information. The Committee reiterated previous requests for information in relation to the number of persons with disabilities in mainstream vocational training, and with regard to measures taken to

---

[64] European Committee of Social Rights, 'Conclusions 2008 (ROMANIA)' (November 2008), <http://www.coe.int/t/dghl/monitoring/socialcharter/conclusions/State/Romania2008_en.pdf>, last accessed 25 February 2009.

assist integration and specialist vocational training facilities.

The Committee deferred its Conclusion on conformity with Article 15(2) pending the receipt of further information. It stated that a failure to provide this information in the next periodic report would result in a Conclusion of non-conformity. The Committee sought accurate statistics on the number of persons with disabilities of working age, in employment (ordinary and sheltered) and the rate of progression from sheltered employment to the open labour market. It also sought information on the implementation of new legislation promoting the employment of persons with disabilities, in particular the implementation of a 'reasonable accommodation' obligation. The Committee noted measures taken to promote employment but urged the government:

> to bear in mind that Article 15(2) of the Revised Charter requires that persons with disabilities be employed in an ordinary working environment; sheltered employment facilities therefore must be reserved for those persons who, due to their disability, cannot be integrated into the open labour market.

3.2.16. Austria - 1961 Charter (reference period: 2003-2006)[65]

National report available at:
<http://www.coe.int/t/dghl/monitoring/socialcharter/Reporting/StateReports/ Austria25_en.pdf>

Article 15(1): Conclusion - deferred.
Article 15(2): Conclusion - deferred.

In deferring its conclusion with respect to Article 15(1), the Committee requested further information on the updating of the two operating definitions of disability. A new classification relating to eligibility of people with disabilities for certain legislative entitlements was to be introduced in July 2008, and the Committee requested information on its operation. The Committee also asked for employment data to be gathered on people with health-caused impairments which reduce placement opportunities and who attend Public Employment Service courses.

The Committee acknowledged the improved situation resulting from the enactment of legislation prohibiting discrimination against people with disabilities and their family members. It sought further information on the role, if any, of the Ombudsman for the Disabled in third party interventions and class actions in discrimination litigation. It also requested data on the number and outcomes of the compulsory arbitration procedure required prior to any court hearings in discrimination cases. The Committee asked that it be kept informed of the practical implementation of the legislation, including case law specific to education and vocational training.

The Committee noted discrepancies in the level of protection from discrimination in the context of access to education in various Austrian states, and sought

---

[65] European Committee of Social Rights, 'Conclusions XIX – 1 (AUSTRIA)' (November 2008), <http://www.coe.int/t/dghl/monitoring/socialcharter/Conclusions/State/ AustriaXIX1_en.pdf>, last accessed 12 May 2009.

clarification. The Committee noted criticisms of the level of physical accessibility of schools and the lengthy delay in addressing this issue.[66] It encouraged Austria to ensure 'reasonable accommodation' for individual students immediately. The Committee acknowledged advances made in the area of vocational training. However, it also noted that the placement rates for people with disabilities who have a medically certified degree of disability exceeding 50%, were higher than for persons with health-caused impairments that reduce placement opportunities. The latter group is used by the Public Employment Service. The Committee sought further information on this issue.

The Committee also deferred its decision on the matter of conformity with Article 15(2). It acknowledged a legislative amendment requiring employers to provide 'reasonable accommodation'. However, the Committee noted a high level of exclusion of people with mental disabilities[67] from the labour market and requested information in the next report, including case law, about measures taken to redress this situation. The Committee noted that employment levels of people with disabilities could not easily be quantified due to the two co-existing definitions of disability, and reaffirmed its request for reliable data and statistics.

3.2.17. Czech Republic - 1961 Charter (reference period: 2005-2006)[68]

National report available at:
<http://www.coe.int/t/dghl/monitoring/socialcharter/Reporting/StateReports/CzechRep5_en.pdf>

Article 15(1): Non accepted provision.
Article 15(2): Conclusion - non-conformity.

The Committee found that the situation in the Czech Republic was not in conformity with Article 15(2) due to the absence of anti-discrimination legislation in the area of employment. It noted that draft anti-discrimination legislation was under discussion in the national parliament, and requested further information about the proposed definition of disability under the legislation. The Committee reiterated the need for such legislation to include a duty of 'reasonable accommodation'.

The Committee also sought information on measures to promote employ-

---

[66] See Report by the Council of Europe Commissioner for Human Rights, Visit to Austria (21-25/05/2007), see paras. 50 and 61 (document Comm. DH(2007)26, 12 December 2007) and Austrian Country Report on measures to combat discrimination (Directives 2000/43/EC and 2000/78/EC), State of affairs up to 8 January 2007, Report drafted by Dieter Schindlauer for the European Network of Legal Experts in the non-discrimination field, <http://europa.eu.int/comm/employment_social/fundamental_rights/policy/aneval/mon_en.htm>, last accessed 12 May 2009.

[67] See s.63 of the Report by the Council of Europe Commissioner for Human Rights quoted above.

[68] European Committee of Social Rights, 'Conclusions XIX – 1 (Czech Republic)' (November 2008), <http://www.coe.int/t/dghl/monitoring/socialcharter/Conclusions/State/CzechRepXIX1_en.pdf>, last accessed 12 May 2009.

ment. It noted that legislation providing for free social rehabilitation was enacted outside the reference period, and requested information on the implementation of this law. Finally, the Committee requested the collection of comprehensive data on people with disabilities in all areas of employment.

3.2.18. Denmark - 1961 Charter (reference period: 2005-2006)[69]

National report available at:
<http://www.coe.int/t/dghl/monitoring/socialcharter/Reporting/StateReports/Denmark27_en.pdf>

Article 15(1): Conclusion - non-conformity.
Article 15(2): Conclusion - conformity.

With respect to Article 15(1), the Committee expressed concern at the absence of anti-discrimination legislation with regard to educational access for people with disabilities. The Committee noted the adoption of relevant legislation outside the reference period and requested that information on the scope and implementation of this legislation be included in the next report, with specific reference to whether the legislation justifies segregated education.

The Committee assessed the mainstreaming provisions in education and vocational training and acknowledged progress made. It requested further information on the impact of vocational training on the integration of people with disabilities in the labour market and the availability of remedies to those excluded or segregated from participating in vocational training.

In concluding that Denmark was in conformity with Article 15(2), the Committee acknowledged the data collected by the Danish National Institute of Social Studies about the employment of people with disabilities and requested that the next report provide updated information on the total number of people with disabilities of working age in employment. It commended the enactment of new legislation prohibiting discrimination against people with disabilities in employment and promoting active employment efforts, and sought clarification as to how this legislation helped employers implement their obligation to provide reasonable accommodation. Details of 'reasonable accommodation' case law, integration of people with disabilities in the open labour market, and numbers of people with disabilities in sheltered employment were also requested.

---

[69] European Committee of Social Rights, 'Conclusions XIX – 1 (Denmark)' (November 2008), <http://www.coe.int/t/dghl/monitoring/socialcharter/Conclusions/State/DenmarkXIX1_en.pdf>, last accessed 12 May 2009.

3.2.19. Germany - 1961 Charter (reference period: 2005-2006)[70]

National report available at:
<http://www.coe.int/t/dghl/monitoring/socialcharter/Reporting/StateReports/
Germany25_en.pdf>

Article 15(1): Conclusion - conformity.
Article 15(2): Conclusion - conformity.

The Committee concluded that German anti-discrimination legislation was in conformity with Article 15(1). The Committee noted a presumption in favour of integration of persons with disabilities into mainstream education unless compelling reasons justified special education. The Committee also noted that special needs education was an integral part of teacher training in Germany, and universities were obliged to ensure access for students with disabilities in order to protect equality of opportunity.

The Committee commended an initiative to provide work experience to young people with disabilities, and requested further information on the impact of another initiative that seeks to raise awareness and improve the situation of people with severe disabilities in employment. The Committee also requested further information relating to specialized training centres and sheltered work environments, including data on the transition of people with disabilities to the open labour market.

The Committee also found the situation in Germany to be in conformity with Article 15(2), due to the existence of 'non-discrimination' legislation in the sphere of employment. However, the Committee requested information on whether the requirement to provide 'reasonable accommodation' was generally carried out in practice by employers. The Committee commended a number of initiatives undertaken in order to promote employment of people with disabilities. For example, Germany requires that employers with twenty work places or more must employ persons with severe disabilities in at least one of those work places. If an employer fails to meet this quota, a compensation levy must be paid to an integration office which promotes the employment of persons with severe disabilities. The purpose of this compensation levy is to encourage companies to recruit more persons with disabilities. The national report indicated that this quota-levy system has led to an increase in the numbers of people with disabilities actually employed.

3.2.20. Greece - 1961 Charter (reference period: 2005-2006)[71]

National report available at:

---

[70] European Committee of Social Rights, 'Conclusions XIX – 1 (Germany)' (November 2008), <http://www.coe.int/t/dghl/monitoring/socialcharter/Conclusions/State/GermanyXIX1_en.pdf>, last accessed 12 May 2009.

[71] European Committee of Social Rights, 'Conclusions XIX – 1 (GREECE)' (November 2008),<http://www.coe.int/t/dghl/monitoring/socialcharter/Conclusions/State/GreeceXIX1_en.pdf>, last accessed 23 July 2009.

<http://www.coe.int/t/dghl/monitoring/socialcharter/Reporting/StateReports/
Greece18_fr.pdf>

Article 15(1): Conclusion - non-conformity.
Article 15(2): Conclusion - deferred.

The Committee concluded that the situation in Greece was not in conformity with
Article 15(1) due to the absence of legislation prohibiting discrimination against
people with disabilities in education. The Committee was critical of the absence
of up-to-date statistics on the number of people with disabilities. It noted that the
definition of disability used in Greece was based on the model endorsed by the
WHO and asked if new draft legislation on special educational needs would also
use this definition. The Committee also sought details as to the reforms proposed
in this draft legislation in relation to compulsory education of persons with disabilities, improvement of the assessment body for determining school placements
and training of educators in special educational needs.

In relation to vocational training, the Committee repeated a request for information on the various training opportunities for people with disabilities and the
remedies available to those who experience discrimination. The Committee also
sought data on the numbers of people with disabilities attending and graduating
from higher education and university.

The Committee deferred its Conclusion on conformity with Article 15(2)
pending the receipt of up-to-date information on the experience of people with
disabilities in a range of employment situations. It noted that legislation had been
enacted prohibiting direct and indirect discrimination against people with disabilities in employment and providing for reasonable accommodation in terms of
access to employment, vocational orientation and training, terms and conditions
of employment and membership or participation in workers' organizations. The
Committee asked that information on the application of this law in practice be
provided in the next report. Further to information provided on the organization
of sheltered employment in Greece, the Committee reaffirmed that 'sheltered employment facilities must be reserved for those persons who, due to their disability,
cannot be integrated into the open labour market. They should aim nonetheless to
assist their beneficiaries to enter the open labour market.'[72]

3.2.21. Iceland - 1961 Charter (reference period: 2005-2006)[73]

National report available at:
<http://www.coe.int/t/dghl/monitoring/socialcharter/Reporting/StateReports/Ice-
land21_fr.pdf>

---

[72]   Ibid, p. 15.
[73]   European Committee of Social Rights, 'Conclusions XIX – 1 (ICELAND)' (Novem-
       ber 2008), <http://www.coe.int/t/dghl/monitoring/socialcharter/Conclusions/State/
       IcelandXIX1_en.pdf>, last accessed 12 May 2009.

Article 15(1): Conclusion - non-conformity.
Article 15(2): Conclusion - non-conformity.

The Committee concluded that the situation in Iceland was not in conformity with Article 15 (1) due to the absence of legislation prohibiting discrimination against people with disabilities in education and training. The Committee was informed of proposals for anti-discrimination legislation which were due to be submitted in 2008. As this was outside the reference period, the Committee requested to be kept informed of any progress in the next report.

Some information on complaints procedures and case law on exclusion from mainstream education was provided to the Committee, and further details on the total numbers of children with disabilities, and on the numbers attending mainstream and special schools or training facilities were requested. The Committee also received information on the judicial and administrative remedies available to people with disabilities who are unlawfully excluded or segregated from vocational training.

The lack of legislation prohibiting discrimination against people with disabilities in employment resulted in the Committee's Conclusion of non-conformity with Article 15(2). Similar to the situation with respect to Article 15(1), proposals for such legislation were expected in 2008, and the Committee highlighted the importance of including requirements for employers to provide 'reasonable accommodation' in such legislation. The Committee requested further information on the impact of measures taken to promote the employment of people with disabilities in the open labour market on the actual numbers of people with disabilities in the open market. These measures included the introduction of legislation providing for employment-related rehabilitation, the collection of statistics on people with disabilities in open and sheltered employment and the facilitation of membership of trade unions for people with disabilities in open and sheltered employment.

The Committee noted that the legislative definition of disability in Iceland took a primarily medical approach, although at policy level, greater emphasis was being placed on people's abilities rather than disabilities. The Committee requested further information as to whether the shift to an ability-focused approach has had an impact in the area of education and training.

3.2.22. Luxembourg - 1961 Charter (reference period: 2005-2006)[74]

National report available at:
<http://www.coe.int/t/dghl/monitoring/socialcharter/Reporting/StateReports/Lithuania5_en.pdf>

Article 15(1): Conclusion - non-conformity.
Article 15(2): Conclusion - non-conformity.

---

[74]   European Committee of Social Rights, 'Conclusions XIX – 1 (LUXEMBOURG)' (November 2008), <http://www.coe.int/t/dghl/monitoring/socialcharter/Conclusions/State/LuxembourgXIX1_en.pdf>, last accessed 12 May 2009.

The Committee concluded that the situation in Luxembourg was not in conformity with Article 15(1) as it was not provided with sufficient information to establish that mainstreaming of people with disabilities in training was effectively guaranteed. The Committee asked to be furnished with statistics on the number of children with disabilities of school age and with details of any case law or complaints relating to discrimination in access to education. The national report also failed to provide information on the number of people with disabilities receiving vocational training in mainstream establishments. The Committee emphasized the national authorities' duty to gather and analyze data on recognized categories of persons who might be discriminated against, including people with disabilities.[75] The Committee also reiterated previous requests for information on any efforts made to reframe the definition of disability in line with the social model endorsed by the WHO.

In respect of Article 15(2) on employment, the Committee noted that anti-discrimination legislation had been adopted prohibiting direct and indirect discrimination against people with disabilities in employment and providing for 'reasonable accommodation.' The Committee requested information on the provision of 'reasonable accommodation' in practice, its effect on people with disabilities entering open employment and any related case law. The Committee also requested information on efforts to address the low number of people with disabilities in employment. The Committee asked whether persons in sheltered employment enjoyed the usual benefits of labour law, including membership of a trade union. The national report stated that no new measures had been adopted and no new information on the number of beneficiaries of employment initiatives was provided. This led to the Committee's Conclusion of non-conformity with Article 15(2), as it failed to establish that persons with disabilities were guaranteed effective equal access to employment.

3.2.23. Poland - 1961 Charter (reference period: 2003-2006)[76]

National report available at:
http://www.coe.int/t/dghl/monitoring/socialcharter/Reporting/StateReports/Poland7App1_en.pdf

Article 15(1): Conclusion - non-conformity.
Article 15(2): Conclusion - non-conformity.

The Committee concluded that Poland was not in conformity with Article 15(1) as the data in the national report indicated that significant numbers of children with disabilities were still attending segregated education, and as there was no data on the numbers attending vocational training. It found that mainstreaming in education and training was not effectively guaranteed.

---

[75]   *European Roma Rights Centre v. Italy*, Collective Complaint No. 27/2004 under the European Social Charter, Decision of 7 December 2005, para. 23.

[76]   European Committee of Social Rights, 'Conclusions XIX – 1 (POLAND)' (November 2008), <http://www.coe.int/t/dghl/monitoring/socialcharter/Conclusions/State/PolandXIX1_en.pdf>, last accessed 12 May 2009.

The Committee noted that it was unclear whether Ministerial regulations providing for the education and care services for children and young people with disabilities prohibited discrimination on the ground of disability. The Committee expressed disappointment at the lack of information on case law relating to discrimination against people with disabilities in education. The figures in the national report showed that the number of children with disabilities attending special schools exceeded those attending mainstream schools. In light of these figures, the Committee reiterated the need for States Parties to provide for inclusive education, and to operate on the presumption that children with disabilities should attend mainstream schools where possible.

In reaching a Conclusion of non-conformity with Article 15(2), the Committee noted that Polish anti-discrimination legislation relating to people with disabilities in employment did not require employers to provide 'reasonable accommodation'. The Committee stated that arrangements in the legislation, which enabled employers to finance the cost of adapting the workplace for people with disabilities, did not amount to a legal obligation to provide 'reasonable accommodation'. The Committee also repeated an earlier request for information on any relevant case law on discrimination in employment on the ground of disability.

The Committee noted a number of measures intended to promote employment of people with disabilities, particularly in the form of sheltered employment initiatives. It requested information on the number of people with disabilities subsequently entering the open labour market, and emphasized that sheltered employment bodies must work to help users to find ordinary employment.

3.2.24. Spain - 1961 Charter (reference period: 2003-2006)[77]

National report available at:
<http://www.coe.int/t/dghl/monitoring/socialcharter/Reporting/StateReports/Spain20_en.pdf>

Article 15(1): Conclusion - non-conformity.
Article 15(2): Conclusion - non-conformity.

The Conclusion of non-conformity with respect to Article 15(1) was reached on the basis that the Committee could not establish whether mainstreaming was effectively provided for people with disabilities in education and training. The national report did not provide up-to-date data on the total number of people with disabilities, including children, the number of children with disabilities attending mainstream schools or training, and the number attending special schools or training, nor did it indicate whether regular teacher training included the study of special needs education. Due to the absence of this information, the Committee was unable to make a Conclusion of conformity.

During the reference period, the definition of disability was amended to cover those who had a degree of disability which was equal to or above 33%.

---

[77] European Committee of Social Rights, 'Conclusions XIX – 1 (SPAIN)' (November 2008), <http://www.coe.int/t/dghl/monitoring/socialcharter/Conclusions/State/SpainXIX1_en.pdf>, last accessed 12 May 2009.

The Committee requested information as to how many persons are recognized as disabled under this definition and how many persons are recognized as having a disability which does not reach this threshold. The Committee also asked if this definition would be used to determine entitlement to services of the National Dependant Care System. It also sought data on grants of personalized assistance to people with disabilities to facilitate their education and training.

The Committee noted Spanish anti-discrimination legislation applying to people with disabilities in education and the arbitration system in place to resolve related complaints. The Committee requested information on any case law or complaint referred to arbitration on discrimination on the ground of disability, in relation to education and training. The Committee also sought information on the implementation of the Second Action Plan for Persons with Disability (2003-2007) and the National Accessibility Plan (2004-2012).

With respect to Article 15(2), the Committee could not establish whether people with disabilities had effective equal access to employment and thus found the situation to be not in conformity. No up-to-date employment figures for persons with disabilities were provided and the Committee requested that these be included in the next report. Although Spain has anti-discrimination legislation that applies to people with disabilities in employment and requires employers to provide 'reasonable accommodation', the Committee queried how the obligation to provide 'reasonable accommodation' was implemented in practice. It asked what practical steps employers may take to ensure effective access to employment.

The Committee noted that a global action strategy on people with disabilities was due to be approved by the government and it requested that further updates on this be included in future national reports. The Committee acknowledged a number of employment promotion initiatives, such as a quota system and financial assistance for employers hiring people with disabilities, and requested further information on the operation of these initiatives in practice.

3.2.25. Former Yugoslav Republic of Macedonia - 1961 Charter (reference period: 2005-2006)[78]

National report available at:
<http://www.coe.int/t/dghl/monitoring/socialcharter/Reporting/StateReports/FY-ROM1_en.pdf>

Article 15(1): Conclusion - non-conformity.
Article 15(2): conclusion - deferred.

A Committee Conclusion of non-conformity with respect to Article 15(1) was based on the inadequacy of legislation to prohibit discrimination against people with disabilities in education. In order to assess the effectiveness of access

---

[78] European Committee of Social Rights, 'Conclusions XIX – 1 (The former Yugoslav Republic of Macedonia)' (November 2008), <http://www.coe.int/t/dghl/monitoring/socialcharter/Conclusions/State/FYROMXIX1_en.pdf>, last accessed 12 May 2009.

to education for people with disabilities, the Committee requested information on the total number of people with disabilities, including children, the number of children with disabilities attending mainstream schools or training, and the number attending special schools or training. The Committee observed that the definition of disability contained in national legislation appeared to be based on medical characteristics or impairments. It asked for the next national report to highlight whether socio-economic aspects of disability were taken into account, and whether any steps were being taken to move towards a more social definition as endorsed by the WHO.

The Committee noted that although national legislation provides for free compulsory education for all children, this did not amount to non-discrimination legislation. The Committee also noted that while there was an explicit prohibition on discrimination on the ground of disability in higher education, this was not the case in primary and secondary education. In terms of mainstream educational provision, the Committee sought further information relating to (1) the extent to which the mainstream curriculum is adjusted to take account of disability, (2) the existence of individual educational plans, (3) whether resources follow the child and (4) how the physical accessibility of school environments is promoted. With regard to special education, the Committee requested information on curriculum design, qualifications received, and subsequent progression of students into further education, or open employment. The Committee expressed concern at the lack of information provided on mainstream vocational training and requested updates on the integration of people with disabilities into vocational training, including higher education.

With respect to Article 15(2), the Committee deferred its Conclusion pending the receipt of further information on the operation of anti-discrimination legislation. The Committee sought clarification as to whether the prohibition of discrimination applied to recruitment, promotion, pay and dismissal and whether employers are obliged to provide 'reasonable accommodation' to people with disabilities. The Committee sought further information on the practical implementation of the legal framework, in particular, in relation to the role of the Commission established by the Minister for Labour and Social Policy, in determining what activities may be performed by people with disabilities in employment. The Committee also requested further information on uptake of financial incentives and tax exemptions in place to promote employment of people with disabilities.

Finally, the Committee noted that most persons with disabilities were employed in 'protected companies' rather than the open labour market. It went on to state that Article 15(2) requires that persons with disabilities be employed in an ordinary working environment.[79]

3.2.26. United Kingdom - 1961 Charter (reference period: 2004-2006)[80]

National report available at:
<http://www.coe.int/t/dghl/monitoring/socialcharter/Reporting/StateReports/

---

[79] Ibid, p.12.
[80] European Committee of Social Rights, 'Conclusions XIX – 1 (UNITED KINGDOM)' (November 2008), <http://www.coe.int/t/dghl/monitoring/socialcharter/Conclusions/State/UKXIX1_en.pdf>, last accessed 12 May 2009.

UK27_en.pdf>

Article 15(1): Conclusion - deferred.
Article 15(2): Conclusion - conformity.

The Committee deferred its Conclusion on Article 15(1), pending the receipt of information relating to the possible reframing of the definition of disability, new initiatives to support early intervention in education, and comprehensive data on vocational training for people with disabilities.

In relation to education, the Committee concluded that legislation providing for mainstreaming was in conformity with the Charter, although it sought further information on how this operated in practice. Information on the practical impact and degree of achievement of recent initiatives, such as the introduction of specific programmes in schools to promote social and behavioural aspects of learning and comprehensive children's mental health services, was also sought by the Committee.

With regard to vocational training, the Committee expressed concern at the lack of comprehensive new information provided in the national report. Further information was requested on the implementation of a new cross government strategy to improve employment rates of persons with learning difficulties and disabilities. The committee also asked for data on the number of people with disabilities in higher education and the percentage of students with a disability entering the labour market.

The Committee's Conclusion of conformity with Article 15(2) was based on improvements made to ensure effective access by people with disabilities to employment without discrimination. The national report detailed a new statutory duty imposed on public bodies to promote equal opportunities for people with disabilities as employers and, crucially, as service providers. The national report also provided information on a number of initiatives to promote the employment of people with disabilities, including a programme which helped people with disabilities in receipt of health benefits to enter lasting paid employment and a sheltered employment programme which facilitated the transition of people with disabilities into open employment.

Finally, the Committee requested information be included in the next report on the implementation of specific measures to promote employment and legislative reforms undertaken outside the reference period.

3.3. RECENT DECISIONS OF THE EUROPEAN COMMITTEE OF SOCIAL RIGHTS ON COLLECTIVE COMPLAINTS AND DISABILITY[81]

The Collective Complaint mechanism has not been used extensively by organizations of persons with disabilities. Yet, as the following two decisions show, it does have great potential in the disability context.

---

[81] Council of Europe 2004-2009, <http://www.coe.int/t/dghl/monitoring/socialcharter/Complaints/Complaints_en.asp>, last accessed 19 February 2009.

3.3.1. *International Association Autism-Europe v. France (Revised Social Charter, Decision of November 2004)*[82]

This case was the first Collective Complaint lodged by a disability group. It was brought under the Revised Social Charter. As previously mentioned, there are eleven registered pan-European disability NGOs who may lodge Collective Complaints. Extracts from the Decision of the Committee of Social Rights are contained in the Annex to this Yearbook.

The complainant, the International Association Autism-Europe, asked the European Committee of Social Rights:

> to rule that France is failing to satisfactorily apply its obligations under Articles 15(1) [on the education of persons with disabilities] and 17(1) [on the provision of services adequate to ensure the education of children and young persons] of Part II of the Revised European Social Charter because children and adults with autism do not and are not likely to effectively exercise, in sufficient numbers and to an adequate standard, their right to education in mainstream schooling or through adequately supported placements in specialised institutions that offer education and related services;[83]

The complainant also sought a finding of discrimination contrary to Article E in conjunction with Articles 15 and 17 of the Revised Social Charter. The complainant alleged that although provision had been made for the education of young persons with autism in law, this had not been implemented in practice. The complainant attributed this to inadequate budgetary provision.

It was argued that there were not enough special education services available to meet the demand and that the budgetary arrangements made it nearly impossible to change this. It was argued that

> because of the budgeting mechanism chosen, persons with disabilities do not in practice (despite the legislation) benefit from the right to education because they cannot do so for as long as the funding of special education placements remains outside the national education system and is treated as 'social assistance' or 'care' to which health or social-action expenditure limits apply.[84]

The complainant alleged that the level of progress being made was insufficient to comply with the Charter, particularly with respect to the process of mainstreaming. It suggested, that at the current rate of progress, it would take a hundred years before the education provision for children with autism matched demand.

The complainant also argued that early intervention measures were inadequate, and that inadequate teacher training and administrative procedures hindered the achievement of legislative goals in the field of special education. In response, the French Government contested many of the statistics put forward by

---

[82]   Collective complaint No 13/2002. Decision of 7 November 2003, <http://www.coe. int/t/dghl/monitoring/socialcharter/Complaints/CC13Merits_en.pdf>, last accessed 23 April 2009.

[83]   Ibid, para. 7

[84]   Ibid, para. 28.

the complainant in support of their arguments.

In its Decision, the Committee considered the complaint as a whole, believing that the relevant Articles of the Social Charter were so intertwined that they could be considered together. In its discussion of Article 15(1), the Committee stated that education plays an important role in the advancement of citizenship rights. It also stated that the concept of mainstreaming in education was a core to Article 17(1).

On the question of discrimination, the Committee interpreted Article E on non-discrimination as including protection against discrimination on the ground of disability even though this is not specifically enumerated in the Article. It reasoned:

> Although disability is not explicitly listed as a prohibited ground of discrimination under Article E, the Committee considers that it is adequately covered by the reference to 'other status'. Such an interpretative approach, which is justified in its own right, is fully consistent with both the letter and the spirit of the Political Declaration adopted by the 2nd European Conference of Ministers responsible for integration policies for people with disabilities (Malaga, April, 2003), which reaffirmed the anti-discriminatory and human rights framework as the appropriate one for development of European policy in this field.[85]

The Committee reasoned that Article E does not provide an independent cause of action. Instead, it functions to ensure the equal enjoyment of the other rights enshrined in the Charter. The Committee was of the view that Article E prohibited both indirect and direct forms of discrimination. It also took the view that a failure to take positive steps to accommodate difference would violate the principle of non-discrimination.[86]

In its assessment of whether sufficient progressive realization of the right to education had been achieved it made the following important statement:

> The Committee recalls, as stated in its decision relative to Complaint No.1/1998 (*International Commission of Jurist v. Portugal*, para. 32), that the implementation of the Charter requires the State Parties to take not merely legal action but also practical action to give full effect to the rights recognised in the Charter. When the achievement of one of the rights in question is exceptionally complex and particularly expensive to resolve, a State Party must take measures that allows it to achieve the objectives of the Charter within a reasonable time, with measurable progress and to an extent consistent with the maximum use of available resources. States Parties must be particularly mindful of the impact that their choices will have for groups with heightened vulnerabilities as well as for others

---

[85]   Ibid, para. 51.

[86]   The Committee referred to the ECtHR's rationale in *Thlimmenos v. Greece* [2000] ECHR 161. For further discussion, see Quinn, 'The European Social Charter and EU Anti-discrimination Law in the Field of Disability: Two Gravitational Fields with One Common Purpose' in G. de Búrca *et al* (eds), *Social Rights in Europe*, (Oxford University Press, 2005).

persons affected including, especially, their families on whom falls the heaviest burden in the event of institutional shortcomings.[87]

This marks a major advance in the case law of the Committee and although it is relevant across the board, it is particularly relevant in the context of disability. Indeed, on the basis of this reasoning, the Committee concluded that France had failed to achieve sufficient progress in the provision of education to persons with autism.

The Committee considered that:

> as the authorities themselves acknowledge, and whether a broad or narrow definition of autism is adopted … the proportion of children with autism being educated in either general or specialist schools is much lower than in the case of other children, whether or not disabled. It is also established, and not contested by the authorities, that there is a chronic shortage of care and support facilities for autistic adults.[88]

It thus concluded that the situation in France violated Articles 15(1) and 17(1) of the Revised Social Charter, whether read alone or alongside Article E on non-discrimination. In response, the French Government issued a statement indicating it would bring the situation into conformity with the Charter and indicated some initial steps being taken to this end.

This Decision was a milestone in the sense that it shows that the Committee has sufficient capacity to assess whether sufficient progress is being made to achieve obligations of conduct – obligations that take both time and resources. Again, while this applies across the board, it is a particularly telling and helpful advance in the context of disability.

3.3.2. Mental Disability Advocacy Centre (MDAC) v. Bulgaria (Revised Social Charter, Decision of June 2008)[89]

This Collective Complaint was lodged by the Mental Disability Advocacy Centre (MDAC) on 20 February 2007.[90] It contended that children with moderate, severe or profound disabilities, resident in 'Homes for Mentally Disabled Children' in Bulgaria received no education on the basis of their disabilities. As such, it was contended that that this constituted a violation of Article 17(2) of the Revised European Social Charter which obliged States Parties to take all appropriate and necessary measures 'to provide to children and young persons a free primary

---

[87]   Collective complaint No 13/2002. Decision of 7 November 2003, para. 53.

[88]   Ibid, para. 54.

[89]   Collective complaint No. 41/2007, Decision of 10 June 2008, <http://www.coe.int/t/ dghl/monitoring/socialcharter/Complaints/CC41Merits_en.pdf>, last accessed 19 February 2009. See also Mental Disability Advocacy Centre, 'Mental Disability Advocacy Centre v. Bulgaria: Analysis and Recommendations' (October 2008), <http:// www.mdac.info/images/page_image/MDAC_v_Bulgaria_summary_and_recommendations.pdf>, last accessed 19 February.

[90]   Collective complaint No. 41/2007, Case Document 1, <http://www.coe.int/t/dghl/ monitoring/socialcharter/Complaints/CC41CaseDoc1_en.pdf>, last accessed 19 February 2009.

and secondary education as well as to encourage regular attendance at schools'.[91] The Collective Complaint also contended that this was a result of discrimination on the basis of disability, thus violating Article E of the Revised Social Charter, which provides for the enjoyment of Charter rights without discrimination. It was noted that the Bulgarian government had ratified both of these articles by June 2000. Extracts from the Decision of the Committee of Social Rights are contained in the Annex to this Yearbook.

MDAC argued that activities in 'Homes for Mentally Disabled Children' did not constitute education. The homes were under the responsibility of the Ministry of Labour and Social Policy, not the Ministry of Education and Science. The complaint contained statistics from the Government on the number of these homes, which varied from twenty-four to twenty-seven with the number of residents ranging from 1,193 to 3,042. These children were considered as ineducable in Bulgarian law until 2002.[92] At that time, the Bulgarian government introduced reform in the way of an obligation upon itself under domestic law to provide education to all children.[93] MDAC, in their complaint, argued that this 2002 law had not been implemented.

The Collective Complaint argued that the right to education was denied in three ways. Firstly, Government statistics themselves showed that only 6.2% of children living in 'Homes for Mentally Disabled Children' were enrolled in schools. Secondly, mainstream schools themselves were not adapted to accommodate the abilities and needs of these children. Thirdly, the homes themselves provided no, or wholly inadequate, education for resident children.

The Collective Complaint argued that Bulgaria could not rely on a lack of resources as a justification for the discriminatory denial of the right to education, since the complaint resulted from serious and unreasonable policy failures on the part of the Bulgarian Government.

The European Committee of Social Rights declared the Collective Com-

---

[91] Article 17 – The right of children and young persons to social, legal and economic protection. "With a view to ensuring the effective exercise of the right of children and young persons to grow up in an environment which encourages the full development of their personality and of their physical and mental capacities, the Parties undertake, either directly or in co-operation with public and private organisations, to take all appropriate and necessary measures designed: ... 2. to provide to children and young persons a free primary and secondary education as well as to encourage regular attendance at schools".

[92] Prior to 2002, education of children with disabilities was regulated by the 1977 Instruction No. 6 on the placement of children and pupils with physical or mental disabilities in special schools and special educational disciplinary establishments of the Ministry of Education and the Ministry of Health Care. According to this, children with mild intellectual disabilities were to be educated in special schools. Children with moderate, severe, and profound intellectual disabilities were classified as incapable of being educated and therefore, denied any form of education.

[93] In August 2002, the Ministry of Education and Science issued Decree No. 6 on the Education of Children with Special Needs and/or Chronic Diseases.

plaint admissible on 26 June 2007[94] and issued its Decision on 10 June 2008.[95] It held that children with moderate, severe and profound intellectual disabilities residing in 'Homes for Mentally Disabled Children' did not have an effective right to education and this was due to discrimination on the ground of disability.

The Committee considered Bulgarian educational standards to be inadequate as the mainstream educational facilities and curriculum were neither accessible[96] nor adapted to the needs of children with intellectual disabilities. Teachers did not receive the appropriate training, and the resources were not available to cater to the educational needs of children with disabilities. Only 3.4% of the children in question attended special classes, which demonstrated that special education was not accessible to the children either. Furthermore, the Committee considered that the absence of primary educational opportunities meant that children with disabilities were unable to obtain secondary school education. The Committee highlighted the poor implementation of legislation and policies designed to respect the educational rights of children with disabilities living in institutions.

One of the main arguments put forward by the Bulgarian Government was that the educational rights of the children were being progressively realized considering the State's financial constraints. The Committee rejected this argument. It considered that the Bulgarian Government had failed to fulfil the criteria it enunciated in the Autism-Europe Decision regarding the 'progressive realization' of rights. The Committee noted that while some progress had been made, it was confined to the introduction of legislation and policies that were not implemented. It found that the Bulgarian Government failed to provide stakeholders with information on the new law and policies, while staff and management of educational institutions, and of this type of home, were not provided with training that would have assisted in realizing the new laws and policies.[97]

The Committee acknowledged that disability is not explicitly listed as a prohibited ground of discrimination in Article E. However, it followed its Decision in Autism-Europe to the effect that the disability ground is adequately covered by the reference to 'other status' in Article E. The Committee went on to state that a failure to take appropriate action to take positive account of human difference may amount to discrimination.

MDAC had provided information on the low number of children residing in the institutions who received education, relative to the non-disabled children

---

94   Collective complaint No. 41/2007, Decision on Admissibility of 26 June 2007, <http://www.coe.int/t/dghl/monitoring/socialcharter/Complaints/CC41Admiss_en.pdf>, last accessed 29 April 2009.

95   Collective complaint No. 41/2007, Decision of 10 June 2008, <http://www.coe.int/t/dghl/monitoring/socialcharter/Complaints/CC41Merits_en.pdf>, last accessed 19 February 2009.

96   Only 2.8% of children with intellectual disabilities residing in institutions were integrated in mainstream primary schools. The Committee also referred to the educational standards established by the United Nations Committee on Economic, Social and Cultural Rights. According to the UN Committee education must fulfil the criteria of availability, accessibility, acceptability and adaptability. This was clearly not the case in respect of the situation in Bulgaria.

97   The European Committee of Social Rights noted that this type of training could have been provided without much expenditure.

population. This was interpreted by the Committee as giving rise to a presumption of discrimination and the onus of proof was reversed onto the Government. The Bulgarian Government was unable to displace this onus. It was unable to provide any evidence or justification explaining why children living in the 'Homes for Mentally Disabled Children' were disproportionately denied their right to education. The European Committee of Social Rights reached the conclusion that the difference between the two groups was so great that it amounted to discrimination against children with disabilities.

This complaint marks the first time that the European Committee of Social Rights found violations of the right to education (Article 17(2)) and the right to non-discrimination (Article E) of the Revised Social Charter, in Central or Eastern Europe. It applies the logic of the Decision in Autism-Europe in the context of education in segregated residential settings. It is, perhaps, simply a matter of time before the very existence of these segregated settings is challenged in a Collective Complaint.

4. EUROPEAN COMMITTEE FOR THE PREVENTION OF TORTURE AND INHUMANE OR DEGRADING TREATMENT OR PUNISHMENT (CPT) AND DISABILITY

Web Resource: http://www.cpt.coe.int/en

4.1. BACKGROUND OF THE CPT

In recent years, the Council of Europe's work in guaranteeing human rights has placed an emphasis on preventing violations. Article 3 of the ECHR inspired the adoption of the European Convention for the Prevention of Torture and Inhuman or Degrading Treatment or Punishment in 1987 (ETS no 126).[98] This Convention provides a non-judicial preventive machinery to protect detainees. Forty-seven Member States have ratified the Convention. Under Protocol No. 1, which entered into force on 1 March 2002, The Committee of Ministers may invite any non-member State to accede to the Convention.

The Convention is based on a system of visits to places where persons are deprived of their liberty by a public authority. These visits are carried out by the European Committee for the Prevention of Torture and Inhuman or Degrading Treatment or Punishment (CPT). The CPT is made up of independent and impartial experts elected in respect of each State Party by the Committee of Ministers. They are elected for a four-year term and may be re-elected twice.

Places of detention include prisons, juvenile detention centres, police stations, holding centres for immigration detainees and psychiatric hospitals. The purpose of the visit is to see how persons deprived of their liberty are treated and, if necessary, to recommend improvements to the relevant State Party.

Visits are carried out by delegations of two or more CPT members. These members are accompanied by members of the Committee's Secretariat and, in some circumstances, by experts and interpreters. No member participates in a

---

[98]   Council of Europe 2004-2009, <http://conventions.coe.int/Treaty/en/Treaties/Html/126.htm>, last accessed 19 February 2009.

delegation visiting the country in respect of which he/she was nominated. CPT delegations visit Contracting States regularly and may organize additional visits if it is deemed necessary. The Committee is required to notify the State concerned, although it is not necessary to specify the period between the notification and the actual visit (Article 8). In exceptional circumstances, this may be carried out immediately after notification is given to the State. A government can only object to the time or place of a visit on the grounds of national defence, public safety, serious disorder, the medical condition of a person or that an urgent interrogation relating to a serious crime is in progress (Article 9 CPT). Under such circumstances, the State must immediately take steps to enable the Committee to visit as soon as possible.

The Convention further provides that CPT delegations have unlimited access to places of detention and the right to move inside such places without restriction. Delegations may interview detainees in private, and communicate freely with anyone who can provide them with information. Recommendations are drafted on the basis of information found during the visit. The information is included in the report sent to the State subject to the visit, which forms the starting point for ongoing dialogue between the State and the CPT (Article 10). Importantly, and in order to counter the possibility of reprisals against those within institutions who interact with the Committee, the report does not contain any personal information (Article 11(3)).

The CPT is guided in its work by the principles of co-operation and confidentiality (Article 13). The CPT co-operates with the national authority, since the principle aim of the Convention is to protect persons deprived of their liberty rather than to condemn States for abuses. For this reason, the Committee meets in camera and its reports are strictly confidential. A State may request the publication of the Committee's report, together with its comments, if so desired. In circumstances where a country fails to co-operate or declines to improve the situation on the basis of the Committee's Recommendations, the CPT may choose to make a public statement.

The CPT also draws up an Annual General Report on its activities for the Committee of Ministers. These reports contain details of the activities of the CPT in the reference period covered and can also indicate the CPT's interpretation of the Convention.

4.2.   THE CPT STANDARDS AND DISABILITY

The CPT has developed 'CPT Standards - the Substantive sections of CPTs' General reports'. In essence, the Standards draw together the CPTs' interpretation of the requirements of the Convention as they have evolved through the reporting procedure (and reflected in the Annual General Reports). The Standards function much like General Comments under the United Nations treaty monitoring system. That is to say, the Standards provide States Parties with guidance as to their obligations under the Convention.

The most recent version of the CPT Standards was published in 2006[99] and

---

[99]   CPT, 'The CPT Standards: Substantive sections of the CPT's General Reports', (October 2006), CPT/Inf/E (2002)1- Rev. 2006, <http://cpt.coe.int/en/docsstandards.htm>, last accessed 19 February 2009.

deals specifically with detention in police custody, prison (including health care services) and involuntary placement in psychiatric institutions. The Standards consider the situation of women, juveniles and foreign nationals detained under aliens' legislation. They also address issues of training of law enforcement personnel as well as the question of combating impunity.

All of the CPT Standards are relevant in the context of disability, although two sections in particular stand out. The first concerns Part II on 'Health Care Services in Prison' (which are based on the 3rd Annual General Report) and the second concerns Part V on 'Involuntary Placement in Psychiatric Establishments' (based on the 8th Annual General Report).

With respect to health care services, the CPT Standards state that detainees should have access to a doctor and medical care that is comparable to that available in the outside community. They draw attention to the duty of care towards patients and note that this requires that medical staff are independent and competent. They also emphasize freedom of consent and respect for confidentiality and offer guidance as to how these rights should be safeguarded. Furthermore, it is noted that health care is not limited to the treatment of sick patients. Instead, it extends to social and preventative medicine encompassing conditions of hygiene, the containment of transmittable diseases, suicide prevention and prevention of violence. The CPT Standards also require that prisoners' contact with the outside world should be fostered.

In the context of health care services, the CPT identifies '[c]ertain specific categories of particularly vulnerable prisoners'[100] whose particular needs must be accommodated. The categories listed are mothers and children, adolescents, prisoners with personality disorders and prisoners unsuited for continued detention. The standards offer examples of this latter category:

Typical examples of this kind of prisoner are those who are the subject of a short-term fatal prognosis, who are suffering from a serious disease that cannot be properly treated in prison conditions, who are severely handicapped or of advanced age. The continued detention of such persons in a prison environment can create an intolerable situation. In cases of this type, it lies with the prison doctor to draw up a report for the responsible authority, with a view to suitable alternative arrangements being made.[101]

In Part V, the CPT Standards focus on the prevention of ill-treatment by staff (including auxiliary staff), living conditions and therapeutic treatment, staffing levels and training as well as safeguards relating to admission, ongoing placement and discharge.

The Standards call for a patients' rights brochure to be distributed to patients and their families. They state that the patient should be able to request that his/her placement be reviewed by a judicial authority.

With respect to means of restraint, the Standards demand that this should be subject to clearly defined policy. They state that, as far as possible, restraint should be non-physical or, if necessary, it should be limited to manual control.[102] The CPT takes the view that instruments of physical restraint should only be used under doctor's orders (or brought to a doctor's immediate attention) and should be

---

[100]   Ibid, para. 64.
[101]   Ibid, para. 70.
[102]   Ibid, para. 47.

removed at the earliest opportunity. The Standards also state that neither instruments of physical restraint nor seclusion should be used as a method of punishment.

Part V of the Standards also contain important rules for the use of electro convulsive therapy (ECT).[103] They state that ECT should only be administered if it fits the particular patient's treatment plan and where adequate safeguards are in place. The Standards state that ECT should never be used in its unmodified form – without anaesthetic and muscle relaxants – and states that this is a degrading practice. If administered, ECT must take place out of view of other patients. With respect to the primacy of individual consent, the Standards are quite explicit:

> 41.   Patients should, as a matter of principle, be placed in a position to give their free and informed consent to treatment. The admission of a person to a psychiatric establishment on an involuntary basis should not be construed as authorising treatment without his consent. It follows that every competent patient, whether voluntary or involuntary, should be given the opportunity to refuse treatment or any other medical intervention. Any derogation from this fundamental principle should be based upon law and only relate to clearly and strictly defined exceptional circumstances.
>
> Of course, consent to treatment can only be qualified as free and informed if it is based on full, accurate and comprehensible information about the patient's condition and the treatment proposed; to describe ECT as 'sleep therapy' is an example of less than full and accurate information about the treatment concerned. Consequently, all patients should be provided systematically with relevant information about their condition and the treatment that it is proposed to prescribe for them. Relevant information (results, etc.) should also be provided following treatment.

The United Nations special Rapporteur on Torture issued a report in 2008 that comes very close to portraying ECT as a form of torture, at least under certain conditions.[104] In this Report the UN Special Rapporteur states:

> (61)…In its modified form, it is of vital importance that ECT be administered only with the free and informed consent of the person concerned, including on the basis of information on the secondary effects and related risks such as heart complications, confusion, loss of memory and even death.

Part V of the CPT Standards also includes an extract from the 16th Annual General Report addressing the issue of means of restraint. In the context of psychiatric and other institutions, the following provisions are of particular relevance:

> 40. Certain mechanical restraints, which are still to be found in some psychiatric hospitals visited by the CPT, are totally unsuitable for such a purpose and could well be considered as degrading. Handcuffs, metal chains and cage-beds clearly fall within this category; they have no rightful place in psychiatric practice and should be withdrawn from use immediately.

---

[103]   Ibid, paras 39-41.
[104]   Interim Report of the Special Rapporteur on Torture, Inhumane and Degrading Treatment or punishment, A/63/175, 28 July 2008, available at <http://www.unhcr.org/refworld/docid/48db99e82.html>.

The use of net-beds, widespread in a number of countries until only a few years ago, appears to be in steady decline. Even in those few countries where they are still in use, net-beds are resorted to on a diminishing basis. This is a positive development and the CPT would like to encourage States to continue making efforts to reduce further the number of net-beds in use.

41. If recourse is had to chemical restraint such as sedatives, antipsychotics, hypnotics and tranquillisers, they should be subjected to the same safeguards as mechanical restraints. The side effects that such medication may have on a particular patient need to be constantly borne in mind, particularly when medication is used in combination with mechanical restraint or seclusion.

4.3. THE 2008 CPT GENERAL REPORT AND DISABILITY

The 18th General Report on the CPT's activities covered the period 1 August 2007 to 31 July 2008 and was published in September 2008.[105] This report details the CPT's visiting activities over the period, noting the level of cooperation it received. It gives an overview of its visits and commends those states that have published its reports in full.

The 2008 report also provides updates on its monitoring activity on behalf of the International Criminal Tribunal for the former Yugoslavia (ICTY). It is monitoring the treatment and conditions of detention of persons who are serving sentences imposed by that tribunal at the ICTY's request. The report also refers to the activity of two *ad hoc* working groups relating to the use of electroshock stun devices and safeguards for persons held under illegal immigration legislation. The CPT reports ongoing contact with the European Court of Human Rights, the Council of Europe's Commissioner on Human Rights, the United Nations Subcommittee on the prevention of torture and the United Nations Special Rapporteur on the promotion and protection of human rights and fundamental freedoms while countering terrorism. The CPT also refers to plans to step up its contact with the European Union stating that it 'believes that there is considerable scope for developing synergy with such institutions, in particular (but not exclusively) in relation to the implementation of recommendations made by the CPT after country visits.'[106] The report also includes recommendations for the drafting of European Rules for juvenile offenders.

The CPT also contributes to the work of the Council of Europe's other intergovernmental activities and committees of experts. The CPT assisted the Expert Committee on Mental Health in the development of a mental health reference tool on ethics and human rights.[107] The draft Recommendation that resulted is due to be presented to the Committee of Ministers in the near future. This is an analytical inventory of the range of existing policy measures related to mental health, as contained in the Council of Europe binding and non-binding documents. It pro-

---

[105] Secretariat of the CPT, '18th General Report on the CPT's activities' (September 2008), <http://www.cpt.coe.int/en/annual/rep-18.htm>, last accessed 29 April 2009.
[106] Ibid, para. 22.
[107] The Committee also assisted in the development of draft guidelines on accelerated asylum procedures and draft European Rules for juvenile offenders.

poses a model framework leading to the development of an integrated policy tool in each country containing a practical compendium based on existing Council of Europe texts. This document places great emphasis on ethical and human rights issues in the area of mental health.

4.4. COUNTRY VISITS OF THE CPT IN 2008 AND DISABILITY

In 2008, CPT organized eighteen visits.[108] Ten periodic visits were organized: Cyprus, Denmark, Finland, Italy, Lithuania, Malta, Montenegro, Portugal, the Russian Federation and the United Kingdom. In addition to examining the situation in police stations, prisons and psychiatric hospitals, the visit programmes for many of the periodic visits included establishments for immigration detainees, juveniles, and persons in need of social protection.

Ad hoc visits were carried out in Albania, Armenia, Azerbaijan, Bulgaria, the Czech Republic, French Guyana, Greece and the former Yugoslav Republic of Macedonia. The Committee deemed these to be necessary under the particular circumstances. This section will outline some of the content of the reports on these visits, which have been made public to date.

4.4.1. CPT Visit to Albania (2008)[109]

This *ad hoc* visit aimed to review Albania's progress in implementing recommendations made after previous CPT visits. It focused on the treatment of persons detained by police, in remand centres and in pre-trial detention centres. It noted improvements in the situation of persons in police custody and in relation to conditions in pre-trial detention centres, the CPT concluded that 'a page was close to being turned'.[110] The Committee went on to call for urgent action in relation to 'conditions of detention in police establishments and the persistent lack of outdoor exercise for adult remand prisoners at Prison No. 313 in Tirana.'[111]

In relation to involuntary hospitalization in psychiatric establishments, the CPT noted that persons who had been declared not to be criminally responsible were to receive compulsory medical treatment in a forensic institution under the Albanian Penal Code.[112] However, such persons were in fact detained in a prison hospital as the appropriate facility was under construction. The CPT recommended that all arrangements necessary be made to ensure that the forensic institution be opened without delay. The CPT also noted that the cases of only four involuntary persons had been subject to review by the courts over the previous eighteen months, and called for confirmation that the detention of all such persons detained for more than one year has been reviewed.

---

[108]   This amounted to 170 days during the twelve-month period. This represents a marked increase in activities as compared to the previous year, during which seventeen visits were carried totalling 157 days.

[109]   CPT, 'Report to the Albanian Government on the visit to Albania carried out by the CPT from 19 to 20 June 2008' (January 2009).

[110]   Ibid, para. 43.

[111]   Ibid.

[112]   Section 46, para. 3 of Albanian Penal Code.

With respect to involuntary patients in psychiatric hospitals, the CPT found that not all patients had been seen by a judge and called for this to be remedied. The CPT also sought clarification as to whether involuntary patients always received a copy of the court decision in their case.

4.4.2. CPT Visit to Denmark (2008)[113]

This scheduled visit included targeted visits to two psychiatric establishments and focused on the use of immobilization in the Maximum Security Department (or Sikringsafdelingen) of one hospital, which receives patients considered too dangerous for other closed or civil wards.

The CPT expressed serious concern about the practice of prolonged physical immobilization and called for its urgent review. It indicated that it should be used only as a last resort and for the shortest possible time. The CPT articulated a number of principles and minimum standards that should be considered in this review. These included the provision of full reasons to the person subject to the intervention as soon as practicable, accurate record keeping of instances of such intervention, continuous supervision of the restrained person and the appropriate training of staff in the use of restraining equipment.

The CPT also noted a particular form of restraint in the Sikringsafdelingen that it considered to be degrading. The CPT sought confirmation that this method, which entails attaching a patient's arms to a belt and their feet to each other by straps, had been discontinued. In response to the report, the Danish Government defended their legislation on immobilization and confirmed that the particular method of restraint condemned by the Committee had been discontinued.[114]

The CPT went on to question the therapeutic grounds for the practice of prolonged confinement. They noted the situation of one man who had been locked in his room for eight months and called for the urgent review of his case. The Danish Government responded by stating that it found no reason to conduct an enquiry and cited medical reasons for his treatment. The Government also stated that a physician may make a decision to confine a patient on the ground of security of others.[115]

With respect to staff in these institutions, the CPT recommended that the number of nursing and psychiatrist staff be increased and that all medical staff should receive improved continuous training. In response, the Danish Government cited efforts to address these concerns.[116] The CPT noted impressive living conditions in the institutions. The delegation noted that access to bathrooms and outdoor exercise could be improved and was informed of plans to do so.

The CPT also restated an earlier position in calling for the opinion of a second doctor to be necessary to transform a voluntary stay into an involuntary stay. The CPT rejected the contention of the Danish Authorities that the existing safeguards were satisfactory and recommended that the safeguards be brought

---

[113]   CPT, 'Report to the Government of Denmark on the visit to Denmark carried out by the CPT from 11 to 20 February 2008' (September 2008).

[114]   CPT, 'Response of the Danish Government to the report of the CPT on its visit to Denmark from 11 to 20 February 2008' (March 2009), pp. 49-51.

[115]   Ibid, p. 54.

[116]   Ibid, p. 52.

into line with those in operation for other involuntary patients. The Danish Government did not change its position in response.[117]

4.4.3. CPT Visit to Czech Republic (2008)[118]

This *ad hoc* visit was carried out from 25 March to 2 April 2008 in order to examine the application of surgical castration on sentenced sex-offenders. The CPT took the view that this amounted to degrading treatment and recommended an immediate end to the practice.[119] The Czech Government has rejected the CPT's opinion and restated that castration is carried out with free and informed consent of the patient, despite the CPT's reservations in this regard.[120]

The visit included a follow-up on the situation of Section E of Valdice prison where persons sentenced to life imprisonment and high security prisoners are accommodated. The CPT noted ongoing serious concerns about conditions of detention. The Czech authorities have provided information on measures taken to implement the CPT recommendations.[121]

4.4.4. CPT Visit to Finland (2008)[122]

The CPT carried out its fourth periodic visit to Finland in April 2008. As part of its visit, the CPT visited a State psychiatric hospital for forensic patients and patients considered challenging or dangerous, and also a Psychiatric Treatment and Research Unit for Adolescent Intensive Care. The CPT noted that the majority of patients interviewed spoke favourably about staff. Nonetheless, they called on the management of Vanha Vaasa State Psychiatric Hospital 'to regularly remind staff that any form of ill-treatment – including verbal abuse – is unacceptable and will not be tolerated.'[123]

Other recommendations relating to Vanha Vaasa State Psychiatric Hospital included more regular interdisciplinary clinical collaboration on individual patient care, the establishment of a register and the seeking of informed consent in advance of electro convulsive therapy (ECT) being given, as well as the initial and refresher training of staff in manual control of agitated patients, and the involvement of patients in closed wards in appropriate therapeutic activities. It also called for additional staff qualified to provide psycho-social rehabilitative activities.

The CPT also suggested there was excessive reliance on seclusion in Vanha Vaasa State Psychiatric Hospital. They suggested that patients in seclusion were

---

[117] Ibid, p. 55.
[118] CPT, 'Report to the Czech Government on the visit to the Czech Republic carried out by the CPT from 25 March to 2 April 2008' (February 2009).
[119] Ibid, para. 44.
[120] CPT, 'Response of the Czech Government to the report of the CPT on its visit to the Czech Republic from 25 March to 2 April 2008' (February 2009), p. 7.
[121] Ibid, pp. 12-20.
[122] CPT, 'Report to the Finnish Government on the visit to Finland carried out by CPT from 20 to 30 April 2008' (January 2009).
[123] Ibid, para. 120.

not always adequately supervised, did not have ready access to toilet facilities, had no means of diversion and, if secluded in their own room, were within view of other patients. This was brought to the attention of the Finnish authorities at the end of the visit who informed the CPT of measures to be taken to rectify and review this situation. The CPT, in its report, asked that it be kept informed as to progress in this regard.[124]

With respect to involuntary hospitalization, the CPT reiterated an earlier recommendation calling for a legislative amendment 'to provide for a psychiatric opinion (independent of the hospital in which the patient is placed) in the context of the initiation and review of the measure of involuntary hospitalization.'[125] The Committee also expressed concern at possible court 'rubber-stamping' of involuntary hospitalizations lasting more than three months. It called for steps to be taken to ensure such reviews are always meaningful and to realize a patient's right to be heard by a judge.[126] In the context of treatment, the CPT called on the Finnish authorities to seek consent from persons who had been involuntarily hospitalized. The CPT recommended that an external psychiatric opinion be required should a patient refuse treatment, and that the patient should have a right to appeal against compulsory treatment.[127]

The CPT restated an earlier call for the systematic distribution of comprehensible information on patients' rights to the patients themselves and to their families. It recommended that steps be taken to ensure access to legal assistance and that this be free of charge where necessary. Finally, the CPT recommended that psychiatric institutions be visited by external inspection bodies responsible for patient care on a regular basis, and that such bodies be given the powers necessary to carry out their function. The results of these inspections ought to be circulated to management.

4.4.5. CPT Visit to the Former Yugoslav Republic of Macedonia (2008)[128]

The CPT carried out an *ad hoc* visit to 'the former Yugoslav Republic of Macedonia' in order to investigate the treatment and conditions of remand and sentenced prisoners. It looked at developments in prison healthcare and the use of restraints. The CPT reported little progress with regard to previous recommendations and emphasized the need for cooperation from national authorities in the form of adequate responses to requests for information.

The Government response detailed its investment in building new prison facilities and in refurbishing existing ones.[129] The Government also reported that the use of restraint was reviewed in meetings with security staff. It was concluded

---

124 Ibid, para. 134.
125 Ibid, para. 138.
126 Ibid, para. 139.
127 Ibid, para. 140.
128 CPT, 'Report to the Government of "the former Yugoslav Republic of Macedonia" on the visit to "the former Yugoslav Republic of Macedonia" carried out by the CPT from 30 June to 3 July 2008' (November 2008).
129 CPT, 'Response of the Government of "the former Yugoslav Republic of Macedonia to the report of the CPT on its visit to "the former Yugoslav Republic of Macedonia from 30 June to 3 July 2008' (November 2008).

that its use would be reduced to a minimum and that restraint was not to be used as a form of discipline. The Government also indicated that a failure by staff to apply existing regulations on the use of restraints would result in sanctions. The Government detailed specific measures to be taken according to the CPT's recommendations.

4.4.6. CPT Visit to Portugal (2008)[130]

In January 2008, the CPT carried out its fifth periodic visit to Portugal. It looked, in particular, at the treatment of persons deprived of their liberty by the police.

With respect to psychiatric institutions, the CPT focused on living conditions, consent to treatment and legal safeguards for involuntary patients. The CPT noted the respectful and relaxed nature of staff-patient relations. It also referred to a new Portuguese Action Plan on the future of public mental health care and asked to be kept up to date on its implementation.

The CPT recommended that patient's rooms be adequately insulated from noise and that outdoor exercise be offered on a daily basis to patients. It noted that the practice of administering medication in some hospitals placed too much responsibility on nurses. It recommended that this practice be reviewed in light of its potential for abuse. The CPT also recommended the formulation of clear policy and detailed record keeping in relation to the use of electro convulsive therapy (ECT). It also called for an end to the over-sedating of new patients at the private Casa de Saúde de São João de Deus. It noted the practice of clothing patients who did not have proper clothes in pyjamas, and recommended an alternative solution be found as this 'is not conducive to strengthening personal identity and self-esteem'.[131]

On the matter of restraint, the CPT called for every instance of this to be detailed on a specific register to which the patient ought to be entitled to add comments. It stated that both public and private hospitals should have a written policy on the use of means of restraint. The CPT recommended that instances of restraint ought to take place out of sight of other patients and that the straps used be stored out of view. It recommended that a member of staff be present to provide assistance if required or, should the patient be in seclusion, a member of staff should be within view and earshot for observation purposes. The CPT noted that in Miguel Bombarda Psychiatric hospital, it was not necessary to consult a doctor in order to restrain a patient. It recommended that this approach be reviewed. It also called for a sufficient number of staff trained to deal with potentially violent patients in the hospital's Forensic Unit.

On the matter of the safeguards surrounding involuntary placement in a psychiatric institution, the CPT asked that access to a lawyer be ensured. It also noted that involuntary patients are not required to give their consent to treatment and recommended that the relevant Portuguese legislation be reviewed to rectify this. The CPT also called for patients' rights information to be drawn up and distributed to all patients on admission and to their families. Finally, it called for

---

[130] CPT, 'Report to the Portuguese Government on the visit to Portugal carried out by the CPT from 14 to 25 January 2008' (March 2009).
[131] Ibid, p. 48.

the powers of the national monitoring commission under the Portuguese Mental Health Act to be increased in relation to hospital visits.

5. THE COUNCIL OF EUROPE HUMAN RIGHTS COMMISSIONER AND DISABILITY

Web Resource: <http://www.coe.int/t/commissioner/>

5.1. BACKGROUND AND ROLE

The initiative for setting up the office of the Commissioner for Human Rights was taken by the Heads of State and Government of the Council of Europe at their second summit in Strasbourg on the 10-11 October 1997. On the 7th of May 1999, at its 104th Session, the Committee of Ministers adopted a Resolution on the 'Council of Europe Commissioner for Human Rights', establishing the office and laying out its fundamental objectives.[132] Under this Resolution, the Commissioner is mandated to promote awareness of, and respect for, human rights and contribute to the promotion of the effective observance and full enjoyment of human rights in Member States.

The Commissioner is mandated to provide advice and information on the protection of human rights and prevention of human rights violations and to facilitate the activities of national ombudsmen and human rights institutions (e.g., human rights commissions or equality bodies). The Commissioner's work also includes identifying possible shortcomings in the law and practice of Member States and addressing reports on specific matters, whenever appropriate, to the Committee of Ministers or to the Parliamentary Assembly.

The Commissioner is a non-judicial institution that functions independently and impartially. The Commissioner cannot act upon individual complaints but may act on any information addressed to the Commissioner by governments, national parliaments, ombudsmen or national human rights institutions. The Commissioner's work is aimed at ensuring reform in the area of human rights promotion and protection. Since his election on the 1st of April 2006, the position of Commissioner has been held by Mr. Thomas Hammarberg.

5.2. RECENT ACTIVITY OF THE COMMISSIONER ON DISABILITY

Periodically, the Commissioner produces Issues Papers. These aim to highlight the human rights dimension of current issues.[133] In October 2008, the Commissioner published an Issues Paper entitled 'Human Rights and Disability: Equal

---

[132] Resolution (99) 50, <https://wcd.coe.int/ViewDoc.jsp?id=458513&BackColorInte rnet=B9BDEE&BackColorIntranet=FFCD4F&BackColorLogged=FFC679>, last accessed 17 February 2009.

[133] Where appropriate, questions are raised, guidelines are set for subsequent work, and suggestions or warnings are included. Issues Papers provide information and stimulus for reflection or debate. It is important to note that they do not have the status of Recommendations or Opinions as prescribed by the Commissioner's terms of reference.

rights for all.'[134] The full text of this Issues Paper is contained in the Annex to the Yearbook.

This Issues Paper outlined the main factual and legal points that the Commissioner thought merited consideration in relation to human rights and disability. The Commissioner acknowledged that for too long, policies concerning persons with disabilities focused on institutional care, medical rehabilitation and welfare benefits. He stated that '[i]t is no longer correct to view persons with disabilities as merely objects of concern. They are citizens with equal rights and have an active role to play in our societies.'

Mr. Hammarberg identified the current challenge as putting this shift in thinking into practice, as he accepted that persons with disabilities are still discriminated against throughout Europe. The Issues Paper went on to make the following recommendations to Member States:

1. [that they should]…Ratify the Convention on the Rights of Persons with Disabilities including the Optional Protocol and start implementing it. Use the Council of Europe Disability Action Plan 2006-2015 as a tool to make the standards a reality.

2. Consult with and include persons with disabilities and their organisations in the planning and monitoring of law and policies that affect them.

3. Develop action plans to remove physical, legal, social and other barriers that prevent persons with disabilities from participating in society. Collect and analyse the necessary data to monitor the effective implementation of the action plans.

4. Adopt non-discrimination legislation covering all relevant areas of society. Include an obligation for employers, teachers and other duty-bearers to take reasonable measures to accommodate persons with disabilities. Provide effective remedies for persons who have had their rights violated. This includes making the judicial system accessible and the legal costs involved affordable.

5. Raise awareness to fight prejudice against persons with disabilities while empowering people to claim their rights. Provide training for teachers, employers and service providers as well as for lawyers and judges on the rights of persons with disabilities.

6. Set up an independent Ombudsman or other equality body with a view to ensuring that persons with disabilities are able to fully enjoy their rights. Mandate such bodies to receive complaints, act as mediators and provide legal assistance to victims.

7. Develop programmes to enable persons with disabilities to live in the community. Cease new admissions to social care institutions and allocate sufficient resources to provide adequate health care, rehabilitation and social services in the community instead.

---

[134] Comm DH/ Issue Paper (2008) 2, <https://wcd.coe.int/ViewDoc.jsp?id=1355349&Site=CommDH&BackColorInternet=FEC65B&BackColorIntranet=FEC65B&BackColorLogged=FFC679>, last accessed 17 February 2009.

8. Review the laws and procedures for involuntary hospitalisation to secure that both law and practise comply with international human rights standards.

9. Set up independent mechanisms equipped to make regular, unannounced and effective visits to social care homes and psychiatric hospitals in accordance with the Optional Protocol to the UN Convention against Torture.

10. Review guardianship legislation to ensure that persons with disabilities can effectively exercise their right to make decisions and have them respected. When necessary and asked for, provide support tailored to individual needs to enable persons to exercise this right together with adequate safeguards to protect them against abuse.[135]

This Issues Paper was accompanied by the release of a Viewpoint written by the Commissioner calling for 'Respect and rights-based action instead of charity for people with Disabilities'.[136] In this Viewpoint, he welcomed the paradigm shift to a human rights-based model of disability but noted that people with disabilities continue to face practical barriers to participation. He commended those states that have implemented a disability strategy and urged those who have not to do so with their particular circumstances in mind. He called for disability strategies to cater for the specific needs of children, elderly persons and persons with mental disabilities. The Commissioner recommended that the ongoing work of equality bodies or Ombudsmen should involve monitoring disability rights. He also called for a review of involuntary hospitalization processes and asked for independent mechanisms to provide for visits to institutions to ensure that the right to freedom from torture, inhuman or degrading treatment is realized. He called for the relevant national standards to be implemented in practice and not just in policy. The Commissioner also noted that persons with disabilities can be victims of hate crimes and recommended that governments take action to tackle this through proactive policing and prompt prosecutions.

Based on this Viewpoint, the Commissioner delivered a keynote speech at the European Conference on 'Protection and promoting the rights of persons with disabilities in Europe: towards full participation, inclusion and empowerment' at the end of October 2008.[137] In his speech, he noted the gap between political rhetoric and reality in the protection of the rights of persons with disabilities. He again called for urgent action in respect to the rights of children, elderly persons and persons with mental disabilities.

On 7 November 2008, the Commissioner gave a speech entitled, 'Bridge

---

[135]   Ibid, para. 8.

[136]   Hammarberg, Viewpoint on 'Respect and rights-based action instead of charity for people with Disabilities', <http://www.coe.int/t/commissioner/Viewpoints/081020_en.asp>, last accessed 29 April 2009.

[137]   European Conference on 'Protection and promoting the rights of persons with disabilities in Europe: towards full participation, inclusion and empowerment' hosted by the Swedish Presidency of the Council of Europe 2008, Strasbourg, 29-30 October 2008.

the gap through inclusive and transparent work for human rights'.[138] The Commissioner noted the real gap between the rights proclaimed in international and regional human rights instruments and the protection being offered in Member States. The focus in this speech was on the full realization of human rights. The Commissioner acknowledged a lack of awareness of human rights, a lack of co-ordination between actors working to ensure human rights and a lack of a human rights perspective in administrative and political procedures, as some of the factors contributing to human rights violations.[139] The Commissioner also recognized the effectiveness of action plans for identifying gaps in protections and targeting such lacunae. The Commissioner encouraged Member States to carry out baseline studies in order to establish the status of human rights protection. Implementation was noted as a problem issue for many Member States. The Commissioner urged co-operation of politicians and authorities at all levels in order to ensure effectiveness and consistency in implementation.

6. COMMITTEE OF MINISTERS AND DISABILITY

Web Resource: http://www.coe.int/t/cm/home_en.asp

This section considers some recent Recommendations and Resolutions in the field of disability.

6.1. RECENT ACTIVITY OF THE COMMITTEE OF MINISTERS ON DISABILITY

On 23 April 2008 the Committee of Ministers adopted a Recommendation entitled, 'Access to public spaces and amenities for people with disabilities.'[140] The Recommendation called on Member States to accept Article 15 of the Revised Social Charter and to sign and ratify the UN Convention on the Rights of Persons with Disabilities. It endorsed the 'universal design' principle and asked that the principle be integrated into Member States' accessibility policies. The Recommendation fully endorsed the Council of Europe Action Plan to promote the rights and full participation of people with disabilities. Interestingly, it also requested that non-governmental disability organizations be provided with financial support 'to enable them to operate properly and work in a network, and encourage the establishment of such organizations where necessary.'

On 12 December 2008, the Committee adopted a Resolution 'on the education and social inclusion of children and young people with autism spectrum

---

[138] Hammarberg 'Bridge the gap through inclusive and transparent work for human rights' (Strasbourg, 2008), CommDH/Speech (2008) 17, available at <https://wcd.coe.int/ViewDoc.jsp?id=1366987&Site=CommDH&BackColorInternet=FEC65B&BackColorIntranet=FEC65B&BackColorLogged=FFC679>.

[139] It is through work of this type that the Commissioner can raise awareness of the rights of people with disabilities and encourage active implementation of those rights.

[140] Recommendation 208 (2007) of the Congress of Local and Regional Authorities of the Council of Europe.

disorders.'[141] It did so under the aegis of the Partial Agreement in the field of social and public health policy. Both the UN Convention on the Rights of Persons with Disabilities and the Decision of the European Committee of Social Rights in Collective Complaint 13 are referenced in the Resolutions' preamble. The Resolution states that

> Member states should provide a legal framework, which ensures the rights of children and young people with disabilities, including people with autism spectrum disorders to receive education - within general schemes wherever possible - that is appropriate to their needs, is non-discriminatory and works towards social inclusion. There is a need to ensure that resources are sufficient for the full implementation of relevant legislation.[142]

The Resolution also refers to consultation with civil society in policy implementation as well as the provision of training for families and educators.

On the same day, the Committee adopted a second Resolution entitled, 'Achieving full participation through Universal Design' relating to promoting the integration of people with disabilities in the community through Universal Design.[143] This Resolution focused on moving towards a user-centric approach in work to improve accessibility, noting that this can lead to greater participation in public life.

7. THE PARLIAMENTARY ASSEMBLY AND DISABILITY

Web Resource: <http://assembly.coe.int/>

The Parliamentary Assembly has ten subject-specific committees. Among the committees of particular relevance to disability are:

- the Committee for Legal Affairs and Human Rights;
- the Committee for Social, Health and Family Affairs;
- the Committee for Culture Science and Education;
- the Committee for Economic Affairs and Development,
- and the Committee for Honouring of Obligations and Commitments by Member States of the Council of Europe (Monitoring Committee).

7.1. RECENT ACTIVITY OF THE PARLIAMENTARY ASSEMBLY ON DISABILITY

Recent resolutions of the Parliamentary Assembly in the field of disability include the following:

A motion for a resolution entitled, 'Regular monitoring of the living condi-

---

[141]   ResAP(2007)4, available at <https://wcd.coe.int/ViewDoc.jsp?id=1226295&Site=C M&BackColorInternet=9999CC&BackColorIntranet=FFBB55&BackColorLogged =FFAC75>.

[142]   Ibid, 'III. Specific considerations' no. 1.

[143]   ResAP(2007)3, available at <https://wcd.coe.int/ViewDoc.jsp?id=1226267&Site=C M&BackColorInternet=9999CC&BackColorIntranet=FFBB55&BackColorLogged =FFAC75>.

tions provided to children with mental and physical disabilities living in institutions', was discussed in the Assembly in June 2008.[144] The motion called for more stringent monitoring of the situation of children with disabilities in institutions. It highlighted the grave situation still existing in many institutions, particularly in central and Eastern Europe and called for action at both the national and international levels. It also reiterated earlier Recommendations to the effect that undue institutionalization is not generally viewed as acceptable, stating that 'nothing can repair the damage caused by social exclusion, segregation and isolation.'[145]

In August 2008, a Resolution was adopted on 'Access to rights for people with disabilities and their full and active participation in society'[146] based on the report of the Social, Health and Family Affairs Committee.[147] The Assembly noted that effective exercise of the rights of persons with disabilities remained largely inadequate and aspirational. The Assembly welcomed the Council of Europe Disability Action Plan 2006-2015 and advised Member States to use it as a practical policy tool in devising new disability-related policies and in implementing the UN Convention on the Rights of Persons with Disabilities. It called for regular reports from Member States on the implementation of the Action Plan. The Assembly urged the inclusion of disability issues in all areas of policy-making and the assurance of sufficient resources for disability-related programmes. The Assembly highlighted a number of key areas of action, which it recommended be given priority in order to effectively realize the rights of persons with disabilities in practice. These included community living, the right to exercise legal capacity, awareness-raising to tackle prejudices and equal access to sustainable employment, education, social and cultural facilities, transport, healthcare and the media. The Resolution also called for the acceptance of Article 15 of the Revised Social Charter (by those States that have yet to opt in) and the ratification of the UN Convention on the Rights of Persons with Disabilities.

---

[144] Parliamentary Assembly Doc. 1165, <http://assembly.coe.int/main.asp?Link=/documents/workingdocs/doc08/edoc11658.htm>, last accessed 26 February 2009.

[145] Ibid, para. 2.

[146] Resolution 1642 (2009), <http://assembly.coe.int/main.asp?Link=/documents/adoptedtext/ta09/ERES1642.htm>, last accessed 26 February 2009.

[147] Parliamentary Assembly Doc. 11694, <http://assembly.coe.int/main.asp?Link=/documents/workingdocs/doc08/edoc11694.htm>, last accessed 26 February 2009.

OTHER EUROPEAN INTERGOVERNMENTAL ORGANIZATIONS AND CIVIL SOCIETY GROUPS

In this section we review some of the recent disability-related policy developments within other European intergovernmental organizations (beyond the EC/ EU and the Council of Europe). We also review some of the recent developments within European civil society organizations.

The European policy landscape is quite complex. There are a number of important intergovernmental organizations beyond the EC/EU and the Council of Europe, dealing with specific topics of cooperation that often explicitly include disability, or which have the potential to do so. An effort is made in this first issue of the Yearbook, to at least draw some of the more prominent of these organizations into view. Subsequent editions will look more closely at the ongoing disability-related work of these bodies. For example, NATO is not yet included in the review, although its forward planning activities may well be relevant in the context of disaster management, which is an important topic under the UN Convention on the Rights of Persons with Disabilities.

Likewise, European civil society is extremely diverse and complex. The first issue of the Yearbook is modest, in that it purports to review the recent work of the most important umbrella group of European disability organizations – the European Disability Forum (EDF). Subsequent issues will be expanded to include reviews of the relevant activities and publications of other European-level NGOs and DPOs (disabled persons organizations - i.e., run by persons with disabilities themselves). Their activities will be reviewed inasmuch as they are relevant to European level policy debates.

1. EUROPEAN INTERGOVERNMENTAL ORGANIZATIONS

1.1. ORGANIZATION FOR ECONOMIC CO-OPERATION & DEVELOPMENT (OECD)

Web Resource: <http://www.oecd.org/>

The Organization for Economic Co-Operation and Development (OECD) is a classic intergovernmental organization that was established in 1961 and currently has a worldwide membership of 30 countries.[1] Seventeen EU countries are

---

[1] As of December 2008, the Member States of the OECD are: Australia (1971), Austria (1961), Belgium (1961), Canada (1961), Czech Republic (1995), Denmark (1961), Finland (1969), France (1961), Germany (1961), Greece (1961), Hungary (1996), Iceland (1961), Ireland (1961), Italy (1962), Japan (1964), Korea (1996),

members. The mission of the OECD is to create a forum for governments committed to democracy and the market economy, in order to 'support sustainable economic growth, boost employment, raise living standards, maintain financial stability, assist other countries' economic development and contribute to growth in world trade.'[2] The OECD works by comparing policy experiences across its membership. It stimulates debate concerning common problems and identifies best practices that can be used to inform domestic and international policies. To this end, the OECD commissions and publishes a large range of economic and public policy research. Its work in the areas of employment, education and social welfare is of particular interest from a disability perspective.

The research agenda of the OECD includes equality of access to education, ensuring effective and accessible health systems, preventing exclusion and unemployment and bridging the 'digital divide' between rich and poor.

In August 2008, the OECD 'Programme on Educational Building' organized a conference entitled 'The Role of 21st Century Learning Environments in Promoting Social Participation and Access to Education for Learners with Special Needs,' in cooperation with the New Zealand Ministry of Education.[3] This event, held in Auckland, New Zealand, aimed to explore the role of infrastructural design in improving inclusion and creating a supportive learning environment for all students. The conference focused on mainstreaming in education and looked at the thematic areas of access, social participation and working together to create meaningful learning environments.

The OECD's Directorate for Employment, Labour and Social Affairs also engages with disability issues. Its 2003 publication, 'Transforming Disability into Ability' analyzed labour market and social protection policies affecting persons with disabilities.[4] Since 2006, it has been conducting a thematic review on 'Sickness, Disability and Work'.[5] A synthesis report of the data collected in country reviews to date will be produced in 2009. In April 2008, the OECD published an issues paper and progress report on the thematic review entitled 'Modernizing Sickness and Disability Policy'.[6] This publication expresses concern that the administration of measures relating to employment supports, aimed at those experiencing various health problems (or alternatively those experiencing dis-

---

Luxembourg (1961), Mexico (1994), Netherlands (1961), New Zealand (1973), Norway (1961), Poland (1996), Portugal (1961), Slovak Republic (2000), Spain (1961), Sweden (1961), Switzerland (1961), Turkey (1961), United Kingdom (1961), United States (1961). The current Accession Countries are: Chile, Estonia, Israel, Russia, and Slovenia. Enhanced engagement countries are: Brazil, China, India, Indonesia and South Africa.

[2]   Article 1 of the OECD Convention, agreed on 14th December 1960 (Paris), <http://www.oecd.org/document/7/0,3343,en_2649_201185_1915847_1_1_1_1,00.html>, last accessed 23 March 2009.

[3]   OECD 2008, <http://www.oecd.org/site/0,3407,en_21571361_37054264_1_1_1_1_1,00.html>, last accessed 23 March 2009.

[4]   OECD, 'Transforming Disability into Ability: Policies to promote work and income security for disabled people' (February 2003).

[5]   OECD 2009, <http://www.oecd.org/els/disability>, last accessed 23 March 2009.

[6]   OECD, 'Modernising Sickness and Disability Policy: OECD thematic review on sickness, disability and work issues paper and progress report' (April 2008).

ability), are inadequately dealt with in the majority of the countries reviewed. It found that the necessary supports are difficult to access or are only available once they are no longer required. The publication deals both with workers who leave the labour market for health-related reasons and those who are not provided with the opportunity to work, due to reduced work capacity arising from health concerns. The publication also highlights a significant increase in the number of persons affected by mental illness, and notes that, in many countries, the relevant services are inadequate to deal with specific conditions affecting young people. The publication focuses on the importance of getting the right services to the right people at the right time and recommends financial incentives for public institutions, outcome-based funding, and fragmented systems of supports to improve the situation.

The publication suggests turning disability benefits into re-employment payments and distinguishes between disability benefit and unemployment benefit. It concludes that, in a small number of countries, ill and disabled persons with partially-reduced work capacity are treated similarly to those who are unemployed and are expected to follow similar job-search requirements. The publication further concludes that the cautious approach to reform that has been taken in some countries has resulted in continued exclusion and lower incomes for persons with disabilities. The publication neither supports the prospect of severing payments to people already experiencing disadvantage nor the possibility of forcing them to take up employment. The publication indicates that this would cost more, as well as have a negative impact on society at large. The publication calls for a joint effort from government, the social partners and civil society to ensure the success of what may be perceived as unpopular reforms.[7] The publication will be discussed at a high-level OECD policy forum in Stockholm in 2009 that will form the basis of the 2009 synthesis report.

In June 2008, the OECD jointly organized a Seminar on Disability in Ireland with the Irish Department of Social and Family Affairs.[8] At this seminar, an OECD draft report was presented on 'Sickness Disability and Work: Breaking the Barriers'. This was the third volume in this series of reports covering disability policy and outcomes in Denmark, Ireland, Finland and the Netherlands. The finalized report was published in December 2008.[9] The report identified the following seven policy concerns:

- controlling incapacity related spending;
- raising employment rates for people with health problems;
- tackling lower incomes of households with disabled persons;
- reducing the inflow into sickness and disability benefits;
- addressing the increase of mental health conditions and issues;

---

[7] Ibid, 8.
[8] OECD 2008, <http://www.oecd.org/document/18/0,3343,en_2649_34747_4099438
     6_1_1_1_1,00.html>, last accessed 23 March 2009.
[9] OECD, 'Sickness, Disability and Work: Breaking the Barriers, Vol.3: Denmark, Finland, Ireland and the Netherlands' (December 2008). Previous volumes considered the situation in Norway, Poland, Switzerland, Australia, Luxembourg, Spain and the United Kingdom.

- raising the outflow from permanent disability benefits;
- and strengthening cooperation and coordination across institutions.

Variable scoring was used to assess each policy concern in the four countries selected. The report identified certain key trends, such as significant under-representation of people with disability in the workforce and an increased likelihood of experiencing poverty.

Some useful policy initiatives presented by the report involve the need for monitoring absence due to sickness, its causes and potential remedies. The role of the general medical practitioner in the assessment process for benefit entitlement was discussed with respect to curbing the increase in numbers on disability benefit. The provision of financial incentives to employers and improving employment assistance services were also identified as important facilitators of transition to employment. The critical challenge of making benefit systems more employment-friendly was raised, as well as the use of tax credits and other mechanisms to complement benefit systems.

1.2. INTERNATIONAL TRANSPORT FORUM (ITF)

Web Resource: <http://www.internationaltransportforum.org/>

The ITF was created in 2006 through the expansion of its predecessor - the European Committee of Ministers for Transport (ECMT). The EMCT was very active on disability issues.

The ITF is now integrated into the OECD, but also has additional Member States in Central and Eastern Europe. The ITF is a platform for co-operation between high-level bodies that govern the transport sector.

The ITF has a dual role. Firstly, through research and policy work, it contributes to the creation of an integrated transport system throughout an enlarged Europe that is economically efficient and meets environmental and safety standards. Secondly, it looks to the future by forecasting the impact of factors such as globalization on transport and how to manage them.

Disability is relevant to the ITF's work in two ways. First of all, the focus of the ITF on road safety is of obvious concern to persons with disabilities, in part to reduce the incidence of disability, and also to ensure that safety measures are adjusted to take account of persons with reduced mobility or with sensory impairments (e.g., through the provision of audible and flashing warnings). Secondly, the goal of achieving accessible transport ensures that the benefits of mobility are widely shared in society.

The ITF hosts a Joint Research Centre on transport with the OECD. It holds an annual 'Transport Summit of the Year' (held in Leipzig). It hosted its first Summit conference in 2008 on 'Transport and Energy: the Challenge of Climate Change'. The 2009 Summit will focus on globalization and transport. It is likely that the ITF will focus increasingly on disability. Furthermore, it is due to publish a report in 2009 on cognitive disability, mental health and public transport.

The work initiated by the ECMT in the field of disability is still relevant to the work of the ITF. The website of the ITF contains a listing of previous EMCT publications. For example, in 1999, the ECMT drafted and agreed a 'Charter on Access to Transport Services and Infrastructure' in Warsaw that underlined Europe's commitment to taking account of the needs of people with disabilities.[10] The Charter refers to the growing number of people with disabilities, and asserts that all persons are entitled to have an opportunity for independent living. It exhorts States to take account of the needs of people with disabilities with respect to all new infrastructure and to ensure that public funding be made conditional on accessibility. It exhorts States to follow accessibility principles that provide, as a minimum, for the needs of wheelchair users, persons with mobility difficulties, blind and partially sighted persons, as well as the deaf community and those who are hard of hearing.

In 2006, the ECMT produced policy messages on 'Improving Transport Accessibility for All'[11] as well as best practice guides for both policy makers and transport personnel. The former looks at how barriers to mobility in public and private transport can be removed, and includes examples of good practice from throughout ECMT Member and Associate Member countries.[12] It drew attention to the importance of creating a 'seamless' system in which disabled people can access, travel on and interchange between modes easily and safely, and access information about services. The guide aims to promote understanding amongst transport personnel on how to appropriately respond to the requirements of people with disabilities.[13] The guide adopts the perspective that it is the environment that causes difficulty and not a person's disability.

In 2007, the ECMT produced a report in conjunction with the International Road Transport Union calling for improved taxi accessibility.[14] This followed a 2001 joint report from the two organizations on the 'Economic Aspect of Taxi Accessibility'.[15] The 2007 report considers how improved accessibility can benefit both taxi users and companies. It examines the options which are open to vehicle converters and manufacturers, and makes recommendations for vehicle design. It also looks at the issue of training taxi personnel, and offers solutions for governments seeking to improve taxi design and infrastructure. The report states that its recommendations, 'do not attempt to produce an ideal solution, but to give practical guidance, which if adopted by national governments, will be of considerable benefit to the more than 45 million disabled people who live in Europe.'[16]

---

[10] European Conference of Ministers of Transport Charter on Access to Transport Services and infrastructure of 19-20 May 1999, <http://www.internationaltransportforum.org/europe/ecmt/accessibility/pdf/tphCharter.pdf>, last accessed 23 March 2009.

[11] European Conference of Ministers of Transport Council of Ministers, 'Access and Inclusion, Improving Transport Accessibility for All: Policy Messages (May 2006), CEMT/CM (2006)7/Final, <http://www.internationaltransportforum.org/europe/ecmt/accessibility/pdf/CM200607Fe.pdf>, last accessed 23 March 2009.

[12] European Conference of Ministers of Transport Council of Ministers, 'Improving Transport Accessibility for All: Guide to Good Practice' (June 2006).

[13] European Conference of Ministers of Transport Council of Ministers, 'Improving Transport Accessibility for All: Guidelines for Transport Personnel' (June 2006).

[14] European Conference of Ministers of Transport and International Roads Transport Union, 'Improving Access to Taxis' (March 2007).

[15] European Conference of Ministers of Transport and International Roads Transport Union, 'Economic Aspects of Taxi Accessibility' (December 2001).

[16] Ibid, 13.

1.3.   ORGANIZATION FOR SECURITY AND CO-OPERATION IN
        EUROPE (OSCE)

Web Resource: <http://www.osce.org/>

The original Conference for Security and Co-operation in Europe (CSCE) was renamed the Organization for Security and Co-operation in Europe in 1995, and it is now the largest regional security organization in the world. The original CSCE was rightly famous for the human rights provisions in the Helsinki Conference on Security and co-operation in Europe (1975) – Final Act. These human rights provisions were contained in a 'basket' of the Final Act that served to embolden civil society groups in Central and Eastern Europe to seek reforms and ultimately the dismantlement of authoritarian Governments. The Charter of Paris of 1990 for a New Europe plotted a new course for the organization in support of the transformation taking place across Central and Eastern Europe. Eventually, it changed its name to the OSCE.

Interestingly, and even before the adoption of the UN Special Rules for the Equalization of Opportunities for Persons Disabilities in 1993, the CSCE was active on disability. The 'Document' of the 1991 Moscow meeting of the Conference on the Human Dimension of the CSCE contains a commitment to the protection of the human rights of persons with disabilities.[17] Article 41 of that document reads as follows:

> The participating States decide:

- to ensure protection of the human rights of persons with disabilities;
- to take steps to ensure the equal opportunity of such persons to participate fully in the life of their society;
- to promote the appropriate participation of such persons in decision-making in fields concerning them;
- to encourage services and training of social workers for the vocational and social rehabilitation of persons with disabilities;
- to encourage favourable conditions for the access of persons with disabilities to public buildings and services, housing, transport, and cultural and recreational activities.

The OSCE now has fifty-six Member States from across Europe, Central Asia and America. It provides a forum for early warning, conflict prevention, crisis management and post-conflict rehabilitation in the member countries. The OSCE's work looks at the politico-military, economic, environmental and human dimensions of security, and also focuses on monitoring and reporting on human rights compliance and democratic practices in member countries.

The 'human dimension' programme of the OSCE is extensive. The programme has an Office for Democratic Institutions and Human Rights (ODIHR),

---

[17]   Document of the Moscow meeting of the Conference on the Human Dimension of the CSCE, 3 October 1991, <http://www.osce.org/documents/odihr/1991/10/13995_en.pdf>, last accessed 24 March 2009.

an Office of Special Representative and Co-ordinator for Combating Trafficking in Human Beings, and an OSCE representative on Freedom of the Media and a High Commissioner for National Minorities. ODIHR focuses on human rights issues that are relevant to security. Its priorities include freedom of movement, prevention of torture and prevention of human trafficking. The OSCE has begun to take an active interest in disability. In October 2007 the Director of 'Mental Disability Advocacy Europe (MDAC)' gave an interview to the OSCE on the inclusion of persons with mental disabilities in elections.[18] It also appears that Albania organized a donor conference in 2004 on disability within the framework of its national disability strategy.

1.4. EUROPEAN BROADCASTING UNION (EBU)

Web Resource: <http://www.ebu.ch/>

The European Broadcasting Union was founded in 1950. It is an association of national public broadcasters and has its headquarters in Geneva. It aims to 'promote cooperation between broadcasters and facilitate the exchange of audiovisual content'. The principal role of the EBU is to ensure that the values of public service broadcasting are acknowledged and to influence future developments in media policy. The EBU has fifty-six member countries in the wider European region.

The EBU promotes debate on technology and media accessibility for people with disabilities in policy discussions. It formed an 'Access Services Project Group' that prepares publications on accessibility issues. In June 2004, this group published a report and a set of recommendations on Access Services for Digital Television.[19] This report reiterates the duty of public broadcasters to the wider community and emphasizes the need to be inclusive of people with disabilities.[20] The focus of the report is on the diversity of accessibility requirements and the necessity of consultation with different groups of people with disabilities, to ensure that specific requirements are clearly identified and due consideration is given to potentially conflicting needs.

The report offers detailed technical guidance as well as addressing the specific areas of subtitling, spoken subtitling, audio description and signing. Importantly, the report emphasizes the centrality of access services, defining them as 'essence' rather than 'metadata' – meaning that they are essential and not optional requirements. The report emphasizes the new opportunities provided by digital television to facilitate accessibility through both open (provided to all) and optional or closed services (which can be turned on/off by the user). The report further highlights the many links in the process, from manufacturing to broadcasting, which impact on accessibility.

---

[18]   Interview available at <http://www.osce.org/conferences/hdim_2007.html?page= 25862> , last accessed 29 May 2009.

[19]   EBU, 'EBU Report on Access Services' (June 2004), <https://www.uer.biz/CMSimages/en/tec_text_i44-2004_tcm6-14894.pdf>, last accessed 19 February 2009.

[20]   For summary information, see de Jong, 'Access Services for digital television', (October 2004), <http://www.ebu.ch/en/technical/trev/trev_300-de_jong.pdf>, last accessed 19 February 2009.

1.5. WORLD HEALTH ORGANIZATION - REGIONAL OFFICE FOR
      EUROPE

Web Resource: <http://www.euro.who.int/>

The World Health Organization (WHO) Regional Office for Europe covers fifty-three European countries. The WHO believes that health is a fundamental human right that encompasses:

> the right to equal treatment and freedom from discrimination, the right to free, meaningful and effective participation, the right to seek and receive information, the right to benefit from scientific progress and its application to disease prevention, health promotion, diagnosis, treatment, rehabilitation and care, the right to a healthy physical and social environment, the right to clean water, safe food and adequate housing, and the right to privacy.[21]

Three areas of the Regional Office's work are of particular relevance to the disability field. The first relates to Violence and Injury Prevention.[22] The WHO reports that injuries arising from traffic accidents, falls, burns, and acts of violence, wars and conflict, may account for one quarter of all disabilities. The Violence and Injury Prevention project aims to reduce the causes of disabilities, as well as address the types of supports required by those who experience injuries, with the aim of improving emergency care and rehabilitation for victims of trauma.

The second area of work relates to modifiable risk factors and the prevention of disability in old age.[23] In light of the aging European demographic, quality of life implications and limited resources, the Regional Office sees prevention of disability in old age as 'a matter of great humanitarian and economic concern.'[24] In 2003, the Regional Office's Health Evidence Network proposed the establishment of effective disability prevention and reduction services, and called for the myth that disability in old age is inevitable, to be dispelled by evidence. The Health Evidence Network's principal policy recommendations at that time were:

> to develop strategic preventive plans at national and community levels, to promote training in gerontology and geriatric medicine for relevant professional groups, to develop programmes to enable older people to cope with disability risk factors and manage chronic illnesses, to create initiatives to stimulate research and development on old age disability.[25]

The third relevant strand of WHO-Europe's work relates to their classification of health and health-related domains. In 2001, the WHO revised their older disability classification and adopted the International Classification of Functioning,

---

[21] World Health Organization Regional Office for Europe 2007, <http://www.euro.who.int/AboutWHO/About/20070627_3>, last accessed 25 March 2009.

[22] World Health Organization Regional Office for Europe 2008, <http://www.euro.who.int/violenceinjury/20080519_1>, last accessed 25 March 2009.

[23] WHO Regional Office for Europe's Health Evidence Network, 'What are the main risk factors for disability in old age and how can disability be prevented? (September 2003).

[24] Ibid, 4.

[25] Ibid, 5.

Disability and Health (ICF).[26] The new classification utilizes the social model of disability and looks at areas of activity and participation, as well as areas of impairment. The WHO has also developed a children and youth version of the ICF, which considers environmental impact on the development of a child.[27] More and more European countries are adopting the ICF in their legislative and policy definitions of disability.

The WHO is currently preparing a World Report on disability and health that is due for publication in 2009. The publication of this report is likely to further animate the activity of the European Office in the disability field.

1.6. EUROPEAN GROUP OF NATIONAL HUMAN RIGHTS INSTITUTIONS – (NHRIS-EG)

Web Resource: <http://www.nhri.net>

National Human Rights Institutions are the bodies set up under the United Nations Paris Principles of 1993. They include human rights commissions, ombudsmen and equality bodies. Their primary purposes are to protect and promote human rights at the domestic level. Although funded by government, they are given a guarantee of functional independence. Forty-six such bodies are organized regionally in the form of the European Group of NHRIs. The Group is, strictly speaking, not part of the government apparatus nor is it an intergovernmental organization. It is included in our review because of the pivotal role it plays in promoting and protecting rights.

NHRIs were in fact especially influential in the drafting of the UN Convention on the Rights of Persons with Disabilities. Moreover NHRIs are given very specific tasks under that Convention (Article 33(2)); namely, to 'protect, promote and monitor' its implementation at the domestic level. It is clear that they are set to become key engines for transmitting the global values of the Convention into the European regional and national settings.

In June 2003, before a commitment to the new UN Convention was confirmed, the European Group attended the second session of the *ad hoc* Committee considering the Convention on the Rights of Persons with Disabilities. It set out in detail why a protocol to existing Conventions would be inadequate and reinforced the benefit of a Convention as a focal point on disability within the UN system.[28]

In August 2005, the European Group was among the proponents of an NHRI 'Draft Text on Monitoring' at the Sixth Session of the *ad hoc* Committee.[29] The draft text proposed a range of comprehensive structures and systems to support

---

[26] The ICF was officially endorsed in Resolution of the World Health Assembly WHA54.21 of 22 May 2001.

[27] World Health Organization Regional Office for Europe 2008, <http://www.euro.who.int/RHN/20080214_2>, last accessed 25 March 2009.

[28] European Coordinating Committee, 'Position Paper of the European National human Rights Institutions' (June 2003), <http://www.nhri.net/pdf/Position-Paper-EU-NHRI's-Disability.pdf>, last accessed 25 March 2009.

[29] National Human Rights Institutions, 'Draft Text on Monitoring' (August 2005), <http://www.nhri.net/pdf/Disability_Proposal_Monitor.pdf>, last accessed 20 February 2009.

the effective implementation of the Convention. These included the requirement of a baseline report on the legislative, judicial, administrative and other measures relevant to the full implementation of the Convention. The Draft Text also suggested the development and implementation of National Action Plans under the Convention. The establishment of national monitoring bodies to oversee the implementation of the Convention was also recommended, as was the establishment of an international monitoring committee to oversee implementation as well as the appointment of a Global Disability Rights Advocate. The draft text recommended a complaints procedure which allows both individual communications and collective complaints, as well an enquiry procedure to protect complainants. Many aspects of this document influenced the drafting of the Convention and particularly the Optional Protocol.[30]

The European Group – as a Group – made its first historic intervention as *amicus curia* before the European Court of Human Rights in February 2008. The issue was legal capacity, which is perhaps one of the most important disability law reform issues in the world today: *DD v. Lithuania*, Application No 13469/06. The text of the *amicus* brief is contained in the Annex. It is likely that more such interventions will occur at both the regional and domestic levels, as the Group seeks to make its presence felt on European disability law reform.

2. EUROPEAN CIVIL SOCIETY ORGANIZATIONS

2.1. EUROPEAN DISABILITY FORUM (EDF)

Web Resource: <http://www.edf-feph.org/>

The European Disability Forum (EDF) describes itself as:

> an independent European non-governmental organization (ENGO) that represents the interests of 50 million disabled people in the European Union and stands for their rights. EDF is the only European platform of disabled people, which is run by disabled people or the families of disabled people unable to represent themselves.[31]

It is widely acknowledged as the main umbrella organization for the European disability movement.

EDF seeks to ensure that no decisions concerning disabled people are taken at a European level without disabled people being centrally involved. Its members include national councils of disabled people from EU and EEA countries (e.g., Norway, Iceland) as well as European non-governmental organizations of disabled persons, of parents of disabled persons, and European non-governmental organizations working for disabled persons.

EDF provides its members and others with a wide range of publications and

---

[30]   Further information on NHRI interventions in the drafting of the Convention on the Rights of Persons with Disabilities is available at <http://www.nhri.net/default. asp?PID=103&DID=0>, last accessed 20 February 2009.

[31]   European Disability Forum 2007, < http://www.edf-feph.org/Page_Generale.asp>, last accessed 25 March 2009.

positions papers, and facilitates the sharing of this information across its membership.

Since April 2000, the EDF has also enjoyed consultative status with the Council of Europe. It is also entitled to submit Collective Complaints under the European Social Charter.

During the European Year for Equal Opportunities 2007, and to mark its tenth year of fighting for disability rights, EDF ran a campaign entitled '1million4disability'. It collected one million signatures 'for a European Union in which disabled people's rights are protected through effective legislation, combating all forms of discrimination and guaranteeing the full inclusion of 50 million citizens with disabilities in the European society'.[32]

In January 2008, prior to the introduction of the Proposed Council Directive on discrimination on the grounds of religion or belief, disability, age or sexual orientation, EDF produced a comprehensive proposal for a disability specific Directive.[33] When it became clear that the proposal from the Commission would include other grounds of discrimination, EDF produced a list of demands regarding the content of the future legislation.[34] It insisted that the specificities of disability be taken fully into account. It also demanded that direct and indirect multiple discrimination, discrimination by association and discrimination in education be specifically prohibited. It further stated that the new proposal must have broad scope and cover a wide range of fields, that the duty to provide accessibility and 'reasonable accommodation' be anticipatory, and it called for an EU strategy on the development of positive action measures.

In September 2008, EDF published its response to the Commission's Proposal for a Council Directive on implementing the principle of equal treatment between persons irrespective of religion or belief, disability, age or sexual orientation, the text of which is contained in the Annex to the Yearbook.[35] Grand Chamber's assessment are contained in the Annex to the Yearbook. EDF insisted that the new directive must be seen as a step towards the implementation of the UN Convention on the Rights of Persons with Disabilities. However, EDF did not consider that this is the case under the current Draft Proposal. The main areas of its reservation, with respect to the draft proposal for a Directive, related to the absence of any reference to multiple discrimination and the absence of a Community definition of disability. EDF proposed adopting the definition of disability contained in the UN Convention on the Rights of Persons with Disabilities- '[p]ersons with disabilities include those who have long-term physical, mental, intellectual or sensory impairments which in interaction with various barriers may hinder their full and effective participation in society on an equal basis

---

[32] European Disability Forum 2007, <www.1million4disability.eu>, last accessed 9 March 2009.

[33] EDF, 'Proposal by the European Disability Forum for a Comprehensive Directive fighting discrimination of Persons with Disabilities' (January 2008).

[34] EDF, 'Absolute demands of the European Disability Forum regarding the future European non-discrimination directive' (June 2008).

[35] EDF, 'Position on the proposal for a Council Directive on implementing the principle of equal treatment between persons irrespective of religion or belief, disability, age or sexual orientation (Article 13 Directive)' (September 2008).

with others.'[36] EDF also specifically called for the inclusion of the concept of 'discrimination by association'.[37]

EDF called for safeguards against arbitrary discrimination in financial services in Article 2 of the Proposed Directive to be made more robust and suggested that the Article 'be amended to allow for a system of checks and balances to prevent arbitrary differential treatment from taking place'.[38] It also stated that '[t]he collection of data on any possible increased risk resulting from disability must always be administered by an independent unbiased institution in a transparent manner and provide for systematic review'.[39]

EDF articulated concerns about the current wording of Article 4 in the Proposed Directive. It saw potential confusion between anticipatory accessibility measures (generic) and 'reasonable accommodation' (individualized), and considered there to be too many possible justifications for failing to take such actions. EDF 'calls for redrafting this provision to narrow down the exceptions from the anticipatory accessibility duty to a single clause, such as disproportionate burden… to be applicable in strictly defined nature of specific services in individual cases'.[40] It sought that 'reasonable accommodation' and the anticipatory duty be decoupled for the purposes of determining what amounts to a disproportionate burden. It asked that the listed criteria to determine what is disproportionate, be applied to 'reasonable accommodation' only. It also called for the 'justifications' for failing to act which related to the small size of an organization and the short life cycle of a product, to be deleted from the Proposed Directive.

With respect to the implementation of the Proposed Directive, EDF expressed concern at the protracted implementation schedules and proposed that these apply to access issues only, and not to 'reasonable accommodations'. Furthermore, EDF 'invite[d] the Commission and the Member States to consider applying the ideas of "accessibility schedules" in the European Directive'.[41]

EDF is also engaged in a campaign for legislation to promote access to mainstream Information and Communication Technologies (ICT) products for the widest audience.[42] EDF notes the importance of ensuring compatibility and interoperability between assistive and mainstream technologies. EDF also emphasizes the reliance of people with disabilities on ICT devices for leisure, access to education, and access to work.

In July 2008, EDF published a Joint Position with the European Association for the Coordination of Consumer Representation in Standardization (ANEC) on Web and eAccessibility legislation.[43] The joint position paper states that although

---

[36]   United Nations Convention on the Rights of Persons with Disabilities, Article 1.

[37]   Building on the important judgment in Case C-303/06 *Coleman v. Attridge Law*, not yet reported.

[38]   EDF, 'Position on the proposal for a Council Directive on implementing the principle of equal treatment between persons irrespective of religion or belief, disability, age or sexual orientation (Article 13 Directive)' (September 2008), 5.

[39]   Ibid.

[40]   Ibid, 9.

[41]   Ibid, 13.

[42]   EDF 2009, <http://www.edf-feph.org/Page_Generale.asp?DocID=13854&thebloc= 18320>, last accessed 25 March 2009.

[43]   EDF and ANEC, 'Joint ANEC – EDF position on Web- and eAccessibility legisla-

non-binding instruments are in place, they might not lead to real eAccessibility, and they ought to be complemented with binding legislation containing standards. While recognizing the value of sector-specific legislation, the Joint Position also calls for general legislation in order to prevent eAccessibility being forgotten in the rapidly developing ICT sector.

EDF issued a significant statement in November 2008, in response to concerns about the potential negative impact of the current economic crisis on people with disabilities. This statement calls on the EU institutions 'to ensure disabled people and their families do not pay for the worldwide economic crisis by the reduction of their income, benefits, employment opportunities or in cuts in support to our representative organizations'.[44] The statement highlights the need for investment in accessible infrastructure to enable people with disabilities to buy goods and services, and thus contribute to overall economic recovery. The statement also draws attention to the obligations under UN Convention on the Rights of Persons with Disabilities that apply with as much force in times of recession. EDF states that society cannot afford to dilute such commitments.

EDF is committed to the full implementation of the UN Convention in the European Union. In October 2008, their Education Task Force issued a Statement entitled 'Inclusive education- Moving from Words to Deeds'.[45] This Statement offers recommendations for actions by both the EU and individual States under each of the provisions of Article 24 of the UN Convention on education. It recommends that States ensure their constitutions guarantee the right to free education for all children, and that the provision of this falls within the remit of the ministry of education in all cases. It calls for legislation to be reviewed and revised where necessary, to ensure compliance with the UN Convention, and adequate protection of the rights enshrined therein. The Statement calls for individualized support, the encouragement of social interaction, and coordination and collaboration between state bodies involved in the right to education. It goes on to make specific recommendations for teacher training, life and social learning, and participation in further education.

The European Research Agendas for Disability Equality (EuRADE) project is led by the European Disability Forum in partnership with Maastricht University (Netherlands) and the University of Leeds (UK).[46] It works towards 'the full participation of disabled people's organizations as equal and active partners in future research initiatives that will support the equality of people with disabilities in Europe'. It seeks to identify research priorities, to gather information about existing research methodologies in the fields of disability equality and non-discrimination, and to look at future collaboration with European research partners on the basis of its findings.

---

tion' (July 2008). This paper followed the EDF and ANEC 'Joint ANEC – EDF position on eAccessibility' (December 2007).

[44] EDF 'Statement on the Economic Crisis: Disabled people must not pay for the crisis' (November 2008)

[45] EDF Education Task Force, 'Inclusive education- Moving from words to deeds' (October 2008).

[46] EuRADE 2008, <http://www.eurade.eu/>, last accessed 26 March 2009.

In 2008, EuRADE undertook a consultation survey to gather information about the research experience of disabled people's organizations at national and European level and European level and their relationship with researchers.

PART III

ANNEX OF KEY DOCUMENTATION

PROPOSAL FOR A
COUNCIL DIRECTIVE ON IMPLEMENTING THE
PRINCIPLE OF EQUAL TREATMENT BETWEEN PERSONS
IRRESPECTIVE OF RELIGION OR BELIEF, DISABILITY,
AGE OR SEXUAL ORIENTATION[1]

(presented by the Commission)

{SEC(2008) 2180}
{SEC(2008) 2181}

THE COUNCIL OF THE EUROPEAN UNION,

Having regard to the Treaty establishing the European Community, and in particular Article 13(1) thereof,

Having regard to the proposal from the Commission,

Having regard to the opinion of the European Parliament,

Having regard to the opinion of the European Economic and Social Committee,

Having regard to the opinion of the Committee of the Regions,

Whereas:

(1) In accordance with Article 6 of the Treaty on European Union, the European Union is founded on the principles of liberty, democracy, respect for human rights and fundamental freedoms, and the rule of law, principles which are common to all Member States and it respects fundamental rights, as guaranteed by the European Convention for the Protection of Human Rights and Fundamental Freedoms and as they result from the constitutional traditions common to the Member States, as general principles of Community law.

(2) The right to equality before the law and protection against discrimination for all persons constitutes a universal right recognised by the Universal Declaration of Human Rights, the United Nations Convention on the Elimination of all forms of Discrimination Against Women, the International Convention on the Elimination of all forms of Racial Discrimination, the United Nations Covenants on Civil and Political Rights and on Economic, Social and Cultural Rights, the UN Convention on the Rights of Persons with Disabilities, the European Convention for the Protection of Human Rights and Fundamental Freedoms and the European

---

1   Brussels, 2.7.2008, COM(2008) 426 final, 2008/0140 (CNS).

Social Charter, to which [all] Member States are signatories. In particular, the UN Convention on the Rights of Persons with Disabilities includes the denial of reasonable accommodation in its definition of discrimination.

(3) This Directive respects the fundamental rights and observes the fundamental principles recognised in particular by the Charter of Fundamental Rights of the European Union. Article 10 of the Charter recognises the right to freedom of thought, conscience and religion; Article 21 prohibits discrimination, including on grounds of religion or belief, disability, age or sexual orientation; and Article 26 acknowledges the right of persons with disabilities to benefit from measures designed to ensure their independence.

(4) The European Years of Persons with Disabilities in 2003, of Equal Opportunities for All in 2007, and of Intercultural Dialogue in 2008 have highlighted the persistence of discrimination but also the benefits of diversity.

(5) The European Council, in Brussels on 14 December 2007, invited Member States to strengthen efforts to prevent and combat discrimination inside and outside the labour market[1].

(6) The European Parliament has called for the extension of the protection of discrimination in European Union law[2].

(7) The European Commission has affirmed in its Communication 'Renewed social agenda: Opportunities, access and solidarity in 21st century Europe'[3] that, in societies where each individual is regarded as being of equal worth, no artificial barriers or discrimination of any kind should hold people back in exploiting these opportunities.

(8) The Community has adopted three legal instruments[4] on the basis of article 13(1) of the EC Treaty to prevent and combat discrimination on grounds of sex, racial and ethnic origin, religion or belief, disability, age and sexual orientation. These instruments have demonstrated the value of legislation in the fight against discrimination. In particular, Directive 2000/78/EC establishes a general framework for equal treatment in employment and occupation on the grounds of religion or belief, disability, age and sexual orientation. However, variations remain between Member States on the degree and the form of protection from discrimination on these grounds beyond the areas of employment.

(9) Therefore, legislation should prohibit discrimination based on religion or belief, disability, age or sexual orientation in a range of areas outside the labour market, including social protection, education and access to and supply of goods and services, including housing. It should provide for measures to ensure the equal access of persons with disabilities to the areas covered.

(10) Directive 2000/78/EC prohibits discrimination in access to vocational training; it is necessary to complete this protection by extending the prohibition of discrimination to education which is not considered vocational training.

(11) This Directive should be without prejudice to the competences of the Member States in the areas of education, social security and health care. It should also be without prejudice to the essential role and wide discretion of the Member

---

[1]   Presidency conclusions of the Brussels European Council of 14 December 2007, point 50.

[2]   Resolution of 20 May 2008 P6_TA-PROV(2008)0212.

[3]   COM (2008) 412.

[4]   Directive 2000/43/EC, Directive 2000/78/EC and Directive 2004/113/EC.

States in providing, commissioning and organising services of general economic interest.

(12) Discrimination is understood to include direct and indirect discrimination, harassment, instructions to discriminate and denial of reasonable accommodation.

(13) In implementing the principle of equal treatment irrespective of religion or belief, disability, age or sexual orientation, the Community should, in accordance with Article 3(2) of the EC Treaty, aim to eliminate inequalities, and to promote equality between men and women, especially since women are often the victims of multiple discrimination.

(14) The appreciation of the facts from which it may be presumed that there has been direct or indirect discrimination should remain a matter for the national judicial or other competent bodies in accordance with rules of national law or practice. Such rules may provide, in particular, for indirect discrimination to be established by any means including on the basis of statistical evidence.

(15) Actuarial and risk factors related to disability and to age are used in the provision of insurance, banking and other financial services. These should not be regarded as constituting discrimination where the factors are shown to be key factors for the assessment of risk.

(16) All individuals enjoy the freedom to contract, including the freedom to choose a contractual partner for a transaction. This Directive should not apply to economic transactions undertaken by individuals for whom these transactions do not constitute their professional or commercial activity.

(17) While prohibiting discrimination, it is important to respect other fundamental rights and freedoms, including the protection of private and family life and transactions carried out in that context, the freedom of religion, and the freedom of association. This Directive is without prejudice to national laws on marital or family status, including on reproductive rights. It is also without prejudice to the secular nature of the State, state institutions or bodies, or education.

(18) Member States are responsible for the organisation and content of education. The Commission Communication on Competences for the 21st Century: An Agenda for European Cooperation on Schools draws attention to the need for special attention to be paid to disadvantaged children and those with special educational needs. In particular national law may provide for differences in access to educational institutions based on religion or belief. . Member States may also allow or prohibit the wearing or display of religious symbols at school.

(19) The European Union in its Declaration No 11 on the status of churches and non-confessional organisations, annexed to the Final Act of the Amsterdam Treaty, has explicitly recognised that it respects and does not prejudice the status under national law of churches and religious associations or communities in the Member States and that it equally respects the status of philosophical and non-confessional organisations. Measures to enable persons with disabilities to have effective non-discriminatory access to the areas covered by this Directive play an important part in ensuring full equality in practice. Furthermore, individual measures of reasonable accommodation may be required in some cases to ensure such access. In neither case are measures required that would impose a disproportionate burden. In assessing whether the burden is disproportionate, account should be taken of a number of factors including the size, resources and nature of the organisation. The principle of reasonable accommodation and disproportion-

ate burden are established in Directive 2000/78/EC and the UN Convention on Rights of Persons with Disabilities.

(20) Legal requirements[1] and standards on accessibility have been established at European level in some areas while Article 16 of Council Regulation 1083/2006 of 11 July 2006 on the European Regional Development Fund, the European Social Fund and the Cohesion Fund and repealing Regulation (EC) No 1260/1999[2] requires that accessibility for disabled persons is one of the criteria to be observed in defining operations co-financed by the Funds. The Council has also emphasised the need for measures to secure the accessibility of cultural infrastructure and cultural activities for people with disabilities[3].

(21) The prohibition of discrimination should be without prejudice to the maintenance or adoption by Member States of measures intended to prevent or compensate for disadvantages suffered by a group of persons of a particular religion or belief, disability, age or sexual orientation. Such measures may permit organisations of persons of a particular religion or belief, disability, age or sexual orientation where their main object is the promotion of the special needs of those persons.

(22) This Directive lays down minimum requirements, thus giving the Member States the option of introducing or maintaining more favourable provisions. The implementation of this Directive should not serve to justify any regression in relation to the situation which already prevails in each Member State.

(23) Persons who have been subject to discrimination based on religion or belief, disability, age or sexual orientation should have adequate means of legal protection. To provide a more effective level of protection, associations, organisations and other legal entities should be empowered to engage in proceedings, including on behalf of or in support of any victim, without prejudice to national rules of procedure concerning representation and defence before the courts.

(24) The rules on the burden of proof must be adapted when there is a prima facie case of discrimination and, for the principle of equal treatment to be applied effectively, the burden of proof must shift back to the respondent when evidence of such discrimination is brought. However, it is not for the respondent to prove that the plaintiff adheres to a particular religion or belief, has a particular disability, is of a particular age or has a particular sexual orientation.

(25) The effective implementation of the principle of equal treatment requires adequate judicial protection against victimisation.

(26) In its resolution on the Follow-up of the European Year of Equal Opportunities for All (2007), the Council called for the full association of civil society, including organisations representing people at risk of discrimination, the social partners and stakeholders in the design of policies and programmes aimed at preventing discrimination and promoting equality and equal opportunities, both at European and national levels.

(27) Experience in applying Directives 2000/43/EC and 2004/113/EC show that protection from discrimination on the grounds covered by this Directive would be strengthened by the existence of a body or bodies in each Member State, with

---

[1]   Regulation (EC) No. 1107/2006 and Regulation (EC) No 1371/2007.

[2]   OJ L 210, 31.7.2006, p.25. Regulation as last amended by Regulation (EC) No 1989/2006 (OJ L 411, 30.12.2006, p.6).

[3]   OJ C 134, 7.6.2003, p.7.

competence to analyse the problems involved, to study possible solutions and to provide concrete assistance for the victims.

(28) In exercising their powers and fulfilling their responsibilities under this Directive, these bodies should operate in a manner consistent with the United Nations Paris Principles relating to the status and functioning of national institutions for the protection and promotion of human rights.

(29) Member States should provide for effective, proportionate and dissuasive sanctions in case of breaches of the obligations under this Directive.

(30) In accordance with the principles of subsidiarity and proportionality as set out in Article 5 of the EC Treaty, the objective of this Directive, namely ensuring a common level of protection against discrimination in all the Member States, cannot be sufficiently achieved by the Member States and can therefore, by reason of the scale and impact of the proposed action, be better achieved by the Community. This Directive does not go beyond what is necessary in order to achieve those objectives.

(31) In accordance with paragraph 34 of the interinstitutional agreement on better law-making, Member States are encouraged to draw up, for themselves and in the interest of the Community, their own tables, which will, as far as possible, illustrate the correlation between the Directive and the transposition measures and to make them public.

HAS ADOPTED THIS DIRECTIVE:

Chapter 1
GENERAL PROVISIONS

Article 1
Purpose

This Directive lays down a framework for combating discrimination on the grounds of religion or belief, disability, age, or sexual orientation, with a view to putting into effect in the Member States the principle of equal treatment other than in the field of employment and occupation.

Article 2
Concept of discrimination

1. For the purposes of this Directive, the "principle of equal treatment" shall mean that there shall be no direct or indirect discrimination on any of the grounds referred to in Article 1.

2. For the purposes of paragraph 1:
(a) direct discrimination shall be taken to occur where one person is treated less favourably than another is, has been or would be treated in a comparable situation, on any of the grounds referred to in Article 1;
(b) indirect discrimination shall be taken to occur where an apparently neutral provision, criterion or practice would put persons of a particular religion or belief, a particular disability, a particular age, or a particular sexual orientation at a particular disadvantage compared with other persons, unless that provision,

criterion or practice is objectively justified by a legitimate aim and the means of achieving that aim are appropriate and necessary.

3. Harassment shall be deemed to be a form of discrimination within the meaning of paragraph 1, when unwanted conduct related to any of the grounds referred to in Article 1 takes place with the purpose or effect of violating the dignity of a person and of creating an intimidating, hostile, degrading, humiliating or offensive environment.

4. An instruction to discriminate against persons on any of the grounds referred to in Article 1 shall be deemed to be discrimination within the meaning of paragraph 1.

5. Denial of reasonable accommodation in a particular case as provided for by Article 4 (1)(b) of the present Directive as regards persons with disabilities shall be deemed to be discrimination within the meaning of paragraph 1.

6. Notwithstanding paragraph 2, Member States may provide that differences of treatment on grounds of age shall not constitute discrimination, if, within the context of national law, they are justified by a legitimate aim, and if the means of achieving that aim are appropriate and necessary. In particular, this Directive shall not preclude the fixing of a specific age for access to social benefits, education and certain goods or services.

7. Notwithstanding paragraph 2, in the provision of financial services Member States may permit proportionate differences in treatment where, for the product in question, the use of age or disability is a key factor in the assessment of risk based on relevant and accurate actuarial or statistical data.

8. This Directive shall be without prejudice to general measures laid down in national law which, in a democratic society, are necessary for public security, for the maintenance of public order and the prevention of criminal offences, for the protection of health and the protection of the rights and freedoms of others.

Article 3
Scope

1. Within the limits of the powers conferred upon the Community, the prohibition of discrimination shall apply to all persons, as regards both the public and private sectors, including public bodies, in relation to:
(a) Social protection, including social security and healthcare;
(b) Social advantages;
(c) Education;
(d) Access to and supply of goods and other services which are available to the public, including housing.

Subparagraph (d) shall apply to individuals only insofar as they are performing a professional or commercial activity.

2. This Directive is without prejudice to national laws on marital or family status and reproductive rights.

3. This Directive is without prejudice to the responsibilities of Member States for the content of teaching, activities and the organisation of their educational systems, including the provision of special needs education. Member States may provide for differences in treatment in access to educational institutions based on religion or belief.

4. This Directive is without prejudice to national legislation ensuring the secular nature of the State, State institutions or bodies, or education, or concerning the status and activities of churches and other organisations based on religion or belief. It is equally without prejudice to national legislation promoting equality between men and women.

5. This Directive does not cover differences of treatment based on nationality and is without prejudice to provisions and conditions relating to the entry into and residence of third-country nationals and stateless persons in the territory of Member States, and to any treatment which arises from the legal status of the third-country nationals and stateless persons concerned.

Article 4
Equal treatment of persons with disabilities
1. In order to guarantee compliance with the principle of equal treatment in relation to persons with disabilities:
a) The measures necessary to enable persons with disabilities to have effective non-discriminatory access to social protection, social advantages, health care, education and access to and supply of goods and services which are available to the public, including housing and transport, shall be provided by anticipation, including through appropriate modifications or adjustments. Such measures should not impose a disproportionate burden, nor require fundamental alteration of the social protection, social advantages, health care, education, or goods and services in question or require the provision of alternatives thereto.
b) Notwithstanding the obligation to ensure effective non-discriminatory access and where needed in a particular case, reasonable accommodation shall be provided unless this would impose a disproportionate burden.

2. For the purposes of assessing whether measures necessary to comply with paragraph 1 would impose a disproportionate burden, account shall be taken, in particular, of the size and resources of the organisation, its nature, the estimated cost, the life cycle of the goods and services, and the possible benefits of increased access for persons with disabilities. The burden shall not be disproportionate when it is sufficiently remedied by measures existing within the framework of the equal treatment policy of the Member State concerned.

3. This Directive shall be without prejudice to the provisions of Community law or national rules covering the accessibility of particular goods or services.

Article 5
Positive action

With a view to ensuring full equality in practice, the principle of equal treatment shall not prevent any Member State from maintaining or adopting specific measures to prevent or compensate for disadvantages linked to religion or belief, disability, age, or sexual orientation.

Article 6
Minimum requirements

1. Member States may introduce or maintain provisions which are more favourable to the protection of the principle of equal treatment than those laid down in this Directive.

2. The implementation of this Directive shall under no circumstances constitute grounds for a reduction in the level of protection against discrimination already afforded by Member States in the fields covered by this Directive.

CHAPTER II
REMEDIES AND ENFORCEMENT

Article 7
Defence of rights

1. Member States shall ensure that judicial and/or administrative procedures, including where they deem it appropriate conciliation procedures, for the enforcement of obligations under this Directive are available to all persons who consider themselves wronged by failure to apply the principle of equal treatment to them, even after the relationship in which the discrimination is alleged to have occurred has ended.

2. Member States shall ensure that associations, organisations or other legal entities, which have a legitimate interest in ensuring that the provisions of this Directive are complied with, may engage, either on behalf or in support of the complainant, with his or her approval, in any judicial and/or administrative procedure provided for the enforcement of obligations under this Directive.

3. Paragraphs 1 and 2 shall be without prejudice to national rules relating to time limits for bringing actions as regards the principle of equality of treatment.

Article 8
Burden of proof

1. Member States shall take such measures as are necessary, in accordance with their national judicial systems, to ensure that, when persons who consider themselves wronged because the principle of equal treatment has not been applied to them establish, before a court or other competent authority, facts from which it may be presumed that there has been direct or indirect discrimination, it shall be

for the respondent to prove that there has been no breach of the prohibition of discrimination.

2. Paragraph 1 shall not prevent Member States from introducing rules of evidence which are more favourable to plaintiffs.

3. Paragraph 1 shall not apply to criminal procedures.

4. Member States need not apply paragraph 1 to proceedings in which the court or competent body investigates the facts of the case.

5. Paragraphs 1, 2, 3 and 4 shall also apply to any legal proceedings commenced in accordance with Article 7(2).

Article 9
Victimisation

Member States shall introduce into their national legal systems such measures as are necessary to protect individuals from any adverse treatment or adverse consequence as a reaction to a complaint or to proceedings aimed at enforcing compliance with the principle of equal treatment.

Article 10
Dissemination of information

Member States shall ensure that the provisions adopted pursuant to this Directive, together with the relevant provisions already in force, are brought to the attention of the persons concerned by appropriate means throughout their territory.

Article 11
Dialogue with relevant stakeholders

With a view to promoting the principle of equal treatment, Member States shall encourage dialogue with relevant stakeholders, in particular non-governmental organisations, which have, in accordance with their national law and practice, a legitimate interest in contributing to the fight against discrimination on the grounds and in the areas covered by this Directive.

Article 12
Bodies for the Promotion of Equal treatment

1. Member States shall designate a body or bodies for the promotion of equal treatment of all persons irrespective of their religion or belief, disability, age, or sexual orientation. These bodies may form part of agencies charged at national level with the defence of human rights or the safeguard of individuals' rights, including rights under other Community acts including Directives 2000/43/EC and 2004/113/EC.

2. Member States shall ensure that the competences of these bodies include:

- without prejudice to the right of victims and of associations, organizations or other legal entities referred to in Article 7(2), providing independent

assistance to victims of discrimination in pursuing their complaints about discrimination,
- conducting independent surveys concerning discrimination,
- publishing independent reports and making recommendations on any issue relating to such discrimination.

CHAPTER III
FINAL PROVISIONS

Article 13
Compliance

Member States shall take the necessary measures to ensure that the principle of equal treatment is respected and in particular that:

(a) any laws, regulations and administrative provisions contrary to the principle of equal treatment are abolished;

(b) any contractual provisions, internal rules of undertakings, and rules governing profit-making or non-profit-making associations contrary to the principle of equal treatment are, or may be, declared null and void or are amended.

Article 14
Sanctions

Member States shall lay down the rules on sanctions applicable to breaches of the national provisions adopted pursuant to this Directive, and shall take all measures necessary to ensure that they are applied. Sanctions may comprise the payment of compensation, which may not be restricted by the fixing of a prior upper limit, and must be effective, proportionate and dissuasive.

Article 15
Implementation

1. Member States shall adopt the laws, regulations and administrative provisions necessary to comply with this Directive by …. at the latest [two years after adoption]. They shall forthwith inform the Commission thereof and shall communicate to the Commission the text of those provisions and a correlation table between those provisions and this Directive.

When Member States adopt these measures, they shall contain a reference to this Directive or be accompanied by such reference on the occasion of their official publication. The methods of making such reference shall be laid down by Member States.

2. In order to take account of particular conditions, Member States may, if necessary, establish that the obligation to provide effective access as set out in Article 4 has to be complied with by … [at the latest] four [years after adoption].

Member States wishing to use this additional period shall inform the Commission at the latest by the date set down in paragraph 1 giving reasons.

Article 16
Report

1. Member States and national equality bodies shall communicate to the Commission, by .... at the latest and every five years thereafter, all the information necessary for the Commission to draw up a report to the European Parliament and the Council on the application of this Directive.

2. The Commission's report shall take into account, as appropriate, the viewpoints of the social partners and relevant non-governmental organizations, as well as the EU Fundamental Rights Agency. In accordance with the principle of gender mainstreaming, this report shall, inter alias, provide an assessment of the impact of the measures taken on women and men. In the light of the information received, this report shall include, if necessary, proposals to revise and update this Directive.

Article 17
Entry into force

This Directive shall enter into force on the day of its publication in the Official Journal of the European Union.

Article 18
Addressees

This Directive is addressed to the Member States.

Done at Brussels,

For the Council
The President

PROPOSAL FOR A
COUNCIL DECISION CONCERNING THE CONCLUSION, BY THE EUROPEAN COMMUNITY, OF THE UNITED NATIONS CONVENTION ON THE RIGHTS OF PERSONS WITH DISABILITIES[4]

(presented by the Commission)

THE COUNCIL OF THE EUROPEAN UNION,
Having regard to the Treaty establishing the European Community, and in particular Articles 13, 26, 47(2), 55, 71(1), 80(2), 89, 93, 95 and 285 in conjunction with the second sentence of the first paragraph of Article 300(2), and the first subparagraph of Article 300(3) thereof,
Having regard to the proposal from the Commission,
Having regard to the opinion of the European Parliament,

Whereas:
(1) In May 2004, the Council authorised the Commission to conduct negotiations on behalf of the European Community concerning the United Nations Convention on the Protection and Promotion of the Rights and Dignity of Persons with Disabilities;
(2) The UN Convention and its Optional Protocol were adopted by the United Nations General Assembly on 13 December 2006 and entered into force on 3 May 2008;
(3) The UN Convention was signed on behalf of the Community on 30 March 2007 subject to its possible conclusion at a later date, in accordance with Decision.../.../EC of the Council of...;
(4) The UN Convention should be approved;
(5) Both the Community and its Member States have competence in the fields covered by the UN Convention. The Community and the Member States should therefore fulfil the obligations laid down by the UN Convention and exercise the rights invested in them, in situations of mixed competence in a coherent manner;
(6) The Community should, when depositing the instrument of formal confirmation, also deposit a declaration under Article 44.1 of the Convention specifying the matters governed by the Convention in respect of which competence has been transferred to it by its Member States;

---

4   Brussels, 29.8.2008, COM(2008) 530 final, 2008/0170 (COD), VOL.I,

HAS DECIDED AS FOLLOWS:

Article 1

1. The UN Convention on the Rights of Persons with Disabilities is hereby approved on behalf of the Community, subject to a reservation in respect of Article 27.1 thereof.

2. The text of the UN Convention is contained in Annex 1 to this Decision. The text of the reservation is contained in Annex 2.

Article 2

1. The President of the Council is hereby authorised to designate the person(s) empowered to deposit, on behalf of the European Community, the instrument of formal confirmation of the Convention with the Secretary-General of the United Nations, in accordance with Article 41 of the UN Convention.

2. When depositing the instrument of formal confirmation, the designated person(s) shall, in accordance with Articles 44.1 and 46.1 of the Convention, deposit the declaration and reservation set out in Annex 2 to this Decision.

Article 3

1. In respect of matters falling within the Community's competence, the Commission shall be a focal point for matters related to the implementation of the UN Convention in accordance with Article 33.1 of the UN Convention.

2. Community institutions may establish a coordination mechanism in accordance with Article 33.1 of the UN Convention.

3. The Council shall decide on the basis of a Commission proposal on designation or establishment of a framework, including one or more independent mechanisms, as appropriate to promote, protect and monitor implementation of the Convention in respect of matters falling within the competence of the Community, in accordance with Article 33.2 of the UN Convention

Article 4

The Commission is hereby authorised to select and nominate an expert to the Committee of the Rights of Persons with Disabilities, on behalf of the Community, in accordance with Article 34 of the UN Convention and to designate the person(s) empowered to submit the nomination to the Secretary-General of the United Nations, in accordance with Article 34.6 of the UN Convention.

Article 5

1. Members States shall submit to the Commission reports in respect of matters falling within the Community's competence for collation and subsequent transmission to the Committee on the Rights of Persons with Disabilities in accordance with Articles 35.1 and 35.2 of the UN Convention. The Commission is empowered to establish the modus operandi for this reporting mechanism.

2. Community institutions shall decide by common agreement on the reporting modalities in respect of the implementation of the UN Convention by the Institutions.

Article 6

In respect of matters falling within the Community's competence, the Commission shall represent the Community at meetings of the bodies created by the UN Convention, in particular the Conference of Parties referred to in Article 40 thereof, and shall act on its behalf concerning questions falling within the remit of those bodies.

Article 7

The Council may decide on the basis of a Commission proposal to submit an amendment to the UN Convention, on behalf of the Community, to the Secretary-General of the United Nations, in accordance with Article 47.1 of the UN Convention.

Article 8

The Council may decide on the basis of a Commission proposal to submit written notification on denunciation of the UN Convention, on behalf of the Community, to the Secretary-General of the United Nations, in accordance with Article 48 of the UN Convention.

Article 9

This Decision shall be published in the Official Journal of the European Union.

Done at Brussels,

For the Council
The President

(Annexes not reproduced)

Issue Paper from the Council of Europe Commissioner for Human Rights on 'Human Rights and Disability: Equal rights for all'

Strasbourg, 20 October 2008

COMMISSIONER'S ISSUE PAPERS

Issue Papers published by the Commissioner for Human Rights are intended to highlight the human rights dimension of certain current issues, outlining the main factual and legal points for consideration. Where appropriate, questions are raised, guidelines are set for subsequent work, and suggestions or warnings are included. These documents provide information and stimulus for reflection or debate. They do not have the status of *Recommendations* or *Opinions* as prescribed by the Commissioner's terms of reference.

INTRODUCTION

It is estimated that 80 to 120 million Europeans are persons with disabilities, that is 10 to 15% of the total population of the Council of Europe member states. For too long policies concerning persons with disabilities have been focused on institutional care, medical rehabilitation and welfare benefits. Such policies build on the premise that persons with disabilities are merely objects of welfare policies, rather than subjects able and entitled to be active citizens. Over the last few decades a shift in thinking has taken place. It is no longer correct to view persons with disabilities as merely objects of concern. They are citizens with equal rights and have an active role to play in our societies.

The challenge is to put this shift in thinking fully into practice. In reality, persons with disabilities are still discriminated against all over Europe and globally. Children with disabilities are denied their educational rights because schools are not equipped to meet their needs. Job opportunities are limited due to discriminatory practices and inaccessible workplaces, making people dependent on social benefits. Flawed systems of guardianship prevent people from making choices and having control over their lives. Several Council of Europe member states still hesitate to close down residential institutions and develop community-based services for persons with disabilities arguing that institutional care is necessary for persons with multiple or "profound" disabilities.

This paper outlines the international human rights framework for the protection of persons with disabilities. It gives a brief description of the situation focusing on key issues for persons with disabilities: the fight against discrimination; the move from institutional care to community living and the right to take decisions about one's personal affairs. This is followed by an overview of measures to create open and accessible societies, with action plans as the working method, and the importance of involving persons with disabilities in the process. It concludes with a set of recommendations to member states.

HUMAN RIGHTS LAW

International human rights instruments protect everybody, regardless of disability. The UN Standard Rules on the Equalization of Opportunities for Persons with Disabilities, adopted in 1993, were for a long time the guiding instrument clarifying state human rights obligations in this area. The purpose of the Standard Rules was to ensure that persons with disabilities could exercise their rights and freedoms on an equal footing with others. It put the obligation on states to act, pointing out that persons with disabilities should be partners in the process.

The UN Convention on the Rights of Persons with Disabilities

The 2008 UN Convention on the Rights of Persons with Disabilities adopted (the Convention) codifies this shift in thinking in a legally binding instrument. Non-discrimination, accessibility, inclusion in society and the freedom to make one's own choices are core principles. The substantive articles set out the basic human rights of persons with disabilities and the requirements on states to ensure full enjoyment of these rights. For example, to guarantee political rights states must ensure that persons with disabilities have the opportunity to participate in the public debate, vote and be elected. States must make sure that voting procedures, polling stations and ballot papers are accessible and easy to understand. The necessary changes to offices have to be made and equipment has to be provided so that politicians with disabilities can hold public positions.

The UN Convention entered into force on 3 May 2008. So far, among the Council of Europe member states Austria, Croatia, Hungary, San Marino, Slovenia and Spain have ratified the Convention. They have also ratified the Optional Protocol to the Convention which allows individuals and groups to bring complaints before the UN Committee on the Rights of Persons with Disabilities, a new body to monitor the implementation on the Convention. Thirty-four other member states of the Council of Europe have signed the Convention[1] and twenty of those also the Optional Protocol.[2] All member states should sign and ratify this Convention

---

[1]   Andorra, Armenia, Azerbaijan, Belgium, Bulgaria, Cyprus, the Czech Republic, Denmark, Estonia, Finland, France, Germany, Greece, Iceland, Ireland, Italy, Latvia, Lithuania, Luxembourg, Malta, Moldova, Montenegro, the Netherlands, Norway, Poland, Portugal, Romania, Russian Federation, Serbia, Slovakia, Sweden, The Former Yugoslav Republic of Macedonia, Turkey and the United Kingdom.

[2]   Andorra, Armenia, Azerbaijan, Belgium, Cyprus, the Czech Republic, Finland,

and the Optional Protocol without delay and develop clear strategies and plans to put the rights into practice.

The European framework

Specific standard-setting and policy-making activities concerning people with disabilities have been carried out at the intergovernmental level at the Council of Europe since 1959. In 1992, a coherent policy for people with disabilities was adopted. This policy laid down general principles on prevention of disabilities, active participation in community life and independence. It covered areas such as health care, education, employment and accessibility in further detail.[3]

Article 15 of the Revised Social Charter ensures the right of persons with disabilities to independence, social integration and participation in the life of the community. To this end State parties must guarantee quality education free of charge, promote access to employment and take action to make transport, housing and cultural activities accessible to all. The European Committee of Social Rights has concluded that non-discrimination legislation covering all these areas and effective remedies for victims are minimum requirements. In addition, action should be taken to remove barriers preventing persons with disabilities from entering public buildings, using public transport and enjoying new communication and information technologies.[4] For those states who have not accepted article 15, the Committee examines persons with disabilities' access to mainstream schooling and work under the articles concerned with the right to education and the right to employment in general.

The Council of Europe Action Plan 2006-2015 to promote the rights and full participation of people with disabilities in society[5] (Council of Europe Disability

---

France, Germany, Iceland, Italy, Lithuania, Luxembourg, Malta, Montenegro, Portugal, Romania, Serbia, Slovakia and Sweden.

[3] Recommendation No. R(92)6 on a coherent policy for the rehabilitation of people with disabilities, adopted by the Committee of Ministers on 9 April 1992 at the 474th meeting of the Ministers' Deputies. Since 1959, some 60 policy recommendations or resolutions have been adopted and about the same amount of reports published. An overview of achievement and activities is given in: Access to social rights for people with disabilities in Europe, Council of Europe Publishing, Strasbourg, November 2003, and in: Thorsten Afflerbach, Council of Europe Disability Policy, Encyclopedia of Disability, Vol. I, SAGE Publications, 2006, pp. 320-322.

[4] European Committee of Social Rights, Conclusions 2005, p 187ff. The unrevised European Social Charter (1961) article 15 protect the rights of persons with mental and physical disabilities to vocational training, rehabilitation and social resettlement.

[5] Recommendation Rec(2006)5 of the Committee of Ministers to Member states on the Council of Europe Action Plan to promote the rights and full participation of people with disabilities in society: improving the quality of life of people with disabilities in Europe 2006-2015, referred to as the Council of Europe Disability Action Plan 2006-2015.

Action Plan 2006-2015) is another significant instrument in this field. The Action Plan is complementary to the UN Convention in so far as it suggests very specific measures, which would facilitate the ratification and the implementation of the UN Convention. The Action Plan can be used to monitor progress in the implementation of disability-related reforms and subsequently help Council of Europe member states in meeting their obligations toward the UN instrument. States are invited to report regularly on their progress to the European Co-ordination Forum.[6]

The EU Employment Framework Directive (2000/78/EC) establishes a general framework for equal treatment in employment and occupation. It protects against discrimination based on disability and obliges employers to make reasonable adjustments to the workplace to cater for the needs of disabled job-seekers and employees.

The case-law of the European Court of Human Rights protecting the rights of persons with disabilities has so far been rather limited which is partly due to the restrictions in the scope of the European Convention itself. The Court has, however, laid down clear criteria for detention of persons in psychiatric hospitals and similar closed facilities. The Court has stated that no-one should be detained "unless it has been reliably shown that he or she has a true mental disorder of the kind or degree warranting compulsory confinement".[7] This means that all such decisions must be based on objective medical expertise. The Court has also laid down a number of procedural requirements. Admission procedures to closed hospitals must be clearly defined in domestic law. Decisions on admission and prolongation must be subject to judicial review, either by giving the individual the right to appeal or by an automatic periodic review. Procedural safeguards including legal representation must be guaranteed, not only formally, but also effectively in practice. In *Malgalhães Pereira v Portugal (44872/98)* a lawyer was appointed to assist a man suffering from schizophrenia during the judicial review of his confinement. However the lawyer did not take part in the proceedings. The Court concluded that merely "assigning counsel does not in itself ensure effective legal assistance" and found a violation of Article 5 § 4 of the Convention. Several cases challenging so called plenary guardianship laws and procedures depriving persons of their basic human rights - such as the right to vote, to marry and make legally binding decisions - are now pending before the Court.[8]

"Nothing about Us, Without Us"

The motto "Nothing about Us, Without Us" has been used for years by the disability movement to achieve full participation and equality of opportunities for,

---

[6]   The Forum is a committee composed of experts from the member states, representatives from Council of Europe bodies and other international organisations and organisations of persons with disabilities.

[7]   European Court of Human Rights, *Winterwerp v. the Netherlands,* 24 October 1979, para 39.

[8]   See also Chapter 5 – The Right to make decisions.

by and with persons with disabilities. The disability movements have played an important and active role in the development of the UN Convention on the Rights of Persons with Disabilities and the Council of Europe Disability Action Plan 2006-2015. Participation of persons with disabilities in all decisions affecting their lives, both at the individual level and through their organisations, is one of the fundamental principles in the Council of Europe's Action Plan. The same principle governs the rights as enshrined in the UN Convention as well as in the provisions concerning the monitoring of national implementation.

DISCRIMINATION

Discrimination of persons with disabilities persists in many spheres of society and can affect people's lives from an early age. Many children with disabilities are still not accepted in the mainstream school system. One problem is the lack of personal support and technical aids. Inaccessible school buildings are another obstacle. The problem also arises in child-care centres, sometimes forcing parents to choose between leaving their children in institutional care or giving up their job in order to care for their child.

Education for all

Even though every child's ability to learn is undisputed, there are still children of school age who are considered to be "uneducable" and denied any form of education. Such practices do not only limit children's options to support themselves as adults, but also their possibilities to become independent and participate in society. Persons with disabilities have the right to receive quality education and no-one should be excluded from schools because of his or her disability. The European Committee of Social Rights interpreted the right to education in *International Association Autism-Europe (IAAE) v. France (13/2002)*. The case concerned the French education system which allowed children with disabilities to be mainstreamed into the general school system or to attend specialised institutions. In practice, only a small number of persons with autism went into the general school system. Since the specialised institutions could not cater for the needs of the majority, they did not receive adequate education. The Committee stated that both legal and practical measures had to be taken to give full effect to the rights protected by the Charter. When implementation is complex and expensive, states must take progressive measures to give full effect to these rights, within a reasonable time using the maximum of its available sources.

A recent decision from the European Committee of Social Rights concerns over 3,000 children with moderate to profound intellectual disabilities living in residential centres for children with disabilities.[9] Less than 3% of the children were integrated in mainstream primary schools, which the Committee noted as extremely low considering that integration should be the norm. In addition, the teachers had not been trained to teach pupils with intellectual disabilities and the

---

[9]   European Committee of Social Rights, *Mental Disability Advocacy Centre (MDAC) v. Bulgaria*, 3 June 2008.

teaching materials were inadequate. Around 3.5% of the children attended special classes and the rest participated in activities at the residential centres. The Committee pointed out that the centres were not educational institutions and that participation in these activities did not entitle the children to any diploma attesting completion of primary school. Thus the children were prevented from entering secondary education. The Committee concluded that the activities provided by the centres could not be considered a form of education. After comparing the rate of children with intellectual disabilities having access to education with data on primary school attendance in general, the Committee held that the children residing at the centres were discriminated against because of the very low percentage who receive any type of education compared to other children.

The labour market

Employment rates regarding persons with disabilities vary considerably across Europe, but they have one thing in common: the activity rates for people with disabilities are significantly below that of people without disabilities. A recent report from International Labour Organization indicates that whereas the average European between 16 and 64 has a 66 % chance of finding a job, Europeans with "moderate" disabilities only have a 47 % chance. A survey published by the European Commission confirms this status. Close to 80% of the approximately 25,000 respondents from the member states of the European Union feel that with equivalent qualifications, a person with a disability stands less chance when it comes to being employed compared to a person without any disability.[10] Once employed, persons with disabilities commonly earn less than their non-disabled peers. One explanation is the lack of relevant education and personal skills, due to past discrimination. Another contributing factor is negative attitudes among employers. Job-seekers with disabilities are still perceived as less productive and more expensive to employ, considering the adjustments that may be needed. There are, however, surveys indicating that employees with disabilities perform equally or better compared with their non-disabled colleagues. Moreover, only a small percentage require adjustments to the workplace and when adjustments are required, the costs are generally negligible over time.[11]

Multiple discrimination

There is increased awareness that a person can be discriminated against on multiple grounds. For example, women with disabilities tend to have lower salaries and be less represented in management positions compared with men with disabilities and women without disabilities. Women and girls are especially vulnerable to physical, sexual and other abuse in residential institutions. The opportunities for children and young people with disabilities to play sport or enjoy recreational and cultural activities are often very limited, especially for those living in rural areas.

---

[10]   European Commission, Special Eurobarometer 263, January 2007, page 18.

[11]   International Labour Organization, Equality at work: Tackling the challenges, Global Report under the follow-up to the ILO Declaration on Fundamental Principles and Rights at Work (2007), page 44ff.

Migrants, Roma and older persons with disabilities are particularly vulnerable to discriminatory practices within the social protection and health care systems. Both the UN Convention and the Council of Europe Disability Action Plan 2006-2015 request states to address such multiple discrimination, and take appropriate action to empower all persons with disabilities.

Combating discrimination

A comprehensive anti-discrimination legislation is the cornerstone of any strategy combating discrimination. A glance at the situation in Europe reveals that only a few countries have legislation covering all relevant areas of society. This may reflect the EU framework directive covering only the labour market. A wider scope of protection against discrimination is being discussed within the European Union.

Disability-based discrimination manifests itself not only through negative attitudes and ignorance. Failure to take reasonable measures to meet a person's needs has the same discriminatory effect. An example of a reasonable measure would be a restaurant owner putting a ramp in the entrance to make it possible for customers using wheelchairs to enter. Another example is a headmaster deciding to adapt the school environment to the needs of blind or deaf children. Effective protection against disability-based discrimination has to include a legal obligation for employers, teachers and other duty-bearers to take such reasonable measures. The legal term for such an obligation is often called "reasonable accommodation".

Enacting relevant legislation is not sufficient. States should establish effective mechanisms to enforce and monitor the legislation to ensure full implementation. The judicial system has to be accessible to victims of discrimination and the legal costs involved affordable. It is also good practice to provide non-judicial mechanisms to assist victims, such as National Human Rights Institutions, Ombudsmen or other equality bodies. These easily accessible bodies should be mandated to receive complaints, act as independent mediators and/or provide legal assistance to the victims of discrimination in court proceedings.

Efforts to raise public awareness are required to fight prejudices and to empower persons with disabilities to claim their rights. In addition, targeted training for teachers, doctors, civil servants, journalists, employers and service providers as well as lawyers and judges is key to prevent discriminatory practices and ensure effective remedies.

THE RIGHT TO LIVE IN THE COMMUNITY

Life in an institution, separating children and adults from their family and their social context, almost inevitably leads to exclusion. Looking at the situation in Europe, countries are at different stages in the process of closing institutions and replacing them with community-based care, education and social services. Where institutions still exist, living conditions and service differ considerably between, and even within countries. Member states have adopted different strategies and approaches to the de-institutionalisation process. The majority prefer community care, while keeping residential institutions, sometimes renovated and/or transformed into smaller units. Only a few countries have managed to close all institutions and replace them with community-based alternatives.

Article 19 of the UN Convention clearly recognizes the right to choose your residence, on an equal footing with others, and to be included in the community. State parties pledge to take action to facilitate full enjoyment of this right and to prevent isolation and segregation.

De-institutionalisation

To live up to these standards, states need to make sure that parents receive support to enable them to raise their children. Childcare centres and schools should be open to all children and equipped to meet different needs. Social services and health care providers in the community must be accessible and competent to care for persons with different disabilities. Such reforms are challenging and require commitment and re-allocation of resources.

Experts on community living recommend that member states establish timetables to stop new admissions to institutions and establish community alternatives. A recent European study on the outcomes and costs of deinstitutionalisation explores the complex relation between needs, costs and quality of services. It concludes that a good care system usually involves substantial costs, whether provided in the community or in institutional settings. There is no evidence that community-based systems are more costly as such. However, once set up and well-managed, they tend to provide better quality services than institutions.[12] Experience also shows that when states succeed in providing proper services in the community, people prefer this form of service over institutional settings. Closure of institutions is not a goal in itself, but it is a method to ensure independence and inclusion for persons with disabilities.

Independent monitoring of closed institutions

As long as people are still living in institutions, their human rights must be protected. Such institutions should have decent living conditions, be adequately staffed and promote maximum contact with the outside world.[13] The European

---

[12]   Mansell J, Knapp M, Beadle-Brown J and Beecham J, Deinstitutionalisation and community living – outcomes and costs: report of a European Study, 2007, p 97ff. See also Recommendations and Guidelines to promote community living for children with disabilities and de-institutionalisation as well as to help families to take care of their disabled child at home, adopted by the Council of Europe Committee on Rehabilitation and Integration of People with Disabilities (Partial Agreement) (CD-P-RR) on 31 December 2007.

[13]   For more details, see: Recommendation (2005)5 of the Committee of Ministers on the rights of children living in residential institutions and Committee on the Rights of the Child, General Comment No 9, para 42-46.

Committee for the Prevention of Torture and Inhuman or Degrading Treatment or Punishment (CPT) is mandated to visit psychiatric hospitals and institutions across Europe. All too often the Committee reports of poor conditions and low quality care. In some reports, the CPT concluded that this amounted to inhuman and degrading treatment.[14] These reports also describe flawed admission procedures into institutions. Lack of legal provisions, delayed and/or superficial procedures to review the necessity of detention and lack of legal assistance are common problems.

Several NGO reports also highlight violations taking place in such institutions.[15] Malpractices, such as keeping persons in bed all day, over-medication and abuse of restraints must be stopped immediately. In addition, all involuntary placement, whether at institutions or psychiatric hospitals, must be in accordance with national law and subject to judicial review. Procedural safeguards as laid down by the European Court of Human Rights must also be guaranteed. The CPT Standards on involuntary placements in psychiatric establishments as well as two recommendations from the Committee of Ministers – Recommendation (2004)10 on the protection of human rights and dignity of persons with mental disorders and Recommendation (2005)5 on the rights of children living in residential institutions – give detailed guidance for evaluating domestic admission and review procedures.[16]

As with all closed settings where the liberty of persons is restricted, effective complaints procedures as well as independent monitoring visits are of crucial importance to ensure that human rights are respected. All member states should ratify the Optional Protocol to the UN Convention Against Torture and other Inhuman or Degrading Treatment or Punishment. Under this Protocol, states are required to establish national inspection systems to monitor all places of detention, including mental health and social care institutions.

THE RIGHT TO MAKE DECISIONS

The right to decide where we want to reside, how to spend our money, whether and with whom to get married is something many of us take for granted. But for

---

[14]   See, for example, CPT report to the Government of the former Yugoslav Republic of Macedonia on the visit to the country 15 to 26 May 2006, para 134 and the CPT report to the Bulgarian Government on the visit to Bulgaria from 16 to 23 December 2003, para 33.

[15]   Mental Disability Advocacy Centre, *Biennial Report 2005-2006;* Mental Disability Rights International, *Torment not Treatment: Serbia's Segregation and Abuse of Children and Adults with Disabilities(2007), Hidden Suffering: Romania's Segregation and Abuse of Infants and Children with Disabilities (2006)* and *Behind Closed Doors: Human Rights Abuses in the Psychiatric Facilities, Orphanages and Rehabilitation Centres in Turkey (2005).*

[16]   See also: Council of Europe Resolution ResAP(2005)1 on safeguarding adults and children with disabilities against abuse, adopted by the Committee of Ministers on 2 February 2005 at the 913th meeting of the Ministers' Deputies.

thousands of Europeans placed under guardianship the reality is very different. In several member states, adults are still deprived – on the basis of a medical diagnosis – of their legal capacity to take binding decisions. The result of such procedures is that these persons can no longer make any decisions with legal effect. They can no longer sign a lease to rent an apartment, consent or refuse medical treatment, cast a vote, marry, or even access a court to challenge this legal incapacitation. More developed systems allow only partial deprivation of legal capacity, while providing proper procedural safeguards and thoroughly regulating the power of guardians. Adequate monitoring procedures should also be in place to protect individuals against financial impropriety or other abuse or neglect.

The European standards

The European Court of Human Rights has acknowledged that the non-recognition of a person's legal capacity severely limits his or her human rights. In a recent case it stated that full deprivation of legal capacity is a very serious interference with the right to private life protected by article 8 of the European Convention on Human Rights. The sole existence of a mental disorder, even a serious one, cannot in itself justify such incapacitation.[17] The case concerned a man in his twenties who was fully deprived of his legal capacity following a request by his mother. The domestic court made its decision without even informing him of the proceedings, violating the right to a fair trial under Article 6 of the ECHR. As a result he was denied the opportunity to act in almost all areas of life. He could, for example, no longer buy or sell, decide where to live, work, travel or marry. He was denied the opportunity to appeal the decision on guardianship. A few days later, he was detained in a psychiatric hospital by the consent of his mother, who was appointed his guardian. He was unable to challenge that decision. Only his guardian could decide on his release. The European Court of Human Rights concluded that the proceedings had been seriously flawed and the applicant had been arbitrarily detained.

The Council of Europe recommendation on the protection of adults with disabilities who need assistance in making decisions in their personal or economic affairs, enumerate basic principles for interfering with a person's legal capacity.[18] The main principles are maximum preservation of capacity and respect for choices as far as possible. Nobody should be automatically deprived of their right to vote, draw up a will, consent or refuse any medical intervention or take decisions of a personal nature. Any measure restricting legal capacity should be tailored to the needs of the person concerned. Some persons need support to handle their financial affairs. Others need assistance to communicate their decisions. Procedural safeguards to protect against abuse should also be provided, including the right to be heard in person during proceedings, the right to appeal and a periodic review of the decision.

---

[17] European Court of Human Rights, *Shtukaturov v. Russia*, 27 March 2008.
[18] Recommendation No (99)4 of the Committee of Ministers on the principles concerning the legal protection of incapable adults, adopted by the Committee of Ministers on 23 February 1999 at the 660th meeting of the Minister's Deputies.

Supported decision-making

Articles 3 and 12 of the UN Convention clearly state that people with disabilities have the right to equal recognition before the law and the right to make their own choices. State parties are obliged to provide the necessary support these people may require to exercise their rights. The focus is on enabling people to make and communicate their decisions. This approach, often called supported decision-making, is strongly advocated by the disability movement globally. It builds on the sound belief that everyone can make choices and communicate them to others, while recognising that sometimes this requires support. Independence and personal autonomy is not about being able to do everything on your own, but about having control of your life and the possibility to make decisions and have them respected by others.

REMOVING BARRIERS

Persons with disabilities face a number of barriers that prevent their participation in society. Children with physical disabilities cannot play with other children at public playgrounds because the playgrounds have not been designed with them in mind. Television programmes without subtitles exclude persons with hearing impairments. The possibility to be politically active may be circumscribed by legal barriers, inaccessible voting procedures or simply because public information is not provided in an accessible format.

To meet these challenges, we all need to change the way we think and act. More effort should be invested in creating a society fit for all. The challenge is to open up our societies, remove physical, legal and attitudinal barriers and avoid creating new ones. Whilst the majority of European countries have laws and standards regarding public buildings and transport systems, these regulations are not sufficient. They are often limited to new buildings or buildings being reconstructed. Requiring owners to make reasonable adjustments to their existing buildings would be a good practice and an effective way of preventing discrimination. There should be appropriate sanctions for those violating the regulations, and remedies for those who are excluded as a consequence of such violations. Moreover, similar standards should be adopted for other areas of society. The needs of persons with disabilities should always be taken into account when designing new products, services, infrastructure and information and communication systems. Both the UN Convention and the Council of Europe Disability Action Plan 2006-2015 build on the premise that systematic and progressive work is necessary to create inclusive and accessible societies. This can be achieved by improving accessibility of existing environments, and also by applying universal design principles to newly created environments and systems. The Council of Europe's Resolution ResAP(2007)3 on achieving full participation through Universal Design provides member states with specific recommendations.

Scarce resources might have an impact on the timetable for this work, but there is no excuse for not making steady progress. Cost of accessible construction is not always high. According to the World Bank reconstructing buildings may be expensive but the cost of making new buildings accessible adds approximately one percent to the total costs.[19] There is also popular support for such action. A recent survey shows that over 90% of EU citizens think that more money should be spent on eliminating physical obstacles that complicate or hinder the daily life of persons with disabilities.[20] In fact, accessible solutions benefit us all. Electronic coffee makers, remote controls and automatic door openers were all originally designed to be assistive devices for persons with disabilities. Today most people use them on a daily basis.

NATIONAL IMPLEMENTATION

Action Plans as the working method

Achieving inclusive societies requires planning and systematic work. It is therefore encouraging that many European states have adopted disability plans and strategies. Every country will need to develop and implement such action plans tailored to its own circumstances inspired by the Council of Europe Disability Action Plan 2006-2015. Experience shows that certain common factors are crucial for success:

- A high level of political support and allocation of adequate budgetary resources.
- A thorough evaluation of existing policies and practices, to identify problematic areas
- Action-oriented national plans and strategies with concrete measures and clear indications on how these measures will improve the existing situation. The plan should designate who is responsible for implementation and indicate time-frames and benchmarks.
- Involvement of all concerned actors during the entire process. This must include all those who are responsible for the implementation at national or local level, people with disabilities and their representative organisations. The participatory approach will contribute to the legitimacy of the plan, create ownership and make implementation effective.
- Effective evaluation of the process. We need to learn from our mistakes and build on our successes.
- Gathering data in all relevant fields.

The benefits of working systematically on human rights issues, as opposed to a less structured *ad hoc* approach, are numerous. A systematic approach increases the chances of sustainable results. It also makes it possible to foresee and plan costs and to allocate resources where they are most needed.

---

[19] World Bank, Social Analysis and Disability: A Guidance Note Incorporating Disability-Inclusive Development into Bank-Supported Projects (2007), p 21.
[20] European Commission, Special Eurobarometer "Discrimination in the European Union" ref 263.

Data collection and analysis

The availability of adequate data relating to persons with disabilities is key to effective policy implementation and monitoring progress. Data collection and analysis can provide information not only on the number of persons with different disabilities but, for example, on their level of enrolment in mainstream education, their situation on the labour market, their level of participation in public life and the barriers they face when exercising their rights. States parties to the UN Convention have undertaken to collect the information needed to give full effect to this Convention. The process must comply with data protection standards to ensure confidentiality and respect the privacy of the persons concerned. The Council of Europe Disability Action Plan 2006-2015 also highlights the importance of including the gender perspective in collecting and analysing data.

An issue that needs to be taken seriously is terminology. Countries use different vocabulary and definitions relating to disability and persons with disabilities. To serve as a tool for identifying barriers, developing action plans and measuring progress, data collection and analysis should be based on a human rights model of disability. This model recognises that a disability is not solely a feature of the person caused by illness or other health condition. The interaction between a person with impairments and the barriers he or she faces in society, is also another feature of disability. The WHO International Classification of Functioning, Disability and Health (ICF), published in 2001, has already adopted this approach.

RECOMMENDATIONS

In implementing the rights of persons with disabilities member states should:

1. Ratify the Convention on the Rights of Persons with Disabilities including the Optional Protocol and start implementing it. Use the Council of Europe Disability Action Plan 2006-2015 as a tool to make the standards a reality.

2. Consult with and include persons with disabilities and their organisations in the planning and monitoring of law and policies which affect them.

3. Develop action plans to remove physical, legal, social and other barriers that prevent persons with disabilities from participating in society. Collect and analyse the necessary data to monitor the effective implementation of the action plans.

4. Adopt non-discrimination legislation covering all relevant areas of society. Include an obligation for employers, teachers and other duty-bearers to take reasonable measures to accommodate persons with disabilities. Provide effective remedies for persons who have had their rights violated. This includes making the judicial system accessible and the legal costs involved affordable.

5. Raise awareness to fight prejudice against persons with disabilities while empowering people to claim their rights. Provide training for teachers, employers

and service providers as well as for lawyers and judges on the rights of persons with disabilities.

6. Set up an independent Ombudsman or other equality body with a view to ensuring that persons with disabilities are able to fully enjoy their rights. Mandate such bodies to receive complaints, act as mediators and provide legal assistance to victims.

7. Develop programmes to enable persons with disabilities to live in the community. Cease new admissions to social care institutions and allocate sufficient resources to provide adequate health care, rehabilitation and social services in the community instead.

8. Review the laws and procedures for involuntary hospitalisation to secure that both law and practise comply with international human rights standards.

9. Set up independent mechanisms equipped to make regular, unannounced and effective visits to social care homes and psychiatric hospitals in accordance with the Optional Protocol to the UN Convention against Torture.

10. Review guardianship legislation to ensure that persons with disabilities can effectively exercise their right to make decisions and have them respected. When necessary and asked for, provide support tailored to individual needs to enable persons to exercise this right together with adequate safeguards to protect them against abuse.

EDF POSITION ON THE PROPOSAL FOR A COUNCIL DIRECTIVE ON IMPLEMENTING THE PRINCIPLE OF EQUAL TREATMENT BETWEEN PERSONS IRRESPECTIVE OF RELIGION OR BELIEF, DISABILITY, AGE OR SEXUAL ORIENTATION (ARTICLE 13 DIRECTIVE)

26 September 2008

INTRODUCTION

The European Disability Forum (EDF) broadly welcomes the proposal for a Directive adopted by the European Commission on 2 July 2008 and recognises that the proposal aims to address gaps in protection against discrimination against certain groups of the population, including persons with disabilities, outside the labour market.

As a general remark, EDF would like to emphasize the importance of respecting the following key principles in the process of negotiating the text of the Directive:

- The Directive must be a step towards implementing the UN Convention on the Rights of Persons with Disabilities, to which all EU Member States are signatories. The Convention aims to promote, protect and ensure the full and equal enjoyment of all human rights and fundamental freedoms by all persons with disabilities (Article 1), including through adoption of all appropriate legislative, administrative and other measures (Article 4(1)(a)).
- The Directive must bring change for disabled persons in all EU countries.
- The Directive must address all specificities unique to disability discrimination, such as structural and architectural barriers or segregation.
- The Directive must protect all people perceived as disabled, including everyone who currently has a disability; people associated with a person with a disability through a family or other relationship; people perceived as disabled; people who had a disability in the past; people who have a genetic predisposition to become disabled and people who may have a disability in the future.

Overall, EDF believes that the proposal in its current form does not meet these principles.

POSITIVE ASPECTS OF THE PROPOSAL FOR A DIRECTIVE

EDF is pleased that some of the suggestions proposed by the shadow EDF disability-specific Directive have been taken onboard by the European Commission, namely:

- Article 3 (1) provides for the broad scope of the directive, which specifically includes social protection, including social security and healthcare, social advantages, access to and supply of goods and other services which are available to the public, including housing, and education.
- Article 2(5) defines the denial of reasonable accommodation as a specific form of unlawful discrimination.
- Article 4 (1)(a) imposes an anticipatory duty to provide measures to ensure effective non-discriminatory access of persons with disabilities in all fields covered by the Directive.

Article 12 introduces a duty to create an equal treatment body (or bodies) for all grounds, addressing them either individually or collectively.

CONCERNS TO BE ADDRESSED IN THE LEGISLATIVE PROCESS

EDF nevertheless has strong concerns regarding several provisions of the directive that relate to persons with disabilities, and believes that if those are not addressed, the directive will have the effect of limiting rather than advancing the rights of persons with disabilities.

MULTIPLE DISCRIMINATION

EDF is surprised that the concept of multiple discrimination, much talked about at the negotiation stage, is not included in the Directive. EDF invites the European Commission to reconsider its decision and include a provision whereby an individual alleging discrimination on two or more grounds is compared to a hypothetical individual having none of the relevant characteristics of the complainant.

PERSONAL SCOPE OF THE DIRECTIVE

EDF calls on the European Commission to clarify who it intends to include in the personal scope of the Directive. While recognising that there is no Community definition of disability, EDF invites the Commission to include in the preamble to the Directive the wording of the UN Convention on the Rights of Persons with Disabilities:

> Article 1 (Purpose) ... Persons with disabilities include those who have long-term physical, mental, intellectual or sensory impairments which in interaction with various barriers may hinder their full and effective participation in society on an equal basis with others.

Such wording, although non-binding if contained in a recital, will give Member States guidance on the definition of disability for the purpose of this Directive.

ARTICLE 2 "CONCEPT OF DISCRIMINATION"- DISCRIMINATION BY ASSOCIATION

EDF invites the European Commission to explicitly extend the definition of discrimination to "discrimination by association", following the important judgment in case C-303/06 Coleman v Attridge Law. There, the European Court of Justice concluded that the Employment Equality Directive is not limited to protecting people who themselves have a disability, but is extended to persons who, not disabled themselves, are treated unfairly because of their association with a disabled person.

ARTICLE 2 "CONCEPT OF DISCRIMINATION" FINANCIAL SERVICES

Article 2(7) provides:

> ...In the provision of financial services Member States may permit proportionate differences in treatment where, for the product in question, the use of age or disability is a key factor in the assessment of risk based on relevant and accurate actuarial or statistical data.

UN Convention on the Rights of Persons with Disabilities:
Article 12(5)

> ...States Parties shall take all appropriate and effective measures to ensure the equal right of persons with disabilities to own or inherit property, to control their own financial affairs and to have equal access to bank loans, mortgages, and other forms of financial credit, and shall ensure that persons with disabilities are not arbitrarily deprived of their property

Article 25(e)

> States Parties shall... prohibit discrimination against persons with disabilities in the provision of health insurance, and life insurance where such insurance is permitted by national law, which shall be provided in a fair and reasonable manner;

EDF understands 'financial services' as inclusive of a variety of services offered by financial institutions (banks, insurance companies), such as current and savings accounts, mortgages, loans, insurance, and others.

BARRIERS

Access to insurance or a good credit rating are often preconditions to own property. However, calculation of risk for people with disabilities by financial institutions is still frequently based on a medical assessment, and relies on a faulty presumption that "disabled is always higher risk". This results in an effective impossibility for many people with disabilities to get life insurance, and therefore, to be eligible for other financial services.

Many disabled persons who do (after much humiliating questioning relating to their 'health status') obtain insurance must often settle for poor insurance rates, high premiums and small payments in the event of an insured situation occurring. This situation only widens the gap between disabled (often people with lower incomes) and non-disabled people.

EDF is concerned that whilst the proposed directive only permits proportionate differences in treatment based on disability where the assessment of risk is based on "relevant and accurate actuarial or statistical data", it does not provide for any system to guarantee the reliability or transparency of the data used, or to assess whether or not disability is a 'key factor' for assessing the risk. Incorrect and inaccurate data could therefore be used to discriminate against persons with disabilities in the provision of financial services. EDF feels this is a major weakness of the proposal, and can leave the door open to continued misperception and miscalculation of risk with regard to financial services and disability.

EDF has been informed by some of its national members that in Member States, where national legislation is worded along the lines of the current proposal for a Directive, people with disabilities continue experiencing undue hardship in accessing insurance and other financial services. In addition, such a proposal is worrying in light of the increasing privatization of certain forms of insurance (such as health) in some countries.

A BETTER MODEL

EDF notes that the Council Directive 2004/113/EC of 13 December 2004 implementing the principle of equal treatment between men and women in the access to and supply of goods and services (Gender Goods and Services Directive) provides stronger protection against discrimination in the provision of financial services. It stipulates in Article 5(2) that

> Member States may decide [before the deadline for transposition of the Directive] to permit proportionate differences in individuals' premiums and benefits where the use of sex is a determining factor in the assessment of risk based on relevant and accurate actuarial and statistical data. The Member States concerned shall inform the Commission and ensure that accurate data relevant to the use of sex as a determining actuarial factor are compiled, published and regularly updated. These Member States shall review their decision five years after [the deadline for transposition of the Directive], taking into account the Commission report [on the transposition of the Directive] and shall forward the results of this review to the Commission.

Without going into the differences between disability and gender concerning insurances, EDF believes that the Gender Goods and Services Directive provides for a safeguard clause and greater transparency against arbitrary use of data to justify differential treatment.

EDF PROPOSAL

The collection of data on any possible increased risk resulting from disability must always be administered by an independent unbiased institution in a transparent manner and provide for systematic review. Given the heterogeneous nature of disability, providers of financial services should provide evidence that a specific disability or chronic illness (all other conditions being equal) constitutes a risk, and completely justifies the difference in treatment (e.g. lower coverage, higher premiums). *EDF therefore calls for Article 2(7) to be amended to allow for a system of checks and balances to prevent arbitrary differential treatment from taking place.*

Furthermore, EDF recalls the Commission's intention "to initiate a dialogue with financial service providers, together with other relevant stakeholders, in order to exchange and encourage best practice", declared in Commission's Communication on non-discrimination and equal opportunities (COM(2008)/420/3). Convinced that the factors relevant to the risk assessment must be agreed between service providers and user representatives, *EDF insists that an official mandate (for example, preparation of a proposal regulating the restrictions on the access of financial services to certain groups) be given to such stakeholder group by the Directive.*

Finally, EDF believes that the Commission should encourage Member States to establish a public fund to provide for basic insurance for such people with disabilities, whose risks cannot be taken up by private insurers, as it is the case in many countries.

Article 3 Material Scope- restrictions on education

Article 3(3) provides:

> This Directive is without prejudice to the responsibilities of Member States for the content of teaching, activities and the organisation of their educational systems, including the provision of special needs education...

UN Convention on the Rights of Persons with Disabilities does not allow for restrictions on the right to education.

Article 24(1)

> States Parties recognise the right of persons with disabilities to education. With a view to realizing this right without discrimination and on the basis of equal opportunity, States Parties shall ensure an inclusive education system at all levels and life long learning.

EDF feels that Article 3(3) effectively excludes many people with disabilities from protection from discrimination in the context of education. The Article is poorly drafted and, if left unamended, may lead to legal uncertainty, and the denial of rights to people with disabilities.

Firstly, the proposed directive does not define 'special needs education'. It is unclear whether the proposal only intends to reserve this concept for specialised schools, or whether it also includes mainstream schools that provide reasonable accommodation (such as an adapted curriculum, or provision of tuition in alternative communication means) for children with special educational needs. EDF insists that reasonable accommodation for pupils with disabilities in mainstream schools must be included in the scope of the directive, subject to the proviso that this must not result in a disproportionate burden. By extension, EDF believes that that special needs education must be part of the general educational system of a Member State – to state otherwise would be against the letter and the spirit of the UN Convention on the Rights of Persons with Disabilities that provide for mainstream schooling as the first choice of education for all children with disabilities.

Secondly, it is unclear if the proposed directive excludes all aspects of "special needs education" from the scope of the directive, or only those aspects which relate to "the content of teaching, activities and organisation" of "special needs education". Only "the content of teaching, activities and organisation" seem to be excluded from the scope of the directive in the context of "mainstream" education.

If all aspects of "special needs education" fall outside the scope of the directive then, for example, a child who experiences harassment at school on one of the prohibited grounds at a mainstream school would be protected, whilst a child who experiences similar harassment in a "special needs" setting would not be. This is clearly unacceptable. All children and adults, whether disabled or not, and whatever kind of education establishment they are attending, must be entitled to an equal level of protection from discrimination.

In relation to the argument of limited competence of the European Communities in the field of education, EDF would firstly like to point out that a precedent of regulating the issue of education exists in the Racial Equality Directive 2000. Secondly, EDF would like to point at the inconsistency of including 'education' in the scope of the Directive in Article 3(1)(c) only to exclude some part of it (i.e special needs education) later in paragraph 3 of the same Article. EDF believes that once 'education' has been included in the scope, certain areas of it should not be left out without justification. While it is true that the European Communities have limited competence regarding "the content of teaching, activities and organisation" of education, its competence to guarantee effective access to education is illustrated by Article 14 of the EU Charter of Fundamental Rights which states that "everyone has the right to education" and that parents have the right "to ensure the education and teaching of their children in conformity with their… pedagogical convictions".

In addition, the Commission actively supports the use of inclusive education in its Communication COM(2008) 425 "Improving competencies for the 21st century: an Agenda for European Cooperation in Schools" that was published on the same day as the proposal for the Directive. In this Communication, the Commission proposes to focus future cooperation on "*providing more timely support and personalised learning approaches within mainstream schooling for students with special needs*", among other things.

The same positive message about the benefits of inclusive education is featured in the "Accessibility" video produced by the European Commission (available at <http://www.youtube.com/watch?v=U86PW0VdxeA>).

EDF PROPOSAL

In light of the above, EDF *strongly calls for the removal of the explicit exclusion of the special needs education from the scope of the Directive.* EDF insists that person with a disability must be entitled to the same level of protection from discrimination in the context of education as all other EU citizens. In accordance with the spirit of the UN Convention, EDF invites the European Commission to consider a proposal in the EDF shadow Disability-specific Directive, which says: *"Member States shall ensure that, in determining which form of education or training is appropriate, the views of the person with a disability are respected. Where the person is a child or adult who is unable to represent himself, the views of their parents, guardians or designated advocates will be considered as a significant factor."*

Article 4 "Equal Treatment of Persons with Disabilities"

Anticipatory measures and reasonable accommodation

The key problem with this article is that two very different notions - anticipatory measures to enable persons with disabilities to have effective and non-discriminatory access, and reasonable accommodation - are confused in *the* text. This will only lead to more confusion at the transposition stage, and, in particular for parties and courts which are called upon to interpret and apply the relevant provisions.

The anticipatory accessibility duty includes general measures applicable to people with disabilities as a class and comparable to accessibility legislation already available in several EU countries and providing for medium- to long-term commitments to make such adaptations to infrastructures as to make them accessible to persons with disabilities. It may also include the obligation to provide assistance or additional staff. Such anticipatory duty is usually subject to strict exceptions which relate, for instance, to the impossibility of adapting the existing infrastructure, or limitations related to technological developments. In cases, when provision of accessibility involves considerable resources and costs (such as adaptations in the public transport system, or all public buildings), the legislation sometimes provides for a schedule of accessibility.

Reasonable accommodations are individual measures that need to be taken in response to a specific need of a specific person with a disability, in order to enable them to access or use a facility or a service, where those needs have not been anticipated by general measures. The duty to provide reasonable accommodation already exists in national laws of the EU Member States in relation to employment and may include such measures as provision of physical access to the place of employment, flexible working hours, personal assistance at work or revision of working tasks. This duty is subject to disproportionate burden defined on the national level. Some Member States also have legislation that provides for reasonable accommodation in other domains, such as provision of goods and services.

FUNDAMENTAL ALTERATION, ALTERNATIVES

Article 4(1)(a) provides:

> In order to guarantee compliance with the principle of equal treatment in relation to persons with disabilities:

- The measures necessary to enable persons with disabilities to have effective non- discriminatory access to social protection, social advantages, health care, education and access to and supply of goods and services which are available to the public, including housing and transport, shall be provided by anticipation, including through appropriate modifications or adjustments. Such measures should not impose a *disproportionate burden*, nor require *fundamental alteration* of the social protection, social advantages, health care, education, or goods and services in question or require the provision of *alternatives* thereto."

UN Convention on the Rights of Persons with Disabilities

> Article 24(2)

> States Parties shall ensure that: (c) reasonable accommodation of the individual's requirements is provided; (d) persons with disabilities receive the support required, within the general education system, to facilitate their effective education;"

> Article 25

> States Parties recognise that persons with disabilities have the right to the enjoyment of the highest attainable standard of health without discrimination on the basis of disability. ... States Parties shall... (f) prevent discriminatory denial of health care or health services or food and fluids on the basis of disability."

> Article 28(2)

> States Parties recognise the right of persons with disabilities to social protection and to the enjoyment of that right without discrimination on the basis of disability, and shall take appropriate steps to safeguard and promote the realization of this right.

The proposed directive requires that the anticipatory measures necessary to enable persons with disabilities to have "effective non-discriminatory access" (not defined by the proposal!) to social protection, social advantages, health care, edu cation and access to and supply of goods and services be taken, but subjects this to three requirements:

- the measures taken must not amount to a disproportionate burden;
- the measures taken must not require a fundamental alteration to the social protection, social advantages, health care, education or goods and services;
- the measures taken must not require the provision of alternatives to the social protection, social advantages, health care, education or goods and services.

EDF feel that establishing a three-tier system of justifications for failing to provide accessibility is excessive, and a single (and restricted) exception should be used instead.

It is extremely problematic that the proposed directive explicitly exempts Member States from imposing an obligation to introduce fundamental alterations (not defined by the proposal) to social protection, social advantages, healthcare, education or goods and services, even if these are inherently discriminatory and inaccessible to people with disabilities. This seems to mean that, in practice, minor problems must be removed, but global, deeply rooted institutionalised discrimination will be allowed to remain because addressing such problems requires fundamental alteration of the system. This is clearly unacceptable, and the following examples illustrate it:

Large closed residential institutions exist in many EU Member States. De-institutionalisation process will never be complete until community services are made inclusive of persons with disabilities. Integration of persons with disabilities in the community requires "fundamental alteration" to the *systems of social protection, social advantages and healthcare.*

Discriminatory practices, such as placing people with intellectual disabilities at the bottom of a waiting list for medical care or denial of gynaecological services to women with disabilities (both motivated by scarcity of resources and distribution of priorities) require "fundamental alterations" to the *healthcare system.*

The policies of excluding children with special educational needs from mainstream education due to physical barriers or absence of special needs curricula require "fundamental alterations" to the *education system.*

The removal of 'benefit traps' that impede people with disabilities from moving to employment and leaving the benefit systems requires "fundamental alterations" to the *social protection system.*

In contrast to the proposed directive, the United Kingdom Disability Discrimination Act (DDA) 1995 (as amended in 2002) only requires a service provider not "to take any steps which would fundamentally alter the *nature* of the service in question or the nature of his trade, profession or business". However, this exception does not apply to public authorities which also provide services. For example, a restaurant has the right to refuse to deliver meal to a person with a disability, unless it provides home delivery to all customers as part of its services. By the same token, a night club with low-level lighting is not required to adjust the lighting to accommodate customers who are partially sighted, as this would fundamentally change the atmosphere of the club. However, whenever an alternative reasonable adjustment which would ensure the accessibility of the services can be made and this would not fundamentally alter the nature of the services, it must be provided.

A similar provision exists in the Americans with Disabilities Act (ADA) of 1990.

The difference between the UK/US provisions and the current proposal for a European Directive is significant: whereas the former apply strictly to providers of specific services who are exempt from fundamentally altering the *nature* of their services, the latter presumably aims to exempt the whole *scope* of the Directive from fundamental alterations, and is far too broad.

EDF PROPOSAL

Firstly, EDF *invites the Commission to provide definitions for new legal terms*, such as "effective non-discriminatory access" (which should comprise "the conditions of access") or "fundamental alterations", in line with the existing UK legislation.

Secondly, EDF *calls for redrafting this provision to narrow down the exceptions from the anticipatory accessibility duty* from the three-tier system to a single clause, such as disproportionate burden (the definition of which should also be revised, as per the next chapter of the present position paper) to be applicable to strictly defined nature of specific services in individual cases.

"DISPROPORTIONATE BURDEN"

Article 4(2) provides:

> For the purposes of assessing whether measures necessary to comply with paragraph 1 would impose a disproportionate burden, account shall be taken, in particular, of the size and resources of the organisation, its nature, the estimated cost, the life cycle of the goods and services, and the possible benefits of increased access for persons with disabilities. The burden shall not be disproportionate when it is sufficiently remedied by measures existing within the framework of the equal treatment policy of the Member State concerned.

Precedent of the Employment Equality Directive 2000
In 2000, during the negotiations on the Employment Equality Directive, EDF argued that the disproportionate burden test must relate purely to the financial implications of making a specific accommodation and should always involve more that a nominal cost to the provider of the 'reasonable accommodation'.
The European Commission, in drafting the Employment Equality Directive, de-

cided *not* to include the definition of 'disproportionate burden' in the body of the Directive, but mention it in a recital instead. Consequently, recital 21 provides that in determining whether a burden is disproportionate, *"account should be take in particular of the financial and other costs entailed, the scale and financial resources of the organisation or undertaking and the possibility of obtaining public funding or any other assistance."*

EDF feels that the precedent of the Employment Directive should not be undermined by the substantially different approach in the draft Directive, which proposes to include the definition in the body and provide a wider list of criteria of disproportionate burden.

Disproportionate burden as applied to 'reasonable accommodation' and to 'anticipatory duty'.
If, despite the arguments above, the European Commission should decide to establish European criteria to define disproportionate burden, they should not be the same for 'reasonable accommodation' and for 'anticipatory duty'. The two concepts are very different in nature, and operate in different settings: provision of reasonable accommodation to a specific disabled client wanting to use the facilities of a small privately-owned shop should not be subject to the same criteria as public transportation accessibility plans designed by a municipality of a Member State, although both are bound by the obligation to accommodate the needs of persons with disabilities.

In relation to reasonable accommodation, EDF would like to see a definition which would be flexible enough not to restrict the application of the concept of 'disproportionate burden' in national contexts of 27 Member States.

In relation to provision of accessibility measures by anticipation, EDF calls the Commission to use only such definition of 'disproportionate burden' that wouldn't jeopardise the legislation in Member States that either permit the application of the 'disproportionate burden' clause in only the most narrow meaning of it (such as Italy), or use a different approach to 'disproportionate burden' than enumerating the criteria for it (such as Malta).

EDF particularly welcomes the Maltese approach and believes that the Maltese Equal Opportunities (Persons with Disability) Act could serve as an inspiration for the European Directive. Article 13(3) of Title 3 – Access of the Act provides that accessibility should be provided *"unless compliance with accessibility provision is impracticable or unsafe and could not be made practicable and safe by reasonable modification of rules, policies or practices, or the removal of architectural, communication or transport barriers or the provision of auxiliary aids or services."*

In any case, EDF insists that application of the defence of 'disproportionate burden' should never serve as an excuse for inaction or indefinite exemption from the duty to provide accessibility. If it is established that provision of accessibility would impose a substantial burden on the provider, the legislation should oblige them to commit to a long-term accessibility plan outlining how they intend to gradually meet their accessibility obligations under the Directive.

Overall, in the view of EDF, some criteria for determining the 'disproportionate burden' proposed by the Commission are problematic and require further consideration:

Size and resources of the organisation

EDF recognises that this criterion is common to many jurisdictions that allow for this consideration when determining whether making an employment-related accommodation would result in a disproportionate burden. However, the scope of the proposed directive goes beyond employment, and the differences between the employment situation and provision of goods, services and facilities, must be acknowledged.

For example, EDF believes that a small web developing company should not be allowed, because of its size, to sell inaccessible design of websites, if a big one next door would not. Neither should a small hairdressing salon be automatically exempt from the accessibility obligation, if the size is the only consideration. Should the size be a major factor in determining the obligations under the Directive, EDF feels that then a greater burden would be placed on large organisations. By the same token, even if it may be easier for a small school to adapt its facilities and teaching materials to meet the needs of disabled pupils than for a large one, both should be obliged to do so.

Overall, EDF believes that a *nature* of the service rendered should be the decisive factor to determine to what extent its provider is bound by accessibility requirements.

Cost

Whereas cost is often a relevant consideration, it should never be automatically deemed to be the determining factor in deciding whether or not to provide accessibility. In 2005, a study conducted by the University of Iowa showed that more than 50% of adjustments needed by people with disabilities in employment cost absolutely nothing. Many employers gave changing a work schedule as an example of a "no-cost" accommodation. Of those accommodations that do cost, the typical expenditure by employers is around $600 (<http://www.jan.wvu.edu/enews/2005/Enews_V3-I4.htm#4>).

It should not be forgotten that the provision of accessibility does not have to include expensive adaptations; often, a change of attitude, inventive approach and training are sufficient. EDF invites to reflect this consideration in the Directive (possibly, in a recital).

Life cycle

Using this criterion to determine whether an accommodation or an accessibility feature amounts to a disproportionate burden will exclude many products and services, such as some Information Technologies tools, promotional goods and services, one-day cultural excursions, from the accommodation / accessibility requirement. It also seems to allow for this exemption to apply for packaging of products, because of its limited life cycle (as the design of the product, and therefore packaging, must change regularly). EDF suggests that this criterion is removed from the definition of disproportionate burden.

Possible benefits of increased access for persons with disabilities
EDF disagrees with the purpose and wording of this criterion. Whereas a similar condition may be relevant in determining the effectiveness of reasonable accommodation measures in relation to a specific individual, whose needs must be accommodated in one (particularly employment-related) situation, it should not be used to determine the qualitative benefits of the *anticipatory* duty to provide accessibility to people with disabilities as a class.

EDF believes that in order to create real equality, accessibility must be provided prima facie and as a common sense consideration.

Furthermore, EDF finds this criterion confusing, as it is unclear who the beneficiaries of increased access could be (persons with disabilities, companies, society in general?) nor how the benefits should be measured.

EDF PROPOSAL

Firstly, EDF would like to see different restrictions to be placed on the obligation to provide reasonable accommodation and the anticipatory duty.
Thirdly, if the list of criteria to determine the disproportionate burden is to be retained, it should only apply in the context of reasonable accommodation, not anticipatory duty. EDF believes that the conditions of "size" and "life cycle" should be removed from the list, and would like to see further clarification regarding beneficiaries of the increased access and the way the benefits are to be measured.

UNIVERSAL DESIGN

UN Convention on the Rights of Persons with Disabilities

Article 2

For the purposes of the present Convention: ... "Universal design" means the design of products, environments, programmes and services to be usable by all people, to the greatest extent possible, without the need for adaptation or specialised design. "Universal design" shall not exclude assistive devices for particular groups of people with disabilities where this is needed.

Article 4(1)(f)

States Parties undertake to undertake or promote research and development of universally designed goods, services, equipment and facilities, which should require the minimum possible adaptation and the least cost to meet the specific needs of a person with disabilities, to promote their availability and use, and to promote universal design in the development of standards and guidelines;"

EDF regrets that neither the concept of *Universal Design (Design For All)* nor accessibility are defined in the proposal. We believe that the Design for All should be the cornerstone of all accessibility processes, as its application at the earliest stage of decision-making with respect to policies, goods, products or services makes accessibility possible at no additional cost to the manufacturer, government agency or service provider, whereas changing a design or the outcome of a decision later to make it accessible can indeed be expensive.

EDF PROPOSAL

EDF proposes to include a definition of universal design or accessibility, inspired by the UN Convention and set out in the Stockholm Declaration of the European Institute for Design and Disability, in the proposed directive. The said Declaration defines Design for all as aiming "to enable all people to have equal opportunities to participate in every aspect of society. To achieve this, the built environment, everyday objects, services, culture and information – in short, everything that is designed and made by people to be used by people – must be accessible, convenient for everyone in society to use and responsive to evolving human diversity. The practice of Design for All makes conscious use of the analysis of human needs and aspirations and requires the involvement of end users at every stage in the design process."

(<http://www.designforall.org/en/documents/Stockholm_Declaration_ang.pdf>).

Consequently, EDF would like to see a provision that would oblige undertakings to identify and eliminate obstacles and barriers and prevention of new obstacles and barriers that hamper the access, on an equal basis with others, of persons with disabilities, irrespective of the nature of the barrier or disability.

STANDARDS

UN Convention on the Rights of Persons with Disabilities

Article 9(2)

States Parties shall also take appropriate measures to: (a) to develop, promulgate and monitor the implementation of minimum standards and guidelines for the accessibility of facilities and services open or provided to the public; (b) to ensure that private entities that offer facilities and services which are open or provided to the public take into account all aspects of accessibility for persons with disabilities;

EDF regrets that the proposed directive does not contain a reference to "standards" that have proved to be very beneficial to making goods and services accessible, available and affordable to people with disabilities.

344

Standards have two main benefits for users and manufacturers. They are a clear signal for the consumers that the products conform to certain specifications and are therefore more trustworthy. Manufacturers also benefit from European standards, when they exist, because the cost of respecting them is smaller than respecting 27 national ones.

EDF PROPOSAL

EDF invites the Commission to include appropriate references to disability accessibility in all "New Approach" directives adopted on the basis of Article 95 EC and in all mandates issued to the European Standardisation Bodies. These instruments should all complement any directive adopted on the basis of Article 13 EC which addresses disability discrimination.

Article 15 "Implementation"

Article 15(2) provides:

> In order to take account of particular conditions, Member States may, if necessary, establish that the obligation to provide effective access as set out in Article 4 has to be complied with by ... [at the latest] four [years after adoption].

Firstly, EDF requests the Commission to make it explicit that whatever extension of the implementation deadline is proposed, it only applies to "access" as provided in Article 4(1), and not reasonable accommodation, and that the general non-discrimination obligation vis-à-vis persons with disabilities becomes binding together with other provisions of the Directive.

Recognising that the obligation to provide accessibility under Article 4 is a complicated one and requires the mobilization of all stakeholders (public and private) on national, regional and local levels, EDF feels that the provision in Article 15 (2) is not the most flexible approach that could be used in this context.

Instead, EDF would like to propose the Commission to consider the approach proposed by EDF in its shadow Disability-specific Directive of February 2008. The said Annex provides for schedules of progressive realization of accessibility requirements for new and existing buildings, telecommunications, electronic communication, transport modes and other public spaces and facilities. The Annex takes into account the existing standards, the concept of universal design and reasonable consumer expectations.

EDF invites the Commission and the Member States to consider applying the idea of 'accessibility schedules' in the European Directive.

Disability as the New Frontrunner in EC Non-Discrimination Legislation?

Report of the Public Hearing at the European Parliament: Future anti-discrimination legislation: what are the specificities of the 'disability' ground 14 May 2008

A. Giantsidou, E. Kallinikou and E. Erlings[1]

Discrimination on the basis of disability is often a distinct kind of discrimination. This is because people with a disability encounter wholly different problems in their daily lives in comparison to people who fall under one of the other grounds addressed by EC anti-discrimination legislation.[2] In order to be able to fully take into account the specificities of disability in new EC anti-discrimination legislation, a public hearing on this topic was convened at the European Parliament on 14 May 2008 to give MEPs, representatives of people with disabilities and other stakeholders the opportunity to comment on the subject. This paper is a reflection on this meeting and aims to shed light on the different opinions which were espoused. At the time of the hearing the Commission's stated plans were to propose a new anti-discrimination directive based on Article 13 EC which only addressed disability. The Commission subsequently revised its plans, and proposed a 'horizontal' directive addressing a variety of grounds.[3]

The opening speech by Richard Howitt MEP (ESP) highlighted what the European Disability Forum – and other 'Article 13 EC' Non-Governmental Organizations - have lobbied for since 2000: namely, the closing of the gaps in existing EC legislation in order to remove (the appearance of) a hierarchy in anti-discrimination legislation. The tension between those striving for a horizontal directive (covering all grounds) and those supporting a disability-specific directive was recognized, yet, at the same time, Richard Howitt made it clear that the aim of the

---

[1] A. Giantsidou, E. Kallinikou and E. Erlings are master students at Maastricht University, The Netherlands.

[2] Art. 13 EC further mentions sex, racial or ethnic origin, religion or belief, age or sexual orientation.

[3] COM(08) 426 final, Proposal for a Council Directive on implementing the principle of equal treatment between persons irrespective of religion or belief, disability, age or sexual orientation.

hearing was to generate information on the specificities of disability in order to provide for the best possible quality of any future EC anti-discrimination legislation which addressed disability.

On behalf of the European Disability Forum, Donata Vivanti gave a forceful speech signalling the many problems that disabled persons face, such as lower incomes, unemployment, an inaccessible environment, being prevented from receiving donor organs, being portrayed in stereotypical ways in the media and having to live in closed institutions without the possibility of being able to leave them.[4] People with disabilities cannot enjoy the fundamental rights guaranteed under the UN Convention on Disability,[5] and many of them are even denied the basic EC right of freedom of movement.[6] The legislation now in force is insufficient:[7] its scope is too limited, it does not cover problems specific to disabled people, nor does it secure their right to employment. Only disability specific anti-discrimination legislation will help disabled people and their families. Legislation should be coherent and not fragmented, so as to avoid a negative impact on consumers and industry. A link should be made between the UN Convention and EC legislation: the EC has signed the Convention and three of its Member States have ratified it already. EC legislation should be used to give guidance on the interpretation of the Convention. Apart from that, the EC should provide for a strong anti-discrimination instrument which ensures compliance with the UN Convention and promotes the recognition of disability issues as a matter of human rights. People with disabilities should not be seen as patients, but as citizens and be recognized as such.

To give an overview of the legal issues related to any new anti-discrimination law addressing disability, a presentation was given by Lisa Waddington, professor at Maastricht University and the leading academic in the field. She mentioned that any new legislation should be based on three core principles. Firstly, it will need to meet the standards of the UN Convention (which the EC has signed and is expected to ratify in 2008/9), in accordance with Article 4 of that Convention (which refers to States' Parties undertaking to ensure and promote the full realization of all human rights and fundamental freedoms for all persons with disabilities). Secondly, the Directive should be explicitly based on the social model of disability. This is necessary to guide the courts and to ensure that case law does not undermine the legislation by interpreting it in a restrictive, medically inspired, manner.[8] And thirdly, a new directive should draw inspiration from provisions

---

[4]   Many of these points were recognized in the Proposal of the European Disability Forum for a Comprehensive Directive to combat discrimination against persons with disabilities (DOC EDF/0108, February 2008) – hereafter: the EDF proposal-, see Arts. 2, 5 and 7.

[5]   United Nations Convention on the Rights of Persons with Disabilities (hereafter: the UN Convention).

[6]   Arts.18 and 39 EC.

[7]   Namely Directive 2000/78 (Employment Equality Directive), [2000] O.J. L 269/15, which only addresses disability discrimination in the context of employment and vocational training.

[8]   Hereby Prof. Waddington implicitly referred to the Judgment of *Chacón Navas*

in existing EC anti-discrimination legislation.[9] However, this new directive will need to diverge from these older instruments when necessary. For example, in addition to the already recognized forms of discrimination, discrimination should also be defined as explicitly covering a failure to make a reasonable accommodation (this would be in line with the UN Convention and the already existing legislation in several Member States). The obligation to make a reasonable accommodation, in addition, has to be anticipatory. This implies that the accommodation is made before the customer or user encounters the problem. Therefore, public and private bodies are required to have anticipated the needs of disabled persons in advance and made their services accessible in advance, as opposed to the existing reactive obligation which only requires accommodation following a specific request from a specific individual with a disability (see Directive 2000/78, Article 5). Additionally, there should be a clear distinction between the obligation to provide for a reasonable accommodation and positive action.[10]

Regarding the material scope, the directive should, at a minimum, cover the fields referred to in Article 3 of the Racial Equality Directive[11] and, in addition, those fields which are specifically relevant in the context of disability. In particular, a key issue for disability law is accessibility; it is important that services are accessible to people with disabilities and that the provision of these services does not impede the independence, social and occupational integration and participation in the life of the community by people with disabilities. None of the other 'Article 13 grounds' face accessibility problems in the same way disabled persons do, namely difficulties regarding physical access and access to information and procedures. Consequently, there are no precedents on this matter in EC law which can inspire provisions in a new anti-discrimination directive. Nevertheless, the UN Convention does refer to accessibility in Article 9.[12] Drawing inspiration from this article, the directive can give guidance on the meaning of the concept of accessibility. Moreover, a failure to provide access should then be regarded as discrimination. However, this obligation can only apply insofar as a specific area falls within the scope of EC law, which implies that accessibility should at least be addressed in the fields of information and procedures and access to the physical infrastructure.[13] As the directive will not leave any room for technical details, Member States and private parties should be presumed to be in compliance with accessibility requirements if accessibility is provided in accordance with current and future European standards, codes of practice, the state of the art and reasonable consumer expectations. Private and public bodies are thus obliged to comply,

---

where the ECJ relied on medical model of disability when interpreting the Employment Equality Directive. The EDF Proposal, however, is based on the social model and even includes chronic illness in the scope of disability (see recital 9 of the preamble to the proposal) –a point regrettably left out in the discussion at the hearing.

[9]   Directive 2000/78 and Directive 2000/43, [2000] O.J. L180/22 (Racial Equality Directive).

[10]   See Art. 2(6) EDF Proposal.

[11]   Social protection, including social security, healthcare, social advantages, education and goods and services available to the public.

[12]   Art. 9 UN Convention.

[13]   EDF proposal, Arts. 4-5.

yet presumed to be in compliance if they reach this threshold. To ensure effective compliance, Member States should, moreover, establish an independent body to monitor compliance. Professor Waddington finally left the people present with several other topics to think about, including the question of who should be protected by the new directive, and the need to pay specific attention to education, a wide scope for positive action and the involvement of representative organizations of people with disabilities.

The next speaker was Daniela Bankier, Head of the Equality and Action against Discrimination: Legal Questions Unit. She noted that it is important to fill the gaps in existing legislation, but emphasized that no decision had been taken yet on whether to fill these gaps with a horizontal directive or by a gradual approach, involving a series of ground specific directives. If a gradual approach were adopted, then disability was a strong candidate for a first directive as there is a lot of relevant data available and it would be an opportunity to ensure coherent implementation of the UN Convention. The directive itself would be inspired by existing legislation[14] with regard to its material scope, its definition of discrimination and procedural rights (such as the burden of proof, access to justice, sanctions and equal treatment bodies) and, where necessary, complemented by disability specific rules on, for example, access and reasonable accommodation. It should be noted, however, that the EC would have to legislate within its competences which means that it cannot cover all aspects of the UN Convention. Moreover, Article 13 EC itself limits certain possibilities as it is a non-discrimination provision, which means that no concrete rules can be made on, for example, product design, as such an area falls outside the scope of Article 13 EC.

Liz Lynne MEP (LIB) advocated quite another view: as rapporteur for the European Parliament Committee on Employment and Social Affairs on equality issues,[15] she had changed her opinion regarding the directive over time. In line with her report, she now insisted on adopting a comprehensive horizontal approach which included disability specific provisions, in order to avoid a hierarchy and leaving other grounds out. Moreover, following a different approach towards disability, as opposed to the other grounds of discrimination, by adopting a disability specific Directive, would mean that it would be more difficult to deal with cases of multiple discrimination, where different rules would apply to each ground. There should thus be a complete package regarding anti-discrimination and access to goods and services. As for the disability specific elements in the directive, these should be based on the UN Convention. Much attention should be paid to implementation and enforcement. Equal treatment bodies are of significant importance. The EU is based on the principles of human rights and anti-discrimination, and in this respect people should not be left behind.

---

[14]   See in particular Directive 1975/117, EEC [1975] O.J. L45/19 (Gender Directive) and Directive 2000/43, [2000] O.J. L180/22 (Racial Equality Directive).

[15]   Parliament Committee on Employment and Social Affairs, 'Report on progress made in equal opportunities and non-discrimination in the EU (the transposition of Directives 2000/43/EC and 2000/78/EC)' (April 2008), A6-0000/2008.

Edit Bauer MEP (EPP) started by stressing that non-discrimination is a basic value of the EU, yet, most states find it very difficult to implement this principle and the existing legislation in their jurisdictions. The importance of implementation and the need for new non-discrimination legislation was highlighted by noting how persons with disabilities are kept from benefiting from their rights with regard to employment and non-discrimination, because of impediments experienced in other areas such as transport. In the case of anti-discrimination with regard to disability, the UN Convention is very important and the EC has made a commitment to comply with this convention. The best way to proceed now is to intensify measures under the existing non-discrimination framework and to enact a disability specific directive. It should be noted though that certain standards, such as reasonable accommodation, go beyond anti-discrimination and enter the realm of positive action. Yet, with a view to full equality, it is better to revisit the notion of positive action rather than to abolish reasonable accommodation. The only problem left is that there are only weak incentives for policy makers to move from anti-discrimination measures to promoting equality.

Stephen Hughes MEP (ESP) insisted that, on the contrary, the opportunities should be seized while the debate is ongoing to obtain commitments for legislative initiatives from the EC. While all forms of discrimination need to be addressed, disability needs extra attention and the current legislation is insufficient. An attitude change is needed with regard to new legislation and the speed at which it should be adopted. For disability, the starting point should be the UN Convention and, even if the EC is subject to legal limitations, with courage and imagination much can be achieved. As far as product design is concerned, the scientific capacity to provide accessibility already exists – even if this is not specifically placed under the flag of non-discrimination. The material scope of the new directive should indeed be based on the Race Directive. The call for an anticipatory obligation to provide reasonable accommodation and special attention for multiple discrimination was supported. With a view to enforcement and remedies, the directive should be given real teeth.

Cveto Urcic on behalf of the Slovenian government – holding the Presidency of the EU at the time - stressed that in Slovenia special attention is given to disability: the constitution of Slovenia explicitly prohibits discrimination on the ground of disability. Slovenia is one of the three EU Member States that has ratified the UN Convention and its Optional Protocol, and further national legislation on equal opportunities is expected to be adopted in 2009. The Slovenian government is convinced that the Article 13 EC package must be completed with an extension to all grounds, but it specifically supports the disability specific directive which should be inspired by the UN Convention, the social model and the older Article 13 EC directives. Words must be turned into deeds.

The floor was then given to the audience, which led to the following reactions.

Michael Cashman MEP (ESP) called for attention to be paid to the negative experiences of the past, when certain groups were favoured over others. Discrimination against one is discrimination against all. According to Mr. Cashman, the

Commission President should live up to his promise concerning the protection against discrimination and deliver one full directive.

Proinsias de Rossa MEP mentioned that the Lisbon Treaty is very important as it will incorporate the Charter of Fundamental Rights within the EU Treaty, which will lead to a whole new Union based on the rights of citizens. This will give a new opportunity to put pressure on the Commission for a horizontal directive. The role of Civil Society was stressed as well since, with their help, a combination of pressure could be put on the Commission.

On behalf of Disabled People's International Jean-Luc Simon pointed out that horizontal legislation may not be the answer as illustrated by the failure of such legislation in France. Instead, specific legislation ought to be made together with the people experiencing the problems in the field. The keyword is participation; without participation the directive will not be effective. Equally imperative is to base the directive on the idea that disability is created not by the impairments, but by the environment.

Evangelia Tzampazi MEP (ESP) noted that it was most important to abolish the hierarchy in anti-discrimination legislation, whether through a horizontal approach covering all grounds or on a step by step basis with specific directives so as to equally and effectively address all grounds. A ground specificities meeting is very important and should be initiated for all other grounds as well. Furthermore, participation is vital: no one is better equipped to highlight the needs, problems and specificities of people with disabilities people than people with disabilities themselves.

Jukka-Pekka Piimies of the EP Disability Support Group underscored two items of importance regarding a disability specific directive. Firstly, a clear definition of access and universal design is needed. At the moment access is merely defined by what it is not (barriers): a positive definition is to be preferred. Secondly, the directive needs to address existing norms, which are often the result of bargaining between unequal partners (many are practically 'instructions to discriminate').

On behalf of the NGO AGE Platform, Etienne Goulley submitted that AGE would welcome a disability specific directive, as this would greatly benefit elderly people who encounter various problems. However, three principles had to be taken into account. Firstly, age related restrictions should only be made in accordance with objective criteria, secondly preferential treatment for certain age categories should be maintained and thirdly, restrictions on healthcare are strongly rejected.

On behalf of the French Disability Council, Bruno Gaudier mentioned that even though disability is not the only ground for discrimination, it has certain specificities which have to be taken into account. If this is not done people with disabilities will never integrate fully into society. Especially the problem of physical accessibility needs particular attention. Moreover, implementation is of the utmost importance - without effective and timely implementation it would be as if the directive never existed.

Lissy Groener MEP (ESP) called for a horizontal directive to avoid a hierarchy of grounds, and ensure that all people can enjoy all possible support and avoid problems with regard to multiple discrimination. A strong lobby should be instigated at the national level for a horizontal directive.

Patricia Prendville, as director of ILGA and Chairperson of the Fundamental Rights and Non-Discrimination Working Group of the Social Platform, expressed the view that a horizontal directive, which would take the specificities of all grounds into account, should be adopted. Of great importance is the inclusion of Civil Society. It was noted that in fact all of the 'Article 13 EC' anti-discrimination networks have presented shadow directives.

Tansy Hutchinson of ENAR welcomed the concern for multiple discrimination and stressed the need for protection across all grounds. She underscored that, despite differences existing, most striking were the similarities between the grounds, and especially the fact that discrimination is caused, not by a person's characteristics, but by society.

Finally, Ask Andersen of the Danish Disability Council emphasized the need for clear definitions of, among others, discrimination and accessibility, rather than waiting for the European Court of Justice to define these concepts.

The floor was then given back to the panel. Mr. Urcic stated that Slovenia supported the specific directive because, at this moment, it is possible to draft it. Ms. Vivanti made clear that EDF never strove to establish a hierarchy, but that existing legislation is insufficient to enable people with disabilities to fully enjoy all rights. Ms. Bankier acknowledged that the issue of multiple discrimination is very important and has to be recognized as such and that accessibility and reasonable accommodation are important but difficult issues. She noted that there may be infringement procedures against Member States in relation to the 2000 directives, but that the majority of these concern technical issues and lastly, that a substantial number of Member States already have national legislation covering all grounds. Prof. Waddington closed by stating that the new proposals may be costly, but that this may not be any excuse for not granting equality and, moreover, that costs will be limited since the competence of the EC is limited (legislation will not apply in all areas). There should not be a hierarchy between the different grounds, but that does not mean that all grounds must be treated in exactly the same way.

From the foregoing the following becomes clear:

- There seems to be a great divide in opinion as to whether there should be a disability specific directive at all this may promote the idea that a hierarchy regarding the different grounds exists.
- Related to this is the need to pay attention to cases of multiple discrimination. A person may find him-/herself in the position where he/she is discriminated against on multiple grounds but is only able to find protection under one ground.

- Furthermore, much attention was paid to the issue of accessibility and that is definitely a disability specificity: no other ground is faced with physical barriers obstructing the exercise of rights.
- A clear divide should be made between reasonable accommodation – a requirement for non-discrimination - and positive action - the absence of which will not necessarily lead to discrimination.
- The view was shared that any legislation with regard to disability has to be based on the UN Convention and that guidance should be derived from previous legislation in the field of anti-discrimination (such as the racial or gender equality directives).
- Lastly, it was agreed that any legislation on disability (and in fact any legislation at all) should be made in consultation with the stakeholders so as to ensure the most effective legislation possible taking into account the needs, problems and demands of those directly concerned.

EXTRACT FROM THE JUDGMENT OF THE EUROPEAN COURT OF JUSTICE (GRAND CHAMBER) OF 11 JULY 2006 IN THE CASE OF SONIA CHACÓN NAVAS V EUREST COLECTIVIDADES SA[1]

(Case C-13/05)

RE:

Interpretation of Council Directive 2000/78/EC of 27 November 2000 establishing a general framework for equal treatment in employment and occupation (OJ L 303, p. 16) – Scope – Dismissal on grounds of sickness – Sickness and disability.

OPERATIVE PART OF THE JUDGMENT

1. A person who has been dismissed by his employer solely on account of sickness does not fall within the general framework laid down for combating discrimination on grounds of disability by Council Directive 2000/78/EC of 27 November 2000 establishing a general framework for equal treatment in employment and occupation.

2. The prohibition, as regards dismissal, of discrimination on grounds of disability contained in Articles 2(1) and 3(1)(c) of Directive 2000/78 precludes dismissal on grounds of disability which, in the light of the obligation to provide reasonable accommodation for people with disabilities, is not justified by the fact that the person concerned is not competent, capable and available to perform the essential functions of his post.

3. Sickness cannot as such be regarded as a ground in addition to those in relation to which Directive 2000/78 prohibits discrimination.

---

[1]   Extract as per O.J. C224/9.

EXTRACT FROM THE JUDGMENT OF THE EUROPEAN COURT OF JUSTICE (GRAND CHAMBER) OF 17 JULY 2008 IN THE CASE OF S. COLEMAN V ATTRIDGE LAW, STEVE LAW[1]

(Case C-303/06)

RE:

Reference for a preliminary ruling — Employment Tribunal — Interpretation of Articles 1, 2(2)(a) and 2(3) of Council Directive 2000/78/EC of 27 November 2000 establishing a general framework for equal treatment (OJ 2000 L 303, p. 16) — Scope of the term 'disability' — Possibility of extending it to a person who is closely associated with a disabled person and has been discriminated against by reason of that association — Employee bringing up a disabled child on her own

OPERATIVE PART OF THE JUDGMENT

1. Council Directive 2000/78/EC of 27 November 2000 establishing a general framework for equal treatment in employment and occupation, and, in particular, Articles 1 and 2(1) and (2)(a) thereof, must be interpreted as meaning that the prohibition of direct discrimination laid down by those provisions is not limited only to people who are themselves disabled. Where an employer treats an employee who is not himself disabled less favourably than another employee is, has been or would be treated in a comparable situation, and it is established that the less favourable treatment of that employee is based on the disability of his child, whose care is provided primarily by that employee, such treatment is contrary to the prohibition of direct discrimination laid down by Article 2(2)(a).

2. Directive 2000/78, and, in particular, Articles 1 and 2(1) and (3) thereof, must be interpreted as meaning that the prohibition of harassment laid down by those provisions is not limited only to people who are themselves disabled. Where it is established that the unwanted conduct amounting to harassment which is suffered by an employee who is not himself disabled is related to the disability of his child, whose care is provided primarily by that employee, such conduct is contrary to the prohibition of harassment laid down by Article 2(3).

---

[1]   Extract as per O.J. 223/6.

EXTRACT FROM THE JUDGMENT OF THE EUROPEAN COURT OF HUMAN RIGHTS (GRAND CHAMBER) OF 13 NOVEMBER 2007 IN THE CASE OF D.H. AND OTHERS V. THE CZECH REPUBLIC

(Application no. 57325/00)

In the case of D.H. and Others v. the Czech Republic,
The European Court of Human Rights (Second Section), sitting as a Grand Chamber

...

Having deliberated in private on 17 January and 19 September 2007,

Delivers the following judgment, which was adopted on the last mentioned date:

...

The Court's assessment

...

182. The Court notes that as a result of their turbulent history and constant uprooting the Roma have become a specific type of disadvantaged and vulnerable minority (see also the general observations in the Parliamentary Assembly's Recommendation no. 1203 (1993) on Gypsies in Europe, cited in paragraph 56 above and point 4 of its Recommendation no. 1557 (2002): 'The legal situation of Roma in Europe', cited in paragraph 58 above). As the Court has noted in previous cases, they therefore require special protection.... As is attested by the activities of numerous European and international organisations and the recommendations of the Council of Europe bodies... this protection also extends to the sphere of education. The present case therefore warrants particular attention, especially as when the applications were lodged with the Court the applicants were minor children for whom the right to education was of paramount importance.

183. The applicants' allegation in the present case is not that they were in a different situation from non-Roma children that called for different treatment or that the respondent State had failed to take affirmative action to correct factual inequalities or differences between them.... In their submission, all that has to

be established is that, without objective and reasonable justification, they were treated less favourably than non-Roma children in a comparable situation and that this amounted in their case to indirect discrimination.

184. The Court has already accepted in previous cases that a difference in treatment may take the form of disproportionately prejudicial effects of a general policy or measure which, though couched in neutral terms, discriminates against a group.... In accordance with, for instance, Council Directives 97/80/EC and 2000/43/EC... and the definition provided by ECRI..., such a situation may amount to "indirect discrimination", which does not necessarily require a discriminatory intent.

...

205. ... [T]he Czech Republic is not alone in having encountered difficulties in providing schooling for Roma children: other European States have had similar difficulties. The Court is gratified to note that, unlike some countries, the Czech Republic has sought to tackle the problem and acknowledges that, in its attempts to achieve the social and educational integration of the disadvantaged group which the Roma form, it has had to contend with numerous difficulties as a result of, *inter alia*, the cultural specificities of that minority and a degree of hostility on the part of the parents of non-Roma children. As the Chamber noted in its admissibility decision in the instant case, the choice between a single school for everyone, highly specialised structures and unified structures with specialised sections is not an easy one. It entails a difficult balancing exercise between the competing interests. As to the setting and planning of the curriculum, this mainly involves questions of expediency on which it is not for the Court to rule.

...

206. Nevertheless, whenever discretion capable of interfering with the enjoyment of a Convention right is conferred on national authorities, the procedural safeguards available to the individual will be especially material in determining whether the respondent State has, when fixing the regulatory framework, remained within its margin of appreciation.

...

207. The facts of the instant case indicate that the schooling arrangements for Roma children were not attended by safeguards... that would ensure that, in the exercise of its margin of appreciation in the education sphere, the State took into account their special needs as members of a disadvantaged class.... Furthermore, as a result of the arrangements the applicants were placed in schools for children with mental disabilities where a more basic curriculum was followed than in ordinary schools and where they were isolated from pupils from the wider population. As a result, they received an education which compounded their difficulties and compromised their subsequent personal development instead of tackling their real problems or helping them to integrate into the ordinary schools and develop the skills that would facilitate life among the majority population. Indeed, the Government have implicitly admitted that job opportunities are more limited for pupils from special schools.

208. In these circumstances and while recognising the efforts made by the Czech authorities to ensure that Roma children receive schooling, the Court is not satisfied that the difference in treatment between Roma children and non-Roma children was objectively and reasonably justified and that there existed a reasonable relationship of proportionality between the means used and the aim pursued.

In that connection, it notes with interest that the new legislation has abolished special schools and provides for children with special educational needs, including socially disadvantaged children, to be educated in ordinary schools.

209. Lastly, since it has been established that the relevant legislation as applied in practice at the material time had a disproportionately prejudicial effect on the Roma community, the Court considers that the applicants as members of that community necessarily suffered the same discriminatory treatment. Accordingly, it does not need to examine their individual cases.

210. Consequently, there has been a violation in the instant case of Article 14 of the Convention, read in conjunction with Article 2 of Protocol No. 1, as regards each of the applicants.

...

FOR THESE REASONS, THE COURT

1. *Dismisses* unanimously the Government's preliminary objection;

2. *Holds* by thirteen votes to four that there has been a violation of Article 14 read in conjunction with Article 2 of Protocol No. 1;

3. *Holds* by thirteen votes to four

(a) that the respondent State is to pay the applicants, within three months, the following amounts together with any tax that may be chargeable:

(i) to each of the eighteen applicants EUR 4,000 (four thousand euros) in respect of non-pecuniary damage, to be converted into the currency of the respondent State at the rate applicable on the date of payment;

(ii) jointly, to all the applicants, EUR 10,000 (ten thousand euros) in respect of costs and expenses, to be converted into the currency of the respondent State at the rate applicable on the date of payment;

(b) that from the expiry of the above-mentioned three months until settlement simple interest shall be payable on the above amounts at a rate equal to the marginal lending rate of the European Central Bank during the default period plus three percentage points;

4. *Dismisses* unanimously the remainder of the applicants' claim for just satisfaction.

(Application no. 44009/05)

In the case of Shtukaturov v. Russia,
The European Court of Human Rights (First Section), sitting as a Chamber

…

Having deliberated in private on 6 March 2008,

Delivers the following judgment, which was adopted on that date:

…

The Law

60. The Court notes that the applicant submitted several complaints under different Convention provisions. Those complaints relate to his incapacitation, placement in a psychiatric hospital, inability to obtain a review of his status, inability to meet with his lawyer, interference with his correspondence, involuntary medical treatment, etc. The Court will examine these complaints in chronological sequence. Thus, the Court will start with the complaints related to the incapacitation proceedings – the episode which gave rise to all the subsequent events, and then examine the applicant's hospitalisation and the complaints stemming from it.

i. Alleged violation of Article 6 of the Convention as regards the incapactitation proceedings

61. The applicant complained that he had been deprived of his legal capacity as a result of proceedings which had not been 'fair' within the meaning of Article 6 of the Convention. Article 6 (1), in so far as relevant, provides:
    In the determination of his civil rights and obligations ..., everyone is entitled to a fair ... hearing ... by [a] ... tribunal...

...

69. It is not disputed that the applicant was unaware of the request for incapacitation made by his mother.

...

70. The Government argued that the decisions taken by the national judge had been lawful in domestic terms. However, the crux of the complaint is not the domestic legality but the 'fairness' of the proceedings from the standpoint of the Convention and the Court's case-law.

71. In a number of previous cases (concerning compulsory confinement in a hospital) the Court confirmed that a person of unsound mind must be allowed to be heard either in person or, where necessary, through some form of representation – see, for example, *Winterwerp* [*Winterwerp v. the Netherlands*, judgment of 24 October 1979, Series A no. 33, para. 73]. In *Winterwerp* the applicant's freedom was at stake. However, in the present case the outcome of the proceedings was at least equally important for the applicant: his personal autonomy in almost all areas of life was at issue, including the eventual limitation of his liberty.

72. Further, the Court notes that the applicant played a double role in the proceedings: he was an interested party, and, at the same time, the main object of the court's examination. His participation was therefore necessary not only to enable him to present his own case, but also to allow the judge to form his personal opinion about the applicant's mental capacity.

....

73. The applicant was indeed an individual with a history of psychiatric troubles. From the materials of the case, however, it appears that despite his mental illness he had been a relatively autonomous person. In such circumstances it was indispensable for the judge to have at least a brief visual contact with the applicant, and preferably to question him. The Court concludes that the decision of the judge to decide the case on the basis of documentary evidence, without seeing or hearing the applicant, was unreasonable and in breach of the principle of adversarial proceedings enshrined in Article 6(1).

...

74. The Court has examined the Government's argument that a representative of the hospital and the district prosecutor attended the hearing on the merits. However, in the Court's opinion, their presence did not make the proceedings truly adversarial. The representative of the hospital acted on behalf of an institution which had prepared the report and was referred to in the judgment as an 'interested party'. The Government did not explain the role of the prosecutor in the proceedings. In any event, from the record of the hearing it appears that both the prosecutor and the hospital representative remained passive during the hearing, which, moreover, lasted only ten minutes.

75. Finally, the Court recalls that it must always assess the proceedings as a whole, including the decision of the appellate court.... The Court notes that in the present case the applicant's appeal was disallowed without examination, on the ground that the applicant had no legal capacity to act before the courts.... Regardless of whether or not the rejection of his appeal without examination was acceptable under the Convention, the Court merely notes that the proceedings ended with the first-instance court judgment of 28 December 2004.

76. The Court concludes that in the circumstances of the present case the

proceedings before the Vasileostrovskiy District Court were not fair. There has accordingly been a violation of Article 6(1) of the Convention.

ii. Alleged violation of Article 8 of the convention as regards the incapacitation of the applicant

77. The applicant complained that by depriving him of his legal capacity the authorities had breached Article 8 of the Convention. Article 8 provides:

1. Everyone has the right to respect for his private and family life, his home and his correspondence.
2. There shall be no interference by a public authority with the exercise of this right except such as is in accordance with the law and is necessary in a democratic society in the interests of national security, public safety or the economic well-being of the country, for the prevention of disorder or crime, for the protection of health or morals, or for the protection of the rights and freedoms of others.

...

85. The Court reiterates that any interference with an individual's right to respect for his private life will constitute a breach of Article 8 unless it was 'in accordance with the law', pursued a legitimate aim or aims under paragraph 2, and was 'necessary in a democratic society' in the sense that it was proportionate to the aims sought.

86. The Court took note of the applicant's contention that the measure applied to him had not been lawful and had not pursued any legitimate aim. However, in the Court's opinion it is not necessary to examine these aspects of the case, since the decision to incapacitate the applicant was in any event disproportionate to the legitimate aim invoked by the Government for the reasons set out below.

...

90. First, the Court notes that the interference with the applicant's private life was very serious. As a result of his incapacitation the applicant became fully dependant on his official guardian in almost all areas of life. Furthermore, 'full incapacitation' was applied for an indefinite period and could not, as the applicant's case shows, be challenged otherwise than through the guardian, who opposed any attempts to discontinue the measure.

...

91. Second, the Court has already found that the proceedings before the Vasileostrovskiy District Court were procedurally flawed. Thus, the applicant did not take part in the court proceedings and was not even examined by the judge in person. Further, the applicant was unable to challenge the judgment of 28 December 2004, since the City Court refused to examine his appeal. In sum, his participation in the decision-making process was reduced to zero. The Court is particularly struck by the fact that the only hearing on the merits in the applicant's case lasted ten minutes. In such circumstances it cannot be said that the judge had 'had the benefit of direct contact with the persons concerned', which normally would call for judicial restraint on the part of this Court.

92. Third, the Court must examine the reasoning of the judgment of 28 December 2004. In doing so, the Court will have in mind the seriousness of the interference complained of, and the fact that the court proceedings in the applicant's

case were perfunctory at best.

...

93. The Court notes that the District Court relied solely on the findings of the medical report of 12 November 2004. That report referred to the applicant's aggressive behaviour, negative attitudes and 'anti-social' lifestyle; it concluded that the applicant suffered from schizophrenia and was thus unable to understand his actions. At the same time, the report did not explain what kind of actions the applicant was unable of understanding and controlling. The incidence of the applicant's illness is unclear, as are the possible consequences of the applicant's illness for his social life, health, pecuniary interests, etc. The report of 12 November 2004 was not sufficiently clear on these points.

94. The Court does not cast doubt on the competence of the doctors who examined the applicant and accepts that the applicant was seriously ill. However, in the Court's opinion the existence of a mental disorder, even a serious one, cannot be the sole reason to justify full incapacitation. By analogy with the cases concerning deprivation of liberty, in order to justify full incapacitation the mental disorder must be 'of a kind or degree' warranting such a measure – see, *mutatis mutandis*, *Winterwerp*, cited above... However, the questions to the doctors, as formulated by the judge, did not concern 'the kind and degree' of the applicant's mental illness. As a result, the report of 12 November 2004 did not analyse the degree of the applicant's incapacity in sufficient detail.

95. It appears that the existing legislative framework did not leave the judge another choice. The Russian Civil Code distinguishes between full capacity and full incapacity, but it does not provide for any 'borderline' situation other than for drug or alcohol addicts. The Court refers in this respect to the principles formulated by Recommendation No. R (99) 4 of the Committee of Ministers of the Council of Europe, cited above in paragraph 59. Although these principles have no force of law for this Court, they may define a common European standard in this area. Contrary to these principles, Russian legislation did not provide for a 'tailor-made response'. As a result, in the circumstances the applicant's rights under Article 8 were limited more than strictly necessary.

96. In sum, having examined the decision-making process and the reasoning behind the domestic decisions, the Court concludes that the interference with the applicant's private life was disproportionate to the legitimate aim pursued. There was, therefore, a breach of Article 8 of the Convention on account of the applicant's full incapacitation.

iii. Alleged violation of Article 5(1) of the Convention

97. Under Article 5(1) of the Convention the applicant complained that his placement in the psychiatric hospital had been unlawful. Article 5, in so far as relevant, provides:

1. Everyone has the right to liberty and security of person. No one shall be deprived of his liberty save in the following cases and in accordance with a procedure prescribed by law:

...

(e) the lawful detention of persons ... of unsound mind...

...

115. … [T]he Court notes that it was submitted on behalf of the applicant that his deprivation of liberty had been arbitrary, because he had not been reliably shown to be of unsound mind at the time of his confinement. The Government submitted nothing to refute this argument…. It appears that the decision to hospitalise relied merely on the applicant's legal status, as it was defined ten months earlier by the court, and, probably, on his medical history. Indeed, it is inconceivable that the applicant remained in hospital without any examination by the specialist doctors. However, in the absence of any supporting documents or submissions by the Government concerning the applicant's mental condition during his placement, the Court has to conclude that it has not been 'reliably shown' by the Government that the applicant's mental condition necessitated his confinement.

116. In view of the above the Court concludes that the applicant's hospitalisation between 4 November 2005 and 16 May 2006 was not 'lawful' within the meaning of Article 5(1)(e) of the Convention.

iv. Alleged violation of Article 5(4) of the Convention

117. The applicant complains that he was unable to obtain his release from the hospital. Article 5(4), relied on by the applicant, provides:

Everyone who is deprived of his liberty by arrest or detention shall be entitled to take proceedings by which the lawfulness of his detention shall be decided speedily by a court and his release ordered if the detention is not lawful.

…

121. The Court recalls that by virtue of Article 5(4), a person of unsound mind compulsorily confined in a psychiatric institution for an indefinite or lengthy period is in principle entitled, at any rate where there is no automatic periodic review of a judicial character, to take proceedings at reasonable intervals before a court to put in issue the 'lawfulness' – within the meaning of the Convention – of his detention.

…

122. This is so in cases where the initial detention was initially authorised by a judicial authority… and it is *a fortiori* true in the circumstances of the present case, where the applicant's confinement was authorised not by a court but by a private person, namely the applicant's guardian.

123. The Court accepts that the forms of the judicial review may vary from one domain to another, and depend on the type of the deprivation of liberty at issue. It is not within the province of the Court to inquire into what would be the best or most appropriate system of judicial review in this sphere. However, in the present case the courts were not involved in deciding on the applicant's detention at any moment and in any form. It appears that Russian law does not provide for automatic judicial review of confinement in a psychiatric hospital in situations such as the applicant's. Further, the review cannot be initiated by the person concerned if that person has been deprived of his legal capacity. Such a reading of Russian law follows from the Government's submissions on the matter. In sum, the applicant was prevented from pursuing independently any legal remedy of judicial character to challenge his continued detention.

124. The Government claimed that the applicant could have initiated legal proceedings through his mother. However, that remedy was not directly acces-

sible to him: the applicant fully depended on his mother who had requested his placement in hospital and opposed his release. As to the inquiry carried out by the prosecution authorities, it is unclear whether it concerned the 'lawfulness' of the applicant's detention. In any event, a prosecution inquiry as such cannot be regarded as a judicial review satisfying the requirements of Article 5(4) of the Convention.

125. The Court recalls its findings that the applicant's hospitalisation was not voluntary. Further, the last time on which the courts had assessed the applicant's mental capacity was ten months before his admission to the hospital. The 'incapacitation' court proceedings were seriously flawed, and, in any event, the court never examined the necessity of the applicant's placement in a closed institution. Nor was this necessity assessed by a court at the moment of his placement in the hospital. In such circumstances the applicant's inability to obtain judicial review of his detention amounted to a violation of Article 5(4) of the Convention.

v. Alleged violation of Article 3 of the Convention

126. The applicant submitted that the compulsory medical treatment he received in hospital amounted to inhuman and degrading treatment. Furthermore, on one occasion physical restraint was used against him, when he was tied to his bed for more than 15 hours. Article 3 of the Convention, referred to by the applicant in this respect, provides:

No one shall be subjected to torture or to inhuman or degrading treatment or punishment.

127. The Court notes that the complaint under Article 3 relates to two distinct facts: (a) involuntary medical treatment and (b) the securing of the applicant to his bed after his attempted escape. As regards the second allegation, the Court notes that it was not part of the applicant's initial submissions to the Court and was not sufficiently substantiated…Therefore, this incident falls outside of the scope of the present application, and, as such, will not be examined by the Court.

128. It remains to be ascertained, however, whether the medical treatment of the applicant in the hospital amounted to 'inhuman and degrading treatment' within the meaning of Article 3. According to the applicant, he was treated with Haloperidol and Chlorpromazine. He described these substances as obsolete medicine with strong and unpleasant side effects. The Court notes that the applicant did not provide any evidence showing that he had actually been treated with this medication. Furthermore, there is no evidence that the medication in question had the unpleasant effects he was complaining of. The applicant does not claim that his health has deteriorated as a result of such treatment. In such circumstances the Court finds that the applicant's allegations in this respect are unsubstantiated.

129. The Court concludes that this part of the application is manifestly ill-founded and must be rejected in accordance with [Article 35(3) and Article 35(4)] of the Convention.

vi. Alleged violation of Article 13 of the Convention

130. The applicant complained under Article 13, taken together with Articles 6 and 8 of the Convention, that he had been unable to obtain a review of his status as a legally incapable person. Article 13, insofar as relevant, provides:
Everyone whose rights and freedoms as set forth in [the] Convention are violated shall have an effective remedy before a national authority notwithstanding that the violation has been committed by persons acting in an official capacity.
131. The Court finds that this complaint is linked to the complaints submitted under Article 6 and 8 of the Convention, and it should therefore be declared admissible.
132. The Court further notes that in analysing the proportionality of the measure complained of under Article 8 it took account of the fact that the measure was imposed for an indefinite period of time and could not be challenged by the applicant independently from his mother or other persons empowered by law to seek its withdrawal…. Furthermore, this aspect of the proceedings was considered by the Court in its examination of the overall fairness of the incapacitation proceedings.
133. In these circumstances the Court does not consider it necessary to re-examine this aspect of the case separately through the prism of the 'effective remedies' requirement of Article 13.

vii. Alleged violation of Article 14 of the Convention

134. The Court notes that under Article 14 of the Convention the applicant complained about his alleged discrimination. The Court finds that this complaint is linked to the complaints submitted under Article 6 and 8 of the Convention, and it should therefore be declared admissible. However, in the circumstances and given its findings under Articles 5, 6 and 8 of the Convention, the Court considers that there is no need to examine the complaint under Article 14 of the Convention separately.

viii. compliance with Article 34 o the Convention

135. The applicant maintained that, by preventing him from meeting his lawyer in private for a long period of time, despite the measure indicated by the Court under Rule 39 of the Rules of Court, Russia had failed to comply with its obligations under Article 34 of the Convention. Article 34 of the Convention provides:
The Court may receive applications from any person, non-governmental organisation or group of individuals claiming to be the victim of a violation by one of the High Contracting Parties of the rights set forth in the Convention or the Protocols thereto. The High Contracting Parties undertake not to hinder in any way the effective exercise of this right.
Rule 39 of the Rules of Court provides:
1. The Chamber or, where appropriate, its President may, at the request of a party or of any other person concerned, or of its own motion, indicate to the parties any interim measure which it considers should be adopted in the interests of

the parties or of the proper conduct of the proceedings before it.

2. Notice of these measures shall be given to the Committee of Ministers.

3. The Chamber may request information from the parties on any matter connected with the implementation of any interim measure it has indicated.

…

149. Having regard to the material before it, the Court concludes that, by preventing the applicant for a long period of time from meeting his lawyer and communicating with him, as well as by failing to comply with the interim measure indicated under Rule 39 of the Rules of Court, the Russian Federation was in breach of its obligations under Article 34 of the Convention.

…

FOR THESE REASONS, THE COURT UNANIMOUSLY

1. *Declares* the complaints under Article 5 (concerning confinement to the psychiatric hospital), Article 6 (concerning incapacitation proceedings), Article 8 (concerning the applicant's incapacitation), Article 13 (concerning the absence of effective remedies), and Article 14 of the Convention (concerning the alleged discrimination) admissible, and the remainder of the application inadmissible;

2. *Holds* that there has been a violation of Article 6 of the Convention as regards the incapacitation proceedings;

3. *Holds* that there has been a violation of Article 8 of the Convention on account of the applicant's full incapacitation;

4. *Holds* that there has been a violation of Article 5 § 1 of the Convention as regards the lawfulness of the applicant's confinement in hospital;

5. *Holds* that there has been a violation of Article 5 § 4 of the Convention as regards the applicant's inability to obtain his release from the hospital;

6. *Holds* that there is no need to examine the applicant's complaint under Article 13 of the Convention;

7. *Holds* that there is no need to examine the applicant's complaint under Article 14 of the Convention;

8. *Holds* that the State failed to comply with its obligations under Article 34 of the Convention by hindering the applicant's access to the Court and not complying with an interim measure indicated by the Court in order to remove this hindrance;

9. *Holds* that the question of the application of Article 41 is not ready for decision;

accordingly,

(a) *reserves* the said question in whole;

(b) *invites* the Government and the applicant to submit, within three months from the date on which the judgment becomes final in accordance with Article 44 § 2 of the Convention, their written observations on the matter and, in particular, to notify the Court of any agreement that they may reach;

(c) *reserves* the further procedure and *delegates* to the President of the Chamber the power to fix the same if need be.

EXTRACT FROM THE DECISION OF THE EUROPEAN COMMITTEE OF SOCIAL RIGHTS OF 4 NOVEMBER 2003 IN THE COLLECTIVE COMPLAINT OF AUTISM - EUROPE V. FRANCE

(Complaint No 13/2002)

Autism - Europe v. France
The European Committee of Social Rights, committee of independent experts established under Article 25 of the European Social Charter (hereafter referred to as 'the Committee'), during its 197th session
...
After having deliberated on the 3 and 4 November 2003,
On the basis of the report presented by Mr Gerard QUINN,
Delivers the following decision adopted on this last date:
...

II. ASSESSMENT OF THE COMMITTEE

47. The Committee considers that the arguments of the complainant alleging the violation of Articles 15(1) and 17(1) and of Article E are so intertwined as to be inseparable. Its assessment, therefore, will deal with the question whether the situation in France is in conformity with Articles 15(1) and 17(1) whether alone or when read in combination with Article E of the Revised Charter.

48. As emphasized in the General Introduction to its Conclusions of 2003 (p. 10), the Committee views Article 15 of the Revised Charter as both reflecting and advancing a profound shift of values in all European countries over the past decade away from treating them as objects of pity and towards respecting them as equal citizens – an approach that the Council of Europe contributed to promote, with the adoption by the Committee of Ministers of Recommendation (92) 6 of 1992 on a coherent policy for people with disabilities. The underlying vision of Article 15 is one of equal citizenship for persons with disabilities and, fittingly, the primary rights are those of 'independence, social integration and participation in the life of the community'. Securing a right to education for children and others with disabilities plays an obviously important role in advancing these citizenship rights. This explains why education is now specifically mentioned in the revised Article 15 and why such an emphasis is placed on achieving that education 'in the framework of general schemes, wherever possible'. It should be noted that Article 15 applies to all persons with disabilities regardless of the nature and origin of

their disability and irrespective of their age. It thus clearly covers both children and adults with autism.

49. Article 17 is predicated on the need to ensure that children and young persons grow up in an environment which encourages the 'full development of their personality and of their physical and mental capacities'. This approach is just as important for children with disabilities as it is for others and arguably more in circumstances where the effects of ineffective or untimely intervention are ever likely to be undone. The Committee views Article 17, which deals more generally, *inter alia,* with the right to education for all, as also embodying the modern approach of mainstreaming. Article 17(1), in particular, requires the establishment and maintenance of sufficient and adequate institutions and services for the purpose of education. Since Article 17(1) deals only with children and young persons it is important to read it in conjunction with Article 15(1) as far as adults are concerned.

50. Autism-Europe also argued that Article E of the Revised Charter is violated since the net result of alleged shortfalls is that persons with autism do not benefit, as effectively as other citizens, from a right to education as embodied both in Articles 15(1) and 17(1).

51. The Committee considers that the insertion of Article E into a separate Article in the Revised Charter indicates the heightened importance the drafters paid to the principle of non-discrimination with respect to the achievement of the various substantive rights contained therein. It further considers that its function is to help secure the equal effective enjoyment of all the rights concerned regardless of difference. Therefore, it does not constitute an autonomous right which could in itself provide independent grounds for a complaint. It follows that the Committee understands the arguments of the complainant as implying that the situation as alleged violates Articles 15(1) and 17(1) when read in combination with Article E of the Revised Charter.

Although disability is not explicitly listed as a prohibited ground of discrimination under Article E, the Committee considers that it is adequately covered by the reference to 'other status'. Such an interpretative approach, which is justified in its own rights, is fully consistent with both the letter and the spirit of the Political Declaration adopted by the 2nd European conference of ministers responsible for integration policies for people with disabilities (Malaga, April, 2003), which reaffirmed the anti-discriminatory and human rights framework as the appropriate one for development of European policy in this field.

52. The Committee observes further that the wording of Article E is almost identical to the wording of Article 14 of the European Convention on Human Rights. As the European Court of Human Rights has repeatedly stressed in interpreting Article 14 and most recently in the Thlimmenos case [*Thlimmenos v. Grèce* [GC], no 34369/97, CEDH 2000-IV, § 44)], the principle of equality that is reflected

therein means treating equals equally and unequals unequally. In particular it is said in the above mentioned case

> The right not to be discriminated against in the enjoyment of the rights guaranteed under the Convention is also violated when States without an objective and reasonable justification fail to treat differently persons whose situations are significantly different.

In other words, human difference in a democratic society should not only be viewed positively but should be responded to with discernment in order to ensure real and effective equality.

In this regard, the Committee considers that Article E not only prohibits direct discrimination but also all forms of indirect discrimination. Such indirect discrimination may arise by failing to take due and positive account of all relevant differences or by failing to take adequate steps to ensure that the rights and collective advantages that are open to all are genuinely accessible by and to all.

53. The Committee recalls, as stated in its decision relative to Complaint No.1/1998, that the implementation of the Charter requires the State Parties to take not merely legal action but also practical action to give full effect to the rights recognised in the Charter.[1] When the achievement of one of the rights in question is exceptionally complex and particularly expensive to resolve, a State Party must take measures that allows it to achieve the objectives of the Charter within a reasonable time, with measurable progress and to an extent consistent with the maximum use of available resources. States Parties must be particularly mindful of the impact that their choices will have for groups with heightened vulnerabilities as well as for others persons affected including, especially, their families on whom falls the heaviest burden in the event of institutional shortcomings.

54. In the light of the afore-mentioned, the Committee notes that in the case of autistic children and adults, notwithstanding a national debate going back more than twenty years about the number of persons concerned and the relevant strategies required, and even after the enactment of the Disabled Persons Policy Act of 30 June 1975, France has failed to achieve sufficient progress in advancing the provision of education for persons with autism. It specifically notes that most of the French official documents, in particular those submitted during the procedure, still use a more restrictive definition of autism than that adopted by the World Heath Organisation and that there are still insufficient official statistics with which to rationally measure progress through time. The Committee considers that the fact that the establishments specialising in the education and care of disabled children (particularly those with autism) are not in general financed from the same budget as normal schools, does not in itself amount to discrimination, since it is primarily for States themselves to decide on the modalities of funding.

Nevertheless, it considers, as the authorities themselves acknowledge, and whether a broad or narrow definition of autism is adopted, that the proportion of children

---

[1]   *International Commission of Jurist v. Portugal*, para. 32.

with autism being educated in either general or specialist schools is much lower than in the case of other children, whether or not disabled. It is also established, and not contested by the authorities, that there is a chronic shortage of care and support facilities for autistic adults.

CONCLUSION

For these reasons, the Committee concludes by 11 votes to 2 that the situation constitutes a violation of Articles 15(1) and 17(1) whether alone or read in combination with Article E of the revised European Social Charter.

EXTRACT FROM THE DECISION OF THE EUROPEAN COMMITTEE OF SOCIAL RIGHTS OF 3 JUNE 2008 IN THE COLLECTIVE COMPLAINT OF MENTAL DISABILITY ADVOCACY CENTER (MDAC) v. BULGARIA

(Complaint No 41/2007)

The European Committee of Social Rights, committee of independent experts established under Article 25 of the European Social Charter ('the Committee'), during its 230th session

...

Having deliberated on 1 April 2008 and 3 June 2008,
On the basis of the report presented by Mrs Polonca Kon'ar,
Delivers the following decision adopted on this last date:

...

i – The alleged violation of Article 17(2) of the Revised Charter

Preliminary remarks

33. Referring to its admissibility decision and the issue of the delimitation of the material scope of Articles 15 and 17, the Committee considers that the fact that the right to education of persons with disabilities is guaranteed by Article 15(1) of the Revised Charter does not exclude that relevant issues relating to the right of children and young persons with disabilities to education may not be examined in the framework of Article 17(2), *inter alia.*

34. The Committee begins by pointing out that both the first and the second paragraphs of Article 17 of the Revised Charter guarantee children's right to education. The Committee considers that Article 17(2) applies fully in this case as it covers all children and hence concerns children with intellectual disabilities. The Committee recalls in this respect that:

> Therefore Article 17 as a whole requires states to establish and maintain an education system that is both accessible and effective. In assessing whether the system is effective the Committee will examine under Article 17: ... whether, considering that equal access to education should be guaranteed for all children, particular attention is paid to vulnerable groups such as children from minorities, children seeking asylum, refugee children, children in hospital, children in care, pregnant teenagers, teenage

mothers, children deprived of their liberty etc. and whether necessary special measures have been taken to ensure equal access to education for these children.[1]

States need to ensure a high quality of teaching and to ensure that there is equal access to education for all children, in particular vulnerable groups.[2]

35. Firstly, as regards taking special account of children with disabilities, the Committee points out that, while it is acceptable for a distinction to be made between children with and without disabilities in the application of Article 17(2) the integration of children with disabilities into mainstream schools in which arrangements are made to cater for their special needs should be the norm and teaching in specialised schools must be the exception.[3]

36. In addition, for any special education that is set up to be in conformity with Article 17(2) the children concerned must be given sufficient instruction and training and complete their schooling in equivalent proportions to those of children in mainstream schools.[4]

37. The Committee considers that all education provided by states must fulfil the criteria of availability, accessibility, acceptability and adaptability. It notes in this respect General Comment No. 13 of the Committee on Economic, Social and Cultural Rights of the United Nations International Covenant on Economic, Social and Cultural Rights on the right to education.... In the present case, the criteria of accessibility and adaptability are at stake, i.e. educational institutions and curricula have to be accessible to everyone, without discrimination and teaching has to be designed to respond to children with special needs.

38. As regards the respect for the right to education of intellectually disabled children residing in HMDCs [homes for mentally disabled children], the Committee takes note of the efforts made by the Government, particularly through the adoption of legislation and the setting up of action plans. It considers this to be a necessary first step but one that is insufficient to bring a situation into conformity with the Revised Charter. It reiterates that 'the aim and purpose of the Charter, being a human rights protection instrument, is to protect rights not merely theoretically, but also in fact'.[5] Consequently, the manner in which this legislation and these action plans are implemented is decisive.

---

[1]   Conclusions 2003, Bulgaria, Article 17(2).
[2]   Conclusions 2005, Bulgaria, Article 17(2).
[3]   *Autism-Europe v. France*, Complaint No.13/2000, decision on the merits of 4 November 2003, para. 49.
[4]   Conclusions 2005, Bulgaria, Article 17(2)).
[5]   *International Commission of Jurists v. Portugal*, Complaint No. 1/1998, decision on the merits of 10 September 1999, para. 32.

39. The Committee points out that when it is exceptionally complex and expensive to secure one of the rights protected by the Revised Charter, the measures taken by the state to achieve the Revised Charter's aims must fulfil the following three criteria: '(i) a reasonable timeframe, (ii) a measurable progress and (iii) a financing consistent with the maximum use of available resources'.[6] It also recalls that 'States Parties must be particularly mindful of the impact that their choices will have for groups with heightened vulnerabilities' and that they must also take 'practical action to give full effect to the rights recognised in the Charter'.[7] Similarly, 'States enjoy a margin of appreciation in determining the steps to be taken to ensure compliance with the Charter, in particular as regards to the balance to be struck between the general interest and the interest of a specific group and the choices which must be made in terms of priorities and resources'.[8]

40. The Committee points out that where precise facts are used to support allegations that a state has infringed the Revised Charter, it is for the Government to answer the allegations using specific evidence such as measures introduced, statistics or examples of relevant case-law.... The MDAC has submitted precise elements to the Committee with a view to demonstrate that the manner in which Bulgaria's legislation and action plans are implemented is highly inadequate. The Committee notes that the Government, however, has failed to provide evidence to refute these.

41. In addition, the Committee notes that the Government describes the situation of children with disabilities in general and not the specific case of children with moderate, severe or profound intellectual disabilities residing in HMDCs, who are the subjects of this complaint.

42. To be able to assess the situation of these children, the Committee must therefore rely on the data referred to in the 2005 report prepared by the Bulgarian national child protection agency, which is mentioned by the MDAC in its complaint and not disputed by the Government.

43. The Committee refers to Order No. 6 on children with special educational needs and/or chronic conditions, 2002, which entitles children with any type of intellectual disability to be educated in special schools or mainstream schools of their parent's or tutor's choice. The Committee notes that only 2.8% of the children with intellectual disabilities residing in HMDCs are integrated in mainstream primary schools, which is extremely low whereas integration should be the norm. Mainstream educational institutions and curricula are not accessible in practice to these children. There also appears to be insufficient evidence to show

---

6   *European Roma Rights Centre v. Bulgaria*, Complaint No. 31/2005, decision on the merits of 18 October 2006, para. 37; *Autism-Europe v. France*, Complaint No.13/2000, decision on the merits of 4 November 2003, para. 53.

7   *Autism-Europe v. France*, Complaint No.13/2000, decision on the merits of 4 November 2003, para. 53.

8   *European Roma Rights Centre v. Bulgaria*, Complaint No. 31/2005, decision on the merits of 18 October 2006, para. 35.

real attempts to integrate these children into mainstream education. The Committee considers therefore that the criterion of accessibility is not fulfilled.

44. For the very few children integrated into mainstream primary schools, the way in which they are dealt with should be suited to their special needs. The Committee finds on this point in particular that teachers have not been trained sufficiently to teach intellectually disabled children and teaching materials are inadequate in mainstream schools. These schools are therefore not suited to meet the needs of children with intellectual disabilities and hence to provide their education. The Committee concludes that neither therefore is the criterion of adaptability met.

45. The Committee notes that only 3.4% of children with intellectual disabilities residing in HMDCs attend the special classes set up for them. Despite the fact that special classes should not be the norm but only an exception to mainstream education, the figure is very low and demonstrates that special education is not accessible to children with intellectual disabilities residing in HMDCs.

46. As to the educational activities that intellectually disabled children follow within the HMDCs, the Committee takes note that the HMDCs are not themselves be regarded as educational institutions, that, consequently, the children are ineligible for a diploma attesting completion of primary school education and that they are therefore prevented from entering secondary education. The Committee notes, in addition, that the programmes of activity implemented at HMDCs were drawn up by the Ministry of Labour and Social Policy before the 2002 reform, at a time when intellectually disabled children were still officially regarded as being uneducable. The Committee also notes that it has been confirmed by various eye-witness reports and studies that the children do not receive any education in the HMDCs. The Committee concludes that the activities pursued by intellectually disabled children living in HMDCs who attend neither a mainstream school nor a special class cannot be considered to be a form of education.

47. As to the Government's argument that the right of children with intellectual disabilities residing in HMDCs to education is being implemented progressively, the Committee is aware of Bulgaria's financial constraints. It notes that any progress that has been made has been very slow and mainly concerns the adoption of legislation and policies (or action plans), with little or no implementation. It would have been possible to take some specific steps at no excessive additional cost (for example HMDC directors and the municipal officials to whom HMDCs and primary schools are accountable could have been informed about and given training on the new legislation and action plans). The choices made by the Government resulted in the situation described above (see in particular para.s 43 et 45). Progress is therefore patently insufficient at the current rate and there is no prospect that the situation will be in conformity with article 17(2) within a reasonable time. Consequently, the Committee considers that the measures taken do not fulfil the three criteria referred to above, i.e. a reasonable timeframe, measurable progress and financing consistent with the maximum use of available resources. In view of this situation, the Committee considers that Bulgaria's financial con

straints cannot be used to justify the fact that children with intellectual disabilities in HMDCs cannot enjoy their right to an education.

48. Consequently, the Committee holds that the situation in Bulgaria constitutes a violation of Article 17(2) of the Revised Charter because children with moderate, severe or profound intellectual disabilities residing in HMDCs do not have the effective right to an education.

ii – The alleged violation of Article 17(2) of the Revised Charter read in conjunction with Article E

49. Article E prohibits any discrimination in the enjoyment of the rights set forth in the Revised Charter. Although disability is not explicitly included in the list of grounds of discrimination prohibited by Article E, the Committee has found previously that it is 'adequately covered by the reference to "other status"'.[1]

50. The Committee has previously observed that:

> The wording of Article E is almost identical to the wording of Article 14 of the European Convention on Human Rights. As the European Court of Human Rights has repeatedly stressed in interpreting Article 14 and most recently in the Thlimmenos case [*Thlimmenos v. Greece* [GC], no 34369/97, ECHR 2000-IV, para. 44)], the principle of equality that is reflected therein means treating equals equally and unequals unequally. In particular it is said in the above mentioned case:
>
> 'The right not to be discriminated against in the enjoyment of the rights guaranteed under the Convention is also violated when States without an objective and reasonable justification fail to treat differently persons whose situations are significantly different'.
>
> In other words, human difference in a democratic society should not only be viewed positively but should be responded to with discernment in order to ensure real and effective equality.[2]

51. Therefore, the Committee notes that failure to take appropriate measures to take account of existing differences may amount to discrimination.

52. The Committee recalls its case law regarding disputes about discrimination in matters covered by the Revised Charter, adopted in the framework of reporting procedure, that the burden of proof should not rest entirely on the complainant, but should be the subject of an appropriate adjustment. It also applies to the collective complaints procedure. The Committee therefore relies on the specific data sent to it by the complainant organisation, such as its statistics which show unexplained differences. It is then for the Government to demonstrate that there is no ground for this allegation of discrimination.

---

[1]   *Autism-Europe v. France*, Collective Complaint No.13/2000, decision on the merits of 4 November 2003, para. 51.

[2]   Ibid, para. 52.

53. The Committee refers to the data cited above, according to which only 6.2% of the intellectually disabled children living in HMDCs are educated in mainstream primary schools or in special schools. It notes that, in reply, the Government states that a high percentage of children in Bulgaria do not go to school and that this does not just apply to children with intellectual disabilities. However, the Government fails to support this assertion with statistical data or to specify whether this is already a problem at primary school level or affects only secondary schools. The Committee underlines that it has already noted that, for the period 1997-2000, primary school attendance rates were 93% for girls and 95% for boys, despite a regrettable, excessively high drop-out rate.[3] The disparity between these figures is so great that it demonstrates that there is discrimination against children with intellectual disabilities residing in HMDCs in comparison with all other children with regard to access to education in Bulgaria.

54. Consequently, the Committee holds that the situation in Bulgaria constitutes a violation of Article 17(2) of the Revised Charter read in conjunction with Article E because of the discrimination against children with moderate, severe or profound intellectual disabilities residing in HMDCs as a result of the low number of such children receiving any type of education when compared to other children.

CONCLUSION

55. For these reasons the Committee concludes

- unanimously that there is a violation of Article 17(2) of the Revised Charter because children with moderate, severe or profound intellectual disabilities residing in HMDCs do not have an effective right to education;
- by 12 votes to 1 that there is a violation of Article 17(2) of the Revised Charter taken in conjunction with Article E because there is discrimination against children with moderate, severe or profound intellectual disabilities residing in HMDCs as a result of the low number of such children receiving any type of education when compared to other children.

---

[3]   Conclusions 2005, Article 17(2), Bulgaria.

The European Yearbook On Disability Law

Aims and Scope: The European Yearbook on Disability Law reviews the significant developments at European level regarding disability law and policy.

The Yearbook contains a series of articles on current challenges and developments from senior analysts and academics working in the field. It aims to provide critical insight in the evolution of European disability law and policy and offers analysis of pressing challenges in a broad range of fields.
The core of the Yearbook consists of a review of the preceding year's significant events, as well as policy and legal developments within the institutions of the European Union. It reviews major EU policy developments, studies and other publications, legislative proposals, and case law from the European Court of Justice and the European Court of Human Rights.

Submission of Articles: The European Yearbook of Disability Law is a peer reviewed publication.
Manuscripts should be submitted in Word form to the co-editor at: lisa.waddington@maastrichtuniversity.nl.
The fact of submission will be taken to mean that the manuscript has not been published, accepted or submitted elsewhere. Once the peer review process is completed, the author will be notified of acceptance, rejection or the need for revision. Acceptance for publication entails the transfer of copyright to the publishers. Articles should be between 8,000 and 10,000 words. Authors are encouraged to contact the co-editor before submitting their article to establish if their paper falls within the scope of the Yearbook. Authors are encouraged to submit their articles by the end of September in the year preceding the issue of the Yearbook in which they wish their article to be published.